CW01460157

THE

# "ELECTRICAL THEORY"

OF THE

# UNIVERSE.

OR

THE ELEMENTS OF

# PHYSICAL AND MORAL PHILOSOPHY.

BY T. S. MACKINTOSH.

---

[FIRST AMERICAN, RE-PUBLISHED FROM THE LONDON EDITION.]

---

BOSTON:
Printed and Published at the Investigator Office, 35 Washington st.
BY JOSIAH P. MENDUM.
1846.

# AMERICAN PUBLISHER'S PREFACE.

The following work is a reprint of the London Edition of 1838, but few copies of which are now to be purchased either in England or the United States. So rarely is the work met with in this country, that we were unable, after the most careful enquiry, to obtain a copy from which to re-publish, and were about abandoning the project, when fortunately a kind friend interested himself in the undertaking, and procured a copy for us from England. Whatever may have been the causes that threw this book out of circulation, or effected its almost entire suppression, within the short period of eight years, we believe it may safely be said that very seldom does a book come from the press which is designed to meet a more urgent want of the liberal community, than this volume by T. S. Mackintosh, Esq., on the Electrical Theory of the Universe, or the Elements of Physical and Moral Philosophy. Its utility cannot fail to be recognised by the liberal public to whom it is offered, and the publisher congratulates himself that he has been enabled to make this addition to the library of useful and scientific works.

This able treatise is peculiarly fitted, by its agreeable and attractive style of illustration, to afford great help to the important studies of Natural and Moral Philosophy. It shows a thorough knowledge of these subjects. The views are strikingly original, generally just, and always clear, and, what is of vast importance in works of this kind, the course of enquiry is every where of a practical character; and being also illustrated by numerous diagrams, it is believed that the sciences here developed are made as plain and as easy to be understood, as the nature of the case will allow. The propriety and advantage of introducing the subjects, here treated of, as a branch of common study and investigation, will not, it is presumed, be questioned by any who are desirous of understanding and explaining many of the every-day occurrences of life and the common phenomena of nature. The want of this kind of knowledge is indeed regretted by every uneducated person; for such persons every day observe facts, which, though now mysterious to them, they could readily explain did they possess but a slight knowledge of Natural Philosophy. This treatise, by Mr. MACKINTOSH, will, in a good degree, impart this desirable knowledge; and those into whose hands it may fall, cannot fail to profit by the enlightened views and useful knowledge with which it abounds.

# AUTHOR'S PREFACE.

In offering to the world a work which professes to show that the Newtonian Philosophy is based upon false principles, I would say in the language of Locke, "Truth has been my only aim, and wherever that has appeared to lead, my thoughts have impartially followed, without minding whether the footsteps of any other lay the same way; not that I want a due respect to other men's opinions, but after all the greatest reverence is due to truth." The system of Newton is now almost generally received, and is *presumed* to rest upon demonstrable principles. But neither the principles nor the methods by which the conclusions are deduced have been duly, if at all, considered by many who have the fullest assurance of the truth of that system. The philosophy of such minds, rests upon *faith*, not upon knowledge; upon the authority of names, and not upon conclusions worked out by the efforts of their own mind. Such is the foundation upon which the opinions of the mass of mankind are based, which led Fontenelle to remark that, "the number of those who believe in a system already established in the world, does not, in the least, add to its credibility."

There is, however, an air of plausibility about the system of Newton, combined with a considerable degree of simplicity, arising from its purely mechanical character, which renders it difficult for those who examine it by mechanical principles alone, to perceive the fallacies which lie at the bottom. Those who may be desirous of investigating the subject for themselves, are recommended to turn their especial attention to the four propositions adverted to in the following letter:

---

"*To the Secretary of the Royal Society:*

Sir,—It having been intimated to me that certain members of your Society hesitate to admit the conclusions to which I have come respecting the fallacies of the Newtonian Philosophy, I hereby respectfully invite such, or any others, members of your body or otherwise, who may feel themselves competent, to meet me in Public Discussion in your Institution or any convenient place,—there, in a friendly way, honestly, openly, and unreservedly, to try the merits of the question. Truth, more especially scientific truth, need not fear investigation. If Newton's fundamental propositions be founded in truth, they will be more fully established by the scrutiny; if founded in error, they must ultimately fall; and they ought to fall, for they deceive mankind.

The following are the Principles which I undertake to prove to be fallacious:—

1st. The Vis Inertiæ of Matter.
2nd. The Vacuity of Space.
3rd. The Primitive Impulse; and
4th. The Centrifugal Force,—its insufficiency to sustain a continued struggle with Attraction.

These being the first principles from which our conclusions are deduced, it behooves us to be well assured of their truth. For false principles lead to false conclusions; false conclusions lead to erroneous action; and erroneous action leads to disappointment, loss and misery.

I am, Sir, yours, respectfully,
T. SIMMONS MACKINTOSH,
60 Oldham street.

Manchester, Oct. 17th, 1838."

—

With respect to the principles advanced in the "Electrical Theory," it is not the province of the author to offer an opinion; at the same time he may be allowed to say, that although he feels the fullest assurance of the correctness of the general principles upon which the Theory is based, he is not so presumptuous as to maintain that it is entirely free from error.

It may be necessary to notice that the title of "Electrical Theory" has not been given by the author, but by a gentleman connected with the Metropolitan press. That title is in some respect inappropriate—although modern science has incontestably proved that, Electrical or Galvanic Action performs important functions in all the operations of nature, whether upon the great or small scale; yet we do not appeal to Electrical Action alone. The principles to which we appeal, are the ultimate and universal forces of attraction and repulsion, under whatever form or modification they may manifest themselves to the senses or minds of men, following the same forces into the mental or moral world, where they put on a purely abstract form.

A clear and correct view of the moral forces by which the mind is actuated, involving as it does, the happiness and progressive advancement of the race, is, in the estimation of the author, of far more importance than that portion of the subject which refers to the purely physical laws, although, no doubt, each is worthy of our attention; for a clear conception of the one, cannot be obtained without some knowledge of the other physics—is, in fact, the basis of morals; but morals have been more neglected, and therefore, demand the greatest care. Every thing in nature is progressive; but the *moral standard* to which every thing is referred, was erected in the dark ages of the world, and is totally unsuited to the advanced state of mind now in existence, and that mind is still advancing.

"Some of those who talk about the wisdom of our ancestors, can see no difference between a people that decided guilt or innocence by the burning plough-shares, and one whose lowest classes read the sentiments of the most eminent men in the kingdom, while they sip their beer. Others, who feel the difference to be fatal to their favorite scheme of policy, endeavor to stultify the nation by retaining usages and forms suggested by the condition of a country emerging from poverty and isolation, after it has fallen into the opposite evil of a plethora of riches.

"The civilized world is now silently undergoing a more wonderful transformation than has ever been dreamed of by the wildest visionary; no man existing can guess the result. But there it a clear path before us.

"Let us watch the reason of mankind, and adapt our conduct to its dictates. The attempts now making, in France and Spain, and England, to retain the errors of a former age, are like the struggles of detached groups in a moving multitude. They disturb the harmony and good humor of the body; but whether maintained for a longer or shorter period, with greater or less energy, is ultimately unimportant; the "vis inertiae" of the mass is sure to triumph.

"So long as it was possible to keep the body of a nation in total ignorance, political institutions could be established, overthrown and modified, according to the pleasure of whomsoever happened to be invested with the power of the sword,—whether legitimate king, popular tribune, or victorious captain; and in the Eastern portion of the globe, this is the case in the present time. But since the art of printing, and the commercial intercourse of the European states, have deprived governments of the power of maintaining popular delusions, opinions have taken the place of the sword; and whatever struggle may arise from the reluctance of this formidable ruler to yield to its flimsy competitor, it is nevertheless in the nature of things, that opinions will finally triumph, and all the waste of human happiness, and the effusion of blood, which must attend the wars maintained in opposition to them, will be 'en pure perte.'

"If a young man sets out in life professing the doctrines of a benighted age, and lending his support to those who delude him into the belief, that what he opposes is an innovation, and will pass away with the season, he will doom himself to that state of suffering which attends the alternative of acting against the judgment and the conscience, or of appearing to be a renegade by renouncing his early sentiments. He will, in the course of nature, be left by those elder politicians, who now support him by their countenance and example; and he will remain amongst his opponents, an isolated object of sneer and sarcasm, as a disciple of those, whose opinions have disappeared from the political world, as the dream of the alchemists have from that of science.

"Let him look considerately around him. What growing and strengthening opinion has ever yet been ultimately extinguished by opposition? Has the reformed religion yielded to force?—the spirit of colonial independence?—the desire of civil equality?—the wish for representative government?—Do we not observe that the leaders of the opposition to all those latter opinions, are now studying only how to retreat with honor?

"At the period when Napoleon was about to leave Paris for his last Austrian war, he reviewed in the square of the Carousa one of the most brilliant assemblages of troops that had ever been collected in Europe. He spent many hours enjoying the effect of his word, or look, in transforming into its various shapes, this mighty instrument of dominion over the nations opposed to his will. A witness of the scene relates, that a little dry old man, in a rusty wig, came near him, and whispered in his ear thus: 'Do you see a little bird flitting about the square, and passing in between those columns and battalions, and squadrons of horse?' 'I see no bird,' said the man. 'But I do, clearly,' replied the other, 'and it is that little bird which will soon overthrow the columns, and the squadrons, and the mind that now directs them.' 'What do you mean?' said his companion. 'I mean,' replied he, 'that public opinion, in the shape of a little bird, is now flitting between all these military masses, and will, before long, be able to subdue both them and their master.' After such a speech, he was soon lost in the crowd, and could never be recognised again by his casual acquaintance."*

The empire of mind is gradually, silently, and surely gaining upon the empire of matter or brute force. The invention of gunpowder reduced men to a state of equality in respect to physical strength. The invention of printing, and the consequent extension of knowledge, are now producing the same result in respect to mental strength. If such result be desirable, as lending to the establishment of equity amongst mankind, it is highly necessary that we should endeavor to obtain a clear perception of the moral forces, or motive powers, by which the individual mind is actuated, for, thereby, we shall, to a considerable extent, be enabled to direct the great moral movement to a happy issue.

* Political Primer.

# CONTENTS.

# INTRODUCTION.

The study of philosophy, both *physical* and *moral*, is simply the study of the BOOK OF NATURE. Written books, the compositions of men, are nothing more than *commentaries* upon this great original; for all the knowledge which men possess, or ever can possess, is derived from this volume, the pages of which are equally open to all, if they would use the eyes of their understandings, and by patience and diligence, learn to know the characters in which it is written, and thereby become qualified to seize the valuable truths which it contains. In written language, the first thing to be learned is to know the letters or alphabet; 2nd. To put two, three, or more letters together, vowels or consonants, so as to form a syllable; 3rd. To put two or three syllables together, so as to form a word, in which word is contained an idea; 4th. To put two, three, or more words or ideas together to form a sentence, in which sentence is contained a proposition; and 5th. Putting sentences together forms a language, in which is comprehended the whole knowledge of the people speaking that language.

Now, the letters or characters of which the alphabet of the book of nature is formed, consists of simple facts; each single fact is a letter, and these must be learned by observation, and by observation alone, by a proper use of those senses of seeing, hearing, feeling, tasting and smelling, with which we have been endowed, for the purpose of enabling us to observe and distinguish facts, so as to discriminate between those things which are useful or hurtful, that we may appropriate to ourselves such as may minister to our happiness; and, on the other hand, learn to reject such as might prove injurious to us; and thus by observation, we accumulate a body of knowledge, by which we secure a power to advance our own individual comfort and prosperity, as well as that of the human species generally. In this sense, knowledge is power. Now, although the facts which constitute the basis of this universal language are numerous, nay, almost numberless, yet we shall find that the language of nature is exceedingly simple, for the great body of single facts may be, and indeed are, referred to a *few general facts*, under each of which the single facts are arranged; by which classification the study of the language is very much facilitated.

These general facts may be called the syllables of the language.

Again, by comparing two single facts with each other, we arrive at a particular conclusion with respect to the qualities or properties of one or both. These particular conclusions may be called the words; for the language now begins to speak its meaning, begins to enter into and exercise the mind; also, by comparing general facts, we arrive at general conclusions, by a like process of reasoning, and these may be named the sentence; and, lastly, we put together the whole of the facts and conclusions, and endeavor to arrive at one universal law that shall comprehend the entire language.

For example, we *see* an apple fall from the branch of a tree—this is a single fact; we *hear* it strike the earth at our feet; we take it up and examine it; we *see* that it is greenish and round; we *feel* that it is somewhat solid, and also that it is round; of its spherical shape we have the evidence of two senses; we *smell* it, it has a certain flavor; and, lastly, we *taste* it, and find that it has a rather sour but pleasant taste. Now let us endeavor to perceive how far these few facts will enable us to read and understand the book of nature; how far they will lead us in our attempts to arrive at particular and general conclusions. In the first place, we must compare this apple with another from the same tree; if the two agree in all the foregoing properties and qualities, we come to the particular conclusion, that these two are of the same nature, and more generally, that all the other apples on the same tree agree with the two which we have examined; and thus we arrive at the general conclusion, that all apples have properties and qualities analogous to these. But, why they possess these qualities, we are yet to learn; and, before we can arrive at this knowledge, new facts must be obtained; and these are to be found in the study of chemistry, which will be treated of in another part of this work. By the study of this science we arrive at a few, or comparatively few, general facts, to which the whole of the almost infinite variety of processes, exhibited in the natural phenomena of the earth may be referred; and thus, that language, which appears so very complicated and abstruse, becomes in reality, exceedingly simple. But there is one circumstance connected with the apple of which we learn nothing by the evidence of the senses. *Why* did it fall from the tree? Why did it fall to the earth? The fact of its falling was visible, but the *cause* is unseen. By the aid of the senses we learn the general fact that all solid bodies do fall towards the earth; but, by the senses alone, we learn nothing more. It is by the aid of the mind, of the intellectual faculties, that we arrive at the general conclusion concerning this cause, by which all solid bodies are moved towards the surface of the earth.

But, before we can venture to decide, we must collect as many facts as we can procure, in order that we may not, in so important and general a conclusion, decide erroneously; for, in proportion as our conclusions become more and more general, so, in proportion, do they become more and more important; because, an error in these, ramifies throughout the whole section which they embrace. Now, before we are prepared to assign a cause for the falling of the apple, we require to know the shape of the earth. The earth, it is known, is a spherical body; its shape is that of the apple itself, and the exterior surface of this sphere is the part which we inhabit; hence, the terms *up* and *down* have no meaning in respect to this earth as a body moving in space; for if we say that a solid body falls *down* upon one side of the earth, we must say that another solid body falls *up* on the *opposite side;* for the two bodies move towards each other;—in falling, both move towards the centre of the spherical earth. What, then, causes them to move in that direction? We come to the conclusion that the earth has a certain power or force within itself, by which all solid bodies are *drawn* towards her—and this power we call the *force of attraction.* We can perceive by the senses the effects resulting from the action of this force, but the force itself is unseen, except by the mind; and, from other general facts which have been observed, we conclude further, that this force of attraction operates throughout the whole universe, and thus we arrive at *one universal conclusion.*

But, although *solid* bodies move or fall *towards* the centre of the earth, *gaseous* bodies move in the opposite direction. Gases are in general invisible, and, therefore, we are not so apt to take notice of their motions; but, if we would read the book of nature with profit, we must endeavor to understand why gaseous bodies do rise from the earth; for unless we can distinctly perceive the cause of the upward motion, we shall not be enabled to comprehend more than half the operations going forward in the world, and even that half will be discerned very imperfectly. As the motion of gaseous bodies is in a direction opposite to that of solid bodies, and as solid bodies move towards the earth by the force of *attraction*, it is obvious that gaseous bodies owe their motion to a force which is directly opposed to attraction, as the motions are directly opposed to each other, and this force is named *repulsion.*

In order that we may obtain a clear perception of the manner in which these two opposing forces act, it becomes necessary to advert to *three general facts* with respect to the form or manner in which matter is presented to our senses. Matter is presented to our notice in three forms, and only three—SOLID, LIQUID, and GAS. Now the solidity of matter is caused by the force of attraction; solid bodies are formed by this force in the first instance, and are maintained in their solid state by the constant exertion of the attractive energy; and the degree of solidity of any body is always in proportion to the degree of attractive energy by which its atoms are attracted or drawn together. If the attractive force were annihilated, all solid bodies would be instantly dissolved, and their atoms scattered throughout universal space by the force of repulsion; neither the earth, moon, nor planets, nor the sun itself could exist as *solid* bodies but for the force of attraction.

Now, as solid bodies owe their existence as solids to the force of attraction, so, on the other hand, gases owe their existence to the force of repulsion. Gases are formed and maintained in their gaseous state by the constant exertion of this force, and the degree of energy of the repulsive force by which its atoms are repelled or pushed from each other. If the repulsive force were annihilated, all gaseous matter, the atmosphere of the earth, and other planets, even the celestial ether which pervades all space, would instantly collapse and be formed into solid matter by the now *unopposed* force of attraction.

It is important, however, to bear in mind, that all matter is at all times and in all places under the action and control of *both* these forces. In a highly expanded gas, the repulsive force greatly predominates over the attractive; but the attractive force, has not, on that account, lost all hold upon the gaseous matter; there is an *ultimate point of expansion* beyond which the force of repulsion cannot carry the expanding or gasifying process: so, on the other hand, in a highly contracted solid, the attractive force greatly predominates over its antagonist force of repulsion; but the repulsive force has not ceased to act in the solid, for no body has ever been known to exist in a state of perfect solidity; there is, therefore, an *ultimate point of contraction* also, beyond which the force of attraction cannot proceed with the contracting or solidifying process. In the liquid form of matter the two forces are in a state of equilibrium.

Seeing, then, that the gaseous medium which pervades all space, filling up the intervals between the solid planetary bodies, owes its existence, as a gas, to the force of repulsion, we conclude, that this force, like attraction, operates throughout the whole universe; and thus we arrive at a *second universal conclusion.*

Now, from these two universal conclusions, we endeavor to discover and determine ONE UNIVERSAL LAW, that shall comprehend every action and re-action, both physical and moral. In short, that shall embrace every variety of phenomena, in matter and mind, which is presented to our notice in the wide field of nature.

---

## UNIVERSAL LAW.

ATTRACTION and repulsion are two ultimate, opposing, and universal forces, inherent in matter, equal in power and extent, and all matter is at all times and in all places under the action and control of both these forces; and thus, every atom, and every aggregate of atoms, being placed between two opposing forces, is held securely in its position, and compelled to occupy the place which it does occupy in the general physical economy of the universe; and sentient beings also, are, in like manner, under the action and control of the same universal ultimate forces, operating upon organized and sentient matter, through the medium of the feeling and thinking mind, by the sensations of pleasure and pain, by which there is exerted an *attractive* force towards pleasing objects, and a *repulsive* force towards those which give pain; and thus, being held between two forces, sentient beings are compelled to occupy the position which they do occupy in the general moral economy of animated nature; and further, if the two forces were at all times and in all places in a state of perfect equilibrium, all nature would remain in a state of rest; no motion could take place, either in animate or inanimate matter; gas would forever remain gas, and solids would ever remain solids; animated beings being attracted in a given direction by pleasure, and repelled in an opposite direction by pain, both forces being equal in energy and intensity, they could not produce motion; hesitation of the mind is caused by the forces being nearly balanced—but the equilibrium of the forces is every where disturbed—the one or the other force is continually gaining upon its antagonist—and MOTION is the effect resulting from that disturbance of equilibrium. When repulsion is the stronger or predominating force, matter continually expands until it has reached the *ultimate point of attraction*—an example of which, is the celestial ether which fills all space; after which, attraction becomes the stronger or predominating force, and matter continually contracts until it has reached the *ultimate point of contraction*—an example of which may be seen in the crystalline matter of which the solid earth is composed. Between these two ultimate points of expansion and contraction, matter continually oscillates without PAUSE or cessation; and all mechanical motion (that is, the motion of matter, which is not itself either expanding or contracting,) is an effect resulting from the expansion or contraction of contiguous matter; and these expansions and contractions are caused by the ultimate universal forces of repulsion and attraction, which are the prime movers of all nature, both animate and inanimate.

# ILLUSTRATIONS OF UNIVERSAL LAW.

---

## PHYSICAL.

Repulsion, acting at the surface, and also at the bottom of the ocean, causes water to expand into vapor; in consequence of which expansion it rises into the atmosphere to a greater or less altitude, in proportion as it is more or less expanded.

The mechanical motion of the piston, beam, fly-wheel, and other parts of a steam engine, derive their motion from this cause, as well as all the machinery which is attached to it; and, if the expanded matter which is continually rising from the ocean could be collected, it would be found more than sufficient to move all the steam-engines in the world, even if they were augmented a thousand-fold.

*Attraction*, acting upon the vapor and gas in the atmosphere, causes it to contract; in consequence of which contraction, it falls or descends to the surface of the earth, in the form of a liquid spherical rain-drop, or in that of a solid hailstone, or in flakes of snow. This rain, or the hail and snow when melted, falling on the tops of mountains, trickles down their sides in small streams, which, continually flowing into larger and larger currents, are at last collected into rivers, and thus carried back into the ocean. We thus find that the moving matter has performed a *circuit*, and that the motion throughout this circuit was derived from the two forces of repulsion and attraction, causing its expansion and contraction.

The mechanical motion of water-wheels and of the machinery thereto attached, is an effect resulting from attraction or the contraction of the water, as that of the steam-engine from its expansion.

The motion of windmills, and of ships upon the sea, result from similar expansions and contractions in the air of the atmosphere which surrounds the earth, producing currents, which also move in circuits like the rain-drop.

Now, in relation to the various processes going forward in the earth, we are enabled by observation, to trace all motion to the expansion and contraction of matter, by which we arrive at a general conclusion, which serves us as a key in our attempts to read and understand this section of the book of nature; and this being the section in which we live, a knowledge of the processes going on here is, to us, of the utmost importance, as our happiness and misery is intimately connected with the amount of knowledge which we possess of every movement going on around us.

These things will be treated of in their proper place: but, as one of the chief objects of the present work is, to deduce from a number of these general conclusions, *one universal conclusion* that shall apply to the whole universe, we proceed to lay before the reader the propositions which we propose to establish, taking the solar system as an example from which, by analogy, we are to deduce the universal conclusion. In the six propositions following, it will be perceived that the matter contained in the solar system is assumed to be passing through a process of expansion and contraction, and performing a circuit similar to that of the rain-drop, to which we have referred; the latter being nothing more than a prototype of the former. The seventh proposition is a corollary coming in, and forming a part of the general conclusion in which it is involved. We shall endeavor to prove:—

1. That a gaseous fluid is continually issuing from the sun, and pervading the whole solar system; without which we could not have either light, heat, or vegetation on the earth.

2. That as matter is indestructible, this gaseous fluid cannot be lost, neither can it return to the sun in the gaseous state; but is contracted or condensed on the outer verge of the solar system, in a manner analogous to the formation of a rain-drop in the earth's atmosphere; and, that the conglomeration of the particles is effected by mutual attraction, aided by a rolling or twisting motion in the solar gaseous fluid in its passage through the field of contracting particles; and, that this rolling or spiral motion, is peculiar to all fluids, even on the surface of the earth.

3. That when the fluid matter has been condensed and collected into a loose pulpy mass, it must, of necessity, be attracted, or fall towards the sun; as a body of gaseous fluid rises from the earth and returns in the condensed form of a rain-drop. This is assumed to be the manner of a comet's formation.

4. But this body being composed of soft, loose and liquid matter, as it approaches the centre, the action of the sun causes the formation of a tail; and, therefore, the comet cannot fall into the sun, but is driven off by the sun, or drawn off by the tail, which the action of the sun has formed, as the car of a balloon is drawn up from the earth by means of the gas which is enclosed in the body of the balloon. The car represents the nucleus of the comet, and the body of the balloon the tail.

5. That the comet continues to condense or harden, and, therefore, at each succeeding revolution, the tail is less and less expanded, and the elliptic or eccentric orbit is continually widened by the action of the sun upon the tail, till, after a series of revolutions, the orbit is reduced to the planetary form, and the pulpy mass is reduced to the consistence of a planet, capable of supporting vegetation.

6. That the planet is continually hardening or contracting, and in the same proportion gradually approaching the sun; that the earth before she reaches the sun will have become a body of solid stone,—all life, both animal and vegetable, will have become extinct; and, as from this solid body no tail can be formed, the earth will fall into the sun, where she will be decomposed, and again issue in the form of a gaseous fluid.

7. That at an early period of the earth's existence she was attended by several satellites, each of which has in the order of their succession, been precipitated upon the earth, and that the remains of these former satellites form the present surface of the earth; that the moon is now approaching, and will finish her course with a similar catastrophe, as will also be the case with the satellites of Jupiter, Saturn, and Uranus.

---

Although these propositions may, at first view, appear extravagant and startling, if the reader will patiently and impartially examine the evidence by which they are supported, he will probably come to the conclusion that they are founded in truth. The chief obstacles to an impartial investigation of the evidence, are the religious and scientific prejudices which we have imbibed in our early infancy, and which more or less influence every conclusion to which we arrive in after-life. From our religious prejudices we cannot conceive the earth to have existed for more than five or six thousand years; but geology has proved that she has been in existence for many, very many millions of years, and that during that time she has undergone many important changes in her internal constitution. Again, from our scientific prejudices, we feel a difficulty in conceiving the possibility of the earth falling into the sun, or the moon to the earth; having been taught in our youth that all the periodical changes of the planetary bodies compensate each other; that the solar system is perfectly balanced in all its relations, and, therefore, will remain forever. Such are the conclusions generated by the Newtonian system of philosophy, in which we have been taught to confide by those who have written commentaries upon that system, and by whom it is asserted, that all the fundamental propositions upon which it rests, have been rigidly demonstrated, and may be safely relied upon. Now the three following objections strike at the very root of that system; if they cannot be fairly answered the Newtonian system is removed, and, of course, the whole superstructure falls to the ground.—It is here objected—

1. That the first impulse which the Newtonian system supposes the planets to have received from the hand of the Creator, and by which impulse the centrifugal force is assumed to have been imparted to the planets, rests upon mere assumption, without any proof whatever, either from philosophy or Scripture.

2. That gravity or attraction is a *real force*, and cannot be destroyed; but, that momentum, or the centrifugal force, as it is called, is *not* a real force, but an *effect* derived from a force, (as from a first impulse) and may be either created or destroyed by an adequate force—that therefore as gravity, the *undiminishable* force is continually contending against momentum, the *diminishable* force, the gravity would destroy the momentum, and the planets would fall into the sun before they had completed one revolution. It is therefore concluded, that gravity and momentum are not the only forces which regulate the motion of the planets.

3. That the Newtonian philosophy assumes that space is a vacuum, and also that light is a fluid filling all space, which is a contradiction in terms.

We will return to these objections again, and will treat them more at length; but in the first place we must proceed to examine the religious prejudices.

*Religious Prejudices.*—If the subject of the Mosaic cosmogony could have been passed over without interfering with the general argument, we should very willingly have foreborne adverting to it in this place, but it lies so completely across our path, that it must be introduced; for if the account of the creation of the earth given in the first chapter of Genesis, is to be accepted in its literal sense, then either that account is a fabrication, or the arguments which we are about to advance have no foundation in nature. If it be not a literal account of the creation, but an allegory containing some hidden and mysterious signification, it is the duty of those whose profession it is to expound the Scriptures, to explain the allegory to such as may desire an explanation; all that we have to do in this place is to show that it neither is, nor could be intended for, a true and literal account of the creation of the earth, inasmuch as it refers to things which never could have had other than an ideal existence. Mention is made of a tree "of the knowledge of good and evil," and also of a "tree of life." Now every one, even the most devout, will at once confess that these trees are mere creations of the mind, that they never had an existence as real, tangible, vegetable creations; indeed, it is not difficult to discern the true allegorical meaning which was intended to be conveyed, for the mention of a tree by which men should be brought to distinguish good from evil, points at once to a moral and not to a physical signification—a relation to mind and not to matter, or the creation of matter; and from this passage we may conclude that the history of the creation as given in Genesis, contains, couched in a kind of figure, some hidden allegorical meaning in relation to morals, and was not intended to convey any information as to the manner in which the earth was called into existence. Many well-informed men of the present day who reject the Mosaic account of the creation in its literal sense, are, nevertheless, sufficiently ready to treat any attempt to trace backward, by natural causes, to the origin of the earth, with ridicule, and to impugn the attempt as an endeavor to exclude the directing energy of the DIVINE MIND from a participation in the operations of the physical and moral universe. In the views and arguments which we are about to advance, we would desire it to be distinctly understood, that our feelings are most decidedly opposed to the introduction of arguments having a tendency to lead to such conclusions; on the contrary, we humbly think that the views of the physical and moral world, which will be disclosed in the course of the work, will infallibly lead the mind to more elevated and sublime conceptions respecting the attributes of the Supreme intelligence, than those views derived from a literal acceptation of the Mosaic account of the creation, by which he is represented in the character of a mere mechanical agent, manufacturing a world as a potter would mould a vessel of clay. But the Jews, who certainly understood the writings of their own language, as well at least as foreigners, reject the Mosaic account in its literal sense.

Marmonides, a learned Jewish Rabbin, in his book entitled "*More Nebachim*," says, "We ought not to understand, or take according to the letter, that which is written in the book of creation, nor to have the same ideas of it with common men; otherwise our ancient sages would not have recommended with so much care to conceal it, and not to raise the allegorical veil which envelopes the truths it contains. The book of Genesis, taken according to the letter, gives the most absurd and most extravagant ideas of the Divinity. Whoever shall find out the sense of it, ought to restrain himself from divulging it. It is a maxim which all our sages repeat, and *above all with respect to the work of six days*. It may happen that some one, with the aid he may borrow from others, may hit upon the meaning of it; in that case he ought to impose silence upon himself; or, if he speak of it, he ought to speak of it in an enigmatical manner as I do myself, leaving the rest to be found out by those who can understand."

Again, Origen, the most eminent defender of the Christian faith, says, "What man of good sense can ever persuade himself that there were at first, a second, and a third day, and that each of these days had a night, when there was neither sun, moon, nor stars? What man can be stupid enough to believe that God, acting the part of a gardener, had planted a garden in the east, that the tree of life was a real tree, and that its fruit had the virtue of making those who eat of it, live forever?" Marmonides was a man of great learning and deep research, and therefore his observations are entitled to the highest respect, as well as on account of his being a Jew, and therefore better calculated to discern, through the idiom of the Hebrew language, the hidden allegorical meaning which the history shadows forth in a dark and ambiguous manner. Origen is one of the most eminent of the fathers of the early Christian Church, a voluminous writer, a steadfast advocate of the faith, and of the authority of the Scriptures, and therefore of all men Origen was the last to advance that which might be calculated to injure the church, of which he was so distinguished a member.

But with respect to the length of time which the earth has been in existence as a planetary body, however formed, we are no longer confined to a period of 5 or 6000 years. Geology has proved in a manner which admits of no dispute, by incontrovertible facts, that she has had an existence, and been the abode of animated beings, millions of years before the human race came into being. "Within the bowels of the earth," says the *Edinburgh Review*, "the geologist has discovered the hieroglyphics of the primeval annals during thousands of years before it was occupied by his own race. Inscribed on marble tablets—encased on the pedestals of the everlasting hills—these symbols have been preserved from the destroying power of man and the elements; and time has respected the only records of its own lengthened duration. Gathered in fragments from remote countries and at distant periods, the elements of this new language were at first rude and mysterious. The few who were first admitted to its secrets, anticipated the conflict between science and religion; and dreaded that the geologist, like the astronomer, might be summoned to the bar of some modern inquisition. Conscious, however, that one truth could never be at variance with another, the patient geologists pursued their labor; and in less than half a century they have created a new deparment of knowledge, which, in point of philosophical and scientific interest, will not yield to the most exalted of the physical sciences."

It was in the Royal Society of Edinburgh that the great battle was fought between the worshippers of fire and water,—between the literal interpreters of Scripture and those gifted men who recognized the hand-writing of the Creator in his works as well as in his word.

Such has been the progress of liberal opinions, that in assemblies composed of Churchmen and Dissenters, and Conservative statesmen, we have heard the walls ring with rapturous joy, when geology renounces her ecclesiastical tenure, and demanded a lease of MILLIONS OF MILLIONS of years for the range of her inquiries.

The truths of religion and of science can never be at variance. A geological truth must command our assent as powerfully as that of the existence of our own minds, or of the Deity himself: and any revelation which stands opposed to such truths, must be false. The geologist, therefore, has nothing to do with revealed religion in his scientific inquiries. It is the office of the divine to interpret the sacred canon; and if he does it with the discrimination and learning it demands, he will never find it at variance with the deductions of science.

At the same time that it is proved that the earth has existed for many, very many millions of years, we have the clearest and most satisfactory evidence that the present state of our planet had a beginning.—"That the present state of things had a beginning," says the same writer, may be inferred from the total absence of organic remains throughout the lowest portions of these strata; and though the Huttonians maintain that no appearance of a beginning were exhibited in the phenomena which they studied, yet the investigation of the subject of fossil remains, which has taken place, principally since their day, has furnished the clearest indications that there was a time when neither animal nor vegetable life existed on our globe.

The reader probably begins to perceive that the Mosaic account of the creation, taken in its literal acceptation, is altogether untenable; we will, therefore, close our observations on this point with an extract from a lecture delivered by Dr. Pye Smith, at the Weigh-house Chapel, London, Nov. 21st, 1837, being an attempt to reconcile the Mosaic account with the discoveries of modern science. Dr. Pye Smith being a man of considerable scientific attainments, especially in the science of geology, admits in the freest and fullest manner that the earth has had an existence of very great duration, probably many millions of years.

In alluding to the first sentence in the book of Genesis, he says, "Now, it is incumbent upon us to come to what I presume was the special design of this occasion—the Mosaic account of the creation. The passage, which has been read, I regard as the grand universal assertion—'In the beginning God created the heaven and the earth.' But it does not tell us *when* that 'beginning' was; it assures us, that at a point in duration past which we cannot ascertain, that point in infinite duration which to the wisdom of the great God seemed best, he was pleased to unfold the majesty of his attributes, and to give existence to a dependent world. The next sentence then takes up this globe, which we inhabit, in the condition to which it had been reduced from (it appears probable) a watery envelopment, putting an end to the last of the strata, lying immediately below that crust of the earth on which we dwell. It may be objected, that the conjunction *and*, connects the following sentence with the preceding—'*And* the earth was without form and void;' but I reply, that this conjunction is used in the Hebrew language with a very remarkable comprehension of meaning; even in tracing its application through but two or three chapters at the beginning of the book of Genesis, I have found it rendered by such expressions as *but—moreover—now*—and with the highest propriety; in point of fact, it introduces a new sentiment, which has connexion with what went before, according to the nature and relation of circumstances. There is nothing at all, therefore, to prevent our supposition of the lapse of immeasurable time—between that 'beginning' and the moment in which the sacred historian takes up this globe, and presents it to us in the condition described by the words—'without form or void.'

"Those words together occur only in two other passages of the Bible; and there they signify ruin and desolation. The former of the two occurs in many other passages, and is used to signify a vast desert, or a ruined city, and other objects in which desolation and destruction are the leading idea. So that we have here presented to us very plainly, this globe in the condition of ruin and desolation, from an anterior state; and then, in the following portions of the chapter, we see the earth made fit for the new purpose, to which God was pleased to appropriate it, by a series of operations, partly the result of attraction, of gravitation, and the chemical affinities, and partly the result of an immediate exertion of divine power."

But there is a prejudice attached to the minds of those who have altogether rejected the Mosaic account, which is, perhaps, even more difficult to remove, than that which we have been now combatting. This prejudice also, is religious, although there may be very little Christian or scriptural faith connected with the mind in which the prejudice exists. Such minds have once received the Mosaic account according to the literal acceptation—but having discovered, or imagining that they have discovered it to be a fallacy, they have now become suspicious and over-cautious, hesitating and doubting, even when a fair chain of reasoning from purely natural phenomena, is presented to their notice. This prejudice can only be removed by facts, and therefore, those who are under its influence must be referred to the body of the work, where they will find the facts, from which they can draw their own conclusions, if those which are connected to those facts should appear unworthy of their acceptance.

*Indian Cosmogony.*—As from the foregoing preconceived opinions operating in the mind and disturbing the judgment, preventing it from drawing a fair and impartial conclusion in respect to the arguments which are about to be advanced in the course of this work, and perhaps constraining it to resist the general conclusion; so also, and for similar reasons, or rather from similar prejudices, would the same arguments be resisted if presented to the mind of a Brahmin or Hindoo.

His mind has been formed by early impressions stamped upon it, by which it retains a certain configuration; it is hardened in this form, as the wax hardens with the force which has been impressed upon it by the seal. Now, before a new impression can be stamped upon the wax, it must be softened, in order to obliterate the previous impression; in order to make the obliteration perfect, the wax ought to be dissolved or liquified, or, more perfect still, gasified. But this process of mental softening, or liquifying, or gasifying, is resisted by the mind with great force. The mind has, and necessarily so, by its very constitution, an antipathy to being dissolved, a horror of dissolution—it clings to its early impressions without any sufficient reason—as the miserable wretch clings to life, when it is no longer worth preserving; and this clinging to opinions, without a sufficient reason, is prejudice; a prejudice is a conclusion received and retained without premises, an opinion unsupported by facts. The minds of the great body of mankind are made up of these opinions and prejudices; if these were removed even from many minds of a superior cast, it would be found that very little remained behind, whilst in those of an inferior class, these prejudices and opinions, unsupported by facts, constitute their very essence; with minds so constituted, reasonable argument avails very little, and such is the mind of the Brahmin, and of many others, too many, who arrogate to themselves a degree of mental superiority far above the Brahmin. Prejudice is the great stumbling-block which lies in the way of the intellectual advancement of the human race, and that which renders the removal of such prejudices most difficult, is, that a very influential body of men derive large emoluments from their propagation. In the sacred writings of the Hindoos, "*The Institutes of Menu,*" a book which is acknowledged to have been written at least eight hundred and eight years before the commencement of the Christian era, an account of the creation of the earth, and indeed of the whole universe, is given in the following words, which, considering the time in which it was written, may be regarded as a wonderful approximation to the true philosophical solution of a problem which has exercised the minds of men in all ages and countries. It distinctly refers to formations and dissolutions of solid matter succeeding each other after long intervals, which, when put into philosophical language, signifies simply the expansions and contractions of matter upon the great scale, these expansions and contractions being controlled and directed by an *infinite and intelligent mind.*

"The Being, whose powers are incomprehensible, having created me (Menu) and this universe, again became absorbed in the Supreme Spirit, changing the time of energy for the hour of repose.

"When that power awakes, then has this world its full expansion; but when he slumbers with a tranquil Spirit, then the whole system fades away.

"For while he reposes, as it were, embodied Spirits endowed with principles of action, depart from their several acts, and the mind itself becomes inert."

Menu next proceeds to speak of the return or absorption of all beings into the Divine essence, which is here considered as the essential substratum of all existence; after this absorption the divine soul is said to sleep and to remain for a season immersed "*in darkness,*" or in what Menu denominates "*the first idea.*"

"Thus," he continues, verse 57, "that immutable power, by waking and reposing alternately, revivifies and destroys, *in eternal succession*, this whole assemblage of locomotive and unmoveable creatures.

"There are creations also and destructions of worlds innumerable; the Being supremely exalted, performs all this with as much ease as if in sport, again and again, for the sake of conferring happiness."—[*Institutes of Hindoo Law; or, Ordinances of Menu.*

"The compilation of the ordinances of Menu was not all the work of one author nor of one period; and to this circumstance, some of the remarkable inequalities of style and matter are probably attributable. There are many passages, however, wherein the attributes and acts of the 'Infinite and incomprehensible Being,' are spoken of with much grandeur of conception and sublimity of diction, as some of the passages above cited may serve to exemplify. There are at the same time such puerile conceits and monstrous absurdities in the same cosmogony, that some may impute to mere accident any slight approximation to truth, or apparent coincidence between the oriental dogmas and observed facts. The pretended Revelation, however, was not purely an effort of the unassisted imagination, nor invented without regard to the opinions and observations of naturalists. There are introduced into the same chapter certain astronomical theories, evidently deduced from observation and reasoning. Thus, for instance, it is declared that at the north pole the year was divided into a long day and night, and that their long day was the northern, and their night the southern course of the sun; and to the inhabitants of the moon it is said one day is equal in length to one month of mortals."—[*Lyell's Principles of Geology.*

*Egyptian Cosmogony.*—"Respecting the cosmogony of the Egyptian priests, we gather much information from writers of the Grecian sects, who borrowed almost all their tenets from Egypt, and amongst others that of the former successive destruction and renovation of the world. We learn from Plutarch, that this was the theme of one of the hymns of Orpheus, so celebrated in the fabulous ages of Greece. It was brought by him from the banks of the Nile; and we even find in this verse, *as in the Indian systems*, a definite period assigned for the duration of each successive world. The returns of great catastrophes were determined by the period of the *Annus Magnus*, or great year; a cycle composed of the revolutions of the sun, moon, and planets, and terminating when these return together to the same sign whence they were supposed at some remote epoch to have set out. The duration of this great cycle was variously estimated. According to Orpheus it was 120,000 years; according to others 300,000; and by Cassander it was taken to be 360,000 years.

"We learn, particularly from the Timæus of Plato, that the Egyptians believed the world to be subject to occasional conflagrations and deluges, whereby the Gods arrested the career of human wickedness, and purified the earth from guilt. After each regeneration, mankind were in a state of virtue and happiness, from which they gradually degenerated again into vice and immorality. From this Egyptian doctrine, the poets derived the fable of the decline from the golden to the iron age. The sects of stoics adopted most fully the system of catastrophes, destined at certain intervals to destroy the world. These they taught were of two kinds—the cataclyism[illegible] destruction by deluge, which sweeps away the whole human race, and annihilates all the animal and vegetable productions of nature; and the ecpyrosis, or conflagration, which dissolves the globe itself. From the Egyptians also, they derived the doctrine of the gradual debasement of mankind from a state of innocence. Towards the termination of each era, the gods could no longer bear with the wickedness of men, and a shock of the elements, or a deluge, overwhelmed them; after which calamity, Astrea descended on the earth to renew the golden age.

"The connexion between the doctrine of successive catastrophes and repeated deteriorations in the moral character of the human race, is more intimate and natural than might at first be imagined. For in a rude state of society, all great calamities are regarded by the people as judgments of God, on the wickedness of man. Thus, in our own time, the Priests persuaded a large part of the population of Chili, and perhaps believed themselves, that the fatal earthquake of 1822 was a sign of the wrath of heaven for the great political revolution just then consummated in South America. In like manner, in the account given to Solon, by the Egyptian Priests, of the submersion of the Island of Atlantes, under the waters of the ocean, after repeated shocks of an earthquake, we find that the event happened when Jupiter had seen the moral depravity of the inhabitants. Now, when the notion had once gained ground, whether from (natural) causes before suggested, or not, that the earth had been destroyed by several general catastrophes, it would next be inferred that the human race had as often been destroyed and renovated. And, since every extermination was assumed to be *penal*, it could only be reconciled with Divine justice, by the supposition that man, at each successive creation, was regenerated into a state of purity and innocence. * * * One extraordinary fiction of the Egyptian Mythology was the supposed intervention of the masculo-feminine principle, to which was assigned the development of the embryo world, somewhat in the way of incubation. For the doctrine was, that when the first chaotic mass had been produced in the form of an egg, by a self-dependent and eternal Being, it required the mysterious functions of this masculo-feminine demi-ourgus to reduce the component elements into organized forms."—[*Lyell's Geology*.

Such were the cosmogonies of the Indians and Egyptians, a strange admixture of wild conceits and of reasonable inferences deduced from natural phenomena. The conceits may excite a smile, but the inferences, so far as they are borne out by observed appearances at the present day, are worthy our attention, as showing that the Brahmins of India and the Priesthood of Egypt were careful observers of nature. Whatever knowledge they either did or could possess, was derived from this source, and could be derived from no other—from the book of nature; and this volume is open now, as it was then; indeed it is more so, for many pages have been turned up since that time by the diligent observers and experimental philosophers who have lived in the intervening ages, which pages were wholly hid from the eyes of the Brahmins and Egyptian Priests. All the writings of these ancient observers are, as has been already observed, *merely commentaries* upon the book of nature; so far as these commentaries agree with the original text, or, by presenting natural phenomena in their ancient aspect, enable us to obtain a wider range of vision, so far we are indebted to these ancient commentators, and so far we may safely coincide with their conclusions; whilst on the other hand, where the comment fails, or is unsatisfactory, we reject the conclusions of the commentator, however ancient, and in whatever degree of respect his commentary may be held, we turn to the original volume, which, if we read it aright, never can deceive us. The book of nature is the most ancient of all works. It is the most sacred of all works—

a thousand times more entitled to the respect and veneration of mankind, than all the *written* commentaries put together, both ancient and modern. If the character and claim of a divine origin be admitted with respect to one or more of the *written commentaries*, how much more is the great original entitled to the admission of that claim where every page bears indelible and incontrovertible evidence of its having been written with the finger of God, and in which is stored up all the knowledge which is necessary to promote the well-being of the human race.

Now, if we compare the Indian, the Egyptian, and the Mosaic cosmogonies, we shall have little difficulty in perceiving that they have one common origin; in each we discern the same leading circumstances:—1st. A creation or renovation by the special intervention of Divine power. 2nd. An overthrow of this creation by a partial or universal deluge.—3rd. Its final dissolution by fire—and 4th. The revolution of nature by a new creation, or, as it is expressed in the scriptures, the creation of a new heaven and a new earth.*—Here are three distinct propositions, (for the fourth is but a reduplication of the first,) and we have to discover whether the ancients could have arrived at these conclusions by the observances of natural phenomena, for unless the conclusions were deduced from observed facts, they were without evidence, and were, therefore, at that time, wholly gratuitous. The only sources from which the ancients could deduce evidences bearing upon these three propositions was, and is, to be sought in the earth itself, and in the motion of the heav-

---

* Although we deprecate the intermixture of *natural* and *Scriptural evidence* so commonly resorted to in ekeing out an argument, resting, as we do, our conclusions on the former alone, it may not be amiss to show, that much authority might be obtained from the latter source if we were disposed to appeal to preconceived opinions:—"And all the host of heaven shall be dissolved, and the heavens shall be rolled together as a scroll; and all their host shall fall down as the leaf falleth from off the vine, and as a falling fig from the fig-tree."—Isaiah xxxiv. 4. "The heavens shall vanish away like smoke, and the earth shall wax old like a garment." Ibid. lxi. 6.

"The stars shall fall from heaven, and the powers of the heavens shall be shaken."—[Matth. xiv. 29.] "But the day of the Lord will come as a thief in the night, in the which the heavens shall pass away with a great noise; and the elements shall melt with fervent heat; the earth also and the works that are therein shall be burned up."—2 Peter, iii. 10. And many more passages might be cited.

enly bodies by which she is surrounded; that is, in the study of the sciences of geology and astronomy. In respect to the latter, their knowledge was pre-eminent,—whilst of the former it was, so far at least as we are enabled to discover, so deficient that we cannot consider it as existing in the character of a science. Geology is strictly a modern science;—yet the evidence upon which the science of geology rests, existed then as it does now—and this evidence was not wholly overlooked by the ancients. They observed marine shells and other fossil remains on the tops of mountains and other situations far removed from the sea, and they concluded, as indeed they could not do otherwise, that the sea had once overflowed the land, that it had covered the highest mountains;—and hence came the conclusion, that the earth had been at a former period covered by the ocean—for they knew that shell-fish neither could nor would leave the sea, their proper element, to travel to the mountain tops, with a view to deposit their remains in the solid rocks, of which those mountain masses are composed;—we thus discover the origin of that almost universally received opinion that the earth, or rather the inhabitants of the earth, had been destroyed by a *universal deluge*,—and this universal opinion was borne out by the evidence to a considerable extent, quite sufficient to warrant the general conclusion; but that evidence is now augmented a thousand fold by the researches of modern geologists. In respect to the ancient and modern geologists, there is this distinction, which ought not to be lost sight of, because it has a most extensive bearing upon the case; the ancient geologists, if their knowledge may entitle them to such appellation, were an ecclesiastical body, and, therefore, the knowledge which they derived from an attentive examination of natural phenomena were upon all occasions turned to account with the people; every circumstance from which a conclusion could be drawn, calculated to advance their influence, their reputation and power, was eagerly seized and appropriated by the body; whilst the modern geologists, having no interested motives, simply examine the facts presented to their notice, and deduce their conclusions accordingly, without any bias or predilection,—retaining the established conclusions so long as they agree with the observed facts, and abandoning them as soon as by new or more satisfactory evidence they are proved to be fallacious. This is a wide and important distinction, which ought not to be overlooked. The ancient priesthood as well as some of the modern, read the book of nature, not to discover the truths which are there revealed, but to search for evidence in support of a preconceived opinion or prejudice, in the propagation of which they were deeply interested. From this consideration it will appear, that if we would arrive at the truth, we must in this case, as in every other, receive the evidence and conclusions of interested parties with extreme caution. But, to whatever end or purpose the Brahmins or Egyptian priesthood might turn the conclusion to which they had arrived with respect to an universal deluge, the conclusion itself was perfectly legitimate, because it rested upon sufficient evidence.

Now this point being established, and it is, or was, firmly established, a creation became necessary. It was proved that the former inhabitants of the earth had been destroyed, and that they had the evidence of their senses, added to the consciousness of their own existence, that the earth was peopled by a new race; the question, therefore, very naturally suggested itself:—how came the former race to be destroyed, and by what power was the new race created which now occupied their place? It is plain that no known natural power could be referred to as competent to bring about such apparently supernatural events, and therefore, then, as now, men had recourse to a creating and destroying power, external to, and, in a certain sense, unconnected with, the visible world;—no visible, natural, or incomprehensible case could be referred to as having effected these great operations, which, notwithstanding, had been effected; and therefore, of necessity, a cause or causes existed somewhere, which being neither visible nor comprehensible, it was concluded must be supernatural. A supernatural cause being established, afforded a resting place to the enquiring mind, which is never satisfied until it has discovered an adequate cause for every effect. The *Divine Intelligent Being*, the *Universal Cause*, therefore, furnishes a home, towards which the aspiring and intelligent mind of man is ever seeking, and in which it finds a resting place,—or it may be compared to an universal solvent, in which all his doubts and difficulties find a ready solution; and so long as but *one doubt* is unsolved, or one effect unaccounted for, so long men will, and must of necessity, refer that one effect to the *universal cause*;—and the connection between the visible and the invisible cause being beyond the reach of the senses, the cause must remain incomprehensible. From these and the like considerations, we may perceive the chain of ratiocination by which two of the three cosmological propositions of the ancients were established. Nor is it in our power to invalidate such conclusions, except in so far as we are prepared to advance evidence whereby some portion of the admitted facts may be referred to secondary causes, guided by Supreme Intelligence. To this extent will the conclusions of the ancients be superseded; but still a very large residuum of these phenomena will remain referrable to the Invisible Power.

The final destruction of the earth by fire was quite as natural a conclusion as either of the preceding. For believing as they did, that in the process of combustion, matter is actually destroyed, that it is annihilated or *consumed*, as we now express it, retaining the error in our language, after it is proved to be incorrect; and seeing burning mountains or volcanoes on various parts of the earth's surface, seeing that the solid mountains were being dissolved by heat, and being *consumed* or annihilated as they imagined, the ultimate dissolvation or annihilation of the earth became a necessary consequence;—and as the seat of the fire or conflagration was hid in the bowels of the earth, apparently consuming its very vitals, they very naturally imagined that it must go on increasing to an unbounded extent, as all conflagrations do, so long as the fire lasts, and thus, to their minds, the ultimate annihilation of the earth by fire, became a necessary, an inevitable consequence. Now, as in the previous case of its destruction by water, from which state of desolation it had evidently been renovated, and as the utter annihilation of the whole visible universe is an idea that could never enter even in the wildest imagination, they were compelled by the necessity of the case to have recourse to an incomprehensible power, capable of creating a world out of nothing; for the matter of which the previous world was composed, is supposed to have been consumed, and by the evidence of a renovation, the analogy of a like renovation after the *purgation* of the earth by fire, pressed itself upon the mind. Although the indestructibility of matter by fire or otherwise is now universally admitted, as also its converse,—that from nothing, nothing can be made,—yet if we would discern the origin of opinions which have had so wide an extension, we must look at the degree of knowledge existing in the world at the time in which they originated,—we must compare the knowledge of Hermes of Egypt, with that of Sir Humphrey Davy, by which we shall perceive, although "the wisdom of the Egyptians" was a proverb in the ancient world, that in the same proportion as the chemical knowledge of the former was inferior to the latter, so must the conclusions deduced from that knowledge be expected to be erroneous.

These opinions, with respect to the destruction and renovation of the earth, were not confined to any particular sect, party, or nation, among the ancients, but were adopted with certain modifications among every people having any pretensions to civilization. It is impossible at this time to say among what people they originated; and as the evidence upon which they rest is not confined to any one country more than another, it is not impossible that the notion might have originated in one nation, without their having any knowledge that a neighboring people had come to a similar conclusion. Whether the Indians originated the idea and gave it to the Egyptians, who adopted it in a modified form, or whether the Egyptians drew their conclusions from geological and astronomical phenomena, cannot be now determined; but of this we are certainly assured, that the Egyptians had an established system of cosmogony before the time that Abraham visited that country, accompanied by his wife, or sister Sarah, as mentioned in Genesis, that is, several centuries before the age of Moses, and therefore, previous to the compilation of the Book of Genesis, in which is to be found the cosmogony commonly called the Mosaic account of the creation, and which account, although rejected in its literal interpretation by the learned Jewish rabbin, Marmonides, will no doubt form the great stumbling block in the way of a theory which professes to trace the origin of this earth, and the other planetary bodies constituting the solar system, by the aid of natural phenomena, which is, after all, precisely the same means by which the several cosmogonies at present adopted in different nations have been compiled, with this difference, that the facts from which the ancients deduced their conclusions, and upon which conclusions they based their cosmogonies, were extremely few, scattered, isolated, and ambiguous, compared with the numerous stories that have been opened to our view by the researches of scien-

3

tific men, and more especially in modern and more recent times.

Seeing that the Egyptian cosmogony had been established prior to the time of Moses, by at least several centuries, a glance at the life of Moses will enable us, perhaps, to trace the origin of the Mosaic account of the creation and universal deluge. Moses, we are informed, was born in Egypt; and that at the time of his birth, by an edict from the court of Pharaoh, it was decreed that every *male* infant, born of an Israelitish woman, should be put to death, and that the midwives of Egypt were strictly enjoined to carry this cruel decree into execution; that the mother of Moses, in order to evade this cruel law, forbore to call the assistance of a midwife, and finding the child to which she had given birth to be a male child, she hid him three months, when finding she could hide him no longer, she put him in an ark, or wicker basket, made water tight by means of pitch daubed upon it, and hid it among the bullrushes; and that she placed her daughter, the sister of Moses, close by to watch the result of her maternal adventures; that shortly after the daughter of Pharaoh, coming to bathe, found the ark with the child; that the sister of Moses now approached, and being, it is presumed, previously instructed, offers to procure a nurse for the child, which being accepted by Pharaoh's daughter, the girl immediately conducts her to her mother, with whom an agreement was concluded to nurse the child for her; and thus the mother of the child not only saved the infant, but also by her ingenious stratagem obtained payment for nursing her own child. This speaks much for the ingenuity of the family of Moses, and is, indeed, strictly characteristic of the natural cunning of the Jews at the present day. When Moses had been suckled by his nurse, he was carried to the court of Pharaoh, and was instructed by the Priesthood, of whom chiefly that court was composed; and as an evidence of his proficiency, we are told in the Epistle of Paul to the Hebrews, that "Moses was learned in all the wisdom of the Egyptians." At forty years of age he slew the Egyptian who had smitten his brother, the Israelite; in consequence of which act, he was obliged to flee from Egypt, into the land of Midian, to Jethro, who afterwards became his father-in-law, and who was also a priest of the Midianites, and with whom, it may be presumed, he increased his previous stock of knowledge. Here Moses remained about forty years, and the remaining forty years of his life was spent in wandering with the children of Israel in the wilderness; so that the life of Moses divides itself into three equal portions of forty years each, the first of which was spent among the priesthood in which he was employed in studying "the wisdom of the Egyptians." There need be, therefore, no wonder if we trace the Egyptian cosmogony in the writings of Moses, and perhaps in this circumstance we may discover the reasons which influenced Marmonides to reject the Mosaic account of the creation, considering it as forming no part of the revelation presumed to be contained in the scriptures of the Old Testament.

The reader will probably begin to perceive that all the cosmogonies now existing or received among the various nations of the world, have been deduced from natural phenomena. That they do not form any part of Divine revelation, properly so called; that in so far as they are formed to accord with known facts and established natural laws, they are entitled to our respect and acceptance, and no farther. That, inasmuch, as the laws of nature are now infinitely better known, and the number of natural facts upon which the knowledge of those laws is based, now recorded, is far greater, out of all proportion, as compared with the times in which those cosmogonies were framed by their various authors, so are we more likely to arrive at correct conclusions respecting the events which have taken place in this earth, and throughout nature generally. And let him ever bear in mind that *the laws of nature are the laws of God;* that we are endowed with certain rational faculties, for the express object of investigating those laws, and that if we neglect to employ those faculties with which we have been endowed, we are, like the servant who hid his talent in the earth, neglecting to fulfil one of the chief ends of our existence. If it be said that the chief end of man's existence is to glorify God, and to do his will, then it may be answered, that no man can glorify God until he has known him, and if he would see him in all his glory, he must view him through the medium of his works, for there he appears in all his majesty,—neither can he do his will, unless he learn to know it, and where shall he learn his will better than in his works? That this revelation of the will of God has not been forged by the arts of the priesthood, all men are certain; and if it appears to some minds to be expressed in terms of a dubious or ambiguous character, it is because they have not studied the language in which it is written; although that language has the exclusive merit of being universal, for it speaks to every people, through every clime. It must also be borne in mind, that in attempting to trace all the operations of the visible universe to secondary causes, and of every event, whether great or small, whether what is denominated creative or destructive, we are in fact elevating the character of the Supreme Being, we are placing him before the mind upon a higher eminence than that which he previously occupied, and showing that all his operations are performed through the agency of fixed laws, which have been, through all time, impressed upon the elements of the material creation, and that He, who was the same yesterday, to-day, and forever, is, in strict conformity with his eternal and immutable character, forever creating and destroying, if indeed such terms may be applicable to that which is, correctly speaking, never at any time either created or destroyed:—in short, that as the creation never had a beginning, so will it never have an end; that the creation or formation of one world, of necessity implies and involves the dissolution of another, as darkly shadowed forth in the Hindoo cosmogony; and this alternate process will continue forever without pause or intermission.

Having examined the cosmogonies of the most ancient nations at some length, it will not be necessary to dwell upon those of others, which, although they occupy a tolerably conspicuous place in the history of the particular nations to which they belong, are obviously and confessedly borrowed from those, to which we have already adverted. The Greeks borrowed nearly all their fables from Egypt; their temples were peopled with Gods from the banks of the Nile. The "wisdom of the Egyptian" charmed and captivated the Greeks, as their own improved version of that wisdom charmed the Romans and other nations who succeeded them, in holding sway over the empire of literature and wisdom; but in the hands of the Greeks, the ancient cosmogonies were stripped of many of their wild and extravagant conceits, and modified to accord with the state of knowledge then existing. In the school of Pythagoras, one of the most ancient of the Greeks, it began to be perceived that matter could not be destroyed or created, that the sum of mortal existence is forever the same, and that though apparently bodies are ever being formed and destroyed, yet that they are not really so, but merely changing their form. Ovid, who in his Metamorphoses professes to give the Pythagorean doctrines, has these words:—

"Nothing perishes in this world; but things merely vary and change their form. To be born, means simply that a thing begins to be something different from what it was before; and dying is ceasing to be that same thing. Yet, although nothing retains long the same image, the sum of the whole remains constant. Solid land has been converted into sea; sea has been changed into land. Marine shells lie far distant from the deep, and the anchor has been found on the summit of hills. Vallies have been hollowed out by running water; and floods have washed down hills into the sea. Marshes have become dry ground; dry lands have been changed into stagnant waters. During earthquakes some springs have been choked up, and new ones have broken out. Rivers have deserted their channels, and have been reborn elsewhere, as the Erasinus in Greece, and the Mysus in Asia. The waters of some rivers formerly sweet, have become bitter. Islands have been connected with the main land by the growth of deltas and new deposits; as in the case of Antissas joined to Lesbos, and Pharos to Egypt. Peninsulas have been divided from the main land, and have become islands, as Leucadia; and according to tradition, Sicily, the sea having carried away the Isthmus. Land has been submerged by earthquakes; the Grecian cities of Helice and Buris for example, are to be seen under the sea, with their walls enclosed. Plains have been upheaved into hills by the confined air seeking vent; as at Trœzen, in the Peloponnesus. The temperature of some springs varies at different periods; the waters of others are inflammable. There are streams which have a petrifying power, and convert the substances which they touch into marble. Extraordinary medical and deleterious effects are produced by the water of different lakes and springs. Some rocks and islands, after floating and having been subject to violent movements, have at length become stationary and immovable; as Delos and the Cyanean isles. Volcanic vents shift their position: there was a time when Ætna was not a burning mountain, and the time will come when it will cease to burn: whether it be that some caverns become closed up by the movements of the earth and others opened, or whether the fuel is finally exhausted."

Ovid next proceeds to trace the generation of races of animals to natural causes, and endeavors to show by the same process of reason and observation of natural things, that such is the progress of natural causes and effects, viewed upon the great scale, both as regards the animate and inanimate world.* With respect to the creation of new species of animals, the Gerbanites, a sect of astronomers who flourished some centuries before the Christian era, taught as follows:—

"That after every period of thirty-six thousand four hundred and twenty-four years, there were produced a pair of every species of animal, male and female, from whom animals might be propagated, and inhabit this lower world. But when a circulation of the heavenly orbs was completed, which is finished in that space of years, other genera and species of animals are propagated; as also of planets and other things: and the first order is destroyed, and so it goes on, forever and ever."

This specious piece of information, furnished by the Gerbanites, must be viewed in the light of a conceit, for no attempt is made to offer any evidence whatever in its support; and no proposition ought to be admitted until the facts—the evidence—has been not only adduced, but also carefully examined and sifted, with a view to detect any error that might creep in unawares. Aristotle con-

---

* Upon this point of the Pythagorean doctrine, Mr. Lyell has the following note:—"It is not inconsistent with the Hindoo mythology to suppose that Pythagoras might have found in the East, not only the system of universal and violent catastrophes and periods of repose in endless succession, but also that of periodical revolutions, effected by the continued agency of ordinary causes;—for Brahma, Vishnoo and Siva, the first, second and third persons of the Hindoo Triad, severally represented the creating, preserving and destructive powers of the Deity. The co-existence of these three attributes, simultaneous operation, might well accord with the notion of perpetual but partial alterations, finally bringing about a complete change. But the fiction before quoted from Menu, of eternal vicissitudes in the slumbers and vigils of the Infinite Being seems accommodated to the system of great general catastrophes, followed by new creations and periods of repose." Mr. Lyell's work being written with the express object of discountenancing "the system of great and general catastrophes," he is naturally adverse to the admission of that system; but facts are stubborn in their support.

sidered great catastrophes occurring at distant intervals of time, a part of the regular course of nature; that deluges and conflagrations alternated with each other, and that the flood constituted the winter of the *annus magnus*, or great astronomical cycle; and the conflagration the summer, or the period of the greatest heat. These opinions were imported into Greece from Egypt, and the doctrines of the east found a genial soil in the mind of the Stagyrite, who from his deep and intimate acquaintance with the operations of nature, both upon the large and small scale, could not fail to perceive that such opinions, supported as they were by numerous and incontrovertible facts, were entitled to be entertained as something more than mere imaginations. They were, however, no longer received with the supernatural accompaniments of the Hindoos; the wild mythological dreams of the earlier nations were stript of their more visionary coloring, and the whole hypothesis was chastened down so as to accord with observed phenomena and philosophical reasoning. Aristotle concludes the twelfth chapter of his Meteorics with the following remarkable and truly philosophical observations:—"*As time never fails, and the universe is eternal*, neither the Tanais nor the Nile can have flowed forever. The places where they rise were once dry, and there is a limit to their operations; but there is none to time. So also of all other rivers; they spring up and they perish; and the sea also continually deserts some lands, and invades others. The same tracts, therefore, of the earth, are not, some always sea, and other always continent, but *every thing changes in the course of time.*"

The cosmological opinions of the Romans are not entitled to much consideration, being derived almost exclusively from the Greeks. Strabo, in the second book of his Geography, examines the opinions of Eratosthenes and other Greek writers, concerning the causes by which marine shells came to be deposited on the tops of mountains and other places at great distances from the sea, and comes to the general conclusion, that these deposits are to be referred to the alternate shifting of the land and sea, by the long protracted operations of ordinary causes,—rejecting the hypothesis as entertained by the ancients. We learn, however, from Strabo, book fourth, that the Druids mentioned in the character of a religious dogma, that the universe was eternal, and that at distant intervals of time it was subject to conflagrations and deluges, from which catastrophes the world was continually renewed or re-produced in youth and vigor, and thus alternately *ad infinitum*.

The opinion of the alternate creation and destruction of the earth by fire and water, is, it would appear, universal; traces of it may be discovered amongst almost every people on the face of the earth. Humboldt informs us that "the Indians of America celebrated after the ideas of an antique superstition, by festivals and dancing, the destruction of the world, and the approaching epoch of its regeneration." Even the idea of a *millennium*, wherein the people of the earth are to enjoy the golden age of peace and happiness, after the iron era of strife and misery shall be finished, has its origin and root in this conceit and universal opinion of the alternate destruction and re-production of habitable worlds,—which destruction and re-production signifies, when expressed in philosophical language, simply the *expansion* of solid matter into an invisible gas, and the *contraction* of an invisible gas into solid matter.

---

## SCIENTIFIC PREJUDICES.

The notions and preconceptions of scientific enquirers do not attach themselves to the mind with so much stubbornness, do not cling and twine around the intellectual faculties with the same tenacity as those of the benighted and bigoted fanatic, whose very judgment is blighted, withered, and dried up by the scorching influence of an all-absorbing superstition. He is to be pitied. His mind has been distorted by false impressions, implanted in his early infancy, by a cunning race of sorcerers and soothsayers, who having discovered that *his* weakness constitutes *their* strength, have planned, and too surely effected, the overthrow of his mind, by taking advantage of the docility and helplessness of infancy. The bigot makes little or no pretension to reason; he is above it, or beyond it, or beneath it; and is, therefore, not strictly amenable to its laws. A philosophical argument falls dead upon his ear, it reaches not the senses, it touches not the mind; he neither feels its truth nor appreciates its value. He can neither perceive its beauties, nor detect its fallacies; nor discriminate between the former and the latter. From all which, it follows that, although he may be a stubborn opponent, he is but a weak antagonist; he strikes all abroad; his shafts fly wide of the mark, and his bootless valor is scorned and despised. Not so, however, with him who is the subject of scientific prejudice. He is a professed reasoner. He brings fact and argument to bear upon the question. Truth he declares to be the object of his search, and that he is willing to receive it wheresoever or by whomsoever it may have been discovered. His opinions and even his prejudices are entitled to respect; they are, to him, honest convictions, which he is justified in holding, until they are superseded by more correct views, founded upon evidence of a more incontrovertible character.

It is not necessary that we should enter into an examination, with a view to the refutation of systems of philosophy which are now exploded. It may be remarked, however, that at each step in the progress of science, the new system has had to contend with the scientific prejudices engendered by that previously established. There was a time when it was universally conceived that the earth was a plain surface, covered with, or surrounded by, a transparent canopy, called a firmament, something like a pewter plate, with a glass dish cover; and no doubt, he who first ventured to suggest that the earth was not a flat surface, but a sphere, was considered by the *scientific* professors of the old or established—the real orthodox system, as a visionary, perhaps a daring and impious innovator, whose object was to unsettle the well established principles of science and religion. Such indeed was the case; but the sphericity of the earth was established notwithstanding;—and why? Because that opinion was founded on truth, and has been confirmed by observation. This was one step. The next innovators propounded that the earth was not a fixed body placed in the centre, with the visible universe revolving round it, as had been formerly conceived; but was moving through space at an immense velocity. This new doctrine was more startling than the former innovation, and was accordingly opposed with great vehemence, especially by the priesthood, as disturbing the locality of those ancient abodes destined for the reception of the departed spirits of the just and unjust, after their liberation from the body. This new doctrine dislodged Jupiter from his fixed abode on high Olympus, and was, therefore, opposed with much energy. But this innovation also has been proved by observation, to be founded in truth, and has, therefore, prevailed, notwithstanding the most violent opposition; and its opposers have been compelled to accommodate their dogmas to the new modification of circumstances. Nature will not bend to the dogmas, and, therefore, the dogmas must bend to nature. The mountain would not come at the bidding of Mahomet, so Mahomet was compelled to go to the mountain. So it has been from the beginning; science and observation have been continually invading the territories of superstition, and the value of the conquered province consists chiefly in its remaining fixed and permanent within the domain of science. Science traces the operations of nature to the agency of secondary causes, by which the supererogatory agencies instituted by superstition are superseded, and the connexion of cause and effect placed upon a rational basis, by which, the cause being known, the effect, in a variety of instances, can be produced at pleasure; and thus men acquire a kind of sovereignty over nature, and are able to make her minister to their wants, which constitutes the chief value of scientific knowledge. But superstition is ever opposed to the advancement of science, because in the same proportion that the empire of the latter is extended or expanded, so is that of the former narrowed and contracted, and thus at every step of her progress, she is opposed by a host of opponents by which her march is more or less retarded; but in the end she always has prevailed. Galileo was cast into a dungeon by the Holy Inquisition, because by the aid of his telescope he discovered that Jupiter was attended by four moons, the whole of which, with their primary, were moving in space, thus bringing the conviction of the motion of the earth and moon home to the mind, confirming the truth of the Copernican theory, and at the same time uprooting the ancient foundations of Purgatory; for which last consideration he was cast into prison, and obliged to renounce the truth, lest a worse fate might befall him, in which he acted wisely,—for philosophy does not require that her truths should be confirmed by the victims of an *auto-da-fe*. *Her* truths will stand alone without the proppage of zeal and sophistry.

The fact of the motion of the earth having been incontrovertibly established, the question very naturally arose

—how was she sustained in her orbit? for it became evident that she rested upon nothing. It might be truly said that "the foundations of the earth were shaken." This is the point with which we have more particularly to deal in the present case; and the consideration of which, will lead us insensibly on to the conclusion to which we propose to arrive. It having been perceived that the moon was a constant attendant upon the earth in her revolutions round the sun, and that the satellites of Jupiter and Saturn revolved in connection with their primaries, the conclusion very naturally suggested itself that they were held together by an *invisible force*, and this force was named attraction. This conclusion was very much strengthened by the long known fact, that the moon produces a tide in the earth's ocean by *drawing* the waters towards her; it was, therefore, conceived that this drawing power must be reciprocal; that as the moon attracted the earth, so the earth must attract the moon with still greater force: the former being the larger body, the attracting energy excited by each upon the other must be in proportion to the magnitude of each, or quantity of matter in each respectively. "If," said Kepler, "the attractive force of the moon reaches to the earth, and be competent to raise the waters of the ocean, the attractive force of the earth must also reach to the moon, and even much farther, in proportion as the earth is greater than the moon." This opinion of an universal attractive force, operating throughout the solar system and the universe generally, began to be entertained by scientific men, as indeed had been the case with some of the ancients; but it was considered merely in the light of an opinion, the absolute truth of which had not been proved or demonstrated. The *demonstration* of the law by which the force of attraction operates,—inversely as the square of the distance,—and the application of this law to the motions of the heavenly bodies, constitutes the great discovery of Sir Isaac Newton, for which his name will ever be held in reverence, even if the system which he established should, by the progress of human knowledge, be to a large extent superseded by more extended views. But although we may honor the name of Newton, and pay respect to his *Commentary* upon the Book of Nature, we must ever recollect that his expositions are entitled to our acceptance so far only as they are found to accord with the great original upon which he has commented; and if by the accumulation of facts which accompanies, and, indeed, constitutes the progress of science, we should discover that Newton's Commentary contains erroneous views, we are bound to reject the comment, and revert to the original text book, for however great may be our respect to the name of Newton, we cannot consent to sacrifice the cause of truth at the shrine of adoration. This unmeasured adoration, and consequent acquiescence in every proposition, however indifferently supported, which is presented under the sanction of a great name, forms the root of that scientific prejudice to which we are now adverting, and the removal of which is essentially necessary in order to prepare the mind for the acceptance of truth. He who rests his religious faith upon the infallibility of the Pope is not more absurd in his belief than he who rests his scientific faith upon the infallibility of Sir Isaac Newton or any other great name.

It was generally believed, and pretty clearly established before the time of Newton, that the solar system, and by analogy the system of the universe, was held together by the force of universal attraction; but it was obvious to those who considered the subject attentively, that there must be some counteracting force to oppose that of attraction, for if the latter force acted alone and unopposed, the necessary result must be, that the satellites would be drawn into their primaries, and the primaries into the sun, and that within a very short space of time. Now, the length of the years and of the lunar months, as well as the periods of the planets generally, showed that if such a consummation were to take place, it must be after a lapse of many ages, for its progress was almost, if not altogether, imperceptible; it was, therefore, concluded, that the force of attraction was really opposed by a counteracting force, and it was very generally believed that the tendency which a heavy body, in rapid motion, has to fly off from the centre round which it revolves, might probably constitute a force sufficient to counteract the centralizing force of attraction. This, it was conceived, might be the opposing force; but the difficulty lay in proving that it really was so. The proof, the demonstration, is said to have been accomplished by Sir Isaac Newton, and the manner in which he proceeded with this proof was as follows:—He proved, first, that a body under the action of *one* force can move only in a right line, which right line will be in the direction in which the force acts. Second, that a body under the action of two equal forces, whose lines of impulse are at right angles to each other, will obey neither force singly, but will take a middle course, at an angle of 45 degrees to the line of each of the two forces. He also showed that a body moving in a curved line, or circular path, must be under the action of a force acting in the centre or focus of that path or curve; and of a force acting at all times at right angles, with the central force;—the latter tending to urge the body onward in a direct line, and the former continually deflecting it from that right line, and thereby retaining it in its circular or curved path—as is very neatly exemplified by a weight at the end of a string when whirled round by the hand. The string represents the attractive force by which the revolving weight is retained in its orbit, and the momentum of the weight, which is kept up by a slight movement of the hand, represents, or rather is the force which urges it onward in its circular path. These are the *centripetal* and *centrifugal* forces of the *Newtonian* philosophy. Now, as no known force can at every instant change its line of action except momentum, it was conceived that the planets were urged on in their orbits by momentum alone; but it must be observed, that in the case of the planets, we have no proof that this momentum is kept up by a continued impulse, as by the slight movement of the hand in the case of the weight and string. Having ascertained that the intensity of the force of attraction is inversely as the squares of the distances, observing the descent of heavy bodies near the earth's surface, he extended this law to the moon, conceiving that if this satellite move under the influence of the same law, she must be deflected from the rectilinear path which she endeavors to pursue by the first law of nature, a given distance in a given time, and that the deflection must be commensurate with the intensity of the attractive force, as estimated by her distance from the earth. The next step was to ascertain the diameter of the earth, in order to estimate the amount of the attractive force which she must exert upon the moon, as well as to express the moon's distance in radii of the earth.

"The corner stone of the whole system of universal gravitation," says a modern writer, "is, that the force which causes a heavy body to descend to the surface of the earth, is the same that retains the moon in her orbit, and makes her deflect from a straight line, and bend towards the earth. All that was requisite to establish the identity of the forces by which these effects were produced, was to prove that the quantity of the effect produced in a certain time upon the moon in thus deflecting from a straight line (taking into consideration the law by which the force varied and *the distance of the moon*), was in due proportion to the effect produced by the *force of gravity* in the same time upon a falling body at the surface of the earth."

"It is evident, therefore, that the determination of this question depended upon, and would, in its solution, be effected by, the distance of the moon from the earth. This distance being expressed only in a number of radii of the earth (about 60), it was necessary to ascertain the length of the earth's radius. This could only be done by means of the proportion which the radius of a circle always bears to the circumference; and the length of the circumference being 360 times that of a degree, the whole matter at last resolves itself into the geodesical operation of accurately measuring a degree upon the earth's surface. The only measure, which in 1666, the time of Newton's first taking up the subject, was that of Norwood's; this exceeded the true length of a degree by little less than 1,000 yards, and as this error would be greatly multiplied in each step of the process, it is not surprising that Newton, whether he used this measure, or the still more incorrect one of 60 miles to a degree, could not reconcile the two phenomena of the falling stone and the revolving moon, so as to refer both to the same cause—namely, the attractive force of the earth. The consequence of this error in the then received length of a degree was, that for many years Newton laid aside his theory of universal gravitation."

"But in 1670, the measurement of an arc of the meridian, by Pickard, took place; by mere accident the length of a degree in latitude 49, was then ascertained to within 35 yards of what is now considered the true length. This new measure brought Newton back to his favorite hypothesis. He then satisfactorily proved that the force of gravity and the force by which the moon is retained in her orbit are one and the same. It is related that towards the end of the calculation, and when he perceived its probable successful issue, he became so much agitated as to be obliged to request a friend to assist him in completing it. Thus, by the aid of a true length of a degree, was established the grand theory of universal gravitation."

Now, that a stone falls to the earth, and that the moon is retained in her orbit by the force of attraction, is universally admitted, and may, therefore, be considered as settled by the common consent of mankind; that both these effects are to be referred to the same universal force in a general sense, may also be considered as a point which has been decided by the same tribunal; but whether they are referrable to the one and the same modification of that universal force of attraction which presents itself to our mind in different aspects, may admit of some doubt, which will be adverted to in another part of this work. It is not, however, on this point that the Newtonian system fails, but upon that of the counteracting or compensating force of momentum, which is said to balance the force of attraction continually struggling against the latter force, thereby preventing the planets from falling into the sun. This is the weak point of the Newtonian philosophy, for a very little reflection will enable us to discern that the momentum or centrifugal *force*, as it is absurdly denominated, is no force whatever, but an *effect* derived from, and dependent upon, a real force, whatever that force may be. But in order that the hollowness of this centrifugal force may be distinctly seen, it will be necessary to advert to the manner in which it is introduced, and the evidence upon which its pretensions to the title of a natural force are based. The Creator, it is said, having formed the earth and moon, impelled them from his hand into space, somewhat after the manner that a man impels a cricket or skittle ball, by which "*primitive impulse*," as it is technically termed, a momentum was created; and space being a vacuum, it is said, this momentum once created, must remain undiminished forever,—because, a body once put in motion, must continue in motion, unless it meet with some resistance from another body to destroy that motion; and further, under the influence of this momentum, as derived from the "primitive impulse," the earth, or moving body, continually endeavors to proceed in a straight line, and would so move, and be thereby carried out of the solar system, were it not that she is continually deflected from this course, and turned towards the sun by the force of attraction. Again, as the earth revolves upon her axis, it is said, that at the time of her receiving the "primitive impulse," she was held, not exactly in the centre, but a little on one side, so that when she received the great heave, she went off with a whirling motion, which she has retained ever since,—just as a stick, held by one end, whirls when thrown from the hand, with this difference, that the stick does not whirl forever. It will scarcely be believed that Laplace, "*Laplace le grand!*" actually entered into an elaborate calculation, with a view to determine at what particular point the Creator held the earth at the time of giving the grand push, and that after a most profound investigation, he arrived at the never-to-be-forgotten conclusion, that when the "primitive impulse" was imparted, the earth was held exactly twenty-five miles from the centre, and hence, quoth Laplace, the earth revolves upon her axis once in twenty-four hours. If she had been held a little nearer to the centre, our days would have been longer, and if a little farther off, she would have revolved with greater velocity, and our days would have been shorter. And this is what we call philosophy! This ridiculous stuff is said to exalt our minds, and to give us sublime conceptions of the power and wisdom of the Supreme Being, representing him in the character of a mechanical agent, rolling up globes of matter and whirling them from his hand, as Jupiter was represented by the heathen world, projecting his thunderbolts from high Olympus. How different is the language of the pious poet, Cowper, who says:—

> ——— "There lives and works
> A soul in all things, and that soul is God;
> ——————— Through all diffused,
> The life of all that lives."

Aye, and that soul is ever active; the creation of God never had a beginning, and will never have an end. He is the same yesterday, to-day, and forever;—and if the progress of his work be not seen and known at the present time, it is because men, blinded by preconceived opinions, neglect to look into the works themselves for the evidence of that progress. Their opinions are formed from the written books of men, and not from the book of nature, which is written with the finger of God himself, and the indelible characters of which no man can forge, or falsify, or obliterate. We have just given a specimen of the most exalted of these human compositions, and what does it exhibit?—a bundle of assumptions, having not one tittle of evidence whereon to rest; and these assumptions comprehend the very essence of what is called the Newtonian philosophy, which has been for the last hundred years trumpeted forth from Halls, Colleges, and Universities, as the most sublime discovery that has ever been made by man; and to crown the absurdity, the world has been gravely assured that every proposition has been rigidly demonstrated. Has it been demonstrated that the earth was pushed off in the manner described? Has it been demonstrated that this push was imparted to the earth 25 miles from the centre? Has it been demonstrated in that space, which is also said to be filled with light, and which is now known to be pervaded by an etherial matter, is a vacuum? And above all, has it been demonstrated that the centrifugal *force*, as it is ignorantly denominated, is imperishable? mere *momentum*, an effect which can be either created or destroyed by the art of man, as every one can *demonstrate* by the simple operation of setting a fly wheel in motion, and again stopping it by resisting its motion;—and yet we are told that every proposition of this system has been "*rigidly demonstrated.*" A barrier has been drawn across the pathway of philosophy by these unwarranted assumptions, and it is high time that it were broken down; the progress of science must not be impeded by a body of self-constituted dictators, who, in the pride of ignorance, hold the reins of knowledge, and check the onward career of mankind. The truth cannot be too widely known, or too loudly proclaimed, for all men are interested in its discovery; and those who have studied the matter most deeply know, that so far from the present age having arrived at the fountain of all knowledge, the world is but just turned into the path that leads to truth, and when a hundred generations shall have passed away, there will still remain much to be discovered; therefore, let no barrier be placed across the path that leads to truth, for truth and happiness are intimately connected with each other;—they are twin sisters—lovely in their lives, and even in their death they ought not to be divided; for although truth in her nature is immortal, she has been often crucified by the arts of men. The Newtonian system of philosophy has held almost undivided sway over men's minds for nearly a century. It has been erected into a kind of second gospel, to doubt the correctness or authenticity of which, has been held as a sort of scientific heresy. The argument has been, "All that is to be known, has been discovered by Newton, and it is presumptuous to seek further." It is now fit and proper the world should know that the me-

*chanical* system of Newton which requires a push to set it going is not the system of nature. It is fit the world should know that there is another natural force, besides attraction, equally extended, equally imperishable, equally active—in short that *attraction* and *repulsion* are *universal forces*, whose co-operation may be seen, and is necessary in every process of nature, whether great or small, in the formation of a plant or moss that clings to the wall, and of a world revolving in the solar system, or any other part of the universe.

Enough has perhaps been advanced to raise a doubt in the mind of the reader as to the soundness of the foundation upon which the Newtonian system rests, especially in respect to the centrifugal force: the subject is, however, of too much importance to be passed over slightly. Those scientific prejudices which it is our present object to remove, are closely interwoven with that system, and unless these prejudices can be shaken or removed, it will be vain to expect that the propositions and arguments which are subsequently to be advanced can be duly appreciated, or examined with a proper spirit. The mind must be cleared of error before it can receive the truth;—the husbandman clears the land before he sows the seed.

---

## NEWTON'S LAW OF MOTION.

The Newtonian system is purely mechanical, and has its root in a certain obscure principle called the *vis inertia* of matter. The expression, *vis inertia*, taken literally, signifies the *power of inactivity*; when taken according to its philosophical application, it signifies the *power of having no power*, which is certainly not very intelligible. Modern commentators, perceiving the absurdity of the expression, have droppped the *vis* (power), retaining the *inertia* only, which signifies simply the negation or absence of power. In this expression a principle is assumed, and attempted to be embodied, in the face of millions of facts to the contrary, that nature has no physical power within herself to produce, or rather to continue motion; but that motion must be generated in a mechanical manner by some force external to nature; and proceeding upon this assumption, the following law is laid down as the thesis or foundation upon which the Newtonian superstructure is to be erected:—

"*If a body be at rest, it will continue at rest; and if in motion, it will continue in motion, and will move uniformly forward in a straight line, if it be not disturbed by the action of some external force.*"

In an abstract and mechanical sense, this law is perfectly true, and may be easily demonstrated; that is, if we grant the *vis inertia* of matter. If a body be at rest, it will continue at rest; because, by the *vis inertia*, it has no power to put itself in motion; and if in motion, it will continue in motion; because, by the *vis inertia*, it has no power to bring itself to a state of rest; and it will move uniformly forward in a right line; because, by the *vis inertia*, it has no power to change its line of motion; therefore, if it deviate from a right line, it is acted upon by some external force.

Now, in the case of planetary motion, what is this force which is said to be external? Attraction. And what is attraction? A property of matter. What then becomes of the *vis inertia*, upon which the whole fabric is based, and which sets out with the assumption that nature contains no power within herself capable of producing, or in any way controlling the motion of matter?

Let us examine this law a little further. If a body be at rest, it will remain at rest. This is true in a mechanical sense. A post set up at the corner of a street, or any body laid upon the surface of the earth, will not move away mechanically in a mass; but do they remain absolutely at rest? Whosoever says they do, must know very little of the laws of nature; indeed, he must shut his eyes, and remain wilfully blind to all that is passing around him. A few revolving seasons are sufficient to remove both the one and the other. Again:—If a body be in motion, it will continue to move uniformly forward in a direct line, if it be not disturbed by the action of some external force. In an abstract and mechanical sense, this also is true; but in what part of the universe is the body to move without being disturbed by the action of external forces? If space were not really a vacuum, and attraction did not exist, it might have a chance to continue in motion; but as space is a perfect vacuum, even according to the Newtonian philosophy, and as the moving body is disturbed and drawn from its rectilinear course by the force of attraction, the law, although true, abstractly considered, has no application to the real circumstances. By the *vis inertia*, the body continues in motion only on condition that it be not retarded or disturbed by external causes; the law is true, but the conditions are not fulfilled.

We find, then, that attraction, which is a property of matter, and is *not* an external force, but is inherent in matter, is competent to produce motion; is, in fact, a *natural force*, and that all matter, under the action of this, moves or is attracted towards a centre. Thus, a stone proceeding from a state of rest, is attracted, and, in consequence moves towards the centre of the earth, until its motion is arrested by the resistance which it meets at the earth's solid surface. But the earth and planets do not move in right lines towards the centre of the sun; if they did, their existence as planets would be of short duration. They move in circular paths or orbits. Now, as a body, under the action of *one* force, can only move in a direct line or path, and as the planets move in curved lines, we are certain they are under the action of two forces, one of which is attraction, a *real* force, capable of putting matter in motion; and the direction in which it acts is towards the centre of the sun. This, in the Newtonian philosophy, is what is called the *centripetal force*, and by which the planets are retained in their orbits.

Let us now examine the *centrifugal force*, which prevents the planets from falling into the sun, by continually striving against the force of attraction, or the centripetal force, and thereby causes them to move in circular orbits. If the centrifugal force be a real force, like attraction, then these two forces are competent to produce the effects ascribed to their operation: if the centrifugal force be not a real force, but simply an effect derived from a force external to nature, then it cannot support an everlasting struggle with a real force, whose efforts are constantly directed to its annihilation, and which force cannot itself be destroyed nor even diminished, by another force acting against it. Now what are the elements of the centrifugal force? Momentum: that is, a certain *quantity* of mechanical motion. The momentum of a body, or quantity of motion, is measured by the quantity of matter and the velocity of the body, taken conjointly; that is, the quantity of any body multiplied by its velocity, is considered as its momentum: thus, if the quantity of matter in one body be represented by 4, and its velocity by 4, and the quantity of matter in another body by 8, and its velocity by 2, the momentum or quantity of motion in each of these two bodies is equal, because 4 times 4 are 16, and 8 times 2 are 16.

Now having ascertained the velocity with which the earth moves in her orbit, if we could determine exactly or nearly the quantity of matter in the terrestrial globe,—whether it be a hollow sphere, or a solid body,—whether its density is the same throughout, or if the density increase or diminish towards the centre, in what ratio it does so increase or diminish; if all these points could be determined, then we could measure the quantity of the earth's momentum, and might proceed to compare this quantity with that of the sun's attraction exerted upon the earth, with a view to decide whether the two forces exactly counterbalance each other; but until these points are settled, it is impossible to obtain a result that shall even approximate the truth, much less such a result as may be relied upon in mathematical investigations. Astronomers proceed upon the assumption that the earth is a solid body; geologists, on the other hand, who have examined the structure of the earth itself, give it as their opinion that it is a hollow sphere, and that the shell or crust bears a very small proportion to the whole diameter.

But even if these points were satisfactorily determined, and it were found that the quantity of momentum were exactly sufficient to counterbalance the force of the sun's attraction, would the quantity of momentum remain forever undiminished, notwithstanding that the force of the sun's attraction is continually tending to the annihilation of the momentum? *This is the great question by which the matter is to be decided.* Now, to make use of a familiar expression, the momentum in the earth, or any other body, is merely a certain quantity of force "bottled up," and will last till the bottle is empty, and no longer: whilst attraction is an inexhaustible fountain of force, from which you may draw forever without any diminution of the original quantity.

When a ball is discharged from a cannon's mouth, its momentum is derived from the explosion of the gunpowder, which, be it observed, is the *expansive or repulsive force.* This expansive force is "bottled up" in the cannon ball, and after it has received the impulse, it would move on forever in a right line if it were not disturbed by the action of some external force. If the momentum were a real force, like attraction, that could not be destroyed; it would move on forever, notwithstanding the action of an equal distributing force, not in a right line, but in a curve, under the action of the two forces: but as the momentum "bottled up" in the cannon ball is not a real force, but simply an effect derived from the "primitive impulse," imparted to it by the expansive force of the gunpowder, and as, by the momentum, the ball continually endeavors to proceed in a right line, whilst the earth's attraction continually bends it downwards towards the surface, the momentum is gradually diminished, and eventually is entirely destroyed, and the ball comes to a state of rest, mechanically speaking, upon the surface. It is on this account that the muzzle of the gun is elevated, when firing at long distances; for although the ball, in rising to the apex, or highest point of its course, has a greater quantity of the momentum destroyed than if it were fired point blank, or at right angles, with the line of attraction, yet, as from the apex the distance to the surface of the earth is considerable, the ball is enabled to proceed to a greater distance before it meets with an obstacle to destroy its motion entirely; but in no part of its course, whether rising or falling, does the attraction in any way add to the *angular* velocity. It is true that the resistance of the atmosphere aids the gravity in a trifling degree; but if the ball moved in a perfect vacuum, the same effect would follow before it had proceeded many yards further in its course. As the Newtonian philosophy assumes that the centrifugal force, or angular velocity or momentum, was imparted to the earth and planets in a similar manner, by an impulse from the hand of the Creator, it is plain, if their angular velocity depended upon this force alone, or rather this effect, for it is not a force, that the same consummation would follow, and that they would be precipitated upon the sun before they had completed one revolution. It is imagined that the Newtonian philosophy provides against this catastrophe, by supposing (without any attempt at proof) that space is a vacuum, forgetting that the sun's attraction would effectually destroy the momentum derived from the supposed "primitive impulse" without the aid of a resisting medium.

It is impossible to comprehend or explain the motion of matter, unless we admit and introduce *two real and natural forces:* attraction is one of these, but momentum is not the other. In a body at rest there is no momentum, and were this body under the action of one force only, it must remain forever at rest; there is no other force to deliver it from the grasp of attraction, and to put it in motion. But although momentum is incompetent to sustain a continuous effort against the force of attraction, it must be taken as an adjunct, and allowance must be made for it as an effect entering into, and in all cases modifying the subject of force and motion more or less. Attraction is one force, and the line of its attraction is towards the centre. Now it is evident that no force can completely counterbalance attraction except repulsion, whose line of action is towards the circumference; *all matter is at all times under the action of both these forces*, and is thus held exactly in the position which it occupies in the universe, as securely as if it were in a blacksmith's vice. If the two forces were at all times, and in all places, in perfect equilibrio, matter would remain at rest; but the equilibrium is continually disturbed, and motion is the result of that disturbance. When the attractive or contractive force predominates, the motion is towards the centre; when the repulsive or expansive force predominates, the motion is from the centre; and in either case the line of motion is modified by momentum. Place a sky-rocket on the earth and it will remain there; the attractive force predominates; apply a lighted match and the expansive force is not created, for it existed before, but is put into a state of high activity, and if the expansive or repulsive force, for they are one and the same, be sufficient to overcome the attractive force, the sky-rocket begins to rise from the earth, without the aid of a "primitive impulse," and so long as the expansive force predominates, the sky-rocket continues to rise till it reaches the highest point, where the two forces are for an instant in equilibrio, after which, the attractive force predominates, and the stick and other parts of the sky-rocket that have not undergone the expansive process, are attracted to the earth's surface. This is a faint and imperfect illustration of the two forces by which all the operations of nature are carried forward.

Again:—in respect to the light and heat of the sun, the explanations or suggestions given are of the most unphilosophical and unsatisfactory description. We have been told, for example, upon the authority of Sir Isaac Newton, that the sun is so many thousands of times hotter than red hot iron; that certain comets when in their perihelia, are exposed to a heat so many thousands of times hotter than red hot iron; and, again, when in their aphelia, they are subjected to a degree of cold so many times colder than ice;--and it has even been suggested that these gaseous bodies may be the abodes of the damned, who are thus alternately roasted and frozen as a punishment for their unbelief! This was a good thought; for as the Catholic priesthood opposed the Copernican system chiefly on account of its having caused the removal of purgatory from its ancient situation, it was perhaps politic to remove their opposition by finding them a new one, fully as good as the one they had lost,—for in the old one there was nothing but roasting carried on, whereas in the newly discovered regions there was the agreeable contrast of freezing superadded. In addition to these very scientific views about the sun and comets being so many degrees hotter than red hot iron, we have, even in recent works, careful calculations to show how very cold the climate of Jupiter must be, and also how hot must be that of Venus and Mercury, all which is readily received, and probably has been written, without much reflection. As we shall devote a chapter to the consideration of light and heat, we shall not enter into the subject at present, to show how erroneous these representations are; we may, however, remark, that the moon has every mark of being a much colder body than the earth, although not more removed from the sun than the latter, and thus we might learn, that the heat of a planet does not depend upon its distance from the sun alone, but upon other circumstances in connexion with that distance, which circumstances are to be sought for in the planet itself. We may also remark, that the supposition of a body or volume of gas, like a comet, being raised to a heat thousands of times hotter than red hot iron, without being dissipated, is contrary to all that we know of the constitution of gaseous matter.

In respect to light, it is said, according to the Newtonian theory, which holds the materiality of light, to move at a velocity which is almost inconceivable, passing from the sun to the earth, at a distance of 95 millions of miles in about eight minutes; but this theory has been now almost superseded by another, called the Undulatory Theory, in which it is held that no material fluid proceeds from the sun, but that light is produced by the undulations of a subtle ether, which being excited by the sun, is kept in a state of continual motion, and thus light is kept up without the expenditure of any matter whatever. This is incomprehensible,—but the most extravagant part of the undulatory theory of light remains to be noticed, which is, that the undulations or vibrations succeed each other so rapidly, that upwards of *seven hundred of million of millions* of these are performed in a single second! Seven hundred millions of millions during one swing of a pendulum! This is the *new light*, and has been very generally received in the scientific world. There are parties of no mean attainments, who absolutely believe in this undulatory theory of light, which is based upon a principle altogether contrary to experience, to philosophy, and to common sense. With respect to the materiality of heat and light, there appears to be some controversy among the chemists; those who contend for its materiality have given it a place among the elementary substances, under the appellation of caloric, while others hold its materiality as too hypothetical to allow it a place. It would perhaps be well if chemists would consent to consider their lists of elements as altogether hypothetical, that is, not in a chemical but in a philosophical light, if it be correct to make such a distinction where some may probably consider there is none. A subject which is not reducible in the crucible, or even by the galvanic battery, is not necessarily a simple body; and further, it is certain that many of the most important phenomena in the vegetable, animal and mineral kingdoms are not explicable upon the hypothesis which considers the present list as elementary substances. Nature forms and dissolves compounds which the chemist's art cannot reach. It is, therefore, by no means impossible that she may go one step further than this, and convert one body considered simple into another also considered simple. If we would study chemistry, or the nature of light and heat, or the laws which regulate the operations of nature upon the great scale, we must look at the processes of nature herself, and not confine our views to the retort, the crucible, and the prism alone, although in some cases they may lend us assistance in our pursuit; in a word, we must extend our views without hesitation, leaving established opinions to stand or fall, according as circumstances may determine. Whatever may be the ultimate result of such a proceeding, it is almost impossible that science can be injured, for a very great proportion of that which now goes by the name is little else than a heap of unmeaning verbiage.

"We know nothing," says Sir Humphrey Davy, "of the true elements belonging to nature; but as far as we can reason from the relations of the properties of matter, *hydrogen* is the substance which approaches nearest to what the elements may be supposed to be. It has energetic powers of combination, its parts are highly *repulsive* as to each other, and *attractive* of the particles of other matter; it enters into combination in a quantity very much smaller than any other substance, and in this respect is approached by no known body. *Oxygen*, next to hydrogen, partakes most of an elementary character. It has a greater energy of attraction, and after hydrogen, is the body that enters into combination in the smallest proportions. All inflammable matter may be similarly constituted, and may contain hydrogen, and on this supposition, they owe these powers of uniting with oxygen, to the attractive force of the combined hydrogen. The probabilities that the metals and inflammable solids may consist of different proportions of hydrogen and an unknown base, are strengthened by the fact, that the metals whose specific gravity is the least, and which, are, therefore, supposed to contain the largest quantity of hydrogen in combination with the unknown base, are the most inflammable, such as potassium, sodium, &c., whilst those, on the other hand, whose specific gravity is greater, as gold and platinum may contain the smallest quantity of the inflammable body of small weight."

There is no impossibility in the supposition, that the same matter in different electrical states, or in different arrangements, may constitute substances chemically different; even if it should be ultimately found that oxygen and hydrogen are the same matter in different states of electricity, or that *two* or *three* elements in different proportions constitute all bodies, the great doctrines of chemistry, the theory of definite proportions, and the specific attractions of bodies must remain immutable. The *causes* of the difference of the form of bodies, supposed to be elementary, must be ascertained before we are justified in the assertion, that they are really simple substances; and if such a step should ever be made, we should have to consider those substances, or some of them, now deemed elementary, as compounded of two or more substances; and such a change could in no way affect the doctrines of chemistry, considered as a science. Whatever decision be ultimately made respecting those views, it is certain that there is matter moving in space, between us and the heavenly bodies, capable of communicating heat, which matter does not enter in the chemist's lists of elementary substances, besides those bodies generally denominated imponderable, the extensive influence and activity of which is confessed by all. In this department of science there is at present almost as many sects and parties as in that of religion; one party maintains that heat is a substance, another opposes this view, holding it to be merely a state of matter. The same difference of opinion exists in respect to light; and even electricity, although capable of rending rocks of vast thickness, and of destroying huge buildings, has been denied a place amongst material existences. The earth and planets are moved in their orbits by a sort of miracle, for contrary to all experience, contrary to all other motion, the celestial movement never tends to a termination, and even the centrifugal force, which we know cannot maintain its existence for any length of time when opposed by another force, is to remain forever.

Now all this jumble of conflicting doctrines arises from the fundamental error of conceiving that the great processes of nature have *now* arrived at a fixed and stationary point;—that the earth revolves in an orbit at a fixed and stationary distance as regards the sun,—that heat is a substance,—and that the bodies called elementary in chemical nomenclature are ultimate principles, because they are the most simple that can be reached or detected by chemical analysis; in all which conclusions the broad, palpable, and unquestionable fact is overlooked:—that every operation, every motion forms a part of a great and universal process, ever in action, ever tending towards the termination or ultimate point of each particular process, again to re-act, to start off in a new direction,—that the earth neither would nor could move in her orbit unless she were moving towards that point in which her process as a planet will terminate, and from which point the re-action will commence as a necessary result of the principles by which the different motions are originated,—that heat is not a substance *per se*, but an effect resulting from the general process, an action of parts upon parts,—and that although the chemist is bound and restricted by the rules of his art, and properly so, to consider those bodies as elementary to which his analysis will reach, which are more or less tangible as objects of sense and experiment, the philosopher is fettered by no such restraints, but on the contrary, he is bound by the principles and terms of that philosophy to which he has devoted himself, to look into the far perspective of nature's deepest arcana. Having carefully reviewed the objects and operations of the visible and tangible world, he takes his cue and ventures boldly into the labyrinth of hidden mysteries. Leaving the region of external sense, he dives into the deepest recesses, guided solely by the inward light of that intellectual lamp which has been carefully trimmed and replenished with oil extracted from the known and accredited operations of the visible creation, and in proportion as his lamp is well trimmed previous to commencing his journey, so may it be anticipated that his researches will be more or less successful.

---

## MIND AND MATTER.

As one of the chief objects of the present work is to show that *all natural phenomena*, both of mind and matter, may be comprehended in *one universal science*, it becomes necessary that we should endeavor to point out where the distinction, and where the connexion exists, the line of demarcation, and the connecting link between the two sciences, in which is included the study of all nature.

Physical philosophy treats of *matter* and *motion* in the most minute as well as in the most extended sense; whilst moral philosophy treats of *mind* and *motives*—of the faculties, feelings and sympathies, by which animated beings are moved. In other words, physical philosophy treats of the *motion of inanimate matter;* moral philosophy of the *motion of animate matter*, and likewise of the *physical and moral forces*, by which these motions are effected, and also of the effects themselves; the former of which is called *physical action*, and the latter *moral action*. Thus these two branches of science are distinguished from each other.

Now, as the sensations of animated beings are excited by the physical action of external objects, and as from these sensations they are conveyed inward to the internal mind and produce moral action, it becomes evident that physical and moral philosophy are connected through the medium of the animal sensations, that the two are but branches of one universal science, and may both be included in the all-comprehensive title—Natural Philosophy—for nature includes all existence, both mind and matter. Physical action proceeds from the external world, *through the senses, to* the internal mind. Moral action proceeds *from* the internal mind, *through the voluntary muscles, to* the external world. By which we may perceive that mind and matter act and re-act upon each other, that they are intimately and indissolubly connected, and form, in fact, but one all-comprehensive science. The unity of this universal science will be rendered still more evident if we further consider, that the motion of all inanimate matter, of atoms, worlds, and systems of worlds, is due to the action and re-action of the ultimate forces of attraction and repulsion, and that the motions or actions of all animated beings, of individuals, families, communities and nations, in short, all animated nature, is due to the action and re-action of the same ultimate and universal forces, through the sensations, a force of moral attraction being manifested towards such objects as give pleasure, and the moral repulsion towards such as give pain.

It may be further remarked, that every change in the disposition, arrangement, or course of action of external objects will produce a corresponding change of the attractive and repulsive sensations, and hence, also, a similar and corresponding change of impressions upon the mind, and of necessity a corresponding change in the motives by which the mind is actuated. The most uncouth and unpolished nature will show some propriety of behavior, if admitted into polite company; and on the other hand, the most finished gentleman will become less polished if surrounded by men of coarse manners; on the same principle the orderly or disorderly arrangement even of inanimate objects exercises an influence upon the conduct and character of animated beings.

As every change of the disposition, arrangement, or physical action of external objects produces a corresponding change in the internal mind upon which they act, so also every change of the disposition, arrangement, or mental action of internal ideas produces a corresponding change in the external world. Mind is modified by matter, and matter is modified by mind. The temples of Greece and the huts of the Indian savages are both of them modifications of matter, emanating from the mind, and the difference of the two is precisely that of the minds from which they emanated. Both the temple and the hut were formed and fashioned in the mind before they had a material existence.

It is not our intention to pursue the connexion of mind and matter further at present; but as systems of philosophy are structures of knowledge, fashioned by the mind, and emanating from it, as much as the Grecian temples or the Indian huts, it becomes us to examine carefully by what channels or conduits that knowledge (the materials of the structure) found its way into the mind in the first instance,—for unless we can connect the reasonings of the mind with existing facts in the visible world, we shall be apt to impose upon ourselves at every step; to take the pure imaginings of the mind for real and tangible existences. From a want of due attention to this important consideration, we have not, even at the present day, mastered the first step of physical philosophy—a definition of matter. Solid extension does not express it, for no matter is *solid;* neither is it defined by summing up its properties as divisibility, &c., for an atom is presumed to be indivisible. In short, there is no definition of matter that will apply under all circumstances, nor are we about to supply the deficiency. Before we attempt to define matter, let us examine and endeavor to understand the nature and power of the instruments with which we propose to investigate its properties. These instruments are:—

I.—The five senses of seeing, hearing, smelling, tasting and feeling, through which we receive impressions from external objects.

II.—The memory into which we collect and retain those impressions, or the ideas which they have generated.

III.—The imagination by which we trace analogies between those things which have passed through the sensations into the memory, and that infinitely larger portion of nature which has not come in contact with our senses.

IV.—The judgment or reasoning faculty by which we compare the whole contents of the mind, correcting the wanderings of the imagination by the facts recorded in the memory.

To these we might perhaps add a fifth, that is, the numerous scientific aids to the senses and faculties, such as telescopes, microscopes, and other instruments, by which the field of observation is greatly enlarged, and our knowledge of the operations of nature proportionately increased.

What information do we receive through the senses in relation to the properties of matter?

Let us examine what kind of impressions those are which we receive through the ear,--what information reaches the mind through this channel? What is that which we hear? Sound; and nothing but sound. Now, what is sound? No one will contend that sound is material,—no one will have the temerity to assert that sound is a substance. What then is sound? It is an *effect* produced by the *action* of matter upon matter; and the intensity of the sound is generally commensurate with the intensity of the action by which it is produced. By the *mechanical* action of the hammer upon the church bell, sound is elicited, and undulates over a surface of several square miles, more or less, in proportion to the intensity of the action of the hammer upon the bell. Whilst the action continues, sound continues to be produced or given out. When the action ceases, the production of sound ceases also, because the sound is an effect of the action. By the *chemical* action produced in the explosion or expansion of a handful of gunpowder stuffed into a cannon, sound is given out and spread over an area of very great extent, and the loudness of the sound or report is, as in the former case, proportionate to the action of which it is an effect.

In whatever way we examine the intimations which we receive through the *ear*, we shall find that by those intimations we receive the evidence of sound, and of sound only; and if we were endowed with this sense of hearing alone, we could not form any correct conceptions of the nature of sound, or how it is produced. But at the same time that we *hear* sound, we *see* that it is produced in connexion with motion or action, and not unfrequently we *feel*, by the agitation of air and other surrounding objects, that a concussion has taken place; and thus although we are unable to determine the nature of the sound by the ear alone, yet by the aid, by the concurring testimony of the other senses, we learn that sound is produced by the action of matter upon matter,—that it is not an existence *per se*, but an *effect* or accompaniment of motion or action, and this effect is at all times in proportion to the action which is the efficient cause by which it is produced. We perceive, then, that without motion or action, if the material world were in a state of perfect repose, we could receive no evidence of the presence or existence of matter through the organ of hearing alone, inasmuch as this organ is acted upon by sound, and sound only; and sound is an effect, a contingent result, which is determined by circumstances, and is not an essential or *constant* property of matter, for matter may exist independent of sound,—although sound cannot be produced independent of matter.

What do we learn through the sense of *taste* concerning the existence of matter? Place a piece of *dry* sugar upon a *dry* tongue, no sense of sweetness or taste of any kind will be excited.—Why? Because there is no *action.* It is the same with every other substance, sweet or bitter. A nauseous drug, in the form of a pill, is passed into the stomach by dropping it into the throat, thus evading the bitter taste which would be excited by the *action* of the drug upon the organs of taste. In a word, the sense of taste, like that of hearing, is excited by *action*, and by action only; and the intensity of taste is at all times in proportion to the intensity of action. When a piece of *hard* sugar candy is put into the mouth, the taste, the sense of sweetness is feebly felt, because the action goes on feebly, and for this reason the teeth is applied to *pound* the materials, as in a mortar, so that a large surface being exposed to the saliva of the mouth, the action goes on more briskly; and the sense of sweetness is perceived more or less vividly in proportion as the action goes on more or less intensely. In short, through the sense of taste we perceive nothing but the action of matter upon matter; we neither do nor can distinguish the existence of matter through that sense alone, because taste is a contingent, and not an essential or *constant* property of matter. The same matter *acting* upon different organizations, will produce different sensations; and the same matter under a new or different chemical combination, will produce a different sensation on the same organization.

The sense of *smell* is analogous to those of taste and hearing. It is excited by *action*, and by action only. There are persons who are without the faculty of perceiving the odors of different substances.—Why? Because there is no *action* going on between their organs of smell and the substances by which they are environed; and in those animals who have this sense excited to an eminent degree, such as Spaniels and Pointers, there is a keen, an intense action going on of which we neither have, nor can have any conception. But this sense, like the two preceding, is excited by the *action*, and not by the mere presence of matter; for without action this sense cannot discern the presence or existence of matter, considered as a substance merely.

We have only two senses to notice, *seeing* and *feeling*; but these are of a higher and more extended nature, and, therefore, demand more careful attention. And first, of the faculty of *sight*. What information do we receive from this channel?

The first and most important is the evidence of *color*. And how do we perceive color? By the medium of *light*. Without light no color can be discerned. How is light produced? By the action of matter upon matter. Without action there is no light. Light is not an existence *per se*, but an effect, like sound, and is produced by action, and action alone. Strike a flint and steel together, you produce a spark, which is light;—this spark is an effect of the *mechanical action* or collision of striking a flint and steel against each other. Whilst the action—the mechanical striking—continues, the sparks, the light, continues to be produced, just as sound continues to be produced by the mechanical striking of the clapper against the bell. But when the action, the striking, ceases, the production of sound or light ceases also, for they are both the effects of action, and nothing more. Again, we perceive that gas, issuing from a common burner or from a fissure in the gas pipe, when unignited gives no light, although it gives an unpleasant smell. Why does it give no light? Because it is not combining with the oxygen of the atmosphere;—the proper action is not going on, for light, like sound and smell, is the result of action, and of action only. When the chemical action is going on, light is produced,—when the action ceases, the production of light ceases also. It is the same with a lamp or common tallow candle. The light given out, or produced, is, in every case, in proportion to the action by which it is produced. In short, light is not a substance, but, like sound and taste, an *effect* of *action*, and is always more or less intense, as the action by which it is produced is more or less intense. And when we have arrived at the proper place, we shall find that the light which we receive through the agency of the sun, is produced in a manner analogous in every respect to that of a gas jet or common tallow candle, viz.: that is, an effect resulting from the chemical or electrical action of matter upon matter, and is produced in the atmosphere of the earth. From these considerations, we perceive that light is the medium of sight, and that light is produced by the action of matter upon matter.

But sight is a double sense; by this faculty we can observe *motion* as well as color. We can perceive bodies shifting their *relative* positions,—and this is all the idea we have of motion. Through the sense of sight we also have or receive some notion of shape or form; but the intimation which we receive of the forms of things through the channels of sight is so mixed and blended with color, that it may be questioned whether we could distinguish by the organ of sight alone, any difference of shape, unless by the mere difference of color. We see a sheet of paper laid upon the table, and we perceive by the faculty of sight that it is of a square form; but we distinguish the form of the sheet of paper merely by the difference of color of the paper and the table upon which it is laid. It appears, then, that through four of the senses,—hearing, tasting, smelling, and seeing, we discover sound, flavor, odor, color, and motion,—neither of which are matter. Nor can we through either of these four senses, arrive at any distinct knowledge of the *absolute existence* of matter, viewed as a substance, in a state of rest. A knowledge of matter in a state of absolute rest could not reach the inward mind through either of these four channels:—for every intimation, every tittle of the evidence which they convey, is the result of motion or action, and without that action, these senses would remain as dead and inactive as the inert matter by which they might be surrounded.

We now approach the fifth, and most important of the five external senses,—that of *feeling*. What then do we feel? We feel heat and cold. Now, is heat matter?—No. Notwithstanding all that has been said by some modern chemists about caloric, or the matter of heat, it requires very little penetration to discern that heat is not material, but merely an effect of action—of the action of matter upon matter. Heat may be produced by the mechanical action of striking or rubbing two bodies together; or by the chemical action of two gasses combining; or by the decomposition of a solid—as the explosion of gunpowder;—but in every case, action of some kind is necessary to the production of heat. In proportion to the intensity of the action, so is the intensity of the heat produced; and when the action ceases, the production of heat ceases also. Heat is not, as is generally imagined, the primary cause of action, but is a necessary accompaniment. Action necessarily produces heat, and this heat, by re-acting, produces a further development of action.

We will go into the question of the materiality of heat more at length, when we come to treat on chemistry. In the meantime, we would observe, as a general principle to which there is no exception, that through the sense of feeling, we receive no evidence of the existence of active heat, except in connexion with action; therefore, so far as we have yet examined the nature of the evidence passing to the mind, through the senses, that evidence bears throughout one common character—it is not the evidence of the existence of matter, considered as a substance, it is merely the evidence of action—of effect; and from evidence which we have yet to notice, we come to the conclusion that these effects result from the action of matter upon matter.

Through the sense of feeling or touch, we receive other evidences besides that of heat:—we perceive and can distinguish different degrees of hardness or solidity of external objects. Now, the perception of hardness or solidity furnishes to the mind the *fundamental idea* of matter; and this idea reaches the mind through the sense of feeling or touch, and through this channel alone. Without the evidence of hardness, of solid extension received through this channel, our ideas of matter would be of the most vague and confused character; for through the other senses we receive the evidence of *action*, and of action only. The mind receives no certain intimation of the absolute existence of matter, except through the sense of feeling or touch, by which we have the conception of solid extension; therefore, the *direct* evidence of the existence of matter, rests upon the testimony of *one witness*. But each of the other senses furnishes a body of *indirect* or *circumstantial* evidence, which, taken in connexion with the direct evidence, gives the mind the fullest assurance of the existence of matter, and enables us, by comparing and contrasting the evidence of one sense with that of another, to acquire a considerable degree of knowledge of the essential and accidental properties of matter, and of the actions and re-actions dependent upon, and resulting from, these essential and accidental properties.

The human mind may be considered in the light of a court of law, sitting upon a case in which there are five witnesses. Each of the witnesses presents his testimony to the court, and that testimony is recorded or noted down in the *memory*. Each of the five witnesses is questioned and cross-questioned; the evidence of each is compared and contrasted with that of the others. The evidence is further examined to see whether the testimony be full and complete, and finally the judgment of the court is formed according to the evidence. Such is the process by which the mind forms a judgment upon any given subject, or rather by which a judgment is formed *in the mind;* for the judgment is not an *act* of the mind, but an *effect* resulting from, and dependent upon, the evidence presented, and the faculty which the mind possesses to sift, examine, compare, and contrast that evidence.

Now, in relation to matter, which is the subject of our present inquiry, we find that we have the *direct* testimony of *one* witness—the sense of touch, by which we have evidence of the absolute existence of matter, independent of action,—and we find that by the other four witnesses, we have the evidence of *action;* and by comparing the whole evidence, one part with another, we arrive at the conclusion with a mental certainty, that, that action, by which the senses are excited, is the action of matter upon matter. Each of these four senses bring us evidence of action of a different character. Through the ear sound,—but sound is not a constant or essential property of matter; so also of the others—we must take the *direct evidence* afforded by the sense of touch, as the basis of our examination: because, through this sense, we receive a knowledge of the constant and essential properties of matter,—of those properties which are essential to its existence, and without which it would no longer be matter,—and these properties are two—*attraction* and *repulsion.*

If we desire to entertain clear and correct notions of matter and motion, we must bring our minds to bear upon the subject in such a manner, as shall enable us to deduce those principles, that are to guide us in our inquiry into the various operations of nature continually going on within us and around us. We have to inquire whether amongst the inherent and essential properties of matter, we can discover *forces competent to originate motion*,—supposing the universe to have been previously in a perfectly quiescent state,—for every operation of nature, the most complicated as well as the most simple, is effected by motion; yet motion is not an existence, but an effect produced by a previously existing cause or *force*. Motion, as an *effect*, may be either created or destroyed,—but not so with the *causes* or *forces* by which it has been so created or destroyed; these forces are eternal and indestructible, as the matter of which they constitute the essential properties is also eternal and indestructible.

The definitions which have been given by the schools, of matter and its properties, convey little or no information to the mind, because in their definitions, they have neglected to include those essential properties or forces by which motion is effected, by which the matter is actuated, and consequently upon which all the varied and ever varying phenomena of nature are dependent. Matter they defined to be *solid extension*, which defines nothing, and might as well have been expressed by the simple truism, that matter is matter, for he who could not clearly understand by the truism all that was intended to be conveyed, would assuredly not be made much wiser by the definition. Again, it has been said, that the *properties* of matter are *impenetrability* and *divisibility*, *mobility* and *inertia*. This is worse than the previous. There is a manifest contradiction:—a body is *impenetrable*, and yet *divisible;* it has *mobility* or *motion*, and also *inertia*, the very essence of which latter property consists in its being devoid of all force.

The ancients, it would appear, were fully aware of this fact in respect to the ever varying aspect of external phenomena, for, after many fruitless attempts to describe and define matter by the evidence of the senses alone, they were at last compelled to abandon the attempt, and betake themselves to their favorite and convenient expedient, that of personifying nature or matter under the character of Proteus, a being who was continually changing his form, never appearing twice under the same garb. Modern chemistry has certainly rent and torn off the mask of Proteus, or at least a considerable portion of it; he is, however, yet sufficiently disguised to render his recognition, in many instances, a point of no small difficulty. The ancients conceived that there were four elementary substances: *earth*, *water*, *air*, and *fire*,—of which, in different proportions, they supposed all bodies to be constituted. But modern chemistry has thrown quite a new light upon this subject. It is proved that water is not an elementary body, but is composed of two gases—oxygen and hydrogen, in the proportions of eight parts of the former to one of the latter. Air also is proved to consist of two gases—oxygen and nitrogen, in the ratio of twenty-eight nitrogen and eight oxygen. Earths, alluvial beds, rocks, and indeed the entire solid crust of the earth, prove to be metallic oxydes, that is, metals compounded with oxygen. Thus, silica consists of eight parts of the metal silicum, combined with eight parts of oxygen; this is a very abundant solid, constituting the chief ingredient of flints, the sands of the sea, and desert, and of very many minerals and rocks;--oxygen, indeed, constitutes more than one half of the whole earth. It forms nearly one half of the more abundant earths, clays, and sands. In nine parts of water, eight is oxygen; and in thirty-six of atmospheric air, eight is composed of the same universal ingredient. Viewed upon the large scale, it appears that the solid earth is a *metallic oxyde*, that the ocean and all the water of the earth is an *oxyde of hydrogen*, and that the atmosphere which surrounds the earth is an *oxyde of nitrogen*.

It is plain, then, that in our attempt to investigate the properties of matter, we must not overlook this important element, which enters so largely into the composition of all bodies, solid, liquid, and gaseous. It is important to note, that although oxygen, *when combined* with other substances, is found in each of the three states of solid, liquid, and gas, yet in the *uncombined* state it exists in the form of gas only, and is attracted to the positive pole of the voltaic battery, by which we learn that oxygen gas is negatively electrified.

Hydrogen, next to oxygen, is the most important elementary substance of modern chemistry, forming, as it does, a considerable portion of the ocean, existing to a certain amount in the atmosphere in the form of vapor and gas, and entering largely into the composition of coal and other mineral bodies. Hydrogen is the lightest of all bodies, being 14½ times lighter than air. Like oxygen, in an *uncombined* state, it exists in the gaseous form only, and is attracted by the negative pole of the voltaic battery, by which it is proved that hydrogen gas is positively electrified.

We have adverted to these two elementary substances

in this place, not only because they hold a very prominent position in chemical analysis and act a conspicuous part in nearly all the operations of nature, but because by an attentive consideration of the three forms in which they are known to exist, the two essential properties of matter, *attraction* and *repulsion*, are disclosed to the mental vision. The atoms of oxygen *repel* each other with a certain force, and, therefore, oxygen, when unmixed with other matter, can exist in the *gaseous form only*. The atoms of hydrogen also *repel* each other with great force, and, therefore, hydrogen uncombined with other matter, can exist only in the gaseous form.

To give an idea of the immense repulsive force in hydrogen gas, reference may be made to the great Vauxhall balloon. It is known that the atmosphere presses upon the surface of all bodies with a weight equal to fifteen pounds to the square inch, being 2,160 pounds to the square foot. Now, the great Vauxhall balloon, when inflated with gas, sustains upon its external surface, an atmospheric pressure equal to twenty millions, four hundred and thirty-three thousand pounds, avordupois, or 9,122 tons. And this enormous pressure is sustained by what? Not by solid matter, for if you were to look up through the balloon you would perceive nothing within it; it looks as if entirely empty, hydrogen gas being invisible: what then sustains the pressure? The *repulsive force*, which is an inherent property of hydrogen gas, as it is of all gases, and indeed of all matter, more or less, for no body has ever yet been known to exist in a perfectly solid form; there are *pores* in all bodies, for even the most solid will absorb liquids and gases, which could not take place if they were perfectly solid and impermeable; therefore, in respect to the force of repulsion, we find that in gaseous matter it is exerted with a very high degree of intensity, whilst the opposite force of attraction is in a very weak and feeble state. The force of attraction is not inactive in the gaseous state, but its strength bears but a small proportion to the opposing force of repulsion. Now hydrogen gas being the lightest or most expanded of all known bodies, we conclude that in this gas the repulsive force is the strongest.

There is, indeed, gaseous matter known to exist, which is, perhaps, as much lighter than hydrogen gas, as the latter is lighter than water,—this is the celestial ether which pervades all space; but of this exceedingly subtle gas, beyond the fact of its existence, we know little or nothing, except by inference and analogy with other gaseous bodies, which come more immediately within the sphere of our observation.

---

## SPACE, TIME, MATTER, MOTION.

In all our investigations, if we desire to obtain a clear and comprehensive view of the subject under consideration, whether physical or moral, it is necessary and essential, in the first place, that we should reduce it to its most simple elements; secondly, from an attentive observation of these elements—and of the effects, as we see them actually occur, we deduce certain fixed principles which are to guide us in our further investigation on the subject; thirdly, we collect and present to the mind an accumulation of facts to strengthen and support these principles, arranging and marshalling each fact under its own appropriate principle; and fourthly, from the facts, we proceed to investigate the nature of the *causes* by which our principles of action are guided, and the observed effects produced. By this mode of investigation we obtain a *systematic view* of the subject, and the perfection of our system is always in a direct ratio with the extent of our knowledge of facts upon any given subject.

Proceeding, then, according to these rules, we find that *all physical science* may be, and indeed is, comprehended under four very common and familiar words:—SPACE,—TIME,—MATTER,—MOTION. Without space there can be no change: for change can only be effected in space. Without time there can be no change: for change is only effected in time. Without matter there can be no change: for then there is nothing conceivable by which, or upon which, the change could be effected. Without motion there can be no change: for no change can take place unless by the motion of matter. When a vegetable is formed or decomposed, it is by the *motion* of *matter* in *space* and *time*. When an animal is formed or decomposed, it is by the *motion* of *matter* in *space* and *time*. When a world is formed or decomposed, it is by the *motion* of *matter* in *space* and *time*. And all these formations or decompositions are guided by the same general laws, the space and time, in each case, being commensurate with, and determined by, the extent of body, and the nature of the process of which it forms the subject.

Of space and time nothing more need be said than that they are both infinite;—space has no boundary; time has neither beginning nor end; universal space is the great laboratory of nature, in which all her operations are performed; universal time—duration without limit—eternity is the era of nature; her operations have no limits either in time or space. But, although space and time are necessarily infinite, our knowledge of both the one and the other is confined within comparatively narrow limits. Of space we cannot be said to know any thing beyond the solar system,—a mere point as compared with the great whole, and much of that we know very imperfectly. Of time, our knowledge is compressed into a few thousand years, and is principally derived from historical records of very doubtful authority; and the accounts which some of these contain of the origin of the earth and the creation of man, and of animal and vegetable life in general, are so palpably absurd, that they do not deserve a serious refutation. The only conclusions to which we can come respecting universal space and time are these:—we see certain conditions exist throughout the solar system, and although we cannot demonstrate that the same conditions prevail throughout universal space, the inference that the same conditions do prevail universally, is legitimate and rational, more especially as every fixed star appears to be the centre of a system. This conclusion, with respect to unseen space, is agreeable to our knowledge of that which is seen: but if we come to the contrary conclusion, then our conclusion is opposed to our knowledge, which is irrational. With respect to time, we learn, not from the writings of men, which might be liable to suspicion, but from astronomical and geological facts, which cannot be distorted either by fraud or error, that a great chain of physical processes, requiring thousands of millions of years for their accomplishment, have been and are now going on in this earth and throughout the solar system, of which the earth forms a part; we, therefore, conclude, that the causes by which these long processes are effected, are coeval with matter itself; that they have been in operation from all eternity, and will continue in operation forever.

We have now disposed of two of the four heads into

which our subject was divided, viz., time and space; matter and motion, are, therefore, all that remain for our consideration.

---

## MATTER AND MOTION.

Matter is presented to our notice in three distinct forms: *solid*, *liquid*, and *gaseous*. The world which we inhabit is made up of these three descriptions of matter:—the *solid earth*, the *liquid ocean*, and the *gaseous atmosphere*. The solar system itself is made up of these three kinds of matter. In the sun and planets are to be found the solids and liquids, with the respective atmosphere of each body; and the whole system is connected together by a gaseous medium of a subtle character, denominated ether, or the etherial medium, which pervades the entire of the intervening spaces between the sun and the different planetary bodies of the solar system. Now experimental philosophy has decided this fact: that all matter may exist in either of these three forms; that the most contracted *solid* may be *expanded* into an invisible gas, and that the most *expanded gas* may be *contracted* into a hard solid. By observations of the most ordinary processes of nature, we learn this further fact: that matter is never at rest, but is continually passing from the gaseous to the solid state, and *vice versa* from the solid to the gaseous state, generally taking the intermediate form of liquid in its transition from the one or the other of the two extremes. These are two simple and well known facts. The first is known to every experimental philosopher, and the second may be known by every one who will but observe the common processes going on around him in the animal, vegetable, and mineral kingdoms of the earth.

All motion of every description may be traced to two distinct sources, attraction and repulsion. These are ultimate forces, and wherever motion is perceived, if we trace it step by step from the effect to the cause, we shall universally find that the entire chain of motion had its origin in one or other of these two ultimate forces. And further, if we observe the ordinary operations of nature, we may perceive that they are carried forward by the continual transference of matter from the dominion of one or other of these two forces to that of the opposite. To use a homely illustration, it may be said that matter is continually being bandied from one side to the other, like a shuttlecock between two battledores, by the two universal forces of attraction and repulsion. The game of battledore and shuttlecock cannot be played by one, nor yet by two, unless they stand opposite each other, and propel the shuttlecock in contrary directions; neither could the system of nature be carried on but by two forces opposing each other in a similar manner. By repulsion, matter is continually being transferred from the solid to the gaseous state,—whilst by attraction, it is continually transferred from the gaseous to the solid; and thus the two forces may be said to play into each other's hands, like two children at battledore and shuttlecock. These two forces are the right and left hands of nature, by which all her operations are carried forward.

A very little consideration will enable us to perceive that neither of these two forces can carry on the operations of nature without the opposite force; and that the two forces must of necessity be equal in power and extent.

It shall be our endeavor to show that *all motion* may be traced to the expansion and contraction of matter; and in the meantime, we shall lay down the following axioms for our future guidance:—

1. Attraction and repulsion are universal and ultimate forces, between which, and by which, every atom of matter and every aggregate of atoms is held securely, and compelled to occupy the place where it does occupy in the visible universe. These two forces are nowhere in a state of perfect equilibrium,—hence arises motion. When repulsion predominates over attraction, matter *expands* into larger volume; when attraction predominates over repulsion, matter *contracts* into smaller volume. When masses of matter are moved without expanding or contracting, which is mechanical motion, their motion is always caused by, and is an effect of, the expansion or contraction of other matter: as the surface of the earth is heaved up in earthquakes by the *expansion*, or when the surface sinks by the *contraction* of matter beneath. Matter is at all times under the control of two opposing forces, one of which is stronger than the other; the stronger is the moving power, the weaker the regulating

power. If the two forces were equal, the motion would cease—if the weaker, or regulating force, were removed, the motion would be headlong.

2. Repulsion is an ultimate force or final cause, co-existent with matter, and its office is to separate solid and liquid bodies, to cause the expansion of matter, the formation of gas by the decomposition of bodies into the ultimate elements, in order to prepare the matter for the operation of the opposite force of attraction.

3. Attraction also is an ultimate force or final cause, whose office is to form solid bodies from gaseous matter, which has been previously prepared by its opponent, or rather coadjutor, repulsion; for the one cannot go on without the other: and as repulsion performs its operation of decomposition more or less perfectly, so may it be anticipated that the formation of the solid will be more or less perfectly effected.

4. Expansion of matter is an effect of the repulsion of atoms, and constitutes chemical decomposition, the ultimate resultant being an invisible gas.

5. Contraction of matter is an effect of the attraction of atoms, and constitutes chemical combination, the ultimate resultant being a solid body.

6. The expansion of matter always tends from a centre towards a circumference, at any distance from that centre; the distance to which the motion proceeds from the centre being greater or less, as the intensity of action or quantity of matter is greater or less.

7. The contraction of matter always tends from a circumference to the centre: the time which the motion continues being greater or less, as the motion is more or less direct, and as the velocity and distance from the centre are greater or less.

8. If expansive motion continually tends from the centre to the circumference, a perpetual expansive motion is impossible; because whatever may be the dimensions of the mass, it must have a centre, at which point expansive action must cease.

9. If contractile motion continually tends from a circumference to a centre, a perpetual contractile motion is impossible; because whatever may be the dimensions of a circle, it must have a centre, at which point the contractile motion must cease.

10. But a perpetual motion may, and does exist, in nature, and is a necessary result of the two forces, viz.,

of the repulsive force tending *from a centre*, and of the attractive force tending *to a centre*, and these two may, and will continue to, produce motion forever.

These axioms might be rendered still more evident by the aid of a diagram, instead of which the following letters may suffice:—

B *a* A *a* B

Let A represent the centre, B B the circumference of a circle, of any given dimensions. Then it is plain that the bodies *a a* if they continue to approach the centre, A, however slowly, cannot continue to move in that direction forever, neither can they move towards circumference B B forever; but they may continue in motion forever, if their motion is alternately from A to B B, and from B B to A. And further, if we consider the bodies *a a* to represent atoms, then their position at A will represent solid or contracted matter, and at B B gaseous or expanded matter. At A they are held together by the force of attraction, and at B B they are held apart by the force of repulsion.

We have noticed the two opposite principles or *causes* of motion, attraction and repulsion, and showed that the ultimate product of attraction is a tangible solid like the earth; and that the ultimate product of repulsion is an invisible gas, like the ether which pervades the solar system. Now it can be proved that in the formation of a solid, there is a point beyond which even nature herself cannot go; that a body may at last become so compact that it cannot be made more solid.—(Axiom 9.) Also in the formation of a gas from a solid, there is a point beyond which it is impossible to go; for whatever may be the dimension of the solid body, it must have a centre, and when the expansive process has reached the centre, the solid is entirely dissipated, and there is nothing left upon which the expansive process can be continued.—(Axiom 8.) There is, therefore, an ultimate point of expansion and an ultimate point of contraction, beyond which it is impossible to go.

These ultimate points are different in different bodies, but in every case the natural ultimate point, which terminates the process, is at an immense distance from the possible ultimate point. Nature never attempts impossibilities. Now, a very ordinary share of observation will enable us to discern that throughout universal nature, there is no portion of matter in a state of *absolute* rest;—all is motion, and the range of that motion is in every case comprised within these two *natural ultimate points*, between the one and the other of which, matter, or the motion of matter, continually oscillates, without pause or cessation. In some cases, an oscillation is finished in a few months, or even less; in others, millions of years are required.

---

## THE CIRCUIT OF MOTION.

We must now advert to a very important element, denominated "THE CIRCUIT OF MOTION." This is the *key* of the system; and in every circuit of motion there must be at least *one expansion* and *one contraction* of matter.

Let us take a familiar case,—that of the common air balloon. This is not a circle of motion formed by nature herself; but we must bear in mind, that every artificial process is nothing more than an imitation of nature; and if all the processes of nature could be imitated, art would have arrived at her highest state of perfection. We cannot go beyond nature;—man can only discover and direct the powers of nature; he can neither create new powers, nor destroy those which exist. The business of philosophy is to discover the powers or forces which now exist, which always have existed, and which always will exist, and to turn them to purposes useful and beneficial to man; all beyond this is mere speculative vanity. However, although the circle of motion of the air balloon is not, strictly speaking, a natural circle, we shall discover abundance of natural circles of motion. Wherever we turn our eyes we may discover them; but in the first place we will take that of the balloon, as being familiar, plain and palpable.

When the great balloon ascends from Vauxhall Gardens, it is driven along by the wind, till the æronaut thinks proper to descend, which he effects, perhaps, in some part of Kent, or wherever else it may be, it matters not. The balloon is then placed upon a vehicle, and brought back to Vauxhall Gardens, the place from which it ascended, and thus the "circuit of motion" is completed. Let us now inquire what powers have been called into action? what forces have been concerned in producing this circuit of motion? and we shall find that every part, except that along the surface of the earth where the cart or other vehicle has been employed, that every portion of the motion is due to the *expansion* and *contraction* of matter, and even the power, and therefore the motion of the animal which dragged the vehicle, may be traced to the same sources; therefore, every part of the motion, throughout this circle, may be traced to the *expansion* and *contraction* of matter.

First, by what power or force does the balloon ascend? By the difference of the specific gravity of the entire balloon and gas, as compared with an equal bulk of atmospheric air, on the well known principles of hydrostatic or ærostatic pressure, it will be replied. True; but this is not the beginning of the process. We have to inquire in the first place, in what way the gas is obtained? for it is from the gas that the ascending power is derived.—With acid and zinc the whole process of ascent and descent may be accomplished by the powers of electricity; but we will take the gas usually employed by æronauts, viz., carburetted hydrogen. Well, having prepared the balloon or envelope to receive the gas, the next thing to be procured is a quantity of coal. Now coal is a *solid mineral body*, and in this solid state gives no ascending power; the balloon will not rise if charged with coal in the solid state;—the solid matter must be *expanded* into gas.—(Axiom 4.)

This expansion is effected by the usual and well known process, and in proportion as the expansion is more or less perfectly effected, so in proportion is this ascending power greater or less. It matters not what materials are used, so that we expand those materials into a permanent gas, whose specific gravity is less than that of atmospheric air. When we say a permanent gas, it must not be understood that this gas would remain forever in the gaseous state in the free open theatre of the universe. On the contrary, all matter is in a state of continual change, from the gaseous to the solid, and from the solid to the gaseous, generally taking the liquid form in its transit from one state to the opposite; and it is by their never ceasing change that all the operations of nature are carried forward: if a solid is forming at one point, there must be of necessity a gas forming at another point, however distant that point may be. When the balloon has been filled with the coal gas, it has received the ascending power, and the gas can only be procured by the expansion of matter; therefore, the ascending motion is due to the expansion of matter, and expanding matter always recedes from the centre of the earth.—(Axiom 6.) This is the first section of the balloon's circle of motion.

When the balloon has risen in the atmosphere, it is driven along by the wind, to the place of descent, in the "air's circle of motion." This completes the second section of the "balloon's circle of motion."

When the balloon has arrived at or over the place of descent, if the æronaut possesses the means of contracting the gas into a solid body (Axiom 5,) as at first, it is plain that the balloon would return to the earth, in consequence of the contraction.—(Axiom 7.) Indeed the condensation of the gas has been frequently recommended as a measure of economy; but not possessing the means of condensing the gas with safety, he suffers it to escape through the valve, and the expanded matter (being now separated from the solid matter, of which the balloon is composed) rises still higher in the atmosphere, or recedes still further from the earth's centre, whilst the car and other solid parts of the balloon return towards the earth's centre.

The balloon is lastly drawn from the place of descent to Vauxhall Gardens, by animal power.

We now find that the circle of motion is divided into four distinct parts or sections, each section being due to a distinct and separate cause.

1. The ascending motion due to the expansion of matter.

2. The horizontal motion [in alto] due to the wind's horizontal motion.

3. The descending motion, due to the contraction of matter.

4. The horizontal motion on the earth's surface, due to animal power.

The first and third of these motions we find due to the expansion and contraction of matter; let us inquire whether we cannot trace the second and fourth to the same two sources?

The second is due to the wind's horizontal motion. Now, what are the forces by which the wind or air is put in motion? Within the tropics, and near the earth's surface, the air is expanded by the heat of the sun, and in consequence rises to the higher regions of the atmosphere, on the same principle that the balloon ascends when filled with gas. This is the point of expansion in the "air's circle of motion." As the column of expanded air rises, it passes into a colder region, and is contracted into even less than its former dimensions. We have here, then, the two points from which we are to trace the motion of the entire circle. Well, the body of contracted air in the higher regions of the atmosphere, cannot descend upon the same point from whence it ascended, for there is a column of expanded air rising immediately under. It therefore descends upon an inclined plane towards the north and south poles, to supply the place of a body of dense air, which rushes along the earth's surface to fill the partial vacuum created by expansion within the tropics; and the body of dense air, is in its turn, expanded and ascends, and thus the process is continued.

Atmospheric currents are modified by a variety of circumstances, as the earth's diurnal motion, by which the point of expansion is continually changing from land to sea, and from sea to land, &c., and thus the currents of air do not move in two great circles from the tropics to the poles *in alto*, and from the poles to the tropics, near the earth's surface, as they would do were those two powers suffered to proceed with their operations undisturbed by other causes. But in this case as in every other, the moving matter performs a circuit in which we find the two opposing processes going on at two distant points, viz., the *expansion* and *contraction* of matter, and upon which two processes the motion of the entire circle depends. Now if we consider the balloon's circle of motion in connexion with the air's circle, we may very readily perceive that the action of one upon the other is precisely the same in kind as that of one spur-wheel upon another, if we choose to view them in this mechanical light. The *lower* section of the aerial circle acts upon the *upper* section of the balloon's circle, and thus the balloon is carried along to the place of descent. The horizontal portion of the balloon (*in alto*) is due to the motion of the wind, and the motion of the wind is due to expansion and contraction of matter.

The fourth section is due to animal power. Now, the animal body is nothing more or less than a bundle of circles of motion. It is a little system within itself, having points of connexion with external nature, working upon the same principles precisely. It contains, or rather consists of a variety of circles, the highest of which is the nervous. The nervous system is the *primary* circle, from which the inferior or secondary circles derive their energy; and this primary circle is actuated, moved, or excited by electrical agency; and in the same manner the inferior or secondary circles of the external world derive their energy from the primary circle, which primary circle is actuated, moved, or excited upon electrical principles.

Let us take, in the first place, the circulation of the blood, which is, perhaps, the most familiar to the ordinary reader. The blood circulates in the animal body through a system of tubes, which tubes are at certain points furnished with valves, so that the blood can flow in one direction only. Those tubes which convey the blood *from* the heart, are called *arteries*, and contain red blood; those which convey the blood *to* the heart, are called *veins*, and contain dark blood. The human heart is double, each side containing cavities that have no connexion with the opposite side. The arterial, or red blood from the lungs, passes through the *left* cavity of the heart. The venous, or dark blood, from the extremities of the body, passes through the *right* cavity. Now, a circuit of motion, like every other circle, has, properly speaking, neither beginning nor end. We may begin any where, but wherever we begin, we must trace it round to the point at which we commenced. In the present case we will begin at the left cavity of the heart.

To the left side of the heart is attached one large tube or artery, through which the blood flows towards the extremities of the body; as we proceed from the heart smaller branches are sent out to the various parts to renovate the system, till at last the arterial tubes finish their course in thousands or millions of ramifications. The blood is now taken up from every part of the body, into the veins, which are ramified in a like manner; each tributary vein continuing to swell the current, till at length the whole is collected in the larger veins, and poured through the orifice into the right cavity of the heart. We have now traced the blood back into the heart, but not into the left cavity, from which we started; we have, in fact, traced one half of the circle only, for before the blood can reach the left side of the heart, it must pass through the lungs. From the right cavity of the heart, the venous or dark blood passes through one orifice or tube, which immediately after leaving the heart divides into two, one passing to each lung, and these tubes ramify into thousands of smaller branches, pervading the entire substance of the lungs, as in the former case, when the ramifications took place at the extremities of the body. Lastly, from these branches or ramifications, the blood is collected into larger and larger tubes and conveyed into the left cavity of the heart, and thus the circuit of motion is complete.

We have now to enquire by what *forces* this circle is kept in motion; that is, we must carefully examine the circle through its entire length, and endeavor to discover the points of expansion and contraction. Now, throughout universal nature, whether in the animal, vegetable, or mineral kingdom, or in the more extended field of what is denominated inorganic nature, there is no single circle of motion working by itself in an isolated state, wholly unconnected with, or independent of, other circles. Nature, considered as a whole, is a beautiful system of wheel work like the interior of a watch, the main-spring of which system is electricity, which, by its alternate attraction and repulsion, is every where producing the contraction and expansion of matter. We find accordingly in the circle of blood, the point of expansion in the ramifications of the venous and arterial systems in the lungs; that of contraction in the ramifications of the venous and arterial systems in the various tissues of the body, where the heat of the blood received in the lungs is again given out to maintain the necessary warmth and muscular energy of the animal frame; and we find the principal point by which this circle is connected with the external world, is also in the lungs, (the point of expansion) and this connexion is carefully and closely maintained by the involuntary expansion and contraction of the lungs, and by the organs of respiration. There are other points where the circles of the blood are connected with the internal operations of the animal economy, as with the lacteals and lymphatics; but these are subordinate to the circulation, and do not demand our special attention. In this place, our object is merely to show that all the operations of nature are guided by the same principles—that all motions are derived from the same forces.

There is nothing mysterious in the circulation of the blood through the animal body, any more than in that of the circulation of a fluid through the steam engine—whoever understands the one may very readily understand the other. When the steam boiler is sufficiently filled with water, and a fire applied to the under surface, the expansion of matter begins within the boiler;—it is in the boiler that the *power is generated*, and unless an exit be provided the boiler must burst, however strong the materials, so great is the expansive force. But an exit being provided through the cylinder the stream rushes through the passage, driving the piston before it—this constitutes the power of the engine. Having exerted its expansive force upon the piston, it rushes into the condenser, a cold vacuum formed by the action of the air-pump, where it is instantly contracted into water; this water is drawn by the air-pump into the hot well, and from thence, by the feeding pump, it is again forced back into the boiler, to be again expanded into steam—and thus the circuit of motion is complete. Now if we compare this with the circulation of the blood, we shall find the two correspond in almost every particular. The lungs correspond with the boilers where the fluid is expanded. The extremities and exterior surface of the body form the condenser, where the blood is contracted; the action of the lungs fulfil the office of the air-pump,—and the heart with its valves is the feeding-pump, to force the blood into the lungs. The heart and lungs are stimulated to action by the nerves, and the nervous power is derived from electrical excitement. This comparison, though plain, is not sufficiently close;—the lungs bear a much closer analogy to a galvanic battery, than a steam boiler.

The entire power of the steam engine is generated in the steam boiler; every subordinate part of the engine, as well as the surplus power which it exerts upon the external part of the machinery, is moved by the expansive force generated by the boiler. So also is the animal mnchine; the entire power which moves every subordinate function is generated in the lungs, as well as the surplus power which the animal exerts upon external objects. In a state of robust health the surplus power is great. Life may continue, however, even when there is no surplus power, so long as sufficient is generated to move the subordinate functions; but if the power should sink beneath this point, the animal machine stops. So also is the steam engine; whilst there is sufficient power generated to work the pumps, and other subordinate parts, the engine may continue to move, although it is incompetent to drive any external machinery. There is no surplus power. If the power sink beneath this point, the engine stops.

Thus far the analogy is complete; but the *manner* in

which the power is generated, is not precisely the same in both cases. In the steam engine boiler, the exciting cause is the heat given out from combustion; in the lungs of the animal body, the exciting cause is galvanic action. In all other respects, the analogy is very close. When extra exertion is required from the steam engine, the boiler, or rather the expansive force in the boiler, must be stimulated; when extra exertion is required from the animal, the lungs must be stimulated by increased respiration. In both cases an extra quantity of heat is generated, and an extra quantity of oxygen or vital air is consumed. If the generation of power in the lungs is stopped, all the subordinate power of muscular action from the heart to the most distant and minute fibre of the body is also arrested. If the generating of power in the steam boiler is stopped, all subordinate action of the pumps and other parts is also arrested. Exclude the air from the fire under the boiler, the fire is extinguished, the expansive process in the boiler is arrested, and the engine stops. Exclude the air from the lungs, the galvanic process in the blood is arrested, the circulation stops, the heart ceases to beat, and the animal dies.

But it will be said, that all this, though true, must be viewed in connexion with the "vital principle:" and what are we to understand by this expression, "vital principle?" If we consider it attentively, we shall very soon discover that it is one of those vague, common-place words, that pass current among men, and which serve rather to cover our ignorance than to advance our knowledge. When we endeavor to trace the "vital principle" to the nervous energy, and the nervous energy to electrical action, we at least endeavor to put our system in a tangible form; but when we profess to explain the animal functions by a "vital principle," our explanation is mere verbiage.

We have already said, that the animal system is a bundle of circles, each connected with the others, like the wheels of a watch, or like the different parts of the steam engine, and that the primary circle, the main-spring, which may be said to originate the animal functions, is the nervous, and that the nervous circle is actuated by electrical agency. The proof of this is derived from plain and simple facts.

The following extract is from the letters of Sir David Brewster, on Natural Magic; and viewed in connexion with the generating of animal force in the lungs, might furnish the basis of a curious and interesting inquiry:—

AN INDIVIDUAL RAISED ON THE FINGERS OF FOUR OTHER PERSONS.—"One of the most remarkable and inexplicable experiments relative to the strength of the human frame, which you have yourself seen and admired, is that in which a heavy man is raised with the greatest facility, when he is lifted up the instant that his own lungs and of the persons who raise him are inflated with air. This experiment was, I believe, first shown in England, a few years ago, by Major H., who saw it performed in a large party at Venice, under the direction of an officer of the American navy. As Major H. performed it more than once in my presence, I shall describe, as nearly as possible, the method which he prescribed. The heaviest person in the party lies down upon two chairs, his legs supported by one and his back by the other. Four persons, one at each leg, and one at each shoulder, then try to raise him, and they find his dead weight to be very great, from the difficulty they experience in supporting him. When he is replaced in the chair, each of the four persons takes hold of the body as before, and the person to be lifted gives two signals by clapping his hands. At the first signal he himself and the four lifters begin to draw a long and full breath, and when the inhalation is completed, or the lungs filled, the second signal is given for raising the person from the chair. To his own surprise and that of his bearers, he is raised with the greatest facility, as if he were no heavier than a feather. On several occasions I have observed that when one of the bearers performed his part ill, by making the inhalation out of time, the part of the body which he tries to raise, is left, as it were, behind. As you have repeatedly seen this experiment, and have performed the part both of the load and the bearer, you can testify how remarkable the effects appear to all parties, and how complete is the conviction, either that the load has been lightened, or the bearers strengthened, by the prescribed process.

"At Venice, the experiment was performed in a more imposing manner. The heaviest man in the party was raised and sustained upon the point of the forefingers of six persons. Major H. declared that the experiment would not succeed if the person lifted were placed on a board, and the strength of the individuals applied to the board. He conceived it necessary that the bearers should communicate directly with the body to be raised. I have not had an opportunity of making any experiments relative to these curious facts; but whether the general effect is an illusion, or the result of known or of new principles, the subject merits a careful investigation."

In the present chapter we propose to show that the vital energy is to be ascribed to galvanic action; and in doing so, we shall confine ourselves chiefly to a statement of facts. To enter into an enquiry concerning the *manner* in which the electrical energy is transmitted to the living animal function, would, from the nature of the subject, require a long and elaborate train of previous inquiry; we must, therefore, for the present be contented with bare facts, which are, after all, the basis of science.

The following extracts are from a paper by Dr. Ure, read before the Glasgow Literary Society, December 10, 1818, and published in the *Journal of Science and the Arts*, of the following January:—

"Convulsions accidentally observed in the limbs of dead frogs originally suggested to Galvani, the study of certain phenomena, which from him have been styled Galvanic. He ascribed these movements to an electrical fluid, or power innate in the living frame, or capable of being evolved by it, which he denominated animal electricity. The *Torpedo Gymnotus* and *Silurus Electricus*, fishes endowed with a true electrical apparatus, ready to be called into action by an effort of their will, were previously known to the naturalist, and furnished plausible analogies to the philosopher of Bologna. Volta, to whom this science is indebted for the most brilliant discoveries, on its principles, as well as for its marvellous apparatus, justly called by his name, advanced powerful arguments against the hypothesis of Galvani. He ascribed the muscular commotions and other phenomena, to the powers of common electricity, by arrangements previously unthought of by the scientific world,—merely by the mutual contact of dissimilar bodies, metal, charcoal and other animal matter, applied either to each other, or conjoined with certain fluids; and at the present day, perhaps, the only facts which seem difficult to reconcile with the beautiful theory of electro motion, invented by the Panian professor, are some experiments of Aldini, nephew of the original discoverer.

"In these experiments neither metal nor charcoal were employed. Very powerful muscular contractions seem to have been excited in some of the experiments, by bringing a part of a warm-blooded and of a cold-blooded animal into contact with each other, as the nerve and muscle of a frog with the bloody flesh of the neck of a newly slain ox. In other experiments, the nerves and muscles of the same animal seem to have operated Galvanic excitation. And again, the nerve of one animal acted with the muscle of another. He deduces from his experiments, in favor of his uncle's hypothesis, that a proper animal electricity is inherent in the body, which does not require the assistance of any external agent for its development.

"According to Ritter, the electricity of the positive pole augments, whilst the negative diminishes the action of life. Tumification of parts is produced by the former; depression by the latter. The pulse of the hand, he says, held a few minutes in contact with the positive pole, is strengthened, that of the one in contact with the negative, is enfeebled;—the former is accompanied with a sense of *heat*, the latter with a feeling of *coldness*;—objects appear, to a positively electrified eye, larger, brighter, and red; while to one negatively electrified, they appear smaller, less distinct, and bluish; colors indicating opposite extremities of the prismatic spectrum. The acid and alkaline tastes, when the tongue is acted on in succession by the two electricities, are well known, and have been ingeniously accounted for by Sir Humphrey Davy in his admirable Bakerian lectures. The smell of oxymuriatic acid, and of ammonia, are said by Ritter to be the opposite odors excited by the two opposite poles, as a full body of sound and a sharp tone are the corresponding effects on the ear. But unquestionably the most precise and interesting researches on the relation between Voltaic electricity and animal life, are those contained in Dr. Wilson Philip's Dissertations in the Philosophical Transactions, as well as in his Experimental Inquiry into the Laws of the Vital Functions.

"The eight pair of nerves distributed to the stomach, and subservient to digestion, were divided by incisions in the necks of several living rabbits. After the operation, the parsley which they ate was removed without alteration in their stomachs; and the animals, after evincing much difficulty of breathing, seemed to die of suffocation. But, when in other rabbits, similarly treated, the galvanic power was transmitted along the nerve below its section to a disk of silver, placed closely in contact with the skin of the animal, opposite to its stomach, no difficulty of breathing occurred, the Voltaic action being kept up for twenty-six hours; the rabbits were then killed, and the parsley was found in as perfectly digested a state as that in healthy rabbits fed at the same time, and their stomachs evolved the smell peculiar to that of a rabbit during digestion; these experiments were several times repeated with similar results. Hence, it appears that the galvanic energy is capable of supplying the place of the nervous influence, so that while under it, the stomach, otherwise inactive, digests food as usual. Dr. Wilson Philip concludes that the identity of galvanic electricity and nervous influence is established by these experiments. The general inferences deduced by him from his multiplied experiments are, that Voltaic electricity is capable of effecting the formation of the secreted fluid, when applied to the blood in the same way in which the nervous influence is applied to it; and that it is capable of occasioning an evolution of caloric from arterial blood. When the lungs are deprived of the nervous influence, by which their function is impeded, and even destroyed; when the digestion is interrupted by withdrawing this influence from the stomach, these two vital functions are renewed by exposing them to the influence of a galvanic trough." "Hence," says Dr. Philip, "galvanism seems capable of performing all the functions of the nervous influence in the animal economy."

These experiments of Dr. Philip will serve as an introduction to the following, of a still more interesting character, which was performed by Dr. Ure, on the body of a condemned murderer, who was executed in Glasgow on the 4th of November, 1817:—

The subject of these experiments was a middle sized, athletic, and extremely muscular man, about thirty years of age. He was suspended from the gallows nearly an hour, and made no convulsive struggle after he had dropped. He was brought to the Anatomical Theatre of our University in about ten minutes after he was cut down. His face had a perfect natural aspect, being neither livid nor tumified, and there was no dislocation of the neck.

Dr. Jeffray, the distinguished professor of anatomy, having on the preceding day requested me to perform the galvanic experiments, I sent to his theatre, with this view, next morning, my minor Voltaic battery, consisting of 270 pairs of four inch plates, with wires of communication, and pointed metallic rods with insulating handles, for the more commodious application of the electric power. About five minutes before the police officers arrived with the body, the battery was charged with a dilute nitrosulphuric acid, which speedily brought it into a state of intense action. The dissections were skilfully executed by Mr. Marshall, under the superintendence of the professor.

Experiment 1.—A large incision was made into the nape of the neck, close behind the *occiput*. The posterior half of the *atlas vertebra* was then removed by bone forcepts, when the spinal marrow was brought into view; a profuse flow of liquid blood rushed from the wound, inundating the floor; a considerable incision was at the same time made in the left hip, through the great gluteal muscle, so as to bring the sciatic nerve into sight; and a small cut was made in the heel; from neither of these did any blood flow. The pointed rod was connected with one end of the spinal marrow, while the other rod was applied to the sciatic nerve; every muscle of the body was immediately agitated with convulsive movements, resembling a violent shuddering from cold. The left side was most powerfully convulsed at every renewal of the electrical contact; on moving the second rod from the hip to the heel, the knee being previously bent, the leg was thrown out with such violence as nearly to overturn one of the assistants, who, in vain attempted to prevent its extension.

Experiment 2.—The left phrenic nerve was now laid bare at the outer edge of the *sternothyroideus* muscle, from three to four inches above the clavicle, the cutaneous incision having been made by the side of the *sternocleidomostoideus*. Since this nerve is distributed to the diaphragm, and since it communicates with its head, through the eight pair, it was expected by transmitting the galvanic power along it, that the respiratory process would be renewed; accordingly a small incision having been made, under the cartilage of the seventh rib, the point of one insulating rod was brought into contact with the great head of the diaphragm, while the other point was applied to the phrenic nerve in the neck. This muscle, the main agent in respiration, was instantly contracted, but with less force than was expected. Satisfied, from ample experience, on the living body, that more powerful effects can be produced in galvanic excitation, by leaving the extreme communicating rods in close contact with the parts to be operated on, while the electric chain or circuit is completed by running the end of the wires along the top of the plates in the last trough of either pole, the other wire being steadily immersed in the last cell of the opposite pole, I had recourse to this method. The success of it was truly wonderful. Full, nay, laborious breathing instantly commenced; the chest heaved and fell; the belly was protruded, and again collapsed with the relaxing and retiring diaphragm. This process was continued without interruption as long as I continued the electric discharges.

In the judgment of many scientific gentlemen who witnessed the scene, this respiratory experiment was perhaps the most striking ever made with a philosophical apparatus. Let it also be remembered that for full half an hour before this period, the body had been well nigh drained of its blood, and the spinal marrow severely lacerated; no pulsation could be perceived meanwhile at the heart or wrist; but it may be supposed that but for the evacuation of the blood, the essential stimulus of that organ, this phenomenon might also have occurred.

Experiment 3.—The supra-orbital nerve was laid bare in the forehead, as it issues through the supra-ciliary foramen in the eye-brow; the one conducting rod being applied to it, and the other to the heel, most extraordinary grimaces were exhibited every time that the electric discharges were made by running the wire in my hand along the edges of the last trough, from the 220th to the 227th pair of plates; thus, fifty shocks, each greater than the preceding one, were given in two seconds; every muscle in his countenance was simultaneously thrown into fiendful action; rage, horror, despair, anguish, and ghastly smiles, united their hideous expressions in the murderer's face, surpassing far the wildest representations of a Fuseli or a Kean. At this period several of the spectators were forced to leave the apartment from terror or sickness, and one gentleman fainted.

Experiment 4.—The last galvanic experiment consisted in transmitting the electrical power from the spinal marrow to the ulnar nerve, as it passes by the internal condyle at the elbow; the fingers now moved nimbly like those of a violin performer; an assistant who tried to close the fist, found the hand to open forcibly in spite of his efforts. When the one rod was applied to a slight incision in the tip of the forefinger, the fist being previously clenched, that finger extended instantly, and from the convulsive agitation of the arm, he seemed to point to the different spectators, some of whom thought he had come to life. About an hour was spent in these operations.

In the preceding account I omitted to state a very essential circumstance.

The positive pole or wire, connected with the zinc end of the battery, was that which I applied to the nerve; and the negative, or that connected with the copper end, was that which I applied to the muscles. This is a matter of primary importance in conducting such experiments."

These experiments are sufficient to satisfy any reasonable mind that electrical action is the great moving principle in the animal economy.

Nor are we compelled to stop here. Modern science has given to this universal power still higher pretensions. The recent discoveries of Mr. Crosse, of Bloomfield, Somerset, prove that electrical power not only governs the living machine, but actually originates the animal functions.

"The public are aware that Mr. Crosse has been recently pursuing a series of researches into the process of crystallization, by means of his galvanic batteries, and that he has made discoveries which have thrown quite a new light upon science. Some weeks ago he prepared a silicious fluid for the purpose of crystallization. He heated a flint to a white heat, and then plunged it in water to pulverize it. The silex, thus reduced, was saturated to excess with muriatic acid. The mixture was placed in a jar, a piece of flannel was suspended in it, one end of which extended over the side, and thus, by capillary attraction, the liquor was slowly filtered, fell into a funnel, and thence dropped on a piece of ironstone from Mount Vesuvius, upon which were laid the two wires connected with either pole of the battery. We should state that the ironstone had been previously heated to a white heat, so that no germs of life could have existed upon it. Mr. Crosse made his daily observations of the wires, to discover the beginning of the process of crystallization. On the 14th day he saw some small white specks upon the stone. Four days afterwards they had elongated and assumed an oval form. He concluded that they were incipient crystals. Great was his surprise on the 22nd day, to find eight legs projecting from each of these white bodies:

still he could not believe that they were living beings. But on the 26th day his surprise was complete; there could be no doubt, they moved, they fed, they were perfect insects. Eighteen or twenty of them have since appeared. Many have seen them, but there is no record of such an insect. It is in form something like a mite; it has eight legs, four bristles at the tail, and the edges of the body are very bristly; its motions are visible to the naked eye; its color is grey; its substance is pulpy. It appears to feed upon the silicious particles in the fluid.

"The most extraordinary circumstance in this phenomenon is the nature of the fluid in which this insect lives and thrives. The acid instantly destroys every other living being.

"But a second trial has confirmed the fact beyond a doubt. Another portion of silex was prepared in the same manner, and reduced to a gelatinous form, but without the acid. A coil of silver wire was suspended in it from one of the poles of the battery, and the other pole was also immersed, so as to send through the mass an incessant stream of the electric fluid. About three weeks afterwards, Mr. Crosse examined the poles to search for crystals, and in one of the coils of wire he found one of these strange insects. This proves that it is produced from the silex, and not from the acid.

"Mr. Crosse, with his usual modesty, has contented himself with stating the fact, without attempting to account for it. He is in correspondence with Professor Buckland upon the subject, and the learned Professor has suggested an explanation, which it will be for future observers, by repeated experiments, to confirm. We should state, that the insects were principally found at the negative pole of the battery."

A great body of similar facts might be adduced, if necessary, tending to show that all animal *motion* may be traced to *electrical action;* enough has, however, been advanced to satisfy those who are willing to be convinced; those who are unwilling, may fall back upon the "vital principle," or some ethereal or spiritual essence, if to their minds such essence furnishes a more satisfactory solution. We do not hope to convince those who are stubbornly bent upon explaining the mysteries of nature, by introducing other mysteries still more incomprehensible than those which they profess to explain. We should not have entered upon the subject but that we are firmly persuaded that before we can hope to elevate the physical and moral condition of man, we must carefully and minutely investigate the laws by which his physical nature is governed, and thereby we shall obtain a sound basis for our moral structure.

To some who may, perhaps, have expected that our remarks would be confined to an exposition of the laws by which the heavenly bodies are guided in their course, it may appear, in some measure out of place, that we should enter into an investigation of those laws which regulate the motion of matter in the animal, vegetable, and mineral kingdoms. We would remind such, that the system which we are now laying before them, is not merely a system of astronomy, which treats of the motions of the heavenly bodies exclusively, but a system of philosophy, which treats of the motion of matter in every form and condition in which it may be presented to the mind; and that our object is to show that the same powers govern and regulate all the motions of matter; that an atom and a world are directed in their motions by the same forces,—in short, that every atom, and every aggregate of atoms, whether in the animal, vegetable, or mineral kingdom, or in the wide field of the universe, is at all times, and in all places, subject to the powers of electricity, the great and universal primary mover of the physical world. In all our studies, before we attempt to comprehend or explain the operations of nature upon the large scale, we should make ourselves familiar with the phenomena which immediately surround us.

In the remarks which we are about to offer upon the vegetable kingdom, it is not our intention to enter into the subject at length, neither is it necessary that we should. Our sole object in the present remarks is, to direct the study of vegetable physiology into the right channel, to show that the vegetable functions are governed by electrical action, as well as every other operation of nature.

A vegetable, like an animal, is constituted of matter existing in the three specific conditions of solid, liquid, and gaseous; and the fluids or vegetable juices in the vegetative process, are assimilated with the solid vegetable matter, according to certain fixed laws, as in the animal body. In the vegetable, however, the flowing of the juices is extremely slow, as compared with the circulation of the blood in warm-blooded animals. The vegetable juices do not, in fact, *circulate*, in the sense in which that term is applied in the animal economy. In the animal body, the blood flows round and round continuously, giving out for the support of the frame, that portion only which has been ærated or laborated in the lungs,—the mass of the liquid current constantly returning to the same point, that another small portion may be ærated and rendered fit for the sustenance of the animal functions. But in the vegetable economy it appears, from the researches of the most eminent vegetable physiologists, that the entire mass of the vegetable juice is laborated and prepared for the formation of solid vegetable matter in one circulation, and that no portion of the juice returns to the point which it previously occupied in the vascular system, or what may be called the veins and arteries of the plant. These vegetable veins and arteries are denominated the *conducting vessels* and *returning vessels*, and are very dissimilar in their structure, to the veins and arteries of the animal body,—not being continuous tubes, but bundles of vessels connected with each other. In the early spring, long before the leaves begin to appear, the vegetable juice or *sap* begins to rise in the *conducting vessels;* but until the leaves have been unfolded, no part of this ascending juice is converted into the substance, of the vegetable; for it is in the leaves that the juice is ærated or laborated, and converted into proper vegetable matter, just as the blood is ærated in the lungs, and converted into proper animal matter. When the vegetable juice has been laborated in the leaf, it is carried downward by the *returning vessels*, which, like the conducting vessels, extend throughout the entire length of the plant, from the highest twig to the most minute fibre of the root. Here, then, as in all other cases, we find that the moving fluid performs a circuit; that the fibres of the root imbibe moisture which is carried upwards to the highest twig or leaf, where a specific change in the sap is effected, after which it is carried down to the smallest fibre of the root; and thus is the process of vegetation carried forward. In this manner is the loftiest tree in the forest formed—by slow and imperceptible degrees; and thus is the moss formed that clings to the damp wall. When we look upon the huge beams of which our ships are formed, or with which our buildings are secured, we do not stop to reflect that every particle of these huge masses have, but a few years previously, passed through the leaves of our forest in the form of a gas, and that, by the influence of so hypothetical a substance as the solar beam, it has been transformed into its present solid form and dimensions.

Mr. Pine, of Maidstone, Kent, and his friend, Mr. Weekes, have for several years been prosecuting experiments, with a view to show that the process of vegetation is due to electrical action, and have been eminently successful. They have proved, beyond all controversy, that in the spring season, the vegetation of the earth drinks in the solar electric fluid with such extreme greediness, that the atmosphere is kept cool and free from thunder storms; but in the autumn, when the vegetative process of the season is finished, when plants and trees are saturated, and no longer able to drink up the supply, the air is surcharged with electrical matter, and accordingly we have thunder and lightning. The following observations are extracted from Mr. Pine's letters, published in the *Mechanic's Magazine*, and which letters are well worthy an attentive perusal:—

"The vast superiority of vegetable over metallic points, in the drawing off and accumulating electric matter, is, I conceive, a subject of great interest and importance. A coated jar, having forty-six inches of metallic surface, was repeatedly charged by the activity of a vegetable point, in four minutes and six seconds, while the same jar, charged to the same degree, required eleven minutes and eighteen seconds to free it from its electric contents by means of a metallic point,—the points in both cases being equi-distant. I find, also, that Bennett's gold-leaf electroscope is powerfully affected by a charged jar at the distance of nearly seven feet, when the brass cap of the instrument is furnished with a branch of the shrub called *butcher's broom*, and which I have found of great use in my experiments. The same delicate instrument when mounted with pointed metallic wires, is not perceptibly affected until the charged jar approaches to within two feet of the cap.

"In order to try the electric action of a vegetable point immediately upon the atmosphere, Mr. Weekes placed 'a large *street-lamp* in an inverted position, mounted with a brass cap, through which passed a stout wire with a brass knob' at its nether extremity, 'and a pair of small pith balls, attached' by threads 'to the wire above the knob.' Within the lamp was placed 'a portable stand, with two metallic discs, one on each side of the wire, and rising to a level with the pith balls.' To the summit of the wire, he attached 'a small branch of the butcher's broom,'

'This apparatus,' he proceeds, 'I have many weeks past had in daily use, nor can I express the pleasure it has afforded to myself and friends, by its frequent indications of atmospheric electricity; for, armed with *vegetable detectors* it has shown symptoms of electricity by the passing of clouds at a great altitude, and under various other circumstances, in which electrometers with metallic points, placed by its side, gave no indication whatever. This appears to me so decided a proof of the superiority of vegetable conductors, that it admits of no contradiction.

"The letter in which these accurate and decisive experiments are related, is dated the 8th of May, 1828; and as they were recently made, they admirably illustrate the electrical state of plants, and their action on the atmosphere in the spring season. This is, no doubt, the season of their greatest electric, as well as vegetative activity, agreeable to which, in my first experiments, made in the month of June, a blade of grass and a metallic point being mutually presented to the prime-conductor, the first continued to be illuminated till it had reached at least four times the distance at which the latter ceased to exhibit any light, that is, at the distance of about fourteen feet from the electrical body; whereas, in a similar experiment, made in October, the grass-point affected the ball of the electrometer, appended to the prime-conductor at a distance only of nineteen inches, when a pointed metal of corresponding length, that is, five inches, would affect it in an equal degree at the distance of nine eight-fourteenths inches.

"It cannot but be evident that very important consequences must flow from such extraordinary conducting energies in plants, more particularly as manifested through the acute extremities of their leaves, buds, and germs, in the spring season.

"The fluid, which, in an uncombined state, by means of artificial excitements, or in the form of lightning, produces electricity, emanates, I conceive, originally from the sun in that state; and that its direct rays either produce electric or galvanic effects;—or, by entering into combination with air, water, or oxygen, obtained by the decomposition of carbonic acid, and, perhaps from the leaves of plants, or being absorbed into the substance of our globe, are neutralized. The air being an electric, a portion of the fluid floats in an uncombined state upon it, which it would do in much greater quantities, more especially in the higher regions, where there is little gravitating matter with which it can combine, were it not continually imbibed by the sap and juices of the plants. Their solid framework, consisting of non-conducting matter, and forming trunks, pierced with an infinitude of capillary tubes, furnishes an admirable passage for the rise of the sap, and for the action of the positive electricity of the atmosphere, in drawing it upwards and towards all the acute extremities of the leaves. The electric matter being thus introduced, is enabled to operate upon all the vital functions of the plants, while its superabundance being transmitted down to the fibrous extremities of the roots, either causes them to imbibe new moisture, or is conveyed by it into the earth, thus maintaining that near approach to an equilibrium on which the general harmony and tranquility of nature depends.

"If the identity of the electric fluid, with that which issues from the sun be admitted, a source is assigned by which, according to the testimonies of those electricians, who have been in the habit of making experiments on the electricity of the atmosphere, and that notwithstanding the immense infinitude of potent conductors which shoot up from its bosom. If it be admitted that plants have their peculiar construction, and are furnished with their conducting points, with the accompanying sap and juices, for the two-fold purpose of causing or promoting their vegetation, and of averting dangerous accumulations of electric matter in the atmosphere, the final and efficient causes of their structure and operations, to a certain extent, will appear. It has been observed by that excellent lecturer on galvanism and other branches of natural philosophy, Mr. Sturgeon, that the rotary motion of our globe and of the other planetary bodies, receives illustration from the action of a galvanic current on bodies capable of receiving its influence placed at right angles to it; and if we allow that the earth actually receives such an influence from the sun, and thus perpetually whirled round with its immense conducting apparatus, for the purpose of imparting a vegetable principle to the system of plants, at the same time that light and warmth are conveyed to the whole creation, while all injurious effects from the effusion of so much electric matter are averted by the near approach to an equilibrium which they constantly maintain, a concurrence of useful causes and effects, in carrying forward the operations of nature, and maintaining its order and harmony, will appear, which seems to reflect credibility on the general conclusion."

The experiments of Mr. Pine are very satisfactory; but if the reader should entertain any doubt, with respect to the agency of electricity in the process of vegetation, let him try the following experiment:—

Let him take a small quantity of mustard or cress seed, and steep it for a few days in diluted oxymuriatic acid; let him sow it in a fine light soil in a garden pot, and cover it with a metallic cover; let him now bring it in contact with the prime-conductor of an electric machine. His seed will spring up as if by magic, and in the course of a *few minutes* his crop will be ready to cut—he will have a salad fit to be put upon the table. The connexion of electricity with vegetation is well worthy of our most serious attention, not merely in relation to speculative science, but as a practical question in which the advancement of our agriculture is deeply involved.

Having seen that original animals have been produced by electrical agency, the reader will not be disposed to doubt that vegetables may be generated by the same powers. Indeed, this is a matter of common occurrence, so common, that, like many others of a similar nature, it escapes our notice. The necessary combination of circumstances for the production of vegetables of the lower order are three, moisture, air, and the solar rays. Whenever these elements are brought in contact, the galvanic process is put in action, and vegetation is the inevitable result. Although the earth has passed that stage in which the higher order of plants can be produced, and is now passing into that stage of old age and barrenness in which it will be impossible that even the lowest orders can be produced, whilst, at the same time, the higher orders will continue to drop off one after another, until ultimately all life, both animal and vegetable, will have ceased upon the face of the earth. We will enter into this subject more at length when we come to treat of geology.

Having endeavored to show that electrical action governs all motion in the animal and vegetable kingdoms, we now approach the mineral kingdom, which, correctly speaking, is the earth itself. Now, although from a superficial observation we might be induced to suppose that the broken and distorted crust of the earth is nothing else than a heap of confusion, yet it is not so. Every atom occupies the place which it has been compelled to occupy by a fixed and determined law. However, we are not about to speak of mountains and rocks upon the large scale in this place, but rather to notice their internal arrangement or organization.

"Most of the solids which compose the mineral crust of the earth are found in the crystallized state. Granite consists of crystals of quartz, felspar, and mica. Even mountain masses, like clay-slate, have regulated forms. Perfect mobility among the corpuscles is essential to crystallization, and may take place either from igneous fusion, or from solution in liquid. In the crystallized state, matter is *contracted* into the smallest space."—[Ure's Dictionary.

The reader will do well to fix in his mind the two important facts contained in the first and last sentences of the above quotation, as these two facts taken conjointly will be of considerable use to him in our further elucidation of the electrical theory.

Now, as rocks are nothing else than immense masses of crystallized matter, we have to inquire by what means crystals are produced; for it is evident that the same power which produces *one* crystal, has, in the long lapse of time, produced all the crystals which *now* form the mountain masses of the earth. We prefer drawing our facts from independent authorities, deeming them more impartial witnesses, than if their evidence had been given with a view to support a theory, and will, therefore, produce an extract upon this point; and as metallic veins also form an important branch of this part of our subject, we will in the same extract give some account of the manner of their formation. It ought to be mentioned, that negative Voltaic electricity instantly determines the crystalline arrangement, while positive Voltaic electricity counteracts it.

"Mr. Fox mentioned the fact, long known to miners, of metalliferous veins, intersecting different rocks containing ore in some of these rocks, and being nearly barren, or entirely so, in others. This circumstance suggested the idea of some definite cause; and his experiments on the electrical magnetic condition of various ores to each other, seems to have supplied an answer, inasmuch as it was thus proved that electro-magnetism was in a state of great activity under the earth's surface, and that it was independent of mere local action between the plates of copper and the ore with which they were in contact, by the occasional substitution of plates of zinc for those of copper, producing no change in the direction of the Voltaic currents. He also referred to other experiments, in which two different varieties of copper ore, with water taken from the same mine, as the only exciting fluid, produced considerable Voltaic action. The various kinds of saline matter which he had detected in water taken from different mines, and also taken from parts of the same mine, seemed to indicate another probable source of electricity; for can it now be doubted, that rocks impregnated with or holding in their minute fissures different kinds of mineral waters, must be in different electrical conditions or relations to each other? A general conclusion is, that in these fissures metalliferous deposits will be determined according to their relative electrical conditions; and that the direction of those deposits must have been influenced by the direction of the magnetic meridian. Thus we find the metallic deposits in most parts of the world having a tendency to an E. and W., or N. E. and S. W. bearing. Mr. Fox added, that it was a curious fact, that on submitting the muriate of tin in solution to Voltaic action to the negative pole of the battery, and another to the positive, a portion of the tin was determined like the copper, the former in a metallic state, and the latter in that of an oxyd, showing a remarkable analogy to the relative position of tin and copper ore with respect to each other, as they are found in the mineral veins.

"The chairman said, it had been observed to them last evening, that the test of some of the highest truths which philosophy had brought to light was their simplicity. He held in his hand a blacking-pot, which Mr. Fox had bought yesterday for a penny, a little water, zinc, and copper, and by these humble means he had imitated one of the most secret and wonderful processes of nature—her mode of making metallic veins. It was with peculiar satisfaction he contemplated the valuable results of this meeting of the Association. There was also a gentleman now at his right hand, whose name he had never heard till yesterday, a man unconnected with any society, but possessing the true spirit of a philosopher; this gentleman had made no less than twenty-four minerals, and even crystalline quartz. He (Dr. Buckland) knew not how he had made them, but he pronounced them to be discoveries of the highest order; they were not made with a blacking-pot and clay, like Mr. Fox's, but the apparatus was equally humble; a bucket of water and a brickbat had sufficed to produce the wonderful effects which he would detail to them.

"Mr. Crosse, of Bloomfield, Somerset, then came forward, and stated that he came to Bristol to be a listener only, and with no idea he should be called upon to address a Section. He was no geologist, and but little of a mineralogist: he had, however, devoted much time to electricity, and he had latterly been occupied in improvements in the Voltaic power, by which he had succeeded in keeping it in full force for twelve months by water alone, rejecting acids entirely. Mr. Crosse then proceeded to state, that he had obtained water from a finely crystallized cave at Holway, and by the action of the Voltaic battery had succeeded in producing from that water in the course of ten days, numerous rhomboidal crystals, resembling those of the cave; in order to ascertain if light had any influence in the process, he tried it again in a dark cellar, and produced similar crystals in six days, with one-fourth of the Voltaic power. He had repeated the experiments a hundred times, and always with the same results. He was fully convinced that it was possible to make even diamonds, and that at no distant period every kind of mineral would be formed by the ingenuity of man. By a variation of his experiments, he had obtained grey and blue carbonate of copper, phosphate of soda, and twenty or thirty other specimens. If any of the members of the Association would favor him with a visit at his house, they would be received with hospitality, though in a wild and savage region on the Quantock Hills, and he should be proud to repeat his experiments in their presence. Mr. Crosse sat down amidst long continued cheering.

"Professor Sedgwick said he had discovered in Mr. Crosse a friend, who some years ago kindly conducted him over the Quantock hills on the way to Taunton. The residence of that gentleman was not, as he had described it, in a wild and savage region, but seated amidst the sublime and beautiful in nature. At that time he was engaged in carrying on the most gigantic experiments, attaching Voltaic lines to the trees of the forest, and conducting through them streams of lightning as large as the mast of a 74 gun ship, and even turning them through his house with the dexterity of an able charioteer. Sincerely did he congratulate the Section on what they had heard.

and witnessed that morning. The operation of electrical phenomena, instances of which had been detailed to them, proved that the whole world, even darkness itself, was steeped in everlasting light, the first-born of heaven. However Mr. Crosse might have hitherto concealed himself, from this time forth he must stand before the world as public property.

"Professor Phillips said, the wonderful discoveries of Mr. Crosse and Mr. Fox would open a field of science in which ages might be employed in exploring and imitating the phenomena of nature."

Seeing that by far the greater proportion of the earth's crust is now in a crystallized form, and that the process of crystallization is still slowly, steadily, and almost imperceptibly proceeding onward, until ultimately the entire mass will pass into the crystallized state, that state in which matter is contracted into the smallest space; and seeing also that the *expansion* and *contraction* of matter are the two most important principles in the electrical theory, and that in this theory it is affirmed that these processes are every where going on unceasingly, more or less, in the hardest rock, and in the most diffused gas; it may be useful and interesting to the reader to peruse the following extract from the letters of Sir David Brewster on Natural Magic, in which it appears that he has discovered the fact, without apparently perceiving the rationale of the subject, that this process is going on in the hardest crystals:—

"In examining with the microscope the structure of mineral bodies, I discovered in the interior of many of the gems, thousands of cavities of various forms and sizes. Some had the shape of hollow and regularly formed crystals; others possessed the most regular outline, and consisted of many cavities and branches united without order, but all communicating with each other. These cavities sometimes occurred singly, but most frequently in groups, forming strata of cavities at one time perfectly flat and at another time curved. Several such strata were often found in the same specimens, sometimes parallel to each other, at other times inclined, and forming all varieties of angles with the faces of the original crystals.

"These cavities, which occurred in sapphire, crysoberyl, topaz, beryl, quartz, amethyst, peridot, and other substances, were sometimes sufficiently large to be distinctly seen by the naked eye, but most frequently they were so small as to require a highly magnifying power to be well seen, and often they were so exceedingly minute that the highest magnifying powers were unable to exhibit their outline.

"The greater number of these cavities, whether large or small, contain two new fluids different from any hitherto known, and possessing remarkable physical properties. These two fluids are in general perfectly transparent and colorless, and they exist in the same cavity in actual contact, without mixing together in the slighest degree. One of them expands *thirty* times more than water, and at a temperature of about eighty degrees of Fahrenheit, it expands so as to fill up the vacuity in the cavity. When heat such as that of the hand is applied to the specimen, the vacuity gradually contracts in size, and wholly vanishes at a temperature of about eighty degrees.

"When the cavities are large compared with the quantity of expansible fluid, the heat converts the fluid into vapor, an effect which is shown by the circular cavity becoming larger and larger till it fills the whole space.

"When any of these cavities, whether they are filled with fluid or with vapor, are allowed to cool, the vacuity re-appears at a certain temperature. In the fluid cavities the fluid contracts, and the small vacuity appears, which grows larger and larger till it resumes its original size. When the cavities are large, several small vacuities make their appearance and gradually unite in one, though they sometimes remain separate. In deep cavities, a very remarkable phenomenon accompanies the re-appearance of the vacuity. At the instant that the fluid has acquired the temperature at which it quits the side of the cavity, an effervescence or rapid ebullition takes place, and the transparent cavity is for a moment opaque, with an infinite number of minute vacuities which instantly unite in one that goes on enlarging as the temperature diminishes.

"Having fallen upon a method of opening the cavities, and looking at the fluids, I was able to examine their properties with more attention. When the expansive fluid rises from the cavity upon the surface of the topaz, it neither remains still like the fixed oils, nor disappears like evaporated fluids. Under the influence, no doubt, of heat and moisture, it is in a state of constant motion, now spreading itself on a thin plate over a large surface, and now contracting itself into a deeper and much less extended drop. These contractions and extensions are marked by very beautiful optical phenomena. When the fluid has stretched itself out into a thin plate, it ceases to reflect light, like the thinnest part of the soap bubble, and when it is again accumulated into a thicker drop, it is covered with the colored rings of thin plates.

"After performing these motions, which sometimes last for ten minutes, the fluid suddenly disappears, and leaves behind it a sort of granular residue. When examining this with a single microscope, it again started into a fluid state, and extended and contracted itself as above. This was owing to the humidity of the hand which held the microscope, and I have been able to restore by moisture the fluidity of these grains twenty days after they were formed from the fluid. This portion was shown to the Rev. Dr. Fleming, who remarked, that had he observed it accidentally, he would have ascribed its apparent vitality to the movements of some of the animals of the genus Planaria.

"After the cavity has remained open for a day or two, the dense fluid comes out and quickly hardens into a transparent and yellowish, resinous looking substance, which absorbs moisture, though with less avidity than the other. It is not volatilized by heat, and is insoluble in water and alcohol. It readily dissolves, however, with effervescence in the sulphuric, nitric, and muriatic acids. The residue of the expansible fluid is volatilized by heat, and is dissolved, but without effervescence in the above mentioned acids. The refracting power of the dense fluid is about 1.295, and of the expansible one 1.131.

"The particles of the dense fluid have a very powerful attraction for each other, and for the mineral which contains them, while those of the expansible fluid have a very slight attraction for one another, and also for the substance of the mineral. Hence the two fluids never mix, the dense fluid being attracted to the angles of angular cavities, or filling the narrow necks by which two cavities communicate. The expansible fluid, on the other hand, fills up the wide parts of the cavities, and in deep and round cavities it lies above the dense fluid.

"When the dense fluid occupies the necks which join two cavities, it performs the singular function of a fluid valve, opening and shutting itself according to the *expansions* or *contractions* of the other fluid. The *fluid valves* thus exhibited in action may suggest some useful hints to the mechanic and the philosopher, while they afford ground of curious speculation in reference to the functions of animal and vegetable bodies. In the larger organizations of ordinary animals, where gravity must in general overpower, or at least modify, the influence of capillary attraction, such a mechanism is neither necessary nor appropriate; but, in the lesser functions of the same animals, and almost in all the microscopic structures of the lower world, where the force of gravity is entirely subjected to the more powerful energy of capillary forces, it is extremely probable that the mechanism of immiscible fluids, and the fluid valves, is generally adopted.

"In several cavities in minerals, I have found crystallized and other bodies; sometimes transparent crystals, sometimes black spicular crystals, and sometimes black spheres, all of which are moveable within the cavity. In some cavities the two fluids occur in an indurated state, and others I have found to be lined with a powdery matter. This last class of cavities occurred in topaz, and they were distinguished from all others by the extraordinary beauty and symmetry of their form. One of these cavities represented a finely ornamented sceptre, and, what is still more singular, the different parts of which it is composed lay in different planes.

"When the gem which contains the highly expansive fluid is strong, and the cavity not near the surface, heat may be applied to it without danger; but in the course of my experiments on this subject, the mineral has often burst with a tremendous explosion, and in one case wounded me on the brow. An accident of the same kind occurred to a gentleman, who put a crystal into his mouth for the purpose of expanding the fluid. The specimen burst with great force, and cut his mouth, and the fluid which was discharged from the cavity had a very disagreeable taste.

"In the gems which are peculiarly appropriated for female ornaments, cavities containing the expansible fluid frequently occur; and if these cavities should happen to be very near the surface or the edge of the stone, the fever heat of the body might be sufficient to burst them with an alarming and even dangerous explosion. I have never heard of such accident having occurred; but if it has, or if it ever shall occur, and if its naturally marvellous character shall be heightened by any calamitous results, the phenomena described in the preceding pages will strip it of its wonder."

Here then we find that electrical action is incessantly going on in the animal, vegetable, and mineral kingdoms; that animals, vegetables, and minerals are produced and maintained each in its own appropriate condition by its agency. Here lies the basis of the electrical theory, to which we shall occasionally appeal, when, in extending our views, we come to treat of electricity as a universal power, by the influence of which the whole universe is kept in everlasting motion.

It may be well to remark in this place, once for all, that in these pages no intention is entertained to interfere in the slightest degree with what, in the religious world, are denominated the dispensations of Divine Providence. This is a point in which philosophy is no wise concerned. Although we have endeavored to show that all *physical* power may be traced to electrical action, we say nothing whatever of the *moral government* of the world, which is presumed to emanate from the Divine mind. These matters pertain to the province of the theologian, and ought never, on any account, to be mixed up with philosophy, for such mixture has ever been productive of evil.

The study of nature, as far as relates to this earth, has been for a length of time classed or divided into three kingdoms, the animal, the vegetable, and the mineral; by a proper attention to which division or classification, the progress of the student is very much facilitated. In the same way, the study of nature *as a whole* ought to be divided into three great empires, the gaseous, the liquid, and the solid; and by this division, equal facility would be obtained in the study of the universe upon the large scale. We shall, therefore, with a view to secure to the student this facility of study, take the liberty of instituting such division, and shall proceed to show that *all matter* is in a state of continual change from the *gaseous empire* to the *liquid empire;* from the *liquid empire* to the *solid empire;* from the *solid empire* to the *liquid empire;* and from the *liquid empire* to the *gaseous empire* again: which round of changes constitutes the *great chain of cause and effect*, or *grand circuit of motion* of the physical universe, of which the smaller operations of nature are but the subordinate links.

The whole universe is full of matter, solid, liquid, and gaseous. The planets are composed of solid and liquid matter, with an atmosphere of gas, which gaseous matter is slowly passing into the solid form. Comets are composed of gas and liquid matter, which is also contracting or passing into the planetary state. The entire of the matter in the solar system, not contained in the sun itself, is gradually contracting or passing into the solid state, and if this process of contracting were to proceed for a series of ages, the operation of the opposite or compensating force of expansion being in the mean time arrested, it is evident that the entire *gaseous empire* would be absorbed into the *solid empire;* and when the contraction of matter had reached the ultimate point, the operations of nature would come to a stand; motion would be at an end; for all mechanical motion, that is, the motion of matter in solid masses, is but an effect resulting from the expansion and contractions of matter; and these latter are also effects resulting from the two opposite and contending principles of repulsion and attraction; which principles are, as far as can be perceived, the ultimate powers or forces from which all motion takes its origin; from which original sources, motion is transferred from body to body in a variety of modifications throughout the whole range of physical existence.

But motion is as imperishable as matter itself. The principles which regulate and control the motions of physical nature, are the first amongst the essential properties of matter; from which principles it is as impossible that matter can be separated, as that sensation can be separated from the living organized animal frame. The two opposing powers are always in action. In proportion as matter is abstracted from the gaseous empire, and absorbed into the solid, in the different planets and comets of the solar system, so, in the same proportion, is matter abstracted from the solid empire and given back to the gaseous by the internal action of the sun himself; and thus is the equilibrium of the two opposite empires maintained, and, for aught we know to the contrary, thus will the equilibrium be maintained to all eternity; worlds after worlds being formed and dissolved in everlasting succession, but the solar system remaining forever.

According to Sir Isaac Newton, matter is almost infinitely divisible; for he conceives that a cubic inch of solid matter, divided or decomposed into its ultimate atoms, may be extended or expanded so as to fill the entire solar system, and yet that no two atoms shall be more than half an inch apart. Although, in this estimate, the expansion of matter is probably carried far beyond what actually takes place in nature; far beyond the *ultimate point of expansion* to which we have already alluded; yet the contemplation of this hypothetical case of Sir Isaac Newton, will enlarge our views, and show us that the expansion and contraction of matter may be carried to an extent which appears almost without limit; that a body of gas sufficient to fill the solar system may be *contracted* into one cubic inch of solid matter; and *vice versa*, that a cubic inch of solid matter may be *expanded* into a gas of sufficient volume to fill the solar system. If man could trace the expansions and contractions of matter through every form and condition, then would all the secrets of nature stand revealed.

Let us pause here, and examine the manner in which these powers work in the earth which we inhabit. Take a common tallow candle, which is formed of solid animal matter, and therefore in that state belongs to the *solid empire*, and which, by the ordinary process of nature, would in time pass off into the *gaseous empire;* but if you light the candle, the process will be quickened. When the candle has been lighted, the solid animal matter begins to decompose, taking the liquid form in the little cup which is formed round the wick immediately under the flame; from the liquid in this little cup it is further decomposed into two or more gases; these gases instantly combine with the oxygen of the atmosphere, and heat and light are given out in the process; or, to speak more correctly, perhaps, we ought to say that heat and light are *effects* resulting from the act of chemical combination. Now, after a certain time, the candle is burned out or consumed, as we say in common language; but not a particle of the solid matter has been lost; the whole has passed off into the *gaseous empire*. Hydrogen and carbon are two of the constituents of the candle, and as it continues to burn, these two bodies continue to combine with the oxygen of the air; the hydrogen and oxygen passing off in the form of steam, and the carbon and oxygen in the form of carbonic acid gas, both gases mixing with the atmosphere. After a time, the steam is condensed or contracted into water, and falls upon the earth;—and the carbonic acid gas, from its specific gravity, floats near the surface. Now, water and carbonic acid are the food of vegetables; therefore, if they fall upon a field of grass, the grass will grow and thrive upon this matter. If sheep or other herbiverous animals are fed in this field, the sheep will thrive and fatten upon the grass, and when the sheep are fatted and killed, we may procure our tallow candle again with which we commenced the process. Here we have the *circuit of motion* again, and every step of this circuit has been carried forward by the expansion and contraction of matter; the matter has passed from the solid to the gaseous empire, and *vice versa*, from the gaseous to the solid empire, in every step throughout the whole process. We have traced the matter through the vegetable and animal kingdoms, but the connexion does not by any means stop here; we may trace the same identical matter through every creek and corner of the solar system; nor is it likely that the connexion stops even here, but that every part of nature is more or less connected, forming one grand harmonious whole.

Again: take a piece of coal, which, in the condition in which it is found, is to be considered a mineral body, although it is evident, upon a very slight inspection, that it once existed upon the surface in the vegetable state. Throw it upon the fire, and as in the former case of the candle, we have carbonic acid and steam, with other gases resulting from the decomposition of the coal, and their combination with the oxygen of the atmosphere; and these gases, obtained from the decomposition of a bed of coal, will feed a forest, which forest may again form a bed of coal. Here we have passed through the vegetable and mineral kingdoms, and here again we have the circuit of motion; each step of which circuit is dependent upon the expansion and contraction of matter. We might go on adding examples without end; but enough has been advanced upon this head, to excite the inquiring mind to further investigation.

Now, it is evident, if in this earth solid matter were dissolved, and passed off into gas in exactly the same proportion that gaseous matter is passing into the solid state, that this alternate action or process, might go on forever, without the whole earth passing into the solid state, as is affirmed by this theory. But such is not the case. In this earth the contractive force is the stronger of the two, just as in the sun the expansive force is the stronger, the effect of which is, that in this earth the solid empire is continually gaining upon the gaseous, and in the sun the gaseous empire is in a like measure gaining upon the solid; and thus the equilibrium of the two is maintained. Every piece of coal which is dug out of the earth, the stones upon which we tread, and of which our buildings are framed, bear witness to this fact, which is broadly and indelibly stamped upon the face of all terrestrial things, that he who will but open his eyes and look around him, cannot misunderstand the language in which it is expressed. The solid rocks which are now deposited many thousand feet beneath the surface of the earth, contain within themselves evidence of the most indubitable character, that the matter of which they are composed has passed from the fluid to the solid form, and the process of contraction is still going on. But this process cannot go on forever; neither is there any known power on earth by which they can be dissolved and given back to the gaseous empire, from which they have been derived, and to which they must return, before the circuit of motion can be completed. There is no power by which they can be dissolved, except electricity, the grand focus of which power is the sun; to which focus the planets are all tending, where their solid materials will be decomposed and again given back to the gaseous empire.

The following example will, in some degree, show the manner in which the solid gains upon the liquid and gaseous empires, on this earth. By the action of the sun upon the surface of the ocean, a small quantity of the water is expanded or formed into vapor or gas, in consequence of which expansion it rises in the atmosphere. This vapor is carried along by the wind, and being now in the higher or colder regions of the atmosphere, the vapor is condensed or contracted into rain drops, which drops, obeying the law of contraction, immediately fall towards the earth's centre, and are scattered upon the surface of the land. This water trickles down the side of the mountain, forming streams and rivulets, till at length the whole is collected into the channels of the great rivers, and thus finds its way back to the ocean, completing the circuit of motion, in which we again find the expansion and contraction of matter. Now, if the *whole* of this water found its way back into the ocean, the ocean might remain forever undiminished, and if such were the case, it would almost seem as if the water were carried round for very little purpose. But nature does not carry on her operations without an ultimate object which is to be attained. A large proportion of this water never returns to the ocean, but is taken up in feeding the vegetation of the earth, where it passes into the solid form, which solid matter is transferred to the mineral kingdom, where it will, in all probability, remain; yet still contracting into a harder state, till it is dissolved into gas at the consummation of all terrestrial things. These views will appear much more plain and intelligible, when the reader has examined the geological facts by which they are supported.

We have endeavored to show that electrical action governs all the motions or processes of the animal, vegetable, and mineral kingdoms. Now, these three kingdoms comprise all the matter of the earth, except *water* and *air;* the first of which constitutes the ocean, seas, lakes, rivers, &c.; and the second, the atmosphere which surrounds the globe. Let us, therefore, endeavor to ascertain whether the processes of these also may not be traced to electrical agency. We shall not, at present, enter into the subject of the tides; that must be allowed to stand over until we have arrived at a more advanced stage of the inquiry. By an attentive consideration of the following experiment, which may be performed by any person possessing but an ordinary share of experimental knowledge, we shall be enabled to perceive much more clearly the nature and manner of the processes going on in the atmosphere, and their connexion with the ocean and other waters of the earth. Take a pint of water, and subject it to the influence of the galvanic battery, in the usual way; the water will be decomposed into its two constituent gases, oxygen and hydrogen, by which it will be *expanded* into about 2,000 times its former volume, that is, the two gases will fill about 2,000 pints. If the experiment be conducted without any preparation for retaining the gases in close vessels, they will escape into the air, and will for a time form a part of the atmosphere. But, if the oxygen and hydrogen gases be collected in two separate vessels, and afterwards passed carefully into one, the gases will, by the laws of chemical attraction, become blended together, though still retaining the gaseous form. If now the electric spark be passed through the mixed gases, a flash and explosion will instantly follow, and the 2,000 pints of gas will be found *contracted* into one pint of water, as at first. Now, in this experiment, what have we exhibited? We have, upon a small scale, imitated the process that is going on in the open theatre of the world: we have, in fact, step by step, prepared the materials for, and finished our experiment with, the exhibition of a small mimic thunder storm. For, if we consider that in this experiment we have brought into action the *two powers* by which all the operations of nature are carried forward, viz., *repulsion* and *attraction*, producing the *expansion* and *contraction* of matter; and if we further consider that the process is constantly going on upon the large scale, without the puny aid of man, we shall be enabled to perceive the nature of those principles by which all the operations of nature are guided. When we see the lightning flash, and hear the thunder roll over our heads, the concussion of elements, finishing with the descent of a vast body of water, we seldom stop to inquire by what physical causes these great effects are brought about. It must not, however, be supposed, that all the water which falls upon the surface of the earth, in the form of rain, has been previously decomposed into its ultimate gases. A very large proportion ascends from the surface into the atmosphere in the state of vapor, where it is held for a time in suspension, until, meeting with a current of cold air, it is contracted into rain drops, in a manner analogous to the condensation of steam. It is known, however, as a fact, concerning which there is no disputing, to which every shower, nay, every drop of rain that falls bears witness, that an immense body of water in the expanded form of vapor and gas, is continually passing from the ocean into the atmosphere. If this process were to cease, the existence of vegetable and animal life must, of necessity, cease also; for it is by the rains, furnished from this circuit of motion, that all vegetable life is supported, and animals derive their subsistence from the vegetable kingdom.

Now, oxygen and hydrogen, combined in certain proportions, constitute water; and oxygen and nitrogen, in certain proportions, constitute the air of the atmosphere, in which there is also suspended, at all times, a certain quantity of carbonic acid, which is a chemical compound of oxygen and carbon. Further, oxygen and hydrogen, combined with carbon and nitrogen, in certain proportions, constitute solid vegetable matter; and oxygen and hydrogen, combined with carbon and nitrogen in certain proportions, constitute solid animal matter; and lastly, oxygen and hydrogen, combined with carbon and nitrogen, and other elements, chiefly metals, constitute the solid matter of the mineral kingdom; that is, the solid matter of the earth itself. By this we learn that these elements exist in the three conditions of solid, liquid, and gas; that in the ocean, they exist in the liquid form; that they pass into the atmosphere in the state of gas; that they pass from the atmosphere into the vegetable kingdom, where they take the solid form; that decayed vegetables do not wholly return to the gaseous state, but that a certain portion, a *residuum* of the vegetable matter, passes into the mineral kingdom, forming beds of earth; and these beds of earth, in the lapse of ages, become beds of stone, and thus we find that the same identical matter which at present constitutes the ocean and atmosphere, is capable of passing into the mineral kingdom, by the silent and almost imperceptible operations of nature. But if this progressive operation be really going on, it is proper that some facts should be brought forward, and in such a shape too that all men may be enabled to estimate the value of evidence upon which the proposition rests. Happily, the facts bearing upon this point are so plain, so numerous, and so utterly beyond the reach of suspicion, that no single proposition, it may be safely asserted, can be supported by so large an amount of evidence, or the nature of which evidence is so incontrovertible.

A bed of coal, now buried some thousands of feet beneath the surface of the earth, contains within it, in a solid state, a vast body of matter, that must, at a former period, have formed a part of the ocean. Almost every person must have it within his power to examine a piece of coal, and may, therefore, easily satisfy himself upon this point. By cleaving a piece of coal, and examining carefully the surface of cleavage, he will readily discern that it consists almost entirely of vegetable matter, in a compressed and mineralized condition. It is utterly impossible that this vegetable matter could have been formed in the bowels of the earth, where it is now found. It must have grown upon the surface either of the earth or of a satellite attending the earth, exposed to the sun and air. Its root must have been supplied with moisture, and that moisture must have been furnished from the atmosphere, and the moisture of the atmosphere is derived from the ocean. But, although this process has been going on for ages, and will go on in this earth for many ages yet to come, it cannot go on forever. Although, to our apprehension, the extent of the ocean seems almost unbounded, yet it is a finite quantity. Every season, a certain quantity of water is drawn from the ocean to sustain the vegetation of the earth, being laborated by the sun's rays, without which, no vegetation can be brought to maturity. When the vegetable dies, and falls upon the surface, a portion of the matter of which it is composed returns to the gaseous empire, from which it has been recently derived; but a very considerable portion passes onward to form vegetable mould. Year after year this mould accumulates, until ultimately a bed of earth is formed, and this bed of earth, in process of time, becomes mineralized into a bed of stone, as is shown to have been the case with a bed of coal, to which we have already alluded, although, in respect to the coal, the vegetable matter has been preserved from passing into the earthy state. The same observations apply to nearly all the stratified rocks composing the crust of the earth, for nearly all of them contain the remains of animals and plants which must have existed upon the surface, exposed to the influence of the sun, the air, and the showers from the atmosphere.

---

## CHEMISTRY.

The study of chemistry, in the abstract sense, is simply the study of the two ultimate forces of *attraction* and *repulsion*. But, as these ultimate forces are invisible,—as they cannot be discerned by the senses,—we are necessitated by the limited nature of our faculties to apply ourselves to the study of the *effects* resulting from the operation of these unseen causes. The causes or forces are invisible; but the effects resulting from their action are tangible and discernable to the senses. These effects are the decomposition or *expansion* of solid bodies into gases by the invisible force of repulsion;—and the decomposition or *contraction* of gaseous matter into solid bodies by the invisible force of attraction. If attraction and repulsion be ultimate forces, then the expansion and contraction of matter are the two *primary effects* of their action; the first visible link in the chain of causation, from which we are to trace downwards all the varied operations going forward in the visible universe.

A cannon ball is discharged from the mouth of a gun, by which a tower is battered down. The materials of the tower fall upon the roof of a contiguous dwelling. The roof is crushed, and the whole mass sinks through the ceiling, and destroys an infant and its mother in the bed-room beneath. Now, can we trace the whole of this process to the ultimate forces of attraction and repulsion? Previous to the explosion or expansion of the gunpowder, all the foregoing objects were relatively at rest, and if the gunpowder had remained in the unexpanded or solid state, the effects could not have followed; what then is that force which caused the expansion or decomposition of the gunpowder? Repulsion evidently;—no other force could effect it. For, although heat, and light, and sound accompany the explosion, these are merely effects elicited by the collision or concussion which takes place in the sudden transition of the matter from the solid to the gaseous form. The efficient force by which matter is expanded, is repulsion, and the sudden exertion of this force in expanding a handful of gunpowder, set in motion the entire chain of objects by which ultimately the mother and infant were destroyed. But, although the ball which battered down the tower was projected from the gun by the force of repulsion, the materials did not descend towards the centre of the earth, breaking down the roof, &c., by the same force, but by its opposite—attraction, the force by which bodies are drawn together; therefore, both these forces were employed in working out the result,—they are the originators and continuators of motion. By the expansion of the gunpowder, the ball was put in motion, and the chain of consequences, of effects, followed. The expansion of the powder was an *effect* of repulsion. The horizontal and mechanical motion of the ball was an *effect* of the expansion. The disturbance or motion of the tower (its horizontal motion), was an *effect* of the motion of the ball. Here the effects originating immediately from repulsion end; the remainder are due to attraction. Solid bodies tend towards the centre of the earth (see the axioms, p. 69); therefore, the descending motion of the materials of the tower is an *effect* of attraction. The breaking down of the roof is an *effect* of the descent of the tower. The breaking through the ceiling may be considered an *effect* forming another link in the chain. The death of the mother and infant is an *effect* of the falling materials. And lastly, the different objects throughout the chain become relatively at rest as at the beginning; and all the effects have been traced to the ultimate forces of repulsion and attraction.

Motion is of two kinds, *chemical* and *mechanical*. By chemical motion, matter expands into a greater or contracts into a lesser volume,—as when a cubic inch of gunpowder is exploded, and thereby expanded into a volume of gas of many hundred cubic inches; or when 2,000 cubic inches of oxygen and hydrogen gases, in the proper proportions, are exploded, and thereby contracted into one cubic inch of water. By mechanical motion, masses of matter are transferred from place to place, but without undergoing any expansion or contraction. The motion of the ball is mechanical; that of the gunpowder chemical. All mechanical motion is an effect of chemical motion; and all chemical motion is due to the forces of attraction and repulsion;—therefore, *all motion* may be referred to these ultimate and universal forces.

We are now about to speak of chemical motion,—of some of the transformations which matter undergoes,—and of the different modifications which it assumes under the hand of the experimental chemist, as well as in the great laboratory of nature.

Of Decomposition.—When solid bodies are to be decomposed, their parts are first separated from each other by the mechanical operation of pounding in a mortar or otherwise,—and in many cases they are further separated by solution; after which the dissolved materials are subjected to a certain degree of heat, by which they are decomposed into their ultimate elements. Such is the ordinary process by which chemical decomposition is effected. But the most powerful instrument yet discovered for effecting chemical decomposition is the Voltaic pile, or galvanic battery. When the galvanic battery is sufficiently powerful, the repulsive and attractive forces are brought so strongly into play, that every substance yields to its decomposing effects,—air, water, metals, earths, and even flints are dissolved by this mysterious agency—in short, every substance; so that with a battery of sufficient magnitude and power, the entire earth might be dissolved and passed off in the form of vapor or invisible gas. We have already noticed the formation of crystals by the galvanic battery of Mr. Crosse, of Somerset. Now, crystals are the hardest or most *contracted* of all bodies;—gases are the softest or most *expanded;* and the galvanic battery has, within itself, the power, when acting on appropriate matter, to transform it into either of these states,—to carry the opposite processes onward to the two *ulti-*

*mate points* of expansion and contraction,—and these powers appertain to it, because in the process, the two forces of attraction and repulsion are brought into active collision with each other; and as the one or the other force predominates, so does the process tend to one or the other ultimate point. Those powers which can form and dissolve a single crystal in a few months, can also form and dissolve a world. There is no distinction between the one and the other process, except in the magnitude of the operation, in respect to the latter, and the time required for its accomplishment; and, when we reflect that eternity is the time allotted to nature for the carrying out her vast purposes, we cease to doubt or even to wonder that results so great as the formation and dissolvation of that, which, to our limited view, appears to be an immense solid globe of matter, should be brought about by the slow and silent operations of two invisible forces.

The galvanic battery has been of eminent service to the science of chemistry. It was chiefly by its aid that Sir Humphrey Davy established his name as the first chemist of the age. It has been the means of introducing a more orderly and scientific classification of the simple substances, or elements, each being classed as electro-negative or electro-positive, according as they are given off at the positive or negative pole of the battery, by which the attractions and repulsions which determine their combinations and decompositions are placed before the mind in an intelligible and scientific form; and the effects of an experiment may be calculated with a certain degree of confidence.

Table of those substances considered elementary, because they have not hitherto been decomposed:—

NON-METALLIC ELEMENTS.

| ELECTRO-NEGATIVE. | Equivalents. | ELECTRO-POSITIVE. | Equivalents. |
|---|---|---|---|
| Oxygen | 8 | Hydrogen | 1 |
| Chlorine | 36 | Nitrogen | 14 |
| Bromine | 75 | Sulphur | 16 |
| Iodine | 124 | Phosphorus | 12 |
| Fluorine | 18 | Selenium | 40 |
| | | Carbon | 6 |
| | | Silicon | 8 |
| | | Boron | 6 |

METALLIC ELEMENTS.

| ELECTRO-POSITIVE. | Equivalents. |
|---|---|
| Mercury | 200 |
| Silver | 110 |
| Gold | 200 |
| Platinum | 96 |
| Palladium | 56 |
| Rhodium | 44 |
| Iridium | ? |
| Osmium | ? |
| Nickel | 30 |
| Lead | 104 |
| Tellurium | 29 |
| Copper | 64 |
| Bismunth | 71 |
| Titanium | ? |
| Cobalt | ? |
| Cerium | ? |
| Uranium | ? |
| Antimony | 44 |
| Columbium | 144 |
| Tungsten | 96 |
| Chromium | 28 |
| Molybdenum | 48 |
| Arsenic | 38 |
| Tin | 59 |
| Iron | 28 |
| Zinc | 34 |
| Cadmium | 56 |
| Manganese | 28 |
| Potassium | 49 |
| Sodium | 24 |
| Lithium | 10 |
| Calcium | 20 |
| Barium | 70 |
| Strontium | 44 |
| Magnesium | 12 |
| Glucium | 20 |
| Yttrium | 34 |
| Almonium | 10 |
| Zinconium | ? |

It will be observed that oxygen and hydrogen stand at the head of the list, and on opposite sides of the table; that is, oxygen is an electro-negative element, and hydrogen electro-positive, and, therefore, as bodies in opposite electrical states, attract each other. These gases have a powerful affinity for each other, and in the act of their combining, the most intense heat and light are exhibited.

They are two most important elements, and enter largely into the composition of the earth, the ocean, and atmosphere; when in an uncombined state, they exist in the form of two invisible gases;—in combination they form water. It will also be noticed that all the metals are in the list of electro-positive elements; oxygen being electro-negative, there is a mutual attraction between oxygen and the metals, and hence we find, that the earth upon which we dwell, is little else than a metallic oxyd. Indeed, all the elements, by either direct or indirect means, will combine with each other, but in those in which the opposite electrical state is more distinct, the affinities are more energetic; and in those cases where two elements of the same electrical class are united, as hydrogen and nitrogen, (ammonia,) it may be that in the indirect process by which the compound is obtained, the electrical states of the elements are masked, modified, or even reversed entirely, as the poles are reversed in the electro-magnetic machine.

Of Chemical Equivalents.—It will be seen in the foregoing table, that a certain number is annexed to each of the elements, except a few of the metals. These numbers represent certain *definite proportions*, by weight, in which the various substances unite with each other. Hydrogen is the standard to which all the others are referred, and its equivalent is represented by 1, whilst that of oxygen is 8. If 1 part of hydrogen gas be mixed with 8 of oxygen, and the electrical spark passed through the mixture, the *whole* of the two gases will combine chemically, and water will be formed. But if more than 8 parts of oxygen to 1 of hydrogen be present, say 10 parts, upon exploding the mixture, the 1 part of hydrogen will combine with 8 parts of oxygen, as before, and 2 parts of the oxygen will remain in the gaseous form; because these two substances, as well as every other, will combine in *definite proportions* only, and this law is never subverted. It is the same on the other side: if too much hydrogen be present, the mixture will combine up to the point of mutual saturation, and the redundant gas will be left in an uncombined state.

Bodies combine, however, in more than one proportion. Hydrogen may be combined with a double dose of oxygen; that is, 1 of the former with 16 of the latter; but they cannot be made to unite in any intermediate or broken number of parts. The same general law holds in respect to all other bodies;—all have their definite proportions in which they mutually saturate each, or in which the mutual attractions of the two are satisfied;—for these proportions are nothing more than the measure by which the energy of the attractions may be estimated;—the representative number indicates the degree of attractive force subsisting between the two. If it were possible to change the intensity of the attractive force, the representative number or chemical equivalent would be changed in the same ratio; for the equivalent expresses the degree of affinity, and not the number or size of the atoms of the combining bodies;—at the same time, it must be admitted that the atomic theory is of considerable utility, as by conceiving, for example, that *one* atom of oxygen combines with *two* of hydrogen to form water, we have presented to our mind a tangible and distinct idea of chemical combination in such a shape as is suited to our capacity. Gases combine in definite proportions by *measure* as well as by weight; thus, a cubic foot of one gas combines with *one*, *two*, or *three* cubic feet of another gas, and will not combine in any intermediate quantity.

*Hydrogen*,—1, electro-positive, is the most expanded or lightest of known bodies,—100 cubic inches weighing about two grains; by which we perceive that the hydrogen formed by nature will ascend to the higher regions of the earth's atmosphere. (See the axioms, p. 68.) Its formation is continually going on upon the surface by the decomposition of solids and liquids, into which it enters as a component.

In describing the properties of different bodies, we shall arrange them in a five-fold division, corresponding to the *five senses* by which those properties are to be examined; and in order to avoid needless repetition, we will in this place number the senses, so that the number may indicate the sense referred to. Thus:—

Touch . . . 1 Taste . . . 2 Smell . . . 3
Sight . . . . 4 Hearing . . . . 5

Agreeable to which, we say, in reference to hydrogen gas,—1. It is elastic, and yields to the touch; indicating thereby, that the atoms do not touch each other, but are held apart by a repulsive force which yields when pressure is applied; and when the pressure is removed, the repulsive force presses out or expands the matter to its former dimensions; by which we may perceive that it is, in fact, the repulsive force which resists the pressure of the hand. 2. It is without taste, that is, it does not *act* upon the nerves of that sense. 3. Has a faint and rather disagreeable smell; and, therefore, does *act* faintly upon the nerves of the organ of smell. 4. When mixed with oxygen, the mixture will explode with a loud report, acting upon the ear. 5. In this explosion light also is exhibited, acting upon the sense of sight, although the gas itself is colorless and invisible. By its small specific gravity, or lightness, or elasticity, or *high degree of expansion*, for they are one and the same, and by its *action* with other matter, by which action our senses are affected, we gather certain particulars relating to it, and are thereby enabled to distinguish it from other bodies.

*Oxygen*,—8, electro-negative. 1. Elastic, or highly expanded. 2. Without taste. 3. No smell. 4. Colorless. 5. Explodes with hydrogen. Oxygen is a *supporter of combustion*, whilst hydrogen is a *combustible*. The former is the highest of electro-negatives, and the latter is the highest of electro-positives. Hence the attractive energy is exerted between them with a very high degree of intensity; therefore, the *action* is of the most intense kind: and as *light* and *heat* are *effects* of action, hence the light and heat elicited by that action is of an intense character, so much so, that almost every known body may be decomposed by the action of the oxy-hydrogen blow-pipe. Oxygen in different proportions enters largely into the composition of almost every body on the earth. 100 cubic inches weigh about 34 grains.

*Water*, (oxygen 8 + hydrogen 1.) Water is a well known compound. By the galvanic battery it may be separated, decomposed, or expanded into the two gases, oxygen and hydrogen;—one pint of water is expanded into about 2000 pints of gas, two-thirds (by measure) being hydrogen, and one-third oxygen; and these 2000 pints of gas may, by means of the electric spark, be again contracted into one pint of water as before,—so that in this case we have the two opposite processes of expansion and contraction effected by electrical agency alone; and these processes are every where going on slowly and silently, and are effected by this universal agent, which is every where in active and unceasing operation.

*Oxygenized Water*, (2 oxy. 16 + 1 hyd. 1.) 1. Liquid; attacks the skin and bleaches it. 2. Metallic taste. 3. Inodorous. 4. Colorless. 5. Explosions are produced by throwing very small bits of silver or platinum wire into the liquid. Little is known of this compound; it is difficult to produce, and cannot be preserved except by surrounding it with ice, as it decomposes very rapidly and at a very low temperature.

*Nitrogen.*—14, electro-positive. This is a very abundant gas, constituting four-fifths of the atmosphere which surrounds the earth. It has been hitherto considered to be an elementary body, but recent facts have tended very much to shake this opinion. Indeed, it is said to have been decomposed by Sir Humphrey Davy, by means of a powerful galvanic battery, and that a metallic body was given off, forming an amalgam with mercury, but which was dissipated so rapidly that it could not be properly examined. It has likewise been noticed by an American chemist, that nitrogen performs some very important functions in the vegetable kingdom, giving rise to the opinion that it is continually being absorbed in the process of vegetation, whilst the supply is kept up by chemical or electrical processes going on in the atmosphere; and that the light and heat which we receive through the agency of the sun does not reach the earth in the character of light and heat, but are effects resulting in this case as in every other, from action, and that the action is going on in the atmosphere of the earth. Nitrogen is distinguished chiefly by its negative properties; it is neither a combustible nor a supporter of combustion, but, like the carbonic acid gas, it possesses the characteristics of a compound which has been formed by the union of the former with the latter;—and if it can be proved that light and heat do not come directly from the sun, but are produced in the atmosphere of the earth, then we might be justified in the assumption that nitrogen is the product of an electro-chemical combustion going on in the atmosphere, and that, therefore, nitrogen being the product of a previous combustion, like carbonic acid gas, it cannot be either a combustible or supporter of combustion; and yet, at the same time, like carbonic acid, it may have very important functions to perform in connexion with the vegetable world, as has been shown to be the case by the experiments of the American chemist already noticed, a more detailed account of which will be given in another part of this work.

1. Nitrogen is an elastic gas. 2. Without taste. 3. No smell. 4. Colorless. 5. ———

*Atmospheric Air*, (2 nitrogen 28 + 1 oxygen 8). The

atmosphere is compounded of four parts, by volume, of nitrogen, and one of oxygen, and this appears to be well adapted to support the animal functions, and to maintain that just tone which is requisite to the healthy action of the system. If the quantity of nitrogen were increased, the vital action would go on more languidly; if the oxygen were wholly withdrawn, or even very much decreased in quantity, the animal machine must stop,—for oxygen is as necessary and essential to the support of the action which goes on in the animal frame, as of that which goes on in combustion. On the other hand, if the proportion of oxygen were greatly increased, or the nitrogen wholly withdrawn, the action would be of that intense kind, that it would be impossible for the animal to withstand it. Rabbits have been immersed in oxygen gas, by which the entire volume of the blood became arterial, and the animals have died in a few hours; we are not, however, justified in concluding that because the present race of animals could not live in an atmosphere differently constituted, that, therefore, no animal could live in the altered circumstances;—every race has its own element. The animals produced by Mr. Crosse, lived in muriatic acid, an element in which no other known animal could live.

*Protoxyd of Nitrogen*, (1 nitrogen 14 + 1 oxygen 8). This gas is also named the nitrous oxyd, and sometimes the *laughing gas*, from the highly exciting effects produced by it upon the animal frame, when inhaled into the lungs, which effects are due to the large proportion of oxygen which it contains. 1. It is an elastic fluid. 2. Has a slightly sweet taste. 3. A faint and rather pleasant smell. 4. Is colorless. 5. Explodes with hydrogen.

*Deutoxyd of Nitrogen*, (1 nitrogen 14 + oxygen 16). This gas, like the preceding, is an elastic fluid, and although it is formed by the addition of one more equivalent of oxygen, yet its properties are in many respects entirely different from the nitrous oxyd. It does not explode with hydrogen. It cannot be respired. It will extinguish flame, although containing so large a quantity of oxygen. Phosphorus and charcoal will burn in it, however, if introduced in a state of high ignition. If small nails, or iron filings be immersed in it, one measure of oxygen will be absorbed by the iron, form oxyd of iron, and the remaining gas will be found to be the protoxyd.

*Hyponitrous Acid*, (1 nitrogen 14 + 3 oxygen 24).—This compound of nitrogen and oxygen is obtained with great difficulty; so much so, that it is questionable whether it has been exhibited in a separate state.

*Nitrous Acid*, (nitrogen 14 + 4 oxygen 32).—1. an elastic fluid. 2. Acid taste. 3. ——— 4. Color, a deep orange.

*Nitric Acid*, (1 nitrogen 14 + 5 oxygen 40).—In this acid we have the highest concentration of oxygen that can be obtained. It is an active and highly corrosive fluid; decomposes animal and vegetable substances, with which the superabundant oxygen of the acid combines, forming new compounds. The usual mode of preparing it is by distilling nitre with strong sulphuric acid; but it may also be prepared by passing a succession of electric sparks through a mixture of the nitrogen and oxygen gases.

The five preceding compounds are all of them compounds of the same elements as atmospheric air, to which if air be added, we have six compounds, all of which are formed from two simple elements, or at least from bodies conceived to be simple, and yet each of these compounds are as distinct from the others, as if they were formed of heterogeneous materials. In looking at this case in a philosophical light, we cease to wonder that so great a variety of substances as we see around us in nature should be formed from a few simple substances. Indeed, those who are most deeply versed in the subject, so far from requiring that the list of simples should be extended, are rather inclined to consider that it may be possible that all bodies are compounds, and that all are formed of two or three simples, which are compounded in various proportions, and that in a sense analagous to that which considers matter to be infinitely divisible, these proportions may be varied in an infinite ratio or series. It must also be ever kept present to the mind, that any new compound can only be formed by the decomposition of another compound. Repulsion separates, decomposes, or expands solids, and the liberated matter sometimes passes off in the form of gas, although in chemical experiments it is more frequently taken up by attraction, and passed into the new compound, whilst the gas is yet in a nascent state, so that the gaseous or liberated state of the matter escapes our observation; yet if we will bring our mind to bear upon the subject in a clear and decided manner, we will perceive that it is impossible for the matter to pass from one solid into another, without passing through the liquid or gaseous form, and that in proportion as the liquefaction or gasefication is well or ill effected, so will the resulting solid or compound be well or ill informed.

*Ammonia*, (1 nitrogen 14 + 3 hydrogen 3). These two gases are both electro-positive, and, therefore, cannot be made to combine directly in any proportions. Their combination may, however, be effected by indirect means; and reasoning from analogy, we might infer that in the process the attractions and repulsions of one or other of the bodies are changed, as the poles are reversed in the electro-magnetic engine. It would appear, however, that the repulsion subsisting between these two electro-positives is but slightly modified, for 100 cubic inches of ammoniacal gas weigh but 18 grains, being little more than half the specific gravity of atmospheric air. The gas is obtained by heating a mixture of *Sal Ammoniac* with unslaked lime in a tube or retort. When the compound has been obtained, it may be again decomposed, and resolved into its ultimate principles (nitrogen and hydrogen), by merely passing electric sparks through it;—by which, it may be presumed, that the elements are restored to their primitive electro-positive state, with respect to each other. A jet of ammoniacal gas may be introduced into oxygen and inflamed;—the product of the combustion is water and nitrogen. Ammonia is generally known by the name of the *volatile alkali.*

We have now introduced to the notice of the reader, two important classes of chemical compounds—*acids* and *alkalis*, a knowledge of which, and of their actions and re-actions, may be considered as the foundation of the study of chemistry. Oxygen, the highest electro-negative, is the basis of the former, and hydrogen, the highest electro-positive, that of the latter. Accordingly, agreeable to the known laws of electrical attraction and repulsion, that bodies in the same electrical state repel each other,—hydrogen, in a pure state, can exist only in the gaseous form, because its atoms being all electro-positive, mutually repel each other: and the same is true with respect to the electro-negative, oxygen. But as bodies in opposite electrical states attract each other, and as oxygen and hydrogen are the highest in the scale of bodies of the opposite class, the attraction exerted mutually between them is of the most energetic character. The positive and negative properties of the different elements, as well as the resulting compounds, are, however, merely relative, and in passing through their various combinations, what may be denominated their original or primitive electrical state, is often disguised, modified, or even reversed in a most mysterious manner.

*Chlorine.*—Electro-negative.—This body being a constituent of sea salt, exists, upon the large scale, chiefly in the ocean, and in those beds of salt, as the salt mines of Nantwich, in Cheshire, and in other countries, from which the inhabitants are supplied with that indispensable household article, common salt; and which beds, we shall, when we come to consider the geological history of the earth, see reason to conclude, have been formed by the evaporation of the water from large basins, lakes, or seas of other ages, like the Caspian sea of the present day; the salt having been left as a deposit in the dried up basin, previous to its entombment beneath the superincumbent strata. Chlorine must, therefore, be considered a marine product, whether found in the existing ocean, or in beds of salt buried beneath the surface of the earth, the deposits of a former ocean.

Chlorine is an electro-negative element, but is less negative than oxygen; and hence, when chloride of sodium is mixed with peroxyd of manganese, and sulphuric acid (in both of these substances oxygen abounds,) poured upon the mixture, the electro-positive and metallic element, sodium, is attracted by the more electro-negative, oxygen, from the less electro-negative, chlorine, and the latter being disengaged from its metallic base, is given off in the gaseous form. The properties of chlorine, agreeable to the five-fold division, corresponding to the five senses, are:—1. It is an elastic or compressible gas—100 cubic inches weigh 76 grains. 2. It has an astringent taste. 3. A strong suffocating smell. 4. Its color is yellowish green. 5. Explodes with hydrogen by the application of flame or of the electric spark, or even by exposing the mixture to the direct rays of the sun.

*Muriatic Acid,* (1 chlorine 36 + 1 hydrogen 1). When chlorine and hydrogen are mixed, and made to combine chemically, by either of the three foregoing means, the resulting compound is muriatic acid. It is,—1. An elastic gas. 2. Taste, intensely acid. 3. Smell, excessively pungent. 4. Transparent, colorless. 5. It does not explode; it is neither a combustible nor a supporter of combustion.

*Chlorine with Oxygen.*—Oxygen and chlorine are both electro-negatives, and have, therefore, no disposition to combine with each other in a direct manner, but their combination may be effected by *indirect* means. There are four compounds of these elements. The protoxyd of chlorine, consisting of (1 chlorine 36 + 1 oxygen 8).—The peroxyd, of (1 chlorine 36 + 4 oxygen 31).—Chloric acid, (1 chlorine 36 + 5 oxygen 40).—And the perchloric acid, consisting of one equivalent of chlorine with eight of oxygen,—(1 chlorine + 8 oxygen 64.)

*Chlorine with Nitrogen.*—Chlorine being less electro-negative than oxygen, and nitrogen less electro-positive than hydrogen, the mutual attraction or chemical affinity exerted between them is of a less energetic character. They may, however, be made to combine, but the equilibrium of their mutual attraction is so easily disturbed, that by very slight causes the compound will explode with great violence. Agreeable to the language which we have adopted in referring the expansion and contraction of matter to the ultimate forces of repulsion and attraction, we should say, that the repulsive force of the two gases is but slightly overcome by the mutual attraction, and that, therefore, that feeble affinity being easily disturbed, the equilibrium of the two ultimate forces is destroyed, and the repulsive force, which is essential to the existence of the ultimate elements in a gaseous form, comes again into full and active operation.

We have now given a slight notice of four of the most important elements of which the *solid earth*, the *liquid ocean*, and the *gaseous atmosphere* are composed. It is not our intention, neither would it be consistent with this work, to teach chemistry as an *art*. Our object is to follow the chemistry of nature, whose laboratory is the universe, and whose operations are as far removed above those of man—of the mere chemist, as the noble and stupendous frame of the solar system is above that of a common Dutch clock. The researches of experimental chemistry are highly instructive, so far as they go. They exhibit to the mind innumerable transformations of matter, guided by laws fixed, definite, and immutable;—and although we cannot as yet trace the transmutations of matter through all that infinite variety presented to our notice in the wide field of nature; yet, by cultivating an acquaintance with experimental chemistry, we are furnished with analysis by which we may trace the general principle, in an abstract sense, even to its ultimate consequences: and this is no small consideration, for the human mind becomes expanded, and the feelings ameliorated by the mere exercise, besides the power which we acquire to direct the powers of nature into channels useful and beneficial to our species. In the instance before us, we perceive that four simple gaseous substances, each of which exert a powerful influence upon the animal frame, enter largely into all the compounds of which the habitable globe is composed. Oxygen and nitrogen, in combination and simple mixture, constitute almost the entire of the atmosphere which surrounds the globe. Oxygen and hydrogen form the water of the rivers, lakes, seas, and ocean; and of that of the *salt sea*, chlorine forms no inconsiderable portion: and when we examine the *solid rocks* of the earth, we find the same elements in combination chiefly with metals, for the solid earth is little less than a metallic oxyd.

THE NON-METALLIC VOLATILE ELEMENTS.—Bromine, Iodine, Fluorine, Sulphur, Phosphorus, and Selenium.—These elements are named *volatile*, because, although at low temperatures, they exist as liquids and solids; yet, by a moderate increase of heat, they rise in the form of vapor, as in the instance of *sulphur*, which must have come under the observation of every person in the igniting of a common brimstone match. Indeed, it is this volatile quality which renders the sulphur fit for that object, as, in consequence of its volatility, it rises in vapor and enters into combustion by combining with oxygen at a lower temperature than the splinter of wood to which it adheres.

*Bromine*—75—electro-negative.—This substance is a liquid at the ordinary temperature. It is a marine product, being obtained from sea-water, and from sea-weeds. It has been recently discovered; it is a rare product; and therefore not important. It unites with oxygen, forming bromic acid, in the proportion of one dose of bromine with five of oxygen; expressed in symbol thus—(4 B 75 + 5 O. 40); and with hydrogen forming hrydo-bromic acid, in the proportion of one equivalent of each, (1 B 75 + 1 H. 1). It also unites with chlorine and forms chloride of bromine.

*Iodine*—127—electro-negative.—This substance, like the preceding, is obtained from sea-weeds. It is a solid, of a dark grey color. It combines with oxygen in the proportion of one iodine and five oxygen, (1. I. 124 + 5.040), forming iodic acid; and with hydrogen in one equivalent of each (1. I. 124 + 1. H. 1), forming hydrodic acid; with nitrogen in the ratio of 3 equivalents of iodine to one of nitrogen, (3 I. 372 + 1 N. 14). It also combines with chlorine and bromine, but the proportions are not decisively known.

*Fluorine*—electro-negative.—The properties of this substance are even less known than either of the two preceding. It is a volatile and highly corrosive fluid. The hardest substances, even glass, may be dissolved by its action. It combines with hydrogen, silicon, and boron, forming the hydro-fluoric, fluosilicic, and fluoboric acids.

*Sulphur*—16.—This is a well-known elementary body. It is found in a pure state in the neighborhood of volcanoes, and exists in the earth in considerable amount in combination with iron and other metals. It melts at a low heat, and is readily volatilized. In combination with oxygen it forms several compounds.

*Sulphurous Acid*—(1 S. 16 + 3 O. 24).—This acid may be formed by mixing sulphurous acid, oxygen, and water; under these conditions the sulphurous acid unites slowly with a further proportion of oxygen, forming dilute sulphuric acid. It is an important and useful acid in the arts. Sulphur also combines with oxygen in the proportion of one equivalent of each (hypo-sulphurous acid) and of two equivalents of the former to five of the latter, (hypo-sulphuric acid,) but they are not easily obtained in a separate form.

*Sulphur with Hydrogen—Sulphuretted Hydrogen*—(1 S. 16 + 1 H. 1).—If sulphuric acid be poured upon a mixture of pounded sulphur and iron filings, sulphuretted hydrogen gas will be produced in considerable abundance; or it may be formed in a direct manner by subliming sulphur in hydrogen gas. It issues from fissures in the earth in many countries, and enters as an ingredient into certain mineral waters, giving them their characteristic smell of rotten eggs. Its properties are:—

1, an elastic gas; 2, acid taste; 3, smell, putrid; 4, transparent and colorless; 5, explodes with oxygen.

*Bisulphuretted Hydrogen*—Is another compound of two elements. It is a *liquid*, heavier than water, and is composed of two equivalents of sulphur with one of hydrogen, (2 S. 32 + H. 1).

*Sulphur with Chlorine—Chloride of Sulphur*—(1 S. 16

+ 1 chl. 36).—These bodies combine directly at a gentle heat. If mixed with water and slightly agitated it is decomposed; muriatic, sulphinous and sulphuric acid being formed—a very considerable heat is given off during the action which takes place.

Sulphur unites with bromine and iodine, but the proportions in which they combine are not distinctly known. No compound of sulphur with nitrogen has ever been obtained.

*Phosphorus.*—Phosphorus has never been found in an uncombined state in nature, but may be obtained by the action of sulphuric acid upon calcined bones—phosphate of lime. The process is difficult and not without danger in unexperienced hands. Its properties, when pure, are—1, it is a soft solid, specific gravity 1.77; 2, without taste; 3, emits the odor of garlic when exposed to the action of the atmosphere; 4, transparent and colorless; 5, explodes in nitric acid by combining suddenly with the excess of oxygen contained in that liquid. Phosphorus is highly inflammable, that is, it has a strong tendency to act or combine with oxygen, hence it is never found in an uncombined state. By a slight rise in temperature, even by the heat of the hand, the tendency to action is excited, so that it inflames spontaneously. Phosphorescent light is given out in consequence of a feeble action resulting from the slow combination of the phosphorus with the oxygen of the atmosphere. In pure nitrogen, phosphorus emits no light. Why? because between phosphorus and nitrogen there is no action. Nitrogen gas is neither a combustible nor a supporter of combustion; and nitrogen constitutes four-fifths of the atmosphere, where a silent and feeble combustion upon a most extensive scale is continually going on by day; that is, whilst the sun is above the horizon, whilst the solar gas which issues from the sun is penetrating the earth's atmosphere, and exciting that chemical action whereby heat and light are given out as in the combination of oxygen and hydrogen; for, as will be shown by and by, there is no *luminous fluid* issues from the sun, but that the light and heat which we experience through the agency of the sun is produced in the earth's atmosphere; and that in this case, as in every other, they are the effects of an electro-chemical action—What, then, is nitrogen? What purpose does it subserve in the economy of nature? Is it the same identical nitrogen that exists in the atmosphere now, that existed three millions of years ago? Does it answer no other end than to dilute the oxygen and make it fit for the respiration of animals? If such were the state of things then nitrogen could be considered an anomaly amongst material existences. Nitrogen is an incombustible, so much so, that it excites no action even with phosphorus, therefore we are not authorized to infer that it is an active agent, although forming so large a proportion of the atmosphere, in the production of that light and heat which we contend, and which we shall prove, is produced in the earth's atmosphere by a process analogous to combustion. But if nitrogen be neither the combustible nor the supporter of the combustion, it may be the *product* of that combustion; and by analogy we are led to conclude that such is the state of the case. Carbon is a combustible, and oxygen is a supporter of combustion, and the *product*, carbonic acid, is neither a combustible nor a supporter of combustion. The same argument holds with respect to the metals, and generally in every case, two bodies combine, heat and light are given out during the action, and the *product*, the *compound* (and Sir Humphrey Davy has shown that nitrogen is a compound) is neither a combustible nor a supporter of combustion. The affinities are satisfied—the action in that direction is finished—and in respect to nitrogen because the elements which have entered into combination were of the most subtle or expanded order, the resulting compound is of the most inert character in reference to the process of combustion; so completely have the combining elements saturated each other, that the compound is incompetent to exert any further action even with that most active body, phosphorus; and on that account we have adverted to nitrogen in this place. We shall recur to this subject in another part of the work. The study of the processes going on in the atmosphere opens to the mind some beautiful analogies, the production of heat and light; the processes of vegetation upon the earth, and even the rotation of the earth upon her axis, are each of them connected with, and dependent upon the continued action excited by the solar non-luminous gas. Indeed, all the terrestrial *circuits* of *motion* are actuated by the *great circuit* of the solar system, and the solar gas is a portion of that circuit.

*Phosphorus with Oxygen*.—If two or three pieces of phosphorus be placed in a funnel inserted into an empty bottle, the phosphorus, by a slow process of combustion, combines with the oxygen of the atmosphere, forming phosphorus and phosphoric acids, which, together with watery vapor also extracted from the atmosphere, falls into the bottle in the form of a liquid. The phosphorus acid contains one equivalent of phosphorus united with one of oxygen, (phos. 12 + 1 oxy. 8=20,) and the phosphoric acid two equivalents of oxygen with one of phosphorus, (1 phos. 12 + 2 oxy. 16=28). There is a third compound, the hypo-phosphorus acid, consisting of two equivalents of phosphorus combined with one of oxygen, (2 phos. 24 + oxy. 8=32).

*Phosphorus with Hydrogen.*—Phosphorus and hydrogen combined in two proportions; one equivalent of the former with two of the latter, forming proto-phosphoretted hydrogen, (1 phos. 12 + 2 hyd. 2=24,) and per-phosphoretted (1 phos. 12 + 1 hyd. 1=13). These two elements are both electro-positives, and by passing a succession of electric sparks through the compound, the affinities by which they are held united, are disturbed, and the compound is resolved into its ultimate principles.

*Phosphorus with Chlorine.*—These two elements combine in two proportions, forming the proto-chloride of phosphorus, (1 phos. 12 + 1 chl. 36=48,) and the per-chloride, (1 phos. 12 + 2 chl. 72=85). Phosphorus being electro-positive and chlorine electro-negative, when presented to each other, action immediately ensues; they inflame and combine spontaneously. The compound acts on water with violence, forming the muriatic and phosphoric acids.

*Phosphorus with Iodine.*—These two bodies unite spontaneously at ordinary temperatures; great heat is given out during the action. The compound is iodide of phosphorus, which is decomposed on being thrown into water, forming hydriodic and phosporic acids.

*Phosphorus with Sulphur.*—Phosphorus and sulphur act upon each other with great energy. Phosphoret of sulphur is formed by agitating the two ingredients under water. It is highly inflammable, and is used for making phosphoric matches.

*Selenium.*—This is a very rare substance. It is obtained from iron pyrites, by treatment with sulphuric acid; in this process a mass of sulphur containing selenium is deposited. It has never been obtained except in very minute quantities, and chiefly in Sweden, at the mines of Fahlun. From its extreme rarity it is not a substance of great importance. Its properties are—1, a brittle solid; 2, no taste; 3, no smell; 4, color, brown.

*Selenium with Oxygen.*—These bodies combine in the proportion of one equivalent of selenium with two of oxygen, forming selenic acid, (1 sel. 40 + 2 oxy. 16=56). During the action accompanying the combustion a peculiar smell like horse-radish is given out. The acid is decomposed with facility, as the base selenium parts with its oxygen very readily. Selenic acid crystallizes at low temperature, forming needle-shaped crystals.

THE NON-METALLIC FIXED ELEMENTS. — *Carbon* — *Silicon*—and *Boron.* These elements are denominated *fixed*, because by the art of the chemist they have not, as yet, been volatilized. They are important elements, if they be in reality elementary bodies, for some eminent chemists have expressed a doubt on this point, conceiving that elementary substances can exist only in the form of a most subtle or expanded gas; and this suspicion, of course, attaches to all solid bodies now deemed elementary. It is, however, necessary and correct, that all bodies which have not been decomposed, should, in chemical language, be considered elementary; and such are the bodies now under consideration. Carbon is a most important element, forming the basis of the organic world, that is, of the vegetable and animal kingdoms. It also exists to a considerable extent in the mineral kingdom in beds of coal, and in combination with oxygen, (carbonic acid,) it enters into the composition of chalk, limestones, and more or less into that of almost every rock composing the solid crust of the earth. In combination with hydrogen it constitutes the common coal gas with which our towns and cities are illuminated.

*Carbon and Oxygen.*—These bodies united in equal proportions, form a gas, (carbonic oxyd,) the properties of which are—1, an elastic gas; 2, smell, highly offensive; 3, without taste; 4, colorless; 5, explodes and combines with oxygen, by passing the electric spark through the mixture, forming carbonic acid.

*Carbonic Acid.*—This gas consists of one equivalent of carbon united with two of oxygen, (1 carbon 6 + 2 oxy. 16=22). It is an important gaseous compound, the formation and decomposition of which is constantly going on in nature upon a very extensive scale. In the process of combustion of common coal, wood and charcoal, it is formed abundantly; and from the animal kingdom it is given out in immense quantities. It is the product of combustion and of animal or vital action, and is fatal to flame and to animal life. It is the resulting product of a specific action; and as the very essence of flame and life is action, of course, the result of the action being the formation of carbonic acid by attraction, the process cannot be repeated until that carbonic acid has been decomposed. Carbon is a combustible, and oxygen a supporter of combustion; or in other words, carbon and oxygen enter into combination with an energetic action, of which heat and light are accompanying effects; and that action, with the effects, is combustion. On this principle it is not difficult to perceive why carbonic acid will not support flame or animal life. The specific action is finished. When the hammer strikes the bell, sound is given out as an effect of the action of one body striking mechanically upon another body; but before the sound can be elicited a second time, the hammer must be lifted away from the bell; and this moving of the hammer from the bell, or the bell from the hammer, as one or the other is more convenient, is nothing else than the *expansion* of *matter*, not in a chemical but mechanical sense; and the returning stroke, by which *sound* is elicited, is a fair and faithful representation of the *contraction of matter*;—at every sudden contraction of the hammer and bell, sound is given out as an *effect* of the *action* of the one upon the other, the action of matter upon matter; and in order that the action and resulting sound may continue, it is necessary that the *mechanical* expansion and contraction of the hammer and bell shall go on incessantly. In a *chemical* sense it is the same with carbonic acid. Let the oxygen be represented by the hammer, and the carbon by the bell; then, whilst the oxygen and carbon are *contracting* or rushing into combination, heat and light are given out as effects of action; and before the action can be repeated, the oxygen must be lifted away from the carbon, or the carbon from the oxygen; and until this separation or expansion is effected by some means or other, carbonic acid cannot support either flame or animal life; for the very essence of flame and of animal life, and indeed of all life, animal, vegetable, and mineral, is action; each being distinguished from the other by a specific action peculiar to its own organization, and the action which accompanies the formation of carbonic acid, is a portion, and an important portion too, of that congeries of actions and reactions which we call animal life.

*Carbon and Hydrogen.*—These bodies by the combinations, form several compounds. Sub-carburetted hydrogen consists of one equivalent of carbon united with two of hydrogen, (1 carbon 6 + 2 hydrogen 2=8,) and carburetted hydrogen (common coal gas) of two equivalents of each, (2 carbon 12 + 2 hydrogen 2=14). Their properties are — 1, elastic gas; 2, tasteless; 3, smell, faint, when pure; 4, colorless; 5, explodes violently with oxygen, by passing the electric spark through the mixture.

*Carbon with Chlorine.*—These elements form several compounds. The per-chloride of carbon consists of two equivalents of carbon with three of chlorine, (2 carbon 12 + 3 chl. 108=120,) chloride of carbon one of each, (1 carbon 6 + 1 chl. 36=42). The sub-chloride of carbon of two carbon with one of chlorine, (2 carbon 12 + 1 chl. 36=48).

*Carbon with Nitrogen.*—A compound is formed by the union of these two bodies, called *cyanogen* or carburet of nitrogen, consisting of two equivalents of carbon with one of nitrogen, (2 carbon 12 + 1 nitrogen 14=26). Its properties are:—1, an elastic gas; 2, ———; 3, smell, pungent and disagreeable; 4, colorless; 5, explodes with oxygen, by passing the electric spark.

This compound exhibits a kind of anomaly in chemistry. It differs from other compounds in this respect, that it combines in a manner in every respect analogous to that of the other gaseous elements, with oxygen, hydrogen, chlorine, sulphur, iodine, bromine, and some of the metals. Some chemists, from this singular property of cyanogen, are inclined to hesitate in admitting the present list of simples as elementary substances; conceiving that as this known compound unites with substances regarded simple, in the manner of a simple, it is probable that those regarded simple may also be compounds, although the chemist's art has not as yet succeeded in decomposing them.

*Carbon with Sulphur.*—Sulphuret of carbon is formed by the combination of these elements in the proportion of one equivalent of carbon to two of sulphur, (1 carbon 6 + 2 sulphur 32=38). Carbon is a fixed body, and at an ordinary temperature sulphur is a solid; whereas the compound of the two is a liquid of a very volatile character. Its properties are:—1, a volatile liquid; 2, acrid taste, slighly aromatic; 3, a most nauseous smell; 4, transparent and colorless; 5, inflames with oxygen.

*Silicon.*—Silix or oxyd of silicon, is one of the most abundant substances in nature. It constitutes the aggregate of sandstones, flints, quartz, and rock crystal, and enters more or less into the composition of almost every rock in the solid crust of the earth; and in the vegetable kingdom it enters as a constituent into reeds, canes, and grasses. The oxygen is separated from the base with much difficulty. The properties of silicon are:—It is 1, a solid; 2, without taste; 3, no smell; 4, color, dark brown; 5, incombustible in oxygen or atmospheric air, but decomposes water by uniting with the oxygen, the hydrogen being set free.

*Silicon with Oxygen.*—These bodies by uniting in the proportion of one equivalent of each, form the oxyd of silicon or silex, as noticed above, (1 silicon 8 + 1 oxygen 8=16). The properties of this compound are:—1, solidity; 2, tasteless; 3, inodorous; 4, perfectly white. It is not acted upon by oxygen, or any acid except the fluoric. Oxyd of silicon or sand, forms the basis of glass, which is formed by fusing it with carbonate of potash, a salt which has yet to be noticed.

*Boron.*—This substance does not hold a very important place in the natural world. It is obtained by heating the metal potassium with boracic acid. The oxygen of the acid combines with the potassium, and the boron is set free. Its properties are:—1, a fixed solid; 2, without taste; 3, inodorous; 4, color, olive-brown; 5, combustible with oxygen.

*Boracic Acid.*—This compound is sometimes found in nature in the neighborhood of volcanoes. When pure it exists in the form of thin crystals. Its properties are:—1, solidity; 2, almost without taste; 3, smell, none; 4, color, greyish and shining.

We have now noticed the *twelve non-metallic* * *elements*, with the principal of what are called their *binary* compounds; that is, the combination of *two* simple substances. These binary compounds which we have noticed, enter however into other and more complex combinations,

* Some writers consider that fluorine has not been sufficiently investigated to be allowed a place as an elementary body; therefore without fluorine the non-metallic elements are twelve.

11

chiefly with *metallic oxyds*, giving rise to a most important class of bodies of a crystalline character, which have been denominated *salts* in chemical language. Before we proceed to speak of these salts, it will be necessary to make a few remarks upon the metals, all of which unite with oxygen, and many with chlorine, forming binary compounds, analogous to those of the non-metallic elements; and these two classes of binary compounds by again uniting, give rise to crystalline forms. Upon the subject of the metals we must be very brief, as a mere notice of each with all its combinations would swell this work to an immoderate size. A distinct notice of each is however, not necessary, as they possess a common character, and the observations which apply to one will almost without modification apply to all.

For convenience of study the metals have been classed in groups: as the *noble metals*, gold, silver, mercury, platinum, and a few others, which have so very little affinity for oxygen, that the oxyds may be reduced by mere heat; The *alkaline metals*, potassium, sodium, calcium, &c., and the *earthly metals*, magnesium, aluminum, &c. Of these, calcium and aluminum are perhaps the most important. The former is the base of all those immense masses of rocks, limestones, chalks, marbles, &c., which are so extensively distributed in the mineral crust of the earth; whilst the latter is the basis of those numerous beds of clay and clay-slates which form an important and interesting portion of the geological study of the earth's mineral crust.

The most important of the binary compounds of the metallic elements, are the *oxyds*, *chlorides*, and *sulphurets*. A short sketch of the principal of these will be sufficient for our purpose.

*Oxyd of Gold.*—If a piece of gold-leaf be exposed to a current of electricity from the galvanic battery, the gold is burnt; that is, it combines with oxygen, giving out heat and light during the action. The oxyd is a powder of a fine purple hue.

*Chloride of Gold.*—Gold-leaf takes fire and burns spontaneously when introduced into chlorine gas. The product of the combustion is a chloride of gold, but the proportions in which they combine is not decisively known.

*Sulphuret of Gold.*—Gold and sulphur being both of them electro-positive elements, will not unite directly; but by passing a current of sulphuretted hydrogen through a solution of the metal, a black powder is thrown down, which is the sulphuret of gold; and is composed of one equivalent of gold united with three of sulphur, (1 gold 200 + 3 sulphur 48=248).

*Oxyd of Silver.*—It may be obtained by dissolving the metal in nitric acid, and mixing limewater with the solution. The oxyd is precipitated in the form of an olive-colored and tasteless powder, insoluble in water. Its composition is, (1 silver 110 + 1 oxygen 8=118).

*Chloride of Silver*—is formed by dissolving the metal in the nitric acid and mixing with a solution of common salt. The chloride is thrown down in the form of a white precipitate, which become black by exposure to light. It is composed of one equivalent of each of the elements, (1 silver 110 + 1 chlorine 36=146).

*Sulphuret of Silver*—is found native in the mines, and may be formed by placing thin plates of the metal and layers of sulphur above each other alternately; at a low red heat, the elements unite, and the sulphuret is formed. It consists of one equivalent of each of the constituents. (1 silver 110 + 1 sulphur 16=126).

To enumerate all the metals, and to follow them through their various combinations, would be wholly inconsistent with the character of the present work. Our object is merely to show that the matter of which the earth is formed, may exist in either of the three forms of solid, liquid, or gas; that gases by attraction form liquids and solids; and that solids by repulsion form liquids and gases; and that whether the matter operated upon be a grain or a world, the general principle is the same.

There are two metals, which, with their compounds, hold a very prominent feature amongst the natural products of the earth. These deserve a more particular notice; and the observations which apply to these will, by analogy, apply to the great body of the metallic elements and their compounds. The metals to which we allude, are calcium and aluminum. Aluminum is the metallic basis of pure clay; calcium is the basis of lime; and if to these we add silicon, concerning the character of which, as to whether it ought to be considered a metallic or non-metallic element, there is some difference of opinion, we have before us the three elements which constitute the basis of by far the largest portion of the solid crust of the earth. But, in order that we may distinctly perceive the manner of the formation of solid rocks, it will be necessary to refer to the oxyd of calcium, which, in combustion with carbonic acid, forms those great masses of limestone rocks which constitute so large a portion of the earth's crust.

*Oxyd of Calcium or Lime.*—Limestone, as dug out of the earth, is composed of oxyd of calcium, the electro-positive base; and carbonic acid, the electro-negative acid, in a state of close combination. When the limestone is burned, the carbonic acid is driven off, and the lime as oxyd of calcium remains. The oxyd of calcium consists of one equivalent of each of the elements, (1 calcium 20 + 1 oxygen 8=28).

It will have been observed, in the list of non-metallic elements, that oxygen holds the highest place amongst the *electro-negatives*, and hydrogen amongst the *electro-positives;* and therefore we find that these two bodies have a very strong affinity for each other, and that whilst existing in combination in the form of water, they are united with so much force that they cannot be separated except by the most powerful counteracting energy, as by the galvanic battery. Now as a general law it is found that the *binary compounds*, that is, compounds formed of *two* simple elements, may also be classed and arranged in a like manner into *electro-negatives* and *electro-positives*, thus:—

| CARBONIC ACID<br>is composed of<br>(1 carbon 6 + 2 oxygen 1 6=22,)<br>and is an<br>electro-negative<br>acid. | OXYD OF CALCIUM<br>is composed of<br>(1 calcium 20 + 1 oxygen 8=28,)<br>and is an<br>electro-positive<br>alkali. |
|---|---|

Therefore, as the negative *element* oxygen, and the positive *element* hydrogen, are attracted to each other in consequence of their opposite electrical conditions, so also the negative *compound*, carbonic acid, and the positive *compound*, lime, or oxyd of calcium, are attracted to each other and form *carbonate of lime*, of which are constituted the immense mountain masses known by the various appellations of chalk, marble, limestone, oolite, dolomite, &c.; and thus we perceive that the entire earth, ocean, and atmosphere, of which the habitable globe is constituted, might, by the application of a sufficient decomposing or repulsive power, be resolved into the primitive elements of which it is formed; and also that it may have been formed by the slow, silent, and progressive combination of those elements through a long series of ages.

The union of two elementary bodies of one description, (non-metallic) gives rise, as we have seen, to one class of compounds, named *acids*, as the nitric, chloric, sulphuric, phosphoric and carbonic acids: so, also, the union of two elementary bodies, one of which is metallic, gives rise to another class of compounds, named *bases*, as the oxyds, chlorides and sulphurets. Again, these binary compounds unite and give rise to other compounds of more complex character, named *salts*. They are so named, because, in uniting, the compound always assumes a certain determinate and *crystalline* form. In the formation of these crystalline compounds, a certain quantity of water enters into composition with the uniting bodies called *the water of crystallization*, and this water always enters in definite proportions in a manner analogous to the definite proportions in which the simple bodies enter into union with each other.

We perceive, then, that by bringing together simple gaseous elements, we can form binary compounds, and that these, with the water of crystallization, will unite and form solid crystalline bodies, and of such the mountains of the earth are formed. On the other hand, these crystal compounds can be decomposed and resolved into their simple gaseous elements; and therefore to form a *solid world* from gaseous matter, and to resolve it again into its ultimate gaseous elements, it is only necessary that the ultimate forces of attraction and repulsion, each alternately predominating, should exert their composing and decomposing energies upon a more extended scale and throughout a longer period of time.

In looking at the results of the chemist's art, satisfactory to a certain extent as they confessedly are, we must ever bear in mind that all his compositions and decompositions are but the results of art; that he cannot approach the intricate and wonderful processes of nature, as exemplified in the animal, vegetable, and mineral kingdoms. He can compose and decompose with astonishing precision, the various elements upon which he operates; but according to observations upon vegetable processes, it would appear that nature has the power of transforming one element into another, that is, substances deemed elementary by the chemist. Seeds have been sown in pure sulphur, watered with distilled water, every source for the supply of the usual elements of vegetable matter being cut off, yet the plants continued to grow and increase, and upon analysis afforded the ordinary proximate principles of the vegetable kingdom. From what source, then, could the matter of which the vegetables were formed, have been derived? Not from the sulphur in which the roots were fixed, for the plant contained no sulphur. Indeed, it is acknowledged by vegetable physiologists that plants do not derive their nutriment from the soil, but rather from the moisture contained in the soil, and from the atmosphere. We have here, then, two sources to which we can look for the material of which the vegetables are formed: the water derived from the ocean and scattered over the earth's surface in the form of rain drops, and the gaseous matter of which the atmosphere is composed. And we find further, that the chemical action necessary to the transformation of the liquid and gaseous matter into a solid vegetable substance, is effected by the laborating influence of the sun; for without the solar influence no vegetable can be brought to a state of maturity. Here, then, are the materials and the power by which those materials are to be transformed, and the result is such as the chemist cannot attain to by the most elaborate processes of his art. Nay, there are plants, as the *air plant* of India, which will grow and flourish suspended by a cord in a moist atmosphere, having no connection whatever with the earth; and yet from these also may be obtained elementary matter, which cannot be detected in the atmosphere in which they grow. Viewing the subject upon the great scale, as having reference to the whole earth, we find that the great bulk of the matter which sustains the vegetable creation, passes through the atmosphere; for the moisture which is absorbed by the root, and without which no vegetable will grow, is carried up from the ocean; is laborated in the atmosphere by the action of the sun; is, in short, to use a familiar expression, *cooked* and prepared as fit food for vegetation. Rain water is the appropriate drink of vegetables, and they live and grow by transforming a portion of this liquid and secreting it in conjunction with other matter derived from the atmosphere, so that the same identical matter which in the early spring exists in the ocean in the form of water, may be found in the fall of the year secreted in the vegetable kingdom and existing in the solid form.

But plants do not live upon that which is absorbed by the root exclusively. It is known that a very considerable portion of their food is inhaled by the leaf from the gaseous atmosphere. Now atmospheric air is composed of *one-fifth* of oxygen, *four-fifths* of nitrogen, and about *one-thousandth* part of carbonic acid. For some time past it has been the received opinion that the carbonic acid contained in the atmosphere is absorbed by the leaf, and furnishes thereby food to the vegetable world. But the demand is greater than the supply. If we take into our consideration the immense forests of vegetation which cover the whole surface of the habitable globe, we shall quickly perceive that one-thousandth part of the atmosphere when contracted into the solid form, would not furnish material for the formation of one of the large South American forests. If the vegetable kingdom depended for its supply of atmospheric food upon this source alone, it would eventually perish of hunger. Besides, it has been recently ascertained by an eminent American chemist, that vegetables absorb and secrete a large amount of nitrogen. Here we have a large and abundant supply amply adequate to the demands of the vegetable kingdom: and as we shall hereafter see reason to conclude, this gas, an important portion of the food of vegetation, is continually reproduced in the earth's atmosphere by the action of the sun, in order to keep up the supply and compensate for that which is taken up in feeding the vegetation of the earth.

By viewing the matter in this light, we find every thing consistent with the great process going forward in the world. Nothing is standing still—all is in a state of progression. Whereas, if we take up the commonly received opinion, that the nitrogen serves only to dilute the atmosphere and render it fit for the respiration of man and animals, a body unchanged and unchangeable, the same nitrogen that "was in the beginning, is now and ever shall be," we assign to it conditions such as appertain to no other known substance. That vegetables absorb carbonic acid, is certain, although the quantity is altogether insufficient to supply food for the whole vegetation of the earth. Now what is carbonic acid? It is, as has been said before, neither a combustible nor a supporter of combustion; but is the product of combustion. Again, what is nitrogen? It is neither a combustible nor a supporter of combustion. Are we, then, justified by the analogy in concluding that this also is a product of combustion? Let us examine what is going on in the earth's atmosphere in connexion with the usual phenomena attendant upon combustion. Combustion is an appearance or condition made manifest in the chemical combination of two bodies; as when the combustible hydrogen and the supporter oxygen are entering into combination, heat and light are developed more or less intense in proportion to the intensity of action, and more or less extended in proportion to the extent of action. If the action be confined to a small point, we have the concentration of light and heat at that point. If the action be diffused over a wide field, we have the same amount of action, and consequently of light and heat spread over a wider field; and in either case the product of the combustion is water, which is neither a combustible nor a supporter of combustion. The light and heat were effects accompanying the action of combination; when the water is formed the action has ceased, and the accompanying effects have ceased also. Now can it be shown that nitrogen is like water or carbonic acid, the product of a kind of atmospheric combination? In the first place, light and heat are effects accompanying the combustion or chemical combination of two bodies, and Sir Humphrey Davy proved by the production of the ammoniacal amalgam, that nitrogen is not a simple but a compound body. Secondly, nitrogen is absorbed by the vegetation of the earth in large quantities, and therefore it is necessary that it be reproduced by some means, or otherwise the atmosphere would be exhausted in a given time.

Thirdly, Sir Humphrey Davy, in the formation of the ammoniacal amalgam, gave the strongest presumptive evidence, that nitrogen is a compound of hydrogen with a metallic basis.

Fourthly, metallic bases have been obtained in the analysis of plants, whose nutriment has been derived exclusively from the atmosphere.

Fifthly, we have light and heat in the earth's atmosphere which is either produced in the atmosphere by a kind of chemical or electro-chemical combustion, or emanates from the sun, and passes from that body to the earth, a distance of 96 millions of miles, in full possession of luminous and calorific properties: and not only to the earth, but also to every other planet and satellite in the solar system, radiating from the sun in every direction, and filling the whole system with light and heat, and thereby precluding the possibility of darkness in any part of space.

There are two doctrines held among scientific men at present with respect to the nature of solar light. The first, adopted by Sir Isaac Newton, is, that an extremely subtle and luminous fluid is continually issuing from the sun with a velocity equal to 96 millions of miles in about eight minutes. Taking this as the true theory of light, let us see where it will lead us. In the first place, as has been already observed, there could be no darkness on the earth at any period of the 24 hours, not even in the middle of the longest night of winter; for although in the middle of the night the sun would be invisible, still the subtle luminous fluid filling, as it must necessarily do, the entire solar system, would be perfectly visible, and would give light upon that side of the earth turned away from the sun. It may be objected, that as in the planetary spaces there is no solid body to reflect the light, that, therefore, we should not expect it to be visible; but if we consider that the solar system, from the centre to the extremities, is at least 2000 millions of miles in depth, and probably much more, nay, even ten times that distance, we shall at once perceive that a body of luminous matter, however subtle, could not be invisible itself nor require any solid body to reflect it back to the earth. Again, in respect to the reflection of this luminous matter by the moon and planets—What kind of body is the moon? A black earthy mass, like the earth, and, as some astronomers have affirmed, devoid, or nearly so, of an atmosphere. And yet she shines with a brilliancy brighter than polished silver. Again, when the moon is totally eclipsed, she is not entirely darkened, but still reflects a dark red light. Whence comes this light? Not directly from the sun, for the earth is interposed between the two bodies. Not from the earth, for the dark side of this body is presented to the moon. Neither can it result from the refraction of the solar light by the terrestrial atmosphere; for the light emitted by the moon is *red*, and the red ray is the least refrangible. This red light emitted by the moon during a total eclipse, must therefore be referred to some other cause. Many more arguments might be advanced, tending to prove that no luminous fluid issues from the sun; and yet, at the same time, we are well assured that the light of day is attributable to the agency of the sun;

that in the absence of the sun there could be no light in the atmosphere of the earth.

The second theory, which has of late become the leading doctrine, is, that the phenomena of light is dependent upon certain undulations of an etherial fluid pervading space, on which accout this is denominated the *undulatory theory*. According to this doctrine there is no emanation from the sun, but the etherial medium is excited and set into a kind of vibratory or undulatory movement like the rising or falling of a wave upon the surface of the ocean. It is assumed that the fluid does not move out of its place, but merely vibrates or undulates in consequence of the excitement of the sun. But the most extravagant part of this doctrine, is, that these vibrations or undulations succeed each other so rapidly, that upwards of 700 *millions of millions* of them are accomplished in a single second of time! This requires no argument to answer it; it is completed by its own absurdity. Besides, it is liable to the same objection as the first: viz., that as the etherial medium pervades all space, and must do so in order that the vibration may reach the distant planets of the system, there could not be darkness at any time upon the earth, or, indeed, in any part of the system. Light produced in this manner, merely by an external vibration, without the expenditure, or rather the expansion and contraction of matter, would be an anomaly in nature; for even in the production of electrical light there is the evident passage of a material substance.

Now if we adopt the hypothesis of a *non-luminous fluid* or gas issuing from the sun, entering into chemical combination with another gas also non-luminous, in the earth's atmosphere, light and heat being given out as effects of that action or weak and extended combustion, of which nitrogen is the product, and this again being essential to the support of the vegetation of the earth; if we view the matter in this light, we shall find every thing consistent and in strict analogy with all the known processes going forward in nature. We shall perceive that the moon andplanets ought to shine with a brilliant light, because the light is generated in the atmosphere of each, and the different colors which they exhibit is to be attributed to the different qualities of the gaseous atmospheres by which they are surrounded;—that the pale silver light of the moon is attributable to a deficiency of atmosphere, although she must be surrounded with an atmosphere of some sort, or otherwise there could be no action, and the light of each planet is dependent upon the action going on in the atmosphere of each. We shall further perceive, that it by no means follows that the distant planets should be either cold or deficient in light, at least in the ratio generally laid down, since the light and heat is not derived directly from the sun, but is produced in the body. And although the quantity of the solar fluid must diminish as the distance from the sun increases, yet this may be, to a great extent, compensated by the internal activity of the body itself.

There is, perhaps, no scientific truth more firmly established, than that heat and light are effects accompanying chemical action; and that these effects are never in any case exhibited except in connection with action of some sort. Therefore in respect to solar light, before we attempt to set up any hypothesis which shall place it without the range of ordinary phenomena, we ought to carefully compare it with the light produced in the usual way by chemical and electro-chemical action.

In the decomposition of nitrogen by Sir Humphrey Davy, one of the constituents was presumed to be hydrogen. Now there cannot be a doubt that hydrogen gas is continually forming on the earth. Indeed there is reason to presume that a very considerable portion of the water which passes from the ocean into the atmosphere, is decomposed in its ultimate gases. Now hydrogen is the lightest of all known bodies, and therefore must have a tendency to occupy the highest place in the atmosphere. Hydrogen is an electro-positive gas. If, then, we have an electro-negative gas issuing from the sun and penetrating the atmosphere of the earth, we have all the elements requisite to the production of the observed effects, which cannot be rationally accounted for by either of the existing hypotheses. We have the electro-negative solar gas, rejecting the electro-negative oxygen, and combining with the electro-positive hydrogen, especially in the higher regions of the atmosphere; and the product of this extended and feeble combustion, nitrogen, in consequence of its greater specific gravity, being a compound of several volumes of expanded gases, now combined or contracted into less volume, descends towards the earth in order to feed the vegetation. It is evident, also, that the watery vapor which ascends into the atmosphere, that which is not decomposed into its elements, undergoes very important and essential changes, in order to prepare and fit it for the nourishment of vegetation. Indeed, it may be affirmed that the currus, cumulus, stratus, and the intermediate clouds, are nothing more than vegetable food in various stages of the process of preparation. There are vast and important processes constantly going on in the atmosphere of the earth, which are essentially necessary to the vegetable creation; and among these, that process which comprehends the production of light is not the least: of which the clearest, and perhaps most pointed manifestation is, that vegetables always seek the light of day, and if they be wholly excluded from it they languish and die. This production of light in the earth's atmosphere in the manner here intimated, is perfectly analogous to that given at the galvanic battery, by two currents of electricity entering into combination or neutralizing each other, or oxygen and hydrogen, or a metal with oxygen, or any other case of chemical union where two active elements combine and form an inactive or neutral compound.

Beginning with the laboration of vegetable food in the atmosphere, as manifested in the formation of clouds, the contents of which are subsequently scattered over the surface of the earth, and following the chain of the process downward, we shall ultimately reach the formation of solid rocks in the mineral kingdom by an easy and natural gradation. All the matter in the atmosphere exists in the gaseous form, or at least must have been in the *expanded* or gaseous state, or otherwise it could not have ascended into the higher regions of the air. But it does not remain permanently fixed in that state, or it could not return to the earth. It is again *contracted*, and in this contraction atmospheric electricity evidently plays an important part, as witnessed in a thunder-storm, which is almost uniformly followed by the descent of a vast body of water or matter, which has been suddenly contracted from its previous expanded or gaseous state; even pieces of solid ice have been precipitated upon the earth at such times, of which an instance has occurred in the present year (1838) at Rochdale in Lancashire, by which most serious damage has been done. Now because a thunder-storm is but an occasional phenomena, we are apt to conceive that the electro-chemical processs going on in the atmosphere is transitory and intermittent. But by the most ample experience it is proved that this process is constant. Thunder-storms occur chiefly in autumn, seldom in spring; and yet at the latter season it is known by experiment that atmospheric electricity is in a state of much greater activity and intensity than in the former. But in the spring and early part of summer the vegetation is in high activity, and drinks in the prepared food with great eagerness. The demand is greater than the supply; the prepared matter does not accumulate, there is no glut or redundancy in the atmosphere, and consequently no thunder-storms. But in the autumn all the circumstances are reversed. The vegetation of the season is finished, but the process in the atmosphere is still going on—the matter accumulates and is dammed back until ultimately it forces its way to the earth with a loud explosion and violent concussion.

If we turn our attention to countries within the tropics, we shall there find all the phenomena here enumerated exhibited upon a magnified scale—more light, heat and activity in the atmosphere, and consequently a more extensive production of atmospheric vegetable food; a more active and luxuriant vegetation, on a scale proportionate to the atmospheric action; and tremendous thunder-storms. As a general principle we may conclude that the principal part of the substance of the vegetable kingdom is derived from the atmosphere;—that although some portion of the food of vegetables is assuredly obtained from the soil, yet the staple of their nutriment comes from the atmosphere; for they may be, and often have been, reared independent of the soil, but never without the aid of moisture and atmospheric air. The quantity or weight of solid vegetable matter formed every year upon the surface of the earth, amounts to many millions of tons. This matter, or the greater portion of it, has come from the ocean; has passed through the atmosphere; and is now solid vegetable matter. Then what becomes of this vegetable matter? It is devoured by the animal kingdom.*

* A friend of the author, Mr. Richard Johnson, of Lambeth, Surrey, a gentleman who has had a large experience in agricultural pursuits, and has been a close observer of nature, holds the opinion that every particle of the vegetable productions of nature, passes through the animal kingdom, coal excepted, and such as are found in a fossil state, and nothing is lost;—that roots and stubble and straw, farm-yard manure and leaves, and even solid timber, are each and all of them devoured by various species of worms and grubs; and that in this manner large addition is every year made to the solid matter of the earth. Myriads of these lit-

The animal kingdom hangs to the vegetable kingdom for support, as the vegetable kingdom hangs to the atmosphere. If we trace the matter from the atmosphere into the vegetable, the change is so striking, the transformation so complete, that we can no longer recognize the same matter, and yet no fact is more firmly authenticated than that the previously gaseous matter of the atmosphere has become solid vegetable substance; so likewise in respect to the next transformation of vegetable into animal matter. A bushel of grain is not a pound of flesh; neither can any art of the chemist transform the one into the other, and yet we know from every-day experience that such transformation takes place by the chemistry of nature. It is true, that analogous elements are afforded by the analysis of vegetable and animal matter, but at the same time it cannot be denied that the two differ in many particulars;—in short, that they are specifically distinguished from each other by well marked lines. If we trace the process onward, from the atmosphere to the vegetable kingdom, from the vegetable kingdom to the animal kingdom, and from the animal kingdom to the mineral kingdom, in the formation of vegetable mould, by the worms existing in the soil, we shall be amazed by each and all of the transformations, but not at one more than another, for all are equally wonderful; and although chemical science fails in its attempts to unravel the mys-

tle creatures have their habitation in the soil, near the surface, and it is well known that they void pure earth, as is evidenced by the common earth-worm; but they do not derive their nutriment from earth. To suppose that they do, is an absurdity, for no animal lives or could live upon the matter which it voids. These worms appear to perform the same functions on the dry land, which the coral insect performs in the ocean. The coral insects form immense masses of calcareous rocks in the depths of the sea, not however, from calcareous matter, for it could not live by eating and voiding the same matter. Its very life is bound up in the process of transformation; indeed, it might be said that its life is that process. Life of every kind, both animal and vegetable, is essentially a process, and is dependent upon the imbibition of one description of matter, and its transformation by an unknown and mysterious process into that of another description; and in this process, even the very elements appear to be changed, as has been already noticed in respect to vegetables. Nor does this process of tranformation stop with the vegetable and animal processes, but descends even to the mineral kingdom, for we find the remains of vegetables and animals in solid rocks of sandstone; therefore, the conclusion is inevitable, that the rock has undergone a transformation in the course of ages.

tery, still the fact of such transformations is plainly and palpably manifested before our eyes. Nor does the great process by which the world is being transformed into solid rock, when we have reached any stage, come to a state of absolute rest at any point. The transformation is going on within the earth, as well as upon the surface; for, as a general law, it is found that the oldest rocks are the hardest or most contracted, although it is plainly demonstrated by the vegetable remains entombed within them, that these identical rocks once formed a portion of the earth's surface, or the surface of a satellite attending the earth. Such are a few of the results of the *chemistry of nature*. The short and imperfect sketch of the *chemistry of art*, which has been introduced, may serve to give a faint illustration as to the *manner* of the great process; with such intention, at least, that sketch was given, being presumed likely to afford a glimpse into the hidden arcana of nature.

But the student of nature must have a care how he pins his faith to the crucible of the chemist. If he would become acquainted with the operations of nature, he must look abroad, and observe the results which she obtains in her own vast laboratory. The instruments with which she works are simple,—and they are but two,—*attraction* and *repulsion*. Yet with these how great and magnificent are the objects which she works out? But she never rests. She is always engaged assiduously. Her progress is slow, silent, and almost imperceptible; but in the end, she overcomes every obstacle, for the time allowed is without limit. To her operations there are no other limits than endless eternity and unbounded space.

The Five Circles of Motion.—That a subtle gaseous fluid of some description is continually issuing from the sun, is generally admitted; and, therefore, it is not necessary that we should proceed formally to the proof of such a proposition. That that portion of this fluid which is arrested in its outward course from the sun, by coming into contact with the earth, (of the other and by far the larger portion we shall speak by-and-by,) produces a specific action in the earth's atmosphere, we have the evidence of our senses:—

1. One of the effects of this action is the expansion of the air;—the ascension of expanded air which is subsequently contracted, and descends, the under-current

sweeping over the surface of the earth and ocean; and thus the motion of the air is performed in a circle, or rather a system of circles is continually in motion in different parts of the atmosphere.

2. A second effect of the solar influence is the expansion of the water at the surface of the ocean, which also rises, and is taken into the circles of the air, in which it is carried round and round, until it is properly prepared for the support of vegetable life; after which it is deposited upon the surface; and thus every portion of the vegetable kingdom is supplied with proper moisture. This requisite nutriment is brought to the vegetable, and it is necessary that it should be so, for vegetables are fixed to the soil by their roots, and cannot travel from place to place to seek their food. The motion and direction of this second circle is dependent upon that of the wind.

3. The vegetable juices move round in a circle, and this third circle is dependent upon the two former.

4. The animal fluids move in circles, which are in a like manner dependent upon the motion of the vegetable circles for the supply of fit and proper matter to keep up the process.

5. In the mineral kingdom we find there is a circulation also, as has been observed by Sir David Brewster; and we have also seen, that (as is exemplified in the formation of vegetable mould and coral rocks), the mineral kingdom receives a supply of appropriate matter from the animal kingdom.

Now, the motion of each of these circles depends upon that which precedes it, and the motion of the whole series is dependent upon the great circle of the solar system; for if the fluid which issues from the sun were suddenly arrested, the action in the atmosphere would also be arrested, and the whole of the circles dependent upon that action would eventually stand still. We shall now proceed to the examination of the great circle of the solar system of which the earth forms a portion. The material has issued from the sun in an expanded form;—is now contracting and returning towards the centre.

# GEOLOGY.

In entering upon this part of our subject, the first consideration which demands our attention, is *the shape of the earth* taken as a whole. It has been found by careful measurement that the earth is flattened at the poles; that the polar axis is, to the equatorial diameter, as 304 to 305,—

| | |
|---|---|
| The equatorial diameter being | 7924 miles, |
| The polar axis about - - - | 7898 " |
| Difference - - - - - - | 26 |

So that the earth is bulged out at the equator, and this shape is such as a fluid body rotating upon an axis would naturally assume. The earth, has, therefore, been named a spheroid of rotation. The natural assumption of this shape, by the revolving earth, necessarily includes the supposition of its having been originally in a fluid state. Such a supposition is one of the fundamental propositions of the Wernerian geology, and, indeed, is a generally admitted principle amongst geologists of the present day. But, although three-fourths of the surface, at least, is still in a fluid state, that portion which is inhabited by man, and terrestrial animals, consists, as we know, of solid rocks, of various degrees of hardness; as a general principle, those nearest the surface being the softest and most friable; the descending series becoming harder and harder as we dig into the earth. Such is the general law, but there are some exceptions, the causes of which will be explained as we proceed. Now, it is evident that the lower rock must have been formed previous to that which rests upon it, and, therefore, as the lower and harder rock is older than the upper and softer, we conclude that these rocks have been for a series of ages, and are now becoming harder and harder, or in other words, that the earth is passing into the solid state, by the continual formation of new rocks, whilst the older rocks are becoming more and more solidified; and that by this slow, silent, and almost imperceptible process, the whole earth is passing onward into the condition of solid or contracted matter. The examination of these rocks, the manner of their formation, the fossils which they contain, and the causes or forces by which they have been thrown into the strange and almost unaccountable positions in which they are now formed, constitute the study of geology.

Our object being to show, by facts and inferences, that the earth has been formed from gaseous matter, which had, in the first instance, issued from the sun, which had subsequently passed from the gaseous to the liquid state, and is now passing from the liquid into the solid form; and as a consequence of that contraction or solidification, is gradually approaching the central sun, from which it originally issued, to be again dissolved and passed off in the gaseous form, it becomes necessary that we should take some notice of the elementary substances of which the solid rocks of the earth are composed. " What is the nature of the mass of the globe?" says Professor Phillips, " is a question to which chemistry and natural philosophy furnish the only answers which our faculties can comprehend." *The nature of matter, in the abstract sense, is not given to man to know.* But instead of this, perhaps useless and certainly unattainable knowledge, we are able to discover differences among the sorts of matter when subjected to the same conditions—differences of weight, of hardness, of fusibility, solubility, crystalline arrangement, and many other important circumstances. These properties define the sort of matter to our senses; and, thus it appears, that many different compounds of matter exist in the earth. The solid rocks of which the crust of the earth is composed, is divided by geologists into two great classes, the *stratified* and the *unstratified;* the former resting upon the latter, and these, for convenience of study, are again subdivided into a number of species, in a manner analogous to the classification of plants and animals, in Botany and Zoology. Amongst the stratified rocks, limestones, sandstones, and clays, hold by far the most conspicuous place. These rocks, as they are denominated, are found in very different states, in respect to their induration or hardness. Chalk and marble are the same in mineral composition, both being carbonates of lime; loose sand and sandstone are likewise formed of the same elementary matter; and soft clay and hard clay-slate are also formed of the same materials. All these beds are, therefore, named rocks by geologists, without any regard to hardness.

By careful analysis of these rocks, they are found to contain, in 100 parts:—

Limestone 52 metallic base + 48 oxygen=100. Sandstone 49 to 53 metallic base + 47 to 51 oxygen=100 Clay-slate metallic base 54 + 46 oxygen=100.

These compounds, by admixture with other oxyds and with each other, give rise to great variety in the mineral composition of rocks, but oxygen enters into the formation of every rock on the face of the earth. Indeed, this *gaseous, element* constitutes more than half of the entire globe, earth, ocean, and atmosphere.

Now, as the stratified rocks rest upon the unstratified, it is evident that the latter must have been formed before the former could have been deposited upon them. To suppose that the upper rocks were formed previous to those upon which they rest, would be about as natural as to imagine that a church or steeple could be built by beginning at the weather-cock, and finishing with the lowest stone of the foundation; and yet there have been geologists who have gravely advanced such an opinion, being led thereto by fallacious appearances, which we shall notice hereafter. These unstratified rocks are the lowest that have been reached. How far they extend towards the centre of the earth it is impossible to determine. If the experiments and calculations which have been made in reference to the density and specific gravity of the earth may be relied on, we should be led to conclude that the crust must be of considerable thickness, the specific gravity being estimated at five times that of water. But to whatever depth they may extend, they were evidently formed previous to the stratified rocks; and the question to which we have to direct our attention at present is, are they composed of the same or similar elementary substances? Granite is the most important of the unstratified rocks. It is composed of crystalline materials,—crystals of quartz, felspar, and mica, which, by analysis, are found to be constituted as under:—

| | | | | |
|---|---|---|---|---|
| Quartz | 48 metallic base | + 52 | oxygen | = 100. |
| Felspar | 54 ditto | + 46 | do. | = 100. |
| Mica | 56 ditto | + 44 | do. | = 100. |

Such is the chemical composition of the component parts of granite, by which we perceive that it differs very little from the stratified rocks in regard to its mineral character. Indeed, many specimens give, by analysis, precisely the same proportion of oxygen with metallic bases as is

12*

found in some of the stratified rocks, the chief difference between the two consisting in the greater number of metals in the granite, in combination with oxygen. De La Beche gives the composition of granite as follows:—

| | |
|---|---|
| Silica | 74,84 |
| Alumina | 12,80 |
| Potash | 7,48 |
| Magnesia | 0,99 |
| Lime | 0,37 |
| Oxyd of Iron | 1,98 |
| Oxyd of Magnesia | 0,12 |
| Fluoric Acid | 0,21 |

Viewed upon the great scale, all the rocks of the earth, stratified and unstratified, may be said to be composed of the same or similar materials. The principal difference appears to consist in the mineral structure or internal arrangement of the constituent elements of which the rocks are composed. Near the surface we have loose sands, soft clays, and chalk; in the old or lower rocks of the series, hard sandstones, clay-slates, and compact limestones; and lower still, we find the same description of matter, of which these three leading rocks are composed, existing in the condition of a hard crystalline unstratified mass of granite.

"It appears," says Professor Phillips, "a probable inference, that the formation of granite was a process which began before the production of any of the strata; was continued during the accumulation of primary, secondary, and tertiary rocks; and is yet in action under particular circumstances in the deep parts of the earth. One of the most remarkable speculations of modern geology is that advocated by Mr. Lyell, who, in his 'Principles of Geology,' defends the somewhat startling speculation, that the granite floor of the stratified crust of the earth is nothing else than the fused and re-consolidated materials of older strata than any which are now visible;—that at this time granite is forming in the same manner, by the fusion of the lower portion of the strata; and that as new stratified rocks, the fruit of water, are slowly deposited above, the older ones which they cover are slowly re-absorbed by the antagonistic element of interior heat, and converted into crystallized granite."

However startling this speculation of Mr. Lyell may appear, it is perfectly consistent with all that we know of the great processes of nature. It might, with safety, be affirmed that no single existence in the universe ever remains during two consecutive instants of time in precisely the same state. All is in motion; a great process is going forward in the earth, in the solar system, and throughout the universe; and the subordinate processes going on in the atmosphere, the vegetable, the animal, and the mineral kingdoms, even down to the granite, the lowest of known rocks, are but the lesser links of that great chain. Nay, our own individual life—the very animal existence which we enjoy, is nothing more than a portion of the great chain of processes going forward in the earth, and every revolution of the blood in the veins and arteries of animated beings carries that process nearer to its termination; for "all nature is linked together—all is dependent—all existence is chained to other existence; and that chain which connects them, and of which we can only see some comparatively insignificant portions, is infinite in extent, time, and space."*

Of the stratified rocks which compose the solid crust of the earth, limestones, sandstones, and clays constitute a very large proportion of the gross bulk, as has been already noticed. Of these, sandstones and clays are considered to be land formations, because they contain the remains of land animals, and plants; whilst limestones, on account of their containing marine remains, are considered to have been formed at the bottom of the sea. The following extract will illustrate, to a certain extent, the manner of formation of the alternating beds of sandstones, clays, and limestones, of which the stratified rocks are composed :—

"The formation of new islands constitutes a distinct and interesting class among the changes to which the surface of the globe is subject. Those which have been raised up by volcanic agency, are comparatively few; but those of coral, which owe their origin to marine insects, (of the class of zoophytes, or *plant-animals*,) are innumerable. Of the different coral tribes, the most abundant is that named the madrepore. It is most common in the tropical seas, and decreases in number and variety towards the poles; it surrounds, in vast rocks and reefs, many of the rocky islands of the South Sea and Indian Ocean, and increase their size by its daily growth. The coasts of the islands in the West Indies, of those to the east of Africa, and the shores and shoals of the Red Sea, are

* Baron Cuvier.

encircled with rocks of coral." Several navigators have furnished us with accounts of the curious manner in which these formations take place. The following is extracted from Captain Basil Hall's narrative of his voyage to the Loo Choo Islands:—

"The examination of a coral reef, during the different stages of one tide, is particularly interesting. When the tide has left it for some time, it becomes dry, and appears to be a compact rock, exceedingly hard and rugged; but when the tide rises, and the waves begin to wash over it, the coral worms protrude themselves from holes which were before invisible. These animals are of a great variety of shapes and sizes, and in such prodigious numbers, that in a short time, the whole surface of the rock appears to be alive and in motion. The most common of the worms at Loo Choo is in the form of a star, with arms, from four to six inches long, which are moved about with a rapid motion, in all directions, probably to catch food. Others are so sluggish, that they may be mistaken for pieces of the rock, and are generally of a dark color, and from four to five inches long, and two to three round.— When the coral is broken, about high water mark, it is a solid hard stone; but if any part of it be detached at a spot which the tide reaches every day, it is found to be full of worms of different lengths and colors; some being as fine as a thread and several feet long, of a bright yellow, and sometimes of a blue color; others resemble snails, and some are not unlike lobsters in shape, but soft, and not above two inches long.

"The growth of coral appears to cease when the worm is no longer exposed to the washing of the sea. Thus, a reef rises in the form of a cauliflower, till its top has gained the level of the highest tides, above which the worm has no power to advance; and the reef, of course, no longer extends itself upwards. The other parts, in succession, reach the surface, and there stop; forming, in time, a level field with steep sides all round. The reef, however, continually increases, and being prevented from going higher, extends itself laterally in all directions. But this growth being as rapid at the upper edge as it is lower down, the steepness of the face of the reef is still preserved. These are the circumstances which render coral reefs so dangerous in navigation: for, in the first place, they are seldom seen above the water; and, in the next, their sides are so steep that a ship's bows may strike against the rock, before any change of sounding has given warning of the danger."

Captain Flinders, who, in 1801, made a survey of the coasts of New Holland, has some observations upon the formation of coral islands, particularly of Half-way Island, on the north coast of that region, which show how, after being raised up, they gradually acquire a soil and vegetation.

"This little Island, or rather the surrounding reef, which is three or four miles long, affords shelter from the south-east winds; and being at a moderate day's run from Murray's Isles, it forms a convenient anchorage for the night to a ship passing through Torres's Strait—I named it Half-way Island. It is scarcely more than a mile in circumference, but appears to be increasing both in elevation and extent. At no very distant period of time, it was one of those banks produced by the washing up of sand and broken coral, of which most reefs afford instances, and those of Torres's Strait a great many. These banks are in different stages of progress; some, like this, are becoming islands, but not yet habitable; some are above high-water mark, but destitute of vegetation; while others are overflowed with every returning tide.

"It seems to me, that when the animalcules which form the coral at the bottom of the ocean cease to live, their structures adhere to each other, by virtue either of their glutinous remains within, or of some property in salt water; and the interstices being gradually filled up with sand and broken pieces of coral, washed by the sea, which also adhere, a mass of rock is at length formed. Future races of these animalcules erect their habitations upon the rising bank, and die in their turn, to increase, but principally to elevate this monument of their wonderful labors. The care taken to work perpendicularly in the early stages would mark a surprising instinct in these diminutive creatures. Their wall of coral, for the most part in situations where the winds are constant, being arrived at the surface, affords a shelter, to leeward of which their infant colonies may be safely sent forth; and to this, their instinctive foresight, it seems to be owing, that the windward side of a reef exposed to the open sea is generally, if not always, the highest part, and rises almost perpendicular from the depth of many fathoms. To be constantly covered with water seems necessary to the existence of the animalcules, for they do not work, except in holes upon the reef, beyond low-water mark; but the coral, sand, and other broken remnants, thrown up by the sea, adhere to the rock, and form a solid mass with it, as high as the common tides reach. That elevation surpassed, the future remnants, being rarely covered, lose their adhesive property; and remaining in a lose state form what is usually called a Key, upon the top of the reef. The new bank is not long in being visited by sea-birds; plants take root upon it, and a soil begins to be formed; a cocoa-nut, or a drop of pandanus, is thrown on shore; land-birds visit it, and deposit the seed of shrubs and trees; every high tide, and still more every gale, adds something to the bank; the form of an island is gradually assumed, and last of all comes man to take possession.

"Half-way Island is well advanced in the above progressive state, having been many years, probably some ages, above the reach of the highest spring-tides, or the wash of the surf in the heaviest gales. I distinguished, however, in the rock which forms its basis, the sand, coral and shells, formerly thrown up, in a more or less state of cohesion. Small pieces of wood, pumice stone, and other extraneous bodies which chance had mixed with the calcareous substances when the cohesion began, were inclosed in the rock, and, in some cases, were still separable from it without much force. The upper part of the island is a mixture of the same substances in a loose state, with little vegetable soil and is covered with the *casuarina*, and a variety of other trees and shrubs, which give food to parroquets, pigeons, and some other birds; to whose ancestors, it is probable, the island was originally indebted for its vegetation."

Here we have nearly all the conditions required for the formation of the successive beds of which the stratified crust of the earth is composed. First, the formation of a limestone rock in the sea, in which we may reasonably expect to find the remains of marine animals and plants Second, the commencement of vegetation and the formation of vegetable soil. All the active processes of the vegetable and animal kingdoms are brought into play, by which, in process of time, the formation of a bed containing the remains of terrestrial animals and plants may be reasonably anticipated. Now, in order to obtain a succession of these beds alternating with each other, it is required that the surface shall be covered by the ocean during the period of the marine deposit, and laid bare to the action of the sun, the rain and the atmosphere, during the period of the terrestrial formation. In order to obtain these alternations in the relative levels of the sea and land, it is necessary either that the surface of solid earth shall be raised and lowered alternately, or that the level of the sea shall be raised and depressed in a manner analogous to that which takes place daily in the ordinary tides. There is reason to suppose that both of these modes of changing the relative levels have been in operation since the earliest times.

Geologists generally attempt to explain the various appearances exhibited in the earth's crust, by alternate elevations and depressions of the land, overlooking the plain and manifest rule which obtains throughout the works of nature:—viz., that in every case the simplest means and mode of action are employed to accomplish the end. Whether then is it easier, more simple, more natural, to raise and depress the level of the liquid ocean so as to cover and uncover different portions of the solid earth at different times, or to elevate and depress the solid rocks so as to accommodate themselves to the liquid ocean? That both of these modes of operation have been employed, there cannot be a doubt; but there is good reason to conclude that the elevation and depression of the ocean has been the rule; of the solid earth the exception.

It is really amusing to observe, with what complacency a modern geologist will set about the raising or sinking of a continent. In order to reach the conclusion at which he aims, he makes no scruple whatever at heaving one half of the continent of Europe up or down a thousand feet or so, and that not once or twice, but as often as suits his convenience, and all this he will accomplish with a few dashes of his pen. There has been some laborious work of this kind performed in the Alps and Pyrenees. These hapless mountains have been tossed, turned, and twisted, in every form and manner, in order to accommodate their relative positions to the particular course of reasoning pursued.

Let us consider what would be the effects consequent upon the shifting of the great mass of the waters of the ocean. If we cast our eye over the map of the globe, we perceive that the southern hemisphere is to a large extent covered by the south sea, and, *vice versa*, that the greater portion of the exposed surface or dry land is situated in the northern temperate zone. Now, we are well assured that limestone rocks are not at present forming on the dry land of the northern hemisphere; at the same time we have evidence that such deposits are now in the process of formation in the south sea. If by any means the conditions of the two opposite hemispheres could be reversed—the northern covered with the ocean, and the southern laid bare to the atmosphere—it is plain that according to the ordinary processes of nature we should have the formation of limestones going on in the northern, and of terrestrial deposits in the southern hemisphere; and the thickness of the respective beds or quantity of matter deposited would bear some proportion to the time during which the supposed conditions remained unchanged.

Now, at the present time, when the earth is in her perihelion, or point nearest the sun, the south pole, and consequently the southern ocean, is presented to that great central attracting body. The earth in the perihelion point is about three millions of miles nearer to the centre than when in the opposite point. We know from observation that the diurnal tides are sensibly affected by the distance of the moon; and, therefore, we are justified in concluding that the great body of the waters are gathered round the south pole by the superior attraction of the sun. But, it will be asked, how are the waters maintained at the south pole during the passage of the earth through the aphelion point? On this head some explanation will be offered when we come to speak of the tides; at present the case is put merely hypothetical. Now, the aphelion and perihelion points of the earth's orbit are not fixed. These points have a progressive motion in space, so slow, that about 114,000 years are required to complete one entire cycle; that is, to bring the two points into the same relative positions, with respect to the fixed stars as at the commencement. Therefore, as the earth's axis never changes its position, in respect to the stars, at the end of a period of 57,000 years, the north pole of the earth will be presented to the sun, whilst the earth is in the perihelion point; and, therefore, according to the inference, the great body of the waters will be drawn around, and will cover the land of the northern hemisphere,—the southern hemisphere being at the same time laid bare to the action of the sun and atmosphere. If such be the course of events, the alternate deposition of marine and terrestrial beds will admit of an easy and natural explication, without doing violence to the laws of nature, by sinking and upheaving continents in order to bring the observed facts to coincide with our preconceived hypothesis; at the same time, we must not attempt to explain every appearance according to the assumption here indicated, but endeavor to refer every phenomena to its own appropriate cause. As the appearances in geology are various, so are the causes by which they are produced. The geological sections of the stratified rocks, whose formation might be referred to the ebbing and flowing of the ocean alternately in the northern and southern hemispheres, are numerous,—an example of which is the "Yore Dale rocks," or upper mountain limestone series.

If all the stratified rocks of the earth were deposited in the above quiet manner upon a horizontal basis, the science of geology, so far as it could reach, which would be very limited, would be an exceedingly simple study. But such is not the case. The rocks are broken, contorted and tumble over each other in the most extraordinary manner; so much so, that it requires the utmost stretch of inductive philosophy to trace the various appearances to their true causes. And this delight, and the intricacy which the intelligent mind experiences in the unravelling of mysterious phenomena, constitute one of the chief pleasures of the study. The pleasure is something akin to that felt by a chess player; the mind is continually on the alert, and kept agreeably active in the endeavor to bring the course of reasoning to a satisfactory conclusion; the turns of the games are so many, and the appearance of check-mate so often presented, that the interest never flags. In order that the reader may enter fairly and fully upon the subject, it is necessary that we should, in a connected view, present a section of the crust of the earth, so far as it is at present known.

We propose to show from an examination of the earth's external crust, strong presumptive evidence that this earth, at an early period of her planetary existence, was attended by three, four, or more moons. We cannot pretend to determine the precise number, but we think we shall be enabled to show, from a geological investigation of the solid crust of the earth, that she was at one time attended by at least five; that the upper strata are principally composed of the wrecks of the first four, which have been precipitated upon her surface at different and indefinitely remote periods of time.

It cannot be supposed that a mere inspection of the simple structure of rocks or beds of gravel will furnish us with a sufficient knowledge whereby to fix the order of their succession, or enable us to draw conclusions of any value. Although the science of geology is merely in its infancy, the body of historical facts that have been already collected, relating to the state of the earth and the various changes it has undergone in past ages, so remote with regard to us, that they may be described as indefinite, are such as must astonish those who are wholly unacquainted with the science. Geology may be considered as furnishing a history of the earth and the events that have occurred upon its surface prior to the creation of man, or the period when sacred history begins. If a casual observer casts his eyes upon the earth and sees confused heaps of gravel, or beds of clay or stone, he cannot discern any symmetry or evidence of design in their formation; but the geologist, by a careful and close examination, discovers that in the mineral kingdom all the various forms and combinations are determined by laws as fixed and immutable as in the most complicated mechanism of organized life, or in the motion of the heavenly bodies. It has been beautifully remarked, that "if astronomy has discovered that the heavens declare the glory of God," as certainly are we assured by geology that "the earth showeth his handi-work."

It has been ascertained by observations in various parts of the world, that the earth's solid crust is composed of a series of parallel layers or strata, having in their internal structure very marked and essential characters, by which they may be readily distinguished from each other. Besides the peculiar features of the elementary composition, or simple structure of the rocks themselves, the greatest proportion may be farther distinguished from each other by containing fragments of pre-existing rocks, shells, and petrified bones of land and amphibious animals and of fishes, and fossil remains of trees and plants.

The following diagram, which represents an imaginary section of the earth's crust, will convey a more intelligible and comprehensive impression to the mind of the reader, than can possibly be given by the most particular and minute verbal description:—

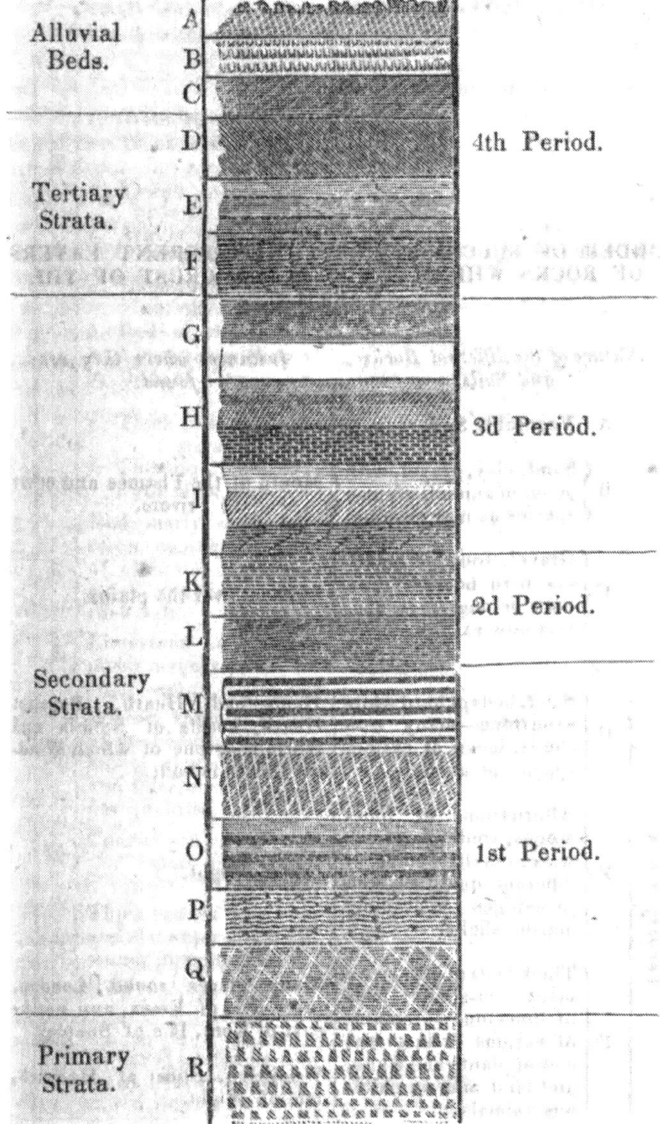
Alluvial Beds.
Tertiary Strata.
Secondary Strata.
Primary Strata.
A
B
C
D
E
F
G
H
I
K
L
M
N
O
P
Q
R
4th Period.
3d Period.
2d Period.
1st Period.

## ORDER OF SUCCESSION OF THE DIFFERENT LAYERS OF ROCKS WHICH COMPOSE THE CRUST OF THE EARTH.

| | | *Nature of the different Rocks and Soils.* | *Instances where they are found.* |
|---|---|---|---|
| | A | Vegetable Soil. | |
| | B | Sand, clay, gravel, with bones of animals of some species as now existing. | Mouth of the Thames and other rivers. |
| | C | Gravel, rounded boulders with bones of animals belonging to species now extinct. | Strewed over the plains. |
| Tertiary Strata. | D | Sand, beds of hard white sandstone—many sea-shells, bones of extinct species of animals. | Hampstead Heath, Bagshot Heath, coasts of Suffolk and Norfolk—stone of which Windsor Castle is built. |
| Tertiary Strata. | E | Alternations of limestones, containing fresh water shells, clays of different qualities, and limestones containing marine shells. | Isle of Wight. |
| Tertiary Strata. | F | Thick beds of clay, with many sea-shells; beds of limestone — remains of various extinct species of plants and fruits, and land and amphibious animals. | Many places round London, great part of Essex, and north-east of Kent, Isle of Shepley.<br><br>Woolwich, Cliffs at Harwich, Isle of Wight. |

| | | | |
|---|---|---|---|
| Secondary Strata. | G | Chalk with flints.<br>Chalk without flints. | Dover Cliffs, Brighton, Hertfordshire.<br>Flamborough Head, Yorkshire. |
| | H | *a.* Chalk marl.<br>*b.* Green sand.<br>*c.* Thick beds of clay.<br>*d.* Yellow sand with beds of iron ore.<br>*e.* Argillaceous sandstone. | Many parts of south coast, Kentish rag.<br>Many parts of Kent and Sussex.<br>The Weald of Kent, Surrey, and Sussex.<br>Neighborhood of Hastings, and Isle of Purbeck.<br>Flat pavement of London, often. |
| | I | *a.* Limestones of different qualities.<br>*b.* Beds of clay.<br>*c.* Limestone with coral<br>*d.* Beds of Clay.<br>*e.* Thick beds of limestone.<br>*f.* Thin do. limestone, and slaty clay. | Portland building stone.<br>Kimmerridge, coast of Dorsetsh.<br>Neighborhood of Oxford.<br>Extensively in Lincolnshire fen clay.<br>Bath building stone.<br>Whitby, Gloucester, Lyme Regis. |
| | K | Red marly sandstone, often containing beds of alabaster or plaster-stone, and also beds of rock-salt. | Great part of East Yorkshire, Nottinghamshire, Stafford, Warwick, Worcester, Cheshire, and neighborhood of Carlisle. |
| | L | Limestone containing much magnesia. | Sunderland, Ferrybridge in Yorkshire, Manisfield, Notts. |
| | M | Coal Measures, containing various seams of coal—beds of ironstone, clay, sandstone and freestones of various qualities. | Newcastle, many parts of Yorkshire, Lancashire, Staffordshire, Somersetshire, vale in which Edinburgh and Glasgow are situated, South Wales. |
| | N | Coarse sandstone and slaty clay. | Millstones of Newcastle and Derbyshire. |
| | O | Thick beds of limestone and slaty clay and sandstone, in many alternations. | Deposits of the lead ore of Derbyshire, Yorkshire, Northumberland, Cumberland, High Peak of Derbyshire, mountains in Yorkshire, Menhip Hills, Somerset. |
| | P | Dark red sandstone with many beds of pebbles. | Great part of Herefordshire, and south-east part of South Wales, Banks of the Wye, south of Scotland. |
| | Q | Thick beds of slate and sandstone, with sometimes impressions of shells, with thick beds of limestone. | Cumberland and Westmoreland mountains, great part of Wales, North Devon, South Devon, and Cornwall, great part of south of Scotland. |

| | | | |
|---|---|---|---|
| Primary Strata. | R | Slates and many hard rocks lying in alternating beds, of great thickness, and the lowest that have been reached. | Chief part of the Highlands of Scotland. |

Here we perceive that the whole series of strata of which the earth's crust is composed, is divided by geologists into three great classes or divisions, by them denominated the primary, secondary, and tertiary strata. This section is merely intended to represent the order of superposition as established by geological observation. There is no instance of *all the strata* having been found together in one place. In some places the primary rocks are found at the surface, the secondary and tertiary being altogether wanting. In very many instances the secondary rocks are found immediately under the vegetable soil, the tertiary alone being wanting; and in every instance that has been observed hitherto by geologists, the series have been found to be incomplete, the upper members of the section represented in the diagram being often found at the surface, whilst many of the lower strata are absent. But wherever the secondary strata are found at the surface, the tertiary are never found under them; nor have the secondary rocks ever been seen lying under the primary.

It must be borne in mind that geology treats of the crust of the earth only;—of the internal constitution of the globe we know comparatively little or nothing. The depth to which science can reach in exploring that crust, amounts in some cases to more than ten miles, and is seldom to be estimated at less than five. This great depth could never be reached by boring or digging. There are no perpendicular precipices on the earth of that altitude, and, therefore, it is manifest that this depth of the crust has never been absolutely explored; yet, from the manner in which the stratified rocks are disposed upon the surface of the earth, we are enabled to determine with a degree of probability, almost amounting to certainty, as to the nature of the rocks at a depth of several miles. If the stratified rocks enveloped the globe with a continuous and unbroken covering, like the coats of an onion, then we could not have become acquainted with more than a few of the upper strata. We could know nothing beyond the depth to which we had actually penetrated. We might speculate concerning the nature of the lower rocks, as we do at present concerning the internal condition of the globe, or that of the distant regions of space to which our observations do not extend. But the stratified rocks do not constitute an unbroken envelope; they are broken and distorted—the ends of the broken beds are presented upon the surface—the beds themselves dipping and stretching away under the surface to a depth of several miles, and their course may, by the aid of science, be followed with almost as much certainty as if they were actually explored by the miner. This will be more clearly understood by reference to the following diagram:—

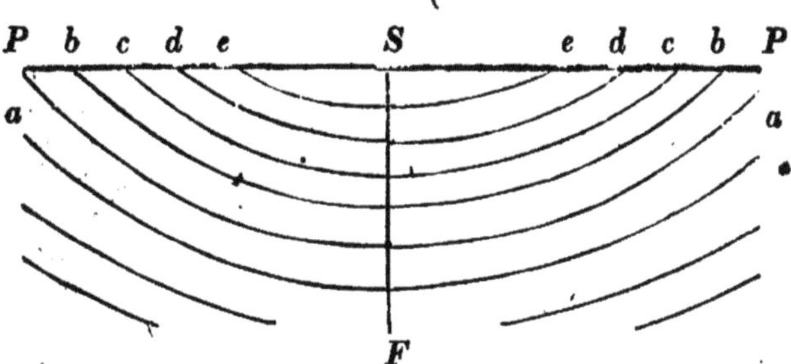


If *a b c d e* be a suit of beds, the broken ends of which are exposed at the surface *S*, and if from *P* to *P* the distance on the surface be twenty miles, then, by measuring the angle of inclination or dip of the bed *a a*, and presuming its continuity from *P* to *P*, we obtain the depth to which it reaches beneath the surface, viz., *F*; and thus we penetrate to a depth equal to the line *S. F*, three, four, five, or any number of miles within a given limit, more or less, according to local circumstances. By these and other means, yet to be noticed, the range of geological inquiry is extended over a wide field, embracing the history of the planet which we inhabit for millions of years previous to its occupation by the human race. When the mind has once entered fully into the geological history of the earth, the *written* records of time, extending to a few thousand years, sink into utter insignificance.

We will now proceed to an examination of the series of rocks of which the earth's crust is composed, so far as they have been observed and investigated by geologists, beginning at the surface, and proceeding downwards, to the lowest that have been reached.

ALLUVIAL DEPOSITS.—If we dig through the vegetable soil, which composes the surface, we come generally to beds of gravel, or clay, or chalk, or other rock, according to the nature of the country in the locality in which we dig. Of these substrata, gravel is the most common. These beds of gravel consist of coarse sand, rolled pebbles, and large stones, with occasionally huge blocks, technically termed "boulders" by geologists. If we examine the various stones with care, we perceive that they have evidently been rolled in water, like the pebbles of the brook or of the sea beach, until the rough corners and projecting angles have been ground away, leaving a smooth stone, more or less rounded. This mechanical rubbing of the stones against each other could not have been effected, if they had, throughout all time, been placed in exactly the same circumstances as at present. They are now at rest, that is, relatively at rest; the grinding process is not going on at present, although it evidently has taken place at some previous period. We have then to look for some natural combination of circumstances by which this grinding could have been effected. If we look to brooks and rivers, and upon a large scale to the ocean, we perceive the process now in active operation. The rivers are continually receiving and carrying small broken fragments of the earth onward to the ocean, where the transported matter is deposited, forming sand banks and shoals.

The "levelling principle" in nature, as in politics, is in constant activity. The mountains, hills, and lesser eminences of surface, are subject to a slow, but certain degradation; and the tendency of this action is to bring the whole surface to nearly the same level; and this, no doubt, would have been the result of this action, were it not counteracted by other causes. If the solid surface were reduced to this perfectly level state, no *land* animals or vegetables could exist, because the sea would cover the entire surface of the earth. If we attentively consider the beds of gravel, of which we are now speaking, we shall see abundant reason to conclude that they once formed the bed of the ocean. No river current could have formed them upon the extensive scale in which they are now found. Nothing less than strong ocean tides and currents, could have rolled about the heavy fragments of rocks and deposited them in the extensive beds of gravel, which at present form a great portion of the surface of

Europe. We are, therefore, compelled to adopt one of two conclusions, either that the surface has been upheaved from the bosom of the deep, or that the sea has retired into the southern hemisphere, where the mass of the waters constitute that which is at present the great south sea. We shall adopt the latter conclusion, as being more consistent with the usual operations of nature. Now, in order to perceive distinctly the manner of the formation of gravel beds or of alluvial strata, it is necessary to advert to the position in which the stratified rocks are found deposited in the earth.

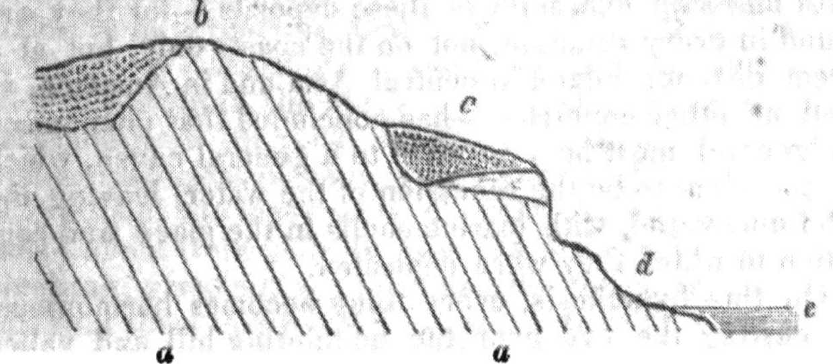


The above is a section of the grauwacke limestones at the Hoe, near Plymouth, where we have an example of three literal formations at different levels;—*a a* the limestone rocks; *b* the highest water level; *c* the intermediate level; *d* the present beach; *e* the present sea level. The maximum elevation of the old beach *c*, is about thirty feet above high water mark. That the beds *b* and *c* are the deposits of an ancient sea beach, is too evident to be disputed, and, therefore, the relative level of the sea and land has been altered, from whatever cause, since the formation of these beds;—and the same appearances may be observed at numerous points along the coasts of Great Britain and Ireland. On the Whittle Hills, near Preston, Lancashire, three hundred feet above the sea level, are found beds of marl, sand, and gravel, (under the ordinary diluvium, with erratic blocks or "boulders"), which are full of the shells of molluscous animals now living in the adjoining sea. On Moel Tryvaen, deposits of marine shells, containing also granite boulders, are seen one thousand feet above the present sea level. At Holderness, in Yorkshire, Murray Frith, in Scotland, Wexford, in Ireland, St. Michael, in France, in Sicily, Greece, and Asia Minor—indeed generally along the sea coasts of Europe, the same phenomena may be observed. In the Baltic, at Lofgrundet, near Upsula, observations have been made, by which it has been determined that the change of level in that locality is about three feet in a century. During that period either the land has been upheaved or the level of the sea has been lowered. Some modern geologists who are accustomed to heave continents up and down, as it suits their convenience, have concluded that the coast around the Baltic has been elevated; but they have omitted to furnish the evidence upon which their conclusion is based. M. Brongniart, on the contrary, (a distinguished name in geology), from the *general* or almost *universal* character of these deposits,—for they are found in every situation, not on the coasts only, but at a great distance inland in central Asia and in America, as well as other countries,—has concluded that phenomena so general must be attributed to a general cause, which he considers to be the recession of the water, leaving the land uncovered, with marine shells in the place and condition in which they were deposited.

On this hypothesis, every thing becomes harmonious. In casting the eye over the undulating hill and valley surface of any country in the world, we notice no abrupt precipices, except in some localities where the intermediate cause can be seen. But in general the hills are smoothed and rounded; the surface is continuous—not broken; the sharp asperities of the fractured ends of the strata are smoothed off and covered by marine deposits; and the general aspect of the country is such as might be expected to result from the long continued action and agitation of an immense superincumbent mass of water. The phenomena are such as could not be produced by rains or any supposable combination of atmospheric causes. "The forms of the valleys," says De La Beche, "are gentle and rounded, and such as no complication of meteoric causes that ingenuity can imagine seems capable of producing; that numerous valleys occur on the lines of faults; and that the detritus is dispersed in a way that cannot be accounted for by the present action of mere atmospheric waters. I will more particularly remark that on great Haldon Hill, about eight hundred feet above the sea, pieces of rock which must have been derived from the lower levels occur in the superficial gravel. They are certainly rare, but may be discovered by diligent search. I there found pieces of red quartziferous porphyry, compact red sandstone, and a compact silicious rock, not uncommon in the grauwacke of the vicinity where all those rocks occur at the lower levels than the summit of Haldon, and where certainly they could not have been carried by rains or rivers, *unless the latter be supposed to delight in running up hill.*"

Seeing that the beds of gravel and other superficial deposits could not have been formed by any of the physical causes now in action in the northern hemisphere; neither by atmospheric action, by rains, streams, nor rivers, we are compelled to admit that these northern countries once formed the ocean bed. This being admitted, we find no difficulty in perceiving that by the long continued action of the great mass of the ocean upon the sharp projecting ends of the strata, the abrupt and angular pieces would be detached from the rock, together with the more loose and friable materials of sand, clays, and marls; that by the tidal action, the loose mass of mixed materials would be rolled about from place to place upon the bed of the sea; breaking, grinding, and rounding the stones and pebbles carrying them to lower levels, and into eddies and quiet corners behind hills, until at length by the retiring of the ocean into the southern hemisphere, the beds were left in the places in which they are found at this day.

From this view of the case before us, we are enabled to form some kind of notion with respect to the age of the earth. These deposits of which we have been treating, are, as compared with the whole crust, a mere outward skin; and if their formation be due to the alternate shifting of the ocean from the one to the other hemisphere as a consequence of the progression of the earth's aphelion point in the ecliptic,—requiring for the completion of the cycle 114,000 years at the present time, and in former ages, when the earth was further from the sun it must have required a still longer period;—if in the formation of the merely external alluvial deposits, a few yards in thickness, a period of 114,000 years has elapsed, and if the whole of the stratified rocks, which, taken together, form, according to Dr. Buckland, a thickness of ten miles, *had been formed upon this planet only*, and by an equally slow process, then, the time which the earth has existed as a planet is so vast, that it exceeds our means of computation.

The beginning of terrestrial things stretches back not through thousands only, but through millions of millions of years, until at length it seems to be lost in an endless eternity. It was the contemplation of the earth's crust, under this point of view, which induced Dr. Hutton to give utterance to the now famous expression—"I see no traces of a beginning or prospect of an end." If Hutton and others who have followed him could not discern the traces of a beginning or prospect of an end, it was because their attention had been directed to the cycle of minor processes going forward on the earth. Their views being confined to this terrestrial cycle, their reasonings necessarily followed the cycle, and returned to the point from which they started in their inquiry. They neglected or overlooked the fact, that the earth is but one of a number of bodies, and is involved in a cycle of processes of still greater magnitude,—a cycle embracing the entire solar system. It is not probable that the knowledge of man will ever become so extensive as to enable him to comprehend all the great processes of the physical world; but certain it is, that if we would obtain a clear and *connected* view of those processes, we must extend the field of observation to the utmost limits of accessible space and time, and endeavor to contemplate nature as one connected whole.

These observations are introductory to another class of phenomena, which appear to be wholly inexplicable, even upon the assumption of the ocean having entirely covered the land of the northern hemisphere. It is required, in order to explain the actual appearances, that the land should be not only submerged, but that the superincumbent waters should be thrown into violent agitation. "Not only are gravels," says De La Beche, "brought from various distances, but even huge blocks, the transport of which, by actual causes into their present situations, seems physically improbable."

These "huge blocks" have been carried along in some instances many hundreds of miles, over ranges of mountains of great altitude, and are found deposited in elevated positions where they could not have been borne by the strongest ocean currents of which we have any knowledge. From the mountainous region of the Lakes in Cumberland, they have been carried along the east coast of England, and are found in the vale of the Severn, near Bridgenorth. They are also scattered over the eastern coast of Yorkshire, and are found at Redcar, Stokesly, Thirsk, the Hambleton Hills, the vale of York, and generally throughout the district; to reach which, they must have passed the central or Penine chain of England, the average altitude of which is at this part not less than 1,500 feet. On the continent of Europe they are found scattered over Saxony, Silicia, and the adjoining countries, and even as far as Moscow, the former capital of the Russian empire, having, as presumed by geologists, travelled from Sweden, where the parent rock from which they have apparently been detached, is found. In North America, also, the same phenomena is observed. Dr. Bigsby has given an account of these "huge blocks," and has shown that from similar causes they are widely scattered over the northern portion of the American continent; so that whatever the cause might be of their distribution over the surface of the northern hemisphere, that cause was not a merely local, but a general cause operating over the entire of the northern hemisphere of the earth. Not only are those "huge blocks," or *boulders*, scattered over the surface of the earth in this extraordinary manner, but large masses of heterogeneous materials are huddled together in a confused way, containing the bones of animals and other fossil remains; and from the manner in which they are thrown together, it is evident that they were not quietly deposited, but were heaped up in a corner as it were, by some violent concussion or catastrophe.

"The most singular circumstance," says Professor Philips, "attending the accumulation of the proper diluvium, is the *extreme confusion* and almost total want of lammillar or stratified structure in the mass; pebbles and fragments of rock of all sizes, of different nature and from different regions, lie mixed indiscriminately in the clay, many yards in thickness, which seem clearly to prove that the whole was rapidly accumulated, and that the particles had not time to be arranged according to magnitude or specific gravity, but were heaped confusedly together by a *force of extraordinary intensity and short duration.*" Geologists have searched the earth in vain to find a force competent to produced the observed effects. No "upheaving" or "downheaving" of islands or continents that even the wildest imagination could conceive, is competent to produce the effects in the order in which they have been noted by observers. An intense force of short duration is required; and, confining our researches to the earth and all the forces contained within it, we can find no cause adequate to the effects. We must, therefore, seek a cause *without* the earth, and *within* the solar system.

TERTIARY ROCKS.—When we have penetrated through the vegetable soil and alluvial beds, we come next upon the tertiary rocks. It must not, however, be understood that the tertiary strata are *every where* found beneath the alluvial beds, or that they are spread continuously over the surface of the earth. They occur in large patches, separated from each other by wide intervening districts. These patches have been named *basins*, as the "London Basin," the Paris Basin, the Hampshire Basin, the Bohemian Basin. The London Basin is upwards of 180 miles in length, extending from above Reading, in Berkshire, to Harwich, in Essex, and of a varying breadth, from a few miles, to 40, 50, 60, or more in some places. The thickness of the tertiary deposits is very irregular. In some places the aggregate thickness amounts to several thousand feet. The strata are more or less disturbed from their original horizontality. At Alum Bay, in the Isle of Wight, the beds are in a vertical position, resting upon an *unbroken* bed of chalk. There is no *visible* evidence of these vertical rocks having been disturbed from their original horizontal position by volcanic agency; indeed, "igneous rocks are no where in England associated with the tertiary strata." Geologists may suppose that the tertiary rocks at Alum Bay and elsewhere have been thrown into their present vertical position by the force of central heat, or any other supposable force, acting from beneath; but before this inference can be received, it is required to be shown by what possibility an internal force could have disturbed the tertiary beds, so as to set them upon their edges, without breaking the stratum of chalk upon which the disturbed beds are deposited. We will not at present insist upon this argument, as we shall recur to it at the close of our geological observations. We could not, however, omit to mention it in this place, meeting with it as we do upon the very threshhold of our geological inquiries; and seeing that such a case involves a principle that must ultimately modify, to a large extent, the science of geology: for, if rocks found in such circumstances could not by any possibility have been disturbed from beneath, it is evident that they must have been deposited from above in the solid form.

The Paris Basin, which is about 180 miles in its greatest length, from north-east to south-east, and about 90 miles from east to west, was carefully examined in 1811, by M. M. Cuvier and Brongniart, and by them arranged into five different formations,—three land or fresh water, with two marine formations intervening, as follows:—

| | |
|---|---|
| 1. Upper land or fresh water formation. | Upper fresh water marls.<br>Silicious millstone with shells.<br>Do. do. without shells. |
| 2. Upper marine formation. | Upper marine marls and limestones.<br>Upper marine sands and sandstones.<br>Gypseous marine marls. |
| 3. Middle formation land or fresh water. | Fresh water marls.<br>Gypsum with bones of animals.<br>Silicious limestones. |
| 4. Lower marine formation. | Calcaire grossier or coarse limestone. |
| 5. Lowest fresh water or land formation. | Sandstone.<br>Lignite.<br>Plastic clay. |

The silicious millstone and sandstones are composed chiefly of silica or oxyd of silicum. The limestones are carbonate of lime, of which an immense mass is deposited in the calcaire grossier, and the gypsum beds (plaster of Paris) are composed principally of sulphate of lime. The formation of these gypsum beds presents a very serious difficulty to geologists. All their conclusions are founded upon the presumption that the tertiary strata have been formed from the wasted materials of the older rocks, which matter has, in the long lapse of ages, been broken off from the upturned ends of the secondary strata, by the action of fresh water and oceanic currents, and by atmospheric influences; and that this matter or detritus, as it is generally named, has been carried by the agency of water into the lower levels of the earth's surface. And hence the sites of the tertiary deposits have been termed "basins," although, as De La Beche remarks, the term is by no means an appropriate one; for the tertiary do not, in fact, repose in basins in the manner of an alluvial deposit, as the term would seem to imply: but, on the contrary, occupy considerable tracts of country in the various quarters of the globe, Europe, Asia, Northern Africa, and America, in the higher as well as in the lower levels, and exhibiting the usual diversity of hill and dale which characterise districts composed of the secondary rocks only. It may be true, that, in respect to the tertiary rocks, the elevations and depressions of hill and valley are upon a scale of less grandeur and magnificence than in countries formed of the older rocks; but still the phenomena are generally and indeed specifically the same, and do not warrant the conclusion that tertiary rocks have been formed in the manner of lacustrine deposits, as generally assumed by geologists.

If the tertiary deposits have been, as assumed, derived from the detritus of the older or secondary rocks, then it may be presumed that we might expect to find some analogy in the mineral composition of the derived rocks with those from which the materials are supposed to have been detached by mechanical action. But we do not find this analogy. The gypsum beds of the tertiary system contain immense masses of sulphate of lime, a compound for which we look in vain in those older rocks of the detritus, of which the gypsum beds are said to have been formed. Again, these gypsum beds contain the fossil remains of animals of a species wholly distinct from any which lived upon the earth previous to the deposition of the tertiary strata, and also unlike any species living upon the earth at the present day. "The osseous gypsum," says De La Beche, "presents us with a decidedly new state of things; singular animals of which the very *genera* are now extinct must have existed some where in the district, the remains of which became in some manner entangled in sulphate of lime, considerable deposits of which were then in progress. The question will arise, whence did such a quantity of sulphate of lime proceed? Certainly it is a new ingredient, at least in any abundance, in this district, and there is no evidence that it was deposited in a sea, as was the case with the carbonate of lime of the calcaire grossier; on the contrary, as it only contains terrestrial and fresh water remains, it would seem to have been formed through the medium of fresh water."

The tertiary strata are widely spread in large isolated patches in every quarter of the world that has been explored or examined geologically. The common hypothesis by which geologists attempt to explain their formation, proceeds from the supposition that they are sedimentary deposits, formed mechanically from detritus derived from older or secondary rocks; that the beds were deposited by subsidence in water upon a horizontal level; and that these horizontal beds were afterwards disturbed and tilted up by an internal force acting from beneath. Let us apply this hypothesis to a section of the shelly crag, near Walton, Suffolk, and many sections might be given presenting similar characters of disturbed stratification.

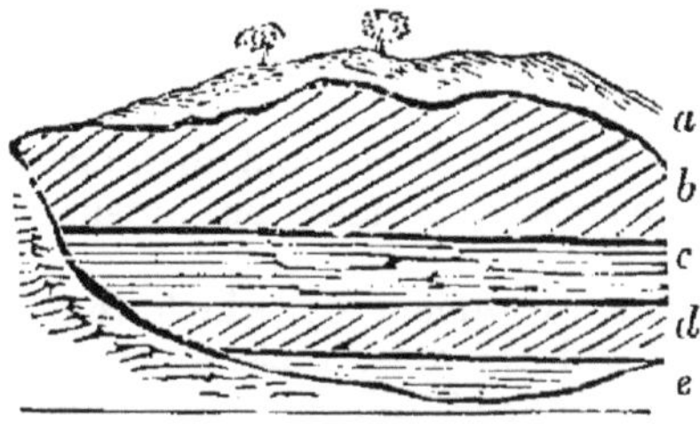


The above diagram is copied from Lyell's Geology, vol. IV., p. 91. Several similar sections are given, upon which he remarks, (p. 93)—"The appearances exhibited in the diagrams are not peculiar to the crag; they may be found in almost every gravel pit; and I have seen sand and pebble beds of all ages, including the old red sandstone, grauwacke, and clay-slate, exhibit the same arrangement." Here, then, the whole doctrine of disturbed stratification upon the great scale, from internal forces, falls to the ground. By no ingenuity can it be shown that the *inclined* strata *b* and *d* could be thrown into their present position without breaking and disturbing the *horizontal* beds *c* and *e*. The upper bed *a* of this section is also instructive. It plainly indicates that at the period of its deposition, the waters of the ocean must have covered the upturned edges of the inclined strata *b*. In denying the sufficiency of internal forces to the production of the phenomena exhibited in this case, and in thousands of others, we do not for a moment seek to impugn the inferences of geologists by which partial and local disturbances are assigned to volcanic action. But, besides the anomaly which would present itself in the above section, if we ascribed all disturbances to internal forces, the confusion, disturbance, contortion, and non-conformity of the strata is too general to admit of explanation by the mere local disturbance caused by a volcano, or even an earthquake. No earthquake, of which we have received any knowledge, could have produced effects upon the stupendous scale observed in the earth's mineral crust. Nor have we a right to draw upon the imagination for internal forces adequate to the observed effects, as geologists have been in the habit of doing. We know of no such forces. To have produced disturbances upon the scale exhibited in the different mountain ranges of the earth by igneous action, would have required that the whole earth should be nothing less than one huge, raging volcano; nor could the disturbances presented in the section we have given be effected even upon that hypothesis. Inclined strata, resting upon an unbroken horizontal foundation, must have been deposited from above, in the solid form, and in a mass, from whatever source the materials may be presumed to have been derived.

The chief argument by which the tertiary system is connected with the older rocks on the one hand, and with the present order of things on the other, is derived from their mineral composition and the fossil remains of animals and plants which they contain. With respect to mineral composition, the analogy fails; for the gypsum beds are composed of sulphate of lime, a compound not found in the older rocks, or at least very sparingly. Besides, seeing that the formation of solid rocks has been going on in the earth for ages, we have a right to infer that a similar process is, and has been, going on in the moon, and that the rocks formed in each of the bodies are, in their mineral composition, to a certain extent analogous; seeing that the primaries and satellites are similarly situated in the solar system, with respect to the sun's influence and other circumstances affecting the vital action of the vegetable, animal, and mineral kingdoms, by which vital influence the specific action is carried forward, and the ultimate product of a solid earth elaborated. Therefore, even if two rocks present some characteristics analogous in respect to their mineral composition, that circumstance alone does not enable us to determine that both rocks were formed upon the primary earth. One may have been formed upon an attendant satellite, and the other upon the primary, and yet, notwithstanding, both rocks may be similar in their mineral composition, seeing that the two bodies were at the same time under the influence of the same or similar influences.

The same argument holds in respect to the fossil remains. If old races have become extinct from time to time, beginning with oldest rocks in which fossil remains are found, and new races have been called into being, each succeeding race being specifically distinguished from its predecessor, and if each succeeding race has been endowed with functions adapting it to the progressive change of circumstances, which has been evidently going on from the beginning, we are justified in the conclusion, that a corresponding progressive development of animal and vegetable life has been going forward in the moon or other attendant satellites; that the progression going on in the satellite has been to a certain extent *parallel* to that going on in the primary, seeing that the two bodies must be *nearly* of the same age; both hold nearly the same local position in the solar system; both have been subjected to the sun's influence in nearly the same degree, and, therefore, the *action*, vital or any other, must have been similar, and a similar product must have been the result of that action. There is nothing, then, in the mere similarity of the tertiary fossils to the existing species, which warrants the conclusion, that they must have lived upon this earth, since all the conditions necessary to their existence might have been equally found in a satellite attending the primary earth.

The number of fossil mollusca found in the tertiary strata is very great. M. Deshayes, who examined this subject with great care, gives the following as the result of his investigation:—

| | |
|---|---|
| Tertiary species . . . | 3036 |
| Living species . . . | 4780 |
| Total . . . | 7816 |

Of these 3036 fossil species, 426 are common to both periods; that is, there are about 426 tertiary fossil shells, and 426 living shells, which appear to be of the same species. All the other, viz., 2610 species, are extinct, and 4354 new species are now living, which do not appear to have had an existence during the period in which the tertiary rocks were in the process of formation. Now, upon this small number, 426 species, about five per cent. of the whole, an argument is founded, by which it is attempted to be shown that the transition from the order of nature, which existed during the tertiary period to the present state in which we now live, has been effected by an easy gradation; although the diluvial beds as well as the disturbed state of the tertiary strata themselves bear witness that between the former and the latter state of things, there has occurred, from whatever cause, a sudden, transitory and overwhelming catastrophe; that the waters of the ocean have rushed over the earth with a degree of force and violence of which it is difficult to form even an indistinct conception.

Let us see how the argument stands in respect to the fossil fish found in the tertiary deposits. "The fishes of the tertiary strata," says M. Agassiz, "are so nearly related to existing forms, that it is often difficult, considering the enormous number (above 8,000) of living species, and the imperfect state of preservation of the fossils, to determine exactly their specific relations. In general, I may say, that *I have not yet found a single species which was perfectly identical with any marine existing fish* except the little species which is found in nodules of clay, of unknown geological age, in Greenland. The species of the Norfolk crag, of the upper sub-appenine formation and of the mollusca, are mostly referable to genera common in tropical regions—such as platax, cartharious, myliobates, &c. In the lower tertiaries of London, the basin of Paris, and Monte Bolca, at least a third of the species belong to genera which are now extinct." At Monte Bolca immense numbers of fossil fish have been found huddled together in such a manner that it is evidently impossible they could have lived in the locality in which they are found. There is evidence of a violent concussion, by which they must have been suddenly destroyed. They are found entire—the fleshy parts not decomposed, which they must have been, if they had died in the usual course of nature. Immediately after death in the ordinary way, decomposition sets in; the soft and fleshy parts are dissolved; the parts are no longer held together, and if in water—the natural element of fish—the bones are scattered far and wide. And, therefore, the entire fossil fishes found at Monte Bolca must have been buried alive and instantaneously, by which their remains have been preserved from decomposing influences, more carefully, than if they had been enclosed in a leaden coffin hermetically sealed. One circumstance marks the sudden transition from life to death and inhumation in a very emphatic manner:—*Fossil fish have been found with their prey half swallowed;* they have been overwhelmed and buried in the act of swallowing their food, and so suddenly, that, that act which requires but a moment for its completion, could not be accomplished; and it is worthy of notice, that the fossil fish thus found, are generally so squeezed and flattened by the immense superincumbent mass under which they have been thus suddenly buried, that their remains are usually a mere film, often not thicker than a sheet of paper, and yet every scale and fin distinctly marked and well defined.

A few remains of birds have been found, which are presumed to have been buried during the tertiary period. They have been discovered chiefly in caverns, such as the Kirkdale cave, in Yorkshire, and in the diluvial beds of the same country. Indeed, it might be fairly questioned whether the different species of the feathered tribe which have been found, may not be referred to the post-tertiary formations. Professor Phillips, in his recent work, (Lardner's Cyclopædia,) justly remarks, "that concerning the date of some of the fossil animals, especially when they occur in lacustrine deposits not interstratified with marine formations, *there is danger of confounding tertiary with diluvial species.*" It is only by taking an extended view of the whole case with all its attendant circumstances, that we can expect to arrive at correct conclusions; by viewing the earth as one of a number of bodies which constitute a solar system, in which system a progressive series of changes have been and are going forward, of equal or greater importance than those which have been going on in the earth herself.

Mr. Lyell has attempted to prove that all the disturbances of the stratified rocks are due to the gradual and continued action of small forces operating throughout a long series of ages. "But," in his own language, "Mr. Conybeare" (and almost every other geologist, he might have added) "has contended that the verticality of the strata in the Isle of Wight and in Purberk, compels us to admit that the movement there was violent; that the vertical strata which have been traced through a district nearly *sixty miles* in length were brought into their present position by a *single convulsion.*" And these sixty miles of vertical strata, be it remembered, rest upon an *unbroken* bed of chalk.

Secondary Strata.—In passing from the present state of things to the fossil remains of the tertiary rocks, we seem to pass into another creation. Thousands of creatures appear to have "lived, moved, and had their being," during the period of the formation of those rocks, some of which bear a kind of resemblance to living species; but by far the greater number of the very races have become extinct. The old creation has passed away, and those which at present exist upon the face of the earth belong to a new order of things. But if the contrast be striking here, when we descend to the secondary rocks it becomes still more so.

Between the tertiary period and the present state of things, we can trace a faint and feeble connexion; but in descending to the secondary rocks, we appear to enter into an entirely new region. Of the animals and vegetables, whose fossil remains are found in the secondary strata, the species and even the genera have ceased to exist. *Their races are all extinct.* And this extinction of the pre-existing species did not take place by graduated steps, by one race dropping off, and another coming on to the stage in slow succession; but suddenly and at once. At this point there appears to be a "snap in the chain" of being; nay, the very rocks themselves are different in their mineral composition. The chalk, the upper member of the series, stands alone, for although it be a carbonate of lime, and, therefore, so far resembling other limestones, it is, notwithstanding, a limestone having peculiar characteristics appertaining to itself, by which it is easily and readily distinguishable from all other limestones.

The whole of the secondary strata, taken together, are of a vast thickness, many thousands of feet, and have, therefore, been classed into groups for convenience of study. These groupings are arbitrary in a certain degree; several have been proposed, but none of them are entirely satisfactory. The following is from Professor Phillips:—

"The secondary rocks comprehend a great variety of different beds of stone, extending from the primary strata to the chalk, which forms the upper or most recent member of the division. There are certain principal groups, which are divisible into subordinate beds, all distinguishable by marked peculiar characters. They occur in the following descending order:—

"The chalk group. The oolite group. The red marl group. The coal group. The mountain limestone group. The old red sandstone group. The grauwacke group.

"We shall briefly describe the leading characters of each group, but in an *ascending* order, from the grauwacke, a German local name for the principal rock among the lowest members of the secondary series. This group occurs extensively in the hilly country of the south of Scotland, in Westmoreland, Wales, and Devonshire.—The *Old Red Sandstone Group* is characterized by its containing a great number of beds composed of water-worn fragments, and sandstone layers of a fine grain, and by its being usually of a deep red color. It contains very few organic remains, but terrestrial plants and marine shells are sometimes found in it. It is the principal rock in Herefordshire, but it is not of very great extent in other parts of England; it is estimated to be in England about 1,500 feet thick. It must not be confounded with another red sandstone which covers a great extent of the midland and northern counties of England, and which belongs to a more recent period, viz., the *Red Marl Group*. Above the old red sandstone comes an important suite of beds, the *Mountain Limestone Group*. The limestone is usually very compact or crystalline, yielding in many places excellent marbles for chimney-pieces, &c. It contains a great variety of organic remains, consisting of corals, and many species of zoophytes and other radiated animals, some species of crustacea, a few remains of fish, and a great variety of marine shells. It forms considerable mountain chains in the north of England, Derbyshire, and Somersetshire, and abounds in many places in valuable ores of lead; it is estimated to have a thickness of 900 feet. Above this limestone comes the important group containing our coal mines. This group must have been produced under very different circumstances from the limestone which it covers, for it rarely contains any marine remains, but a vast profusion of plants of many genera and species. The united thickness of the Coal Group, is, probably, not less than 1,700 feet. The *Red Marl Group* consists of a number of beds of a red marly sandstone, often variegated by stripes and patches of grey, blue, and white, which occupy a great extent of country in England; there is an almost uninterrupted line of it from Hartlepool, in the country of Durham, to Exeter, and it covers the greater part of Nottinghamshire, Warwickshire, Staffordshire, Shropshire, Worcestershire, and Cheshire. In the two last counties it contains valuable mines of common salt, and copious brine-springs of the same, and in other places great quantities of alabaster or plaster-stone. In this group are found considerable beds of limestone of a peculiar quality, from containing a large proportion of the earth called magnesia. The sandstones of the grey group contain very few organic remains, but the limestones abound in those of marine animals, among which have been found the bones of gigantic amphibious reptiles like crocodiles. The group is estimated at not less than 2,100 feet of thickness. The *Oolite Group* is so called from the prevalence in it of a kind of limestone composed of small round grains, like the eggs in the roe of a fish, whence oolite, from two Greek words, signifying egg and stone. It contains about twelve alternations of subordinate beds, or rather systems of beds, consisting of limestones of different qualities and of clays, their united thickness being about 2,600 feet, of which 1,100 are formed by two beds of clay of 500 and 600 feet each. The whole group contains a vast abundance of animal remains, which are almost exclusively marine, consisting of numerous genera and the species of the molluscous animals, crustacea, insects, echini, zoophytes, and skeletons of several species of gigantic reptiles analogous to the crocodile. The celebrated stones of Bath, Ketton, and Portland, and most of the building stones of the middle and south of England, are found in this group, which covers a great part of the country that lies between a line drawn from the mouth of the river Tees to Watchet, on the south coast of the Bristol Channel, and another line drawn from Lynn in Norfolk, to Poole in Dorsetshire. The last or uppermost of the secondary rocks is the *Chalk Group*, which is separated from the Oolite Group by several beds of sand, clays, and sandstones, and including these, has been estimated to be 1,900 feet thick. It is unnecessary to say any thing of the composition of the principal member of the group, as it must be so familiar to all our readers. It covers a great extent of country, forming low hills and downs from the Flamborough Head in Yorkshire to Weymouth, in a curvilinear sweep, the convexity directed to the S. E., and in many places E. S. E., and S. of that line. The whole group abounds in organic remains of the same *classes* as those found in the Oolite Group below.

"It thus appears that the secondary rocks consist of an extensive series of strata, of limestones, sandstones, and clays, all of which contain either rounded fragments of pre-existing rocks or organic remains, or both; and each group, and all the subordinate members of the groups, are distinguishable by characters of great constancy and certainty, derived from the peculiar nature of the enclosed fossils. They must all have been deposited in a horizontal position, but there are parts of them which have undergone greater or less disturbance, being often thrown into a vertical position, and broken, twisted, and disturbed in the most extraordinary manner."

*Chalk Group.*—We have seen in our examination of the tertiary rocks cases of disturbed stratification in which it appears impossible that the disturbed beds could have been thrown into their present position by any force acting from beneath. No sooner do we enter into the secondary strata, than we find evidence of the same character. The following is a section of the valley of Kingsclere, in Berkshire, from Lyell's Geology, vol. 4, p. 261:

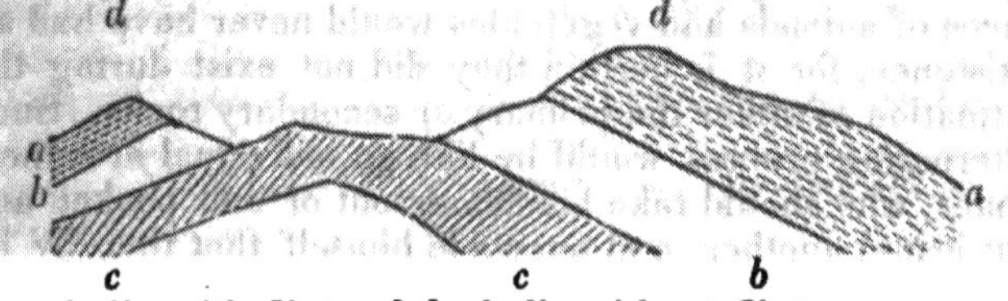


*a a* chalk with flints; *b b* chalk without flints; *c c* upper green sand or firestone; width of the valley from *d* to *d* about two miles. Now, that the strata *a a* and *b b* were once continuous, and have been subsequently broken by some cause, will be granted. But how have the *two miles* of solid chalk been scooped out, and what has become of the material? Geologists informs us that the matter was scooped out by the long continued action of rivers and streams. When it is objected that in that case the river must have run along the *top of the hill*, since previous to the scooping out there could be no banks to confine it in its course, or bed in which it could flow; and worse still, the river must have *flowed up the side of the hill*, in order to get at the top before the scooping process could begin. When such objections are started, the geologist gravely sets to work, lowers a chain of mountains, heaves up a county or two, and having levelled and adjusted the surface to his mind, and formed a channel for his imaginary stream—like a genuine navigator cutting a canal—he conjures up a supply of water, the stream begins to flow, and the scooping commences.

Now really this reasoning is too ridiculous, and yet such is the manner in which some men would account for the appearances presented in the above diagram; and it is by no means impossible that those same men will repudiate the attempt to explain such geological difficulties by the deposition of a satellite. But what has become of the two miles of solid matter, which is said to have been scooped out? This, it is said, has gone towards the formation of the tertiary strata. Now laying no stress upon the argument, that if this *see-saw* process of breaking up one rock to form another had been the *only* resource which nature possessed whereby to form the immense masses of stratified and unstratified rocks which *now* exist, a planet originally liquid, must have remained liquid, the natural progression of all terrestrial processes must have stood still, and the earth would have remained in her primitive state to all eternity. The human race and many other races of animals and vegetables would never have had an existence, for it is certain they did not exist during the formation of either the primary or secondary rocks. Such alternating process would be like an individual or a merchant, who should take his money out of one pocket and put it into another, and persuade himself that thereby he was adding a vast accumulation to his stores, or one who should pull down one house in order to build two of equal magnitude with the old materials. By such process, the solid rocks of the earth never could have been accumulated as they evidently have been. That the conglomerates and other mechanical rocks have been formed from the detritus of the old rocks may be safely admitted, but such admission cannot be made with respect to limestones and others of chemical origin.

But still the argument remains to be answered—What became of the material? We know that the chalk is rich in fossil remains, and if the matter had gone towards the formation of the tertiary rocks, we might expect to find the secondary fossils in the tertiary strata, not a shell here and there, but in considerable quantities. But it is not so. Neither the fossil remains nor the mineral composition of the tertiary strata bear out the conclusion that they have been formed from the wasted materials of the secondary rocks.

The chalk group is widely spread over the surface of the earth. It is seen in England, Ireland, France, Spain, Italy, Germany, Sweden, Denmark, Russia, both in Europe and Asia, and generally throughout the old continent. In America it is seen on the Atlantic coast in New Jersey, whence it may be traced through Delaware, Virginia, Maryland, North and South Carolina, Georgia Florida, Alabama, Mississippi, Tennesee, Louisiana, Arkansas and Missouri; and according to Mr. Rogers, "by specimens brought from time to time from the interior of the continent, it will appear to occur abundantly in the far west, towards the Rocky Mountains."

The disturbances of the chalk group have been in some places upon the great scale, and present in several localities strange anomalies. At the quarry of Weinbohla, on the Danube, a granite or syenite rock rests upon a horizontal bed of chalk; and on the Pyrenees the chalk is associated with granite and serpentine, and pierced with mineral veins.

| Formation | Thickness | Strata | Group |
|---|---|---|---|
| | | TERTIARY STRATA. | |
| Chalk Formation. | 600 Feet. | Upper Chalk with flints. | CHALK GROUP. |
| | | Middle Chalk, of an intermediate character. | |
| | | Lower Chalk, harder, and less white; red in the north of England. | |
| | | Chalk Marl; a soft clayey chalk. | |
| Green Sand Formation. | 600 Feet. | Upper Green Sand, or fire stone, with nodules of chert. | |
| | | Golt, or Folkstone clay; soft and marly with green grains. | |
| | | Lower Green Sand; rocks of chalky limestone; Fuller's earth. | |
| | | Oolite Group. | |

*The Oolite Group* is an interesting series of beds, rich in the remains of animals and plants of an extraordinary character. The highest bed or division of the group, is that of the weald clay (wolds of Sussex) or wealden rocks. These rocks are characterised by the presence of abundant fresh water and *terrestrial* fossil remains, forming a strong contrast with the *marine* fossils of the superincumbent green sands of the chalk group.

In the Isle of Wight, where fine sections of the wealden clay may be seen, it is composed of slatey clay and limestones, with which are associated beds of ironstone.

Beneath the wealden clays, we find the *Hastings sands*, which contain innumerable fragments of vegetables in a carbonized state, attesting that these sands are also of land or fresh water origin. Beneath the Hastings sands are the *Purbeck beds*, composed of limestone strata, alternating with marls. The limestones of this formation are used extensively in paving the streets of London. The upper bed of the Purbeck strata contains a large proportion of green earth, with calcareous matter, the latter being apparently derived from the fragments of a bivalve shell. Descending in the series, we come upon the *Portland Oolite*, associated with which is the remarkable *Dirt bed*. This dirt bed appears to be the remains of an ancient forest. Trees and plants are found apparently in the very position in which they grew. They are for the most part, prostrate or inclined, but some are found in an upright position; the upright portions being sometimes partly included in the limestone strata above.

One conclusion respecting the dirt bed of Portland may be relied upon, viz., that at the period in which the trees and plants grew and flourished, that part of the earth's surface was dry land; that this land was subsequently submerged; and from the state in which the vegetable fossils are found, it would appear that the submergence was effected somewhat suddenly. Had it taken place very gradually,—that is, had it been the work of many ages, it might be supposed that the trees would have been torn up by the roots and scattered from the locality in which they grew. The dirt bed is not a mere local formation. Dr. Fitton has observed an earthy bed in precisely the same geological position, in the cliffs of Boulonnois, and also in Buckinghamshire, and in the vale of Wardour. It therefore appears that a forest so widely extended over the surface could not be overwhelmed by any partial or merely local catastrophe. The cause of submergence, whether sudden or gradual, must have been general and extensive as the effects.

Rocks of the Oolite group are found in England, Scotland, France, Germany, Sweden, the Alps north and south, from which they stretch through Illyria, Dalmatia, Albania, and Greece. They may also be traced on the south slope of the Hymalaya mountains in Upper India, and generally over the surface of the earth in very extensive tracts. The period of the formation of the Oolite group appears, upon the whole, to have been one of comparative repose; limestones, clays, and marls succeed each other throughout the series, in which are found the remains of animals and plants, quietly entombed. It must not, however, be imagined that these rocks are undisturbed. *Since* the period of their formation they have been broken, twisted, or contorted, and tumbeld over each other in the most extraordinary manner. Sections are seen in the Alps where an upper rock of the group is covered by one of older date, the mass appearing to have been, by some cause, turned upside down.

The following section exhibits the group in a state, perhaps, as little disturbed as any that could be selected :— *a* Wealden; *b* Upper Oolite; *c* Middle Oolite; *d d* Lower Oolite; *e* Lias.

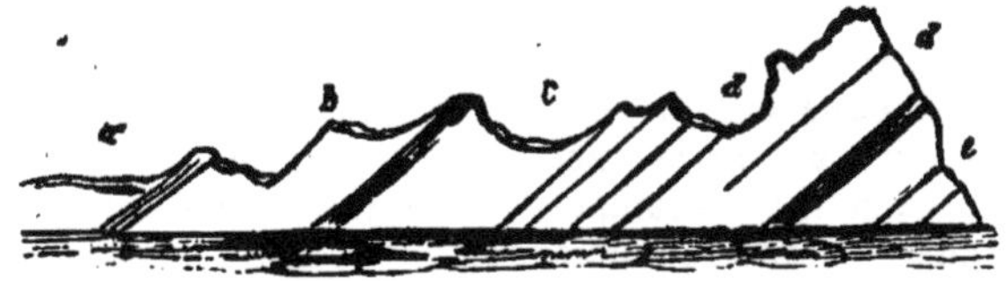


Now, as on the one hand it is evident, from the quiet manner in which the fossils are entombed, that this group was formed during a period of comparative repose, so on the other, it is manifest that since their formation, they have been broken and upheaved by some tremendous force, or they have been deposited from above in the solid form, and in a mass. In the lias, the lowest of the group, some strange circumstances appear. Remains of animals are found, which, judging from appearances, must have been entombed alive. "In the lias of Lime Regis, the Ichthyosauri, Plesiosauri, and many other animals, seem to have suffered a somewhat sudden death; for in general the bones are not scattered about and in a detached state, as would happen, if the dead animals had descended to the bottom of the sea to be decomposed or devoured piecemeal, as indeed might also happen, if the creature floated for a time on the surface, one animal devouring one part, and another carrying off a different portion; on the contrary, the bones of the skeleton, though frequently compressed, as must arise from the enormous weight to which they have been so long subjected, are tolerably connected, frequently in perfect, or nearly perfect order, as if prepared by the anatomist. *The skin, moreover, may*

*sometimes be traced, and the compressed contents of the intestines may at times be also observed—all tending to show that the animals were suddenly destroyed, and as suddenly preserved.* Not only has this apparently happened to these reptiles, which, breathing air, might, under favorable circumstances, be drowned simultaneously in great numbers, but also to the mollusca, to which constant or nearly constant immersion in water is absolutely necessary. Among the multitudes of ammonites discovered in the lias, I have often observed individuals, of which the large terminating chamber of the last whorl, where the body of the animal seems to have been placed, was hollow for half its distance upwards towards the aperture or mouth, as if the animal, when overwhelmed, had retreated as far as possible into this part of the shell, so that the muddy water was prevented from completely filling it. This idea is rendered more probable from the condition of the calcareous matter filling the remaining part of the great cavity which is exceedingly bituminous, as would happen from the decomposition of the animal within the remainder of the chamber."* "It may be remarked that the destruction of the animals whose remains are known to us by the name of Belemnites, was exceedingly great at this place. When the *upper part* of the lias was deposited, multitudes seem to have perished simultaneously, as is attested by a bed composed of little else, beneath Golden Cap, a cliff between Lyme Regis and Bridport harbor. Not only are millions entombed in this bed, but in the *upper part* of the lias generally."†

These fossil remains, although occurring in great abundance at Lyme Regis, are not confined to that locality. They have also been found in several places on the continent, especially at Wurtemburg. Annexed is a skeleton of the Ichthyosaurus, as restored by Mr. Conybeare.

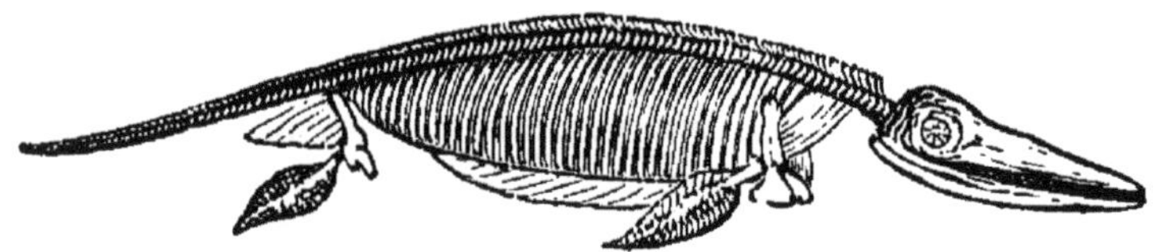

* Geological Manual, p. 346. † Ibid.

Dr. Buckland discovered some bones of a gigantic animal in the quarry of Stonesfield, near Woodstock, in Oxfordshire. They were examined by Cuvier, who declared them to belong to an animal measuring forty feet in length, and having a bulk equal to that of an elephant seven feet high. The numerous interesting and remarkable fossil remains of the oolite group have been treated of largely in different geological works; but our limits will not permit us to enter into a detailed account of them.

The following synopsis, by Professor Phillips, is extracted from the Encyl. Metrop., p. 653:—

| | | | |
|---|---|---|---|
| *Plants* | Marine | 4 | In limestone chiefly. |
| | Terrestrial Cyptogamous | 39 | In sandstones and shales chiefly. |
| | Monocotyledenous | 33 | |
| | Gymnospermous uncertain | 4 | |
| *Polyparia* | Fibrous | 75 | Chiefly in the limestones, but rarely in the lias. |
| | Corticiferous and Celluciferous | 44 | |
| | Lamelliferous | 59 | |
| *Radiaria* | Crinoidea | 31 | Chiefly in the limestones, rarely in the lias. |
| | Stellerida | 17 | |
| | Echinida | 47 | |
| *Conchifera* | Plagimyona | 189 | |
| | Mesamyona | 134 | |
| | Brachiopoda | 61 | |
| *Mollusca* | Gasteropoda | 114 | |
| | Cephalopoda | 273 | |
| | Annulosa | 55 | |
| | Crustacea | 22 | Chiefly astacidæ. |
| | Insects | 20 | Solenhofin & Stonefield. |
| | Fishes | 40 | |
| | Reptiles | 40 | |
| | Mammalia | 2 or 3 | Only in the lower Oolite formation at Stonesfield. |

Now, whence came the material of which the vast accumulation of the rocks of the oolite group are composed? From the wasted material of older rocks, say the geologists. "May we venture to suppose," says Professor Phillips, "that the primary tracts of the Scandinavian peninsula and Scotland, with other land, now sunk beneath the German ocean, has been the source of most of the arenaceous and argillaceous deposits of the carboniferous oolite, and wealden formations of England? In this point of view, the local strata of Brora, the thick coal series of Bornholm, the oolitic coral tracts of Yorkshire and Westphalia, the wealden of Boulogne, Beauvais, Sussex, Dorset, Wilts, are all partial and local deposits, due to a similar succession of causes, and arising from the same or neighboring physical regions, as the materials of some of the older coal strata. In Bornholm, coal occurs with marine beds of all geological ages, from the transition era to the cretaceous group; and the dependence of its deposits on the waste of the Scandinavian mountains is decided. The dependence of the other deposits on the waste of land in the north, is a probable inference; and if we imagine, what is probably true, that the Scottish and Scandinavian coasts were once united, the whole of the phenomena are as intelligible as varied deposits on the shore of one limited sea."

The only weight that can be attached to this argument is derived from the coal and marine beds of Bornholm; and, after all, it is neither "intelligible" nor satisfactory. Let us hear what another geologist says in reference to the derivation of the materials of which the oolite rocks are formed. "Still," says De La Beche, "the question whence all this great mass of carbonate of lime was derived remains unanswered. To attempt to account for it by means of springs, neither more numerous nor abundant than those we now see, seems quite unphilosophical; and to consider it entirely due to animals which have separated lime from the water, leaving their shells, produced through *millions of ages*, to be gradually converted into limestone, appears also a cause inadequate to the effect required, though it cannot be denied that the mass of many limestones is nearly made up of organic remains. With every allowance for the limestone deposits of the oolite series, formed by springs and organic bodies, there remains a mass of calcareous matter to be accounted for, distributed generally over a large surface, which requires a very general production or rather deposit, of carbonate of lime, cotemporaneously, or nearly so, over a great area." * Even if we should grant that the material of the oolite group had been derived from the older rocks, which would be granting a great deal more than has been proved,—indeed it would be allowing a proposition which is

* Geological Manual, p. 387.

at variance with many geological facts,—yet, granting even this, the phenomena could not be rationally accounted for by the hypothesis. No stream or current of which we have any knowledge, could have distributed the matter over the surface of the earth in the extensive manner in which it is found in the sandstone, clays, and limestone of the oolite group.

CHALK GROUP.

| | | |
|---|---|---|
| Wealden Formation. | Wealden clay.<br>Hastings sands.<br>Purbeck beds.<br>Portland dirt bed. | OOLITE GROUP. |
| Upper Oolite Formation. | Portland oolite.<br>Calcareous sands.<br>Kimmeridge clay. | |
| Middle Oolite Formation. | Upper calcareous grit.<br>Coral rag.<br>Lower calcareous grit.<br>Oxford clay.<br>Cornbrash: clayey limestone. | |
| Lower Oolite Formation. | Upper sandstone, shale, and coal.<br>Bath oolites, or great oolite.<br>Lower sandstone, shale and coal.<br>Inferior oolite, ferruginous. | |
| Lias Formation. | Upper lias shales.<br>Marlstone stone beds.<br>Middle lias shales.<br>Lias limestone.<br>Lower lias shals. | |

Red Marl, or New Red Sandstone Group.

Red Marl, or New Red Sandstone Group.—This group (by some authors named also the *saliferous group*, from containing extensive beds of rock-salt, one of which is in Cheshire), is one of very considerable thickness, and appears at the surface in different localities over a considerable portion of the earth. It shows itself in England upon a very extensive scale, and is also seen in Ireland, Scotland, and Wales. But on the continent of Europe, especially in Germany, it is traced over areas of enormous extent. It is seen all around the Hartz, and among the primary ranges of the Alps. It stretches from the vale of the Danube, by Rottenhann and Radstadt, to near Innspruck. It is seen in the West India Islands, and on the new continent extends from Mexico far into the heart of North America.

In this group, as well as the others, we have alternations of marls, sandstones, limestones; the sandstones and marls, however, greatly predominating: hence the name *Red Marl*, or *Sandstone* group. The rocks are clearly distinguishable from those of the oolite group above, as also from the coal group below. The great difference exhibited both in the chemical and mechanical rocks of this group, as compared with those of the oolitic group above, prove incontestably that the two groups must have been formed under circumstances as widely different as the differences manifested in the mineral composition of the rocks themselves. But if the difference of the mineral composition be striking, that of the fossil remains is much more so. In the oolitic rocks, the species of fossils are much more numerous, and the remains abundant. In the red marl group the conditions are reversed; the fossil species are few, and the remains rarely met with. In this group certain fossil fishes of genus Paleoniscus appear for the last time, and for the first time the remains of oviparous animals begin to appear. Hence the red marl group is considered to hold a kind of middle position, as regards the gradual rise and development of animal life upon the face of the earth.

In the oolitic group above, this development of animal life appears upon a magnificent scale; and in the coal group below, vegetable life has been unfolded to an extent of luxuriance which has never been seen upon the face of the earth since that time; whilst in the intermediate red marl group the evidence of the existence of life, both vegetable and animal, is of the most meagre kind. How is this great hiatus in the scale of geological series to be accounted for? Neither volcanoes, nor earthquakes, nor internal forces of any description could have caused so wide a distinction as that observed, in respect to fossil remains as well as mineral composition, between these rocks and those which immediately precede and follow them in the series. In the copper-slate, near the bottom of the group, a certain genus of fishes, named Paleothrissum, and also marine vegetables, are found entire, not in scattered portions, proving that they must have been buried alive, by which their decomposition has been prevented.

The extensive deposits of rock-salt contained in the red marly group is worthy of consideration, although they are not peculiar to this group, as was formerly imagined.—They are found in the county of Chester, in a tract not much raised above the level of the sea; in the Carpathian mountains, at a considerable higher elevation; in Wurtemberg and central Germany; and at Bex, in an ancient valley above the lake of Geneva, it is found at an elevation of more than a thousand feet above the present level of the sea. The question is, how were these beds formed? If we turn to the Caspian sea, and suppose that the different rivers which pour into that basin were by any cause or impediment to have their channels choked up, and were thus compelled to take another course, as towards the Mediterranean and Red sea, we seem to have all the conditions that are requisite for the formation of a bed of rock-salt. For, as the evaporation from the surface would certainly go on, and as we have every reason to presume that the bottom is not a level, but is covered with hill and valley like the dry land, as the evaporation proceeded, the liquid brine would continually subside into the valleys or lower level, carrying the whole, or nearly the whole of the salt with it in solution, and thus a bed of some extent and thickness would be formed in the lowest part of the Caspian basin. And yet it seems scarcely possible, even if the whole of the waters of the Caspian were evaporated, and the deposit left in one small valley, that a bed of salt could be formed equal in thickness to those of Cheshire; and these are by no means the thickest known. "The Cheshire deposits of salt lie along the line of the valley of the river Weaver, in small patches, about Northwich. There are two beds of rock-salt lying beneath forty yards of colored marls, in which no traces of animal or vegetable fossils occur. The upper bed of salt is twenty-five yards thick; it is separated from the lower one by ten and a half yards of colored marls, similar to the general cover; and the lower bed of salt is thirty-five yards thick, but has no where been perforated. Whether any other beds lie beneath these two, is at present unknown. *They lie horizontal, or nearly so, and both beds of salt are below the level of the sea.* They extend into an irregularly oval area, in length one mile and a half, in breadth about 1,300 yards, ranging from N. E. to S. W."*

Dr. Holland supposes that the salt beds of Cheshire have been formed by repeated inroads of the neighboring Irish sea, by the alternate depression and upheaving of the intervening land. This supposition is wholly gratuitous; besides which, it will not account for the formation of salt beds far from the ocean, and those which are situated a thousand feet and upwards above the present level of the sea.

Although the period of the formation of the red marl group is, geologically speaking, one of comparative repose, yet, we can trace effects for which, in the present state of things, we look around us in vain with a view to discern adequate causes.

The following section will exhibit the state in which they are found in some places:—*a* fractured limestone; *b* beds of fine conglomerate sandstone and red marl; *c* red conglomerate, extending many miles; *f* a fault, or dislocation of the strata:—

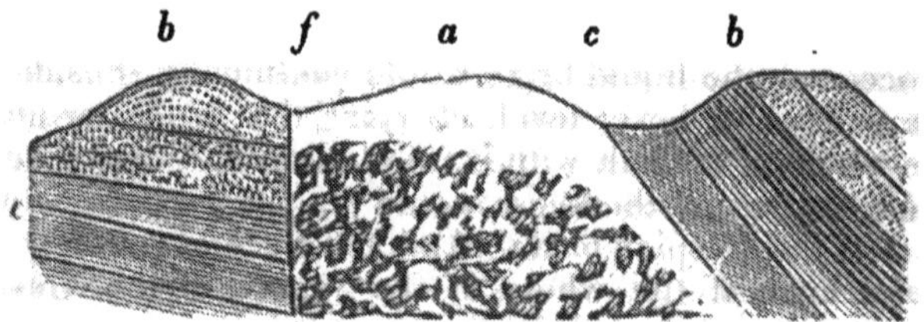


*Petit Tor, Babbacombe Bay, Devon.*

OOLITE GROUP.

| | | |
|---|---|---|
| *Red Sandstone Formation.* | Variegated Marls.<br>Lamillated Clays, or Marls with Salt beds.<br>Muschelkalk.—*German.*<br>Variegated Sandstones. | RED MARL GROUP. |
| *Magnesian Limestone Formation.* | Upper Limestone<br>Gypseous Marls.<br>Magnesian Limestone.<br>Copper or Marl Slate.<br>Lower Red Sandstone. | |

COAL GROUP.

* Phillips in Lardner's Cyclopædia.

Coal Group.—Coal is a well known mineral deposit. It is found extensively in this country; and from this circumstance England derives, in a great degree, her ascendency over the neighboring nations, both in a commercial and political point of view. This deposit, drawn from the deep caverns of the earth, in which it has for ages been buried up, by actuating that beautiful and stupendous instrument of power, the steam engine, sets in motion those millions of wheels and spindles which supply the food of our extended commerce. Applied to the locomotive, it enables us, on the railway, to sweep over the surface of the earth at an immense velocity; and, mining engines, by drawing water from the mines, it even aids in its own excavation. Coal is, therefore, in every point of view, an object of interest. At present we have to inquire concerning its origin and manner of formation. Coal is of vegetable origin. The following analysis, by Dr. Thomson, will show its chemical composition:—

| *Carbon.* | *Hydrogen.* | *Oxygen.* | *Nitrogen.* |
|---|---|---|---|
| NEWCASTLE CAKING COAL. | | | |
| 75.28 | 4.18 | 4.58 | 15.96 |
| GLASGOW SPLINT COAL. | | | |
| 75.00 | 6.25 | 12.50 | 6.25 |
| GLASGOW CHERRY COAL. | | | |
| 74.45 | 12.40 | 2.93 | 10.22 |
| CANNEL COAL. | | | |
| 64.72 | 21.56 | 0.00 | 15.72 |

From the above analysis, as well as from other circumstances, we are assured that a bed of coal is nothing else than a compressed mass of vegetable matter, which must have been produced upon the surface, by the action of the solar and atmospheric influences, in the ordinary way. These vegetables could not have grown beneath a superincumbent mass of solid rocks, ten hundred feet thick; neither has the matter passed through the animal kingdom, for it is still vegetable matter.

The question then, is, how has it been produced; and by what circumstances has it been preserved from those countless myriads of little animated creatures, which, on the land, as the coral insects in the ocean, are ever ready to seize the smallest particle of vegetable matter, and pass it onward to the mineral kingdom, the *action* accompanying which transportation constitutes the very essence of their animal life? In this action they live, move, and have their being; and the moment the action of transformation ceases, then life, motion, and existence, as animated beings, are at an end. But the matter of which the coal deposits are composed, has never, in this planet at least, ministered to the action of animal life. The matter has passed onward as far as the *circuit of motion* of the vegetable kingdom, and there its progress has been arrested.

Can we turn to any analagous process going on upon the surface of the earth at the present day, which will throw a light upon the origin and manner of formation of the coal beds? The peat-bogs of Ireland, Chat-moss in Lancashire, with similar *land* formations in other countries, will perhaps enable us to come to some conclusion with respect to the manner of formation of the coal beds; bearing in mind that the temperature of the earth, the activity of vegetation, and several other circumstances are considerably changed since the period of the formation of the coal beds; that the rich and luxuriant vegetation of that period no longer exists any where upon the earth, not even within the tropics; that the species of plants of which the coal strata are composed are all extinct — all have passed away, and, at the present day, we have upon the surface of the earth a new creation, both of the vegetable and animal kingdoms.

In a peat-bog we find a short "brush" of vegetation covering the surface. It is, however, in those parts only which are immediately exposed to the influence of the sun and atmosphere, that any signs of freshness are exhibited. The under portions which are screened from those influences appear dead, dried, and withered, are crumbling from the stem, falling upon, and adding to the surface of the bog below. This seems a slow process; and yet by these apparently humble means, great depths of peat-bog may be formed in the course of ages. Several feet in thickness are thus accumulated in the comparitively short space of a century. In Ireland, as well as in some other countries, there are large tracts of peat-bogs, having in some places, a thickness of thirty and forty feet, which, if buried for a series of ages beneath a mass of solid rock, would, in its then compressed state, furnish a seam of coal of considerable thickness. This transformation of peat into coal, is now attempted to be accomplished by art. Powerful presses are employed, one of which is the invention of Lord Willoughby, into which the wet soft peat is placed in pieces, about as large as a common brick. The pressure being applied, the moisture is expelled, and the compressed peat, on being withdrawn, is found to be nearly as solid as a piece of coal, and may be used as a substitute for coal in many processes in which it could not be applied in its ordinary or uncompressed condition. A seam of coal is then nothing else than an ancient peat-bog, which has been formed upon the surface in a manner somewhat similar to that which may be seen at the present day; after its formation it has been buried up by some means, and has been for a long series of ages subjected to an immense pressure. Such is the view of De Luc, Brongniart, and many other eminent geological writers.

But, if it be a general law that the mass of the vegetable productions pass through the animal kingdom, and is thus carried onward to the mineral world, especially by the agency of innumerable worms existing in the soil, by what circumstances are those peat-bogs preserved in their vegetable condition, thus forming an exception to the general rule? That they are preserved, is simply a fact. A peat-bog and a bed of coal are, both of them, vegetable remains; the latter has been compressed, the former is still in a soft state, and this, it appears, constitutes almost the only difference between the two. Roots and stubble in arable land, which is comparatively dry or merely moist, are soon devoured by the worms and grubs, and the vegetable matter which they consume is voided in the form of vegetable mould. The soil being moist, that is, strictly speaking, neither wet nor dry, seems congenial to their nature, and consequently, in such situations, they exist in myriads; they pervade the soil as the locusts cover the surface of the countries of the East, and every particle of vegetable matter is appropriated. But in peat-bogs we have a different combination of circumstances. A bog is a swamp; not merely moist, but overcharged with wet. Such a condition is unfavorable to animal life; but, besides this unfavorable degree of moisture, the liquid of a bog is not of the bland nature of rain water: it is highly charged with resinous, oily, and other matter, which appear to exercise a very pernicious influence on animal life. By these, and probably other, circumstances, peat-bogs, and their predecessors, the coal beds, have been preserved in the vegetable state to this day.

Some geologists have been of opinion that the coal beds have been formed from timber which has been drifted down rivers into the sea, and deposited in hollow basins on the bottom, and that these collections of vegetable matter have been subsequently carried up by the drifting of the sands, &c.; but this hypothesis, besides being very clumsy is not borne out by the evidence.

The coal formation attains in many places to a thickness of a thousand yards, and is chiefly composed of six kinds of rocks; sandstones, limestones, and clays, form the principal mass, interstratified with which is found coal, ironstone, and chert. The following arrangement of the New Castle coal field, by Mr. Westgarth Forster, in which the coal beds are distinguished from the rocks with which they are associated, will give a tolerably correct idea of the alternations which are found in the coal formation:—

| | *yds.* | *ft.* | *in.* |
|---|---|---|---|
| Brown post, or Grindstone sill | 24 | 0 | 0 |
| Coal - - - | 0 | 0 | 6 |
| Rock measures - - | 10 | 0 | 0 |
| Coal - - - | 0 | 0 | 8 |
| Rock measures - - | 22 | 0 | 0 |
| Coal - - - | 0 | 0 | 6 |
| Rock measures - - | 15 | 2 | 6 |
| Coal - - - | 0 | 1 | 0 |
| Rock measures - - | 11 | 1 | 0 |
| Coal - - - | 0 | 0 | 0 |
| Rock measures - - | 7 | 1 | 0 |
| Coal - - - | 0 | 0 | 8 |
| Rock measures - - | 6 | 1 | 0 |
| Coal - - - | 0 | 0 | 8 |
| Rock measures - - | 19 | 1 | 0 |
| Coal - - - | 0 | 1 | 0 |
| Rock measures - - | 16 | 0 | 0 |
| Coal (high main) - - | 2 | 0 | 0 |
| Rock measures - - | 11 | 0 | 0 |
| Coal (metal coal) - - | 1 | 7 | 0 |
| Rock measures - - | 10 | 1 | 2 |
| Coal (stone coal) - - | 0 | 1 | 2 |
| Rock measures - - | 19 | 0 | 7 |
| Coal (yard coal) - - | 1 | 0 | 0 |
| Rock measures - - | 7 | 1 | 3 |
| Coal - - - | 0 | 0 | 6 |
| Rock measures - - | 18 | 0 | 11 |
| Coal (Bensham) - - | 1 | 0 | 3 |
| Rock measures - - | 26 | 0 | 6 |
| Coal - - - | 1 | 0 | 6 |

| | | | |
|---|---|---|---|
| Rock measures - - | 9 | 1 | 10 |
| Coal - - - | 1 | 0 | 2 |
| Rock measures - - | 1 | 1 | 0 |
| Coal - - - | 0 | 0 | 9 |
| Rock measures - - | 9 | 2 | 9 |
| Coal (low main) - - | 2 | 0 | 6 |
| Rock measures - - | 27 | 0 | 0 |
| Coal - - - | 0 | 1 | 6 |
| Rock measures - - | 15 | 0 | 0 |
| Coal - - - | 0 | 0 | 0 |
| Rock measures - - | 6 | 0 | 0 |
| Coal - - - | 0 | 0 | 2 |
| Rock measures - - | 10 | 0 | 0 |
| Coal - - - | 0 | 0 | 6 |
| Rock measures - - | 4 | 0 | 0 |
| Coal - - - | 0 | 0 | 6 |
| Rock measures - - | 12 | 0 | 0 |
| Coal (Whickham St.) - | 2 | 0 | 0 |
| Rock measures - - | 10 | 0 | 0 |
| Coal (Brockwell) - - | 1 | 0 | 2 |
| Various rock measures - | 50 | 2 | 0 |
| Millstone grit - - | | | |
| Total, | *yds.* | *ft.* | *in.* |
| Rock measures | 380 | 0 | 6 |
| Coal seams | 15 | 2 | 3 |

The above table will give a very good general idea of the arrangement and thickness of the different coal seams and the intermediate rock measures. It must not, however, be supposed that every seam continues throughout of the same unvarying thickness; on the contrary, the variations are considerable. A good seam will sometimes thin down to a few inches, and in other places will swell out to a great thickness.

But that which more particularly demands our attention is the great number of coal seams. Here we have twenty-five, and in some places there have been found as many as sixty. How were they formed? There cannot be a doubt that the coal beds are land formations, for they consist of the remains of land plants; at the same time, it is clear that the associated limestones were formed in the bottom of the sea, for they contain marine shells in considerable quantity. "In most coal districts," says Professor Phillips, "there are from twenty to sixty seams of coal, alternating with sandy and argillaceous strata, for each series of which, (coal, sandstone, shale,) the land must have been raised, decomposed to soil, covered by forests or peat, and then again submerged to receive sediments from the land or littoral agitation; and *these numerous risings and fallings of the bed of the sea have left no independent proof of their occurrence.*"

That the surface was covered and uncovered by the sea sixty times during the formation of the coal beds, is certain; that during that long period no disturbance of the crust occurred, is also certain; and that *after* the formation of the *whole series* a tremendous concussion was experienced, by which the whole was broken at once, is evident, — not in one place only, but the entire mass has been shattered in a thousand places; as the following section of the Jarrow colliery, near Newcastle, will witness.

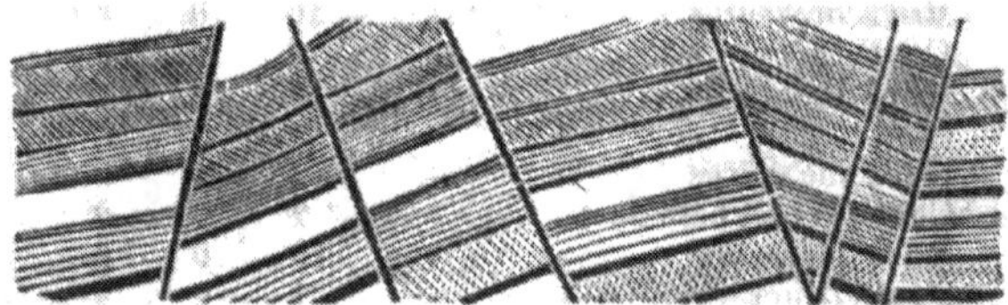

This is a very instructive section. The faults, or lines of dislocation, run continuously throughout the whole formation, proving that the concussion, whatever it was, acted at once. The lines of stratification correspond in every part of the broken mass, thereby proving that during the period of their formation no disturbance of any kind took place; so that, throughout a long period, in which a mass of rocks a thousand yards in thickness were forming, probably many millions of years, there was a state of repose on this earth, such as we now witness; and at the close of that period, there was a violent shock, of such intensity as to shatter that mass into many thousand fragments. There is no force in this earth, of which we have, or ever had, any knowledge, competent to produce effects upon a scale so stupendous as that before us; and even if we were to grant the existence of such a force *within the earth*, it must have slept in perfect repose for many ages, and at length having awakened, like a giant from his sleep, and having exerted its energy with a momentary and tremendous effort, have again sunk into a long and silent repose. Such suppositions are wholly inconsistent with all that we know of terrestrial forces. If we would satisfactorily unravel the mystery, we must turn to the heavens, recollecting the now well-established fact, that the moon is at this moment approaching the earth; and, as will be shown hereafter, that the earth, under the influence of the same law, is also approaching the sun.

One circumstance connected with the vegetation of this early period, deserves to be noticed. The plants required a very hot climate for their growth. Fossil plants have been found in the far north freezing latitude of Melville Island, in North America, which required for their growth a temperature so high, that it is questionable whether they could be reared in the hottest parts of the earth at the present day. This seems to militate with the opinion of the gradual approach of the earth to the sun. If heat and light came *directly* from the sun, the approach of the earth towards the heating body, with at the same time, a decreasing temperature, would be a manifest paradox. But it has been shown, that heat and light are in every case the effects of action; that those sensible manifestations which we call solar heat and light are not emanations of luminous and calorific matter, for beyond the atmosphere of the earth and other planets, neither light nor heat can be discerned; that that which we call solar light, is, more correctly, terrestrial light, for it is an effect of a specific action going on in the atmosphere of the earth; that this light is, notwithstanding, *indirectly* derived from the sun, for the continuance of the atmospheric action is dependent upon a continuous supply of the solar fluid, as the continuance of the *action* of ordinary combustion, by which heat and light are made manifest, is dependent upon a continuous supply of oxygen gas; and, as in every case the intensity of the heat and light is proportionate to the intensity of action, we conclude that at an early period, when the earth was young, less solid, more gaseous, the intensity of the terrestrial action was greater, and, as a consequence, the vegetation more luxuriant, notwithstanding the greater distance of the earth from the sun, the *indirect* source of light and heat.

In the animal kingdom we find a close analogy. The child's body is warmer, of a higher temperature, than the aged. Why? Is it because the infant is nearer to the sun? The very question is ridiculous. No; but the infant, the newly formed being, begins its existence as that of the world or any other planet began, *in a liquid state*. When it emerges from its hidden abode, it is still but a juicy mass; the bones are soft; the muscles are pulpy and full of juice; the circulation is rapid; the internal action is intense, and the temperature of the infant is in the same proportion high. As age creeps on, the action, and, consequently, the temperature of the animal, decreases; the bones become hard, like the rocks of the earth; the muscles become ossified, like indurated clay; the juices become scanty; the ossified muscles cease to be excited, or to act; the circulation becomes languid; the gradual solidification of the animal organization, which has been going on from the first instant of its existence as an independent being, is near its completion; the process must at length come to a termination;—solid, cold, and inactive, the machine stops. And in all this we see but a model of that which has been going on in the earth herself for ages,—is now going on, and will continue for many ages yet to come.

Beneath the coal measures is the *Mountain Limestone*, or, as it is sometimes called, the *Carboniferous Limestone*. It is a marine formation. In some places the shells are so abundant, that the rock appears to be entirely composed of them. It is a compact limestone, and affords good marble. Veins of led ore, beds of coal, shale, and sandstone have been found in it, on which account it is generally accounted a lower portion of the coal group. It is of great thickness, and occupies a large extent of surface.

Beneath the mountain limestone, comes the *Old Red Sandstone*, also of great thickness and extent. Few organic remains are found in this rock, and those observed appear to belong to the same species as those in the mountain limestone above, and in the grauwacke beneath. This rock is also referred to the carboniferous system; the three formations,—the old red sandstone, the mountain limestone, and the coal measures, forming together a mass of rocks many thousand feet in thickness.

GRAUWACKE GROUP.—The grauwacke rocks are generally considered the oldest of the secondary series, although there is little propriety in the usual distinction between the secondary and primary. The mineral composition of the rocks is the same, but in the grauwacke, the remains of animals and vegetables appear for the last time in the descending series; in the primary rocks no traces of fossil remains are discerned, and on this circumstance the distinction between secondary and primary is founded, although, as some geologists think, and with good reason, we are not justified in coming to the conclusion, that no animal or vegetable life existed upon the earth during the formation of the primary rocks, because their fossil remains are not now discernable; all analogy leads us to the contrary conclusion. The grauwacke group consists of hard, slaty, crystalline rocks; indeed, as a general principle, the older rocks are, as might be anticipated, the hardest and most compact. Those rocks are the hardest in which the indurating process has been longest in action; so that the same mineral substances which are found in the tertiary and upper portions of the secondary, in the condition of soft clay, loose sand, and chalk, in the older rocks exist in a highly crystalline state, in the condition of hard clay-slates, compact sandstones, and marbles.

"It is by no means an uncommon circumstance," observes De La Beche, "for the laminæ of the slates of this group to be so arranged as to form various angles with other lines, which may be considered as those of the beds, or of stratification. Of this structure the annexed section of grauwacke slates, at Bovey Sand Bay, on the east side of Plymouth Sound, affords us an instructive example:—

"*a a* curved beds of slate, the laminæ of which meet the *apparent lines* of stratification at various angles, being even perpendicular to them. The beds are cut off by the fault (*f*) from the slates *c*, the laminæ of which are more confusedly disposed, having however a general horizontal arrangement. The whole is covered by a detritus (*b b*,) composed of fragments of the same kind of slate as that on which it reposes, and of the various grauwacke rocks of the hill behind."

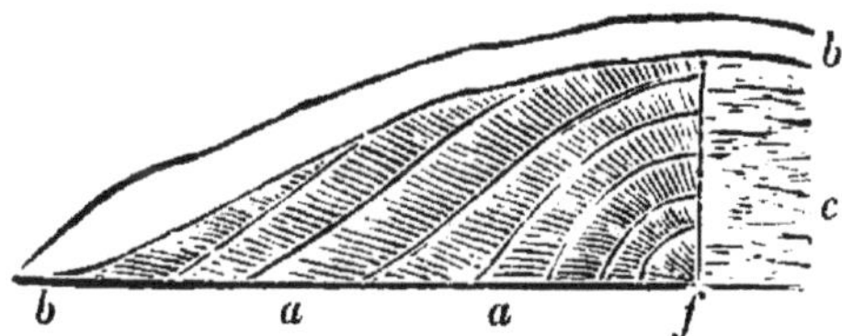


Here the ancient lines of stratification becomes less distinct. The laminated, slaty, and crystalline texture becomes more apparent. It may perhaps be regarded as a kind of transition state from the stratified to the unstratified and still older rocks.

Whence came the materials of which the rocks of this group were formed, — consisting as they do of the usual mineral characters of sandstone, limestones, and clays, or rather clay-slates, although not in the layers so clearly distinguished from each other as in the newer rocks of the secondary and tertiary systems? The materials are more or less intermingled; but still the same calcareous, arenaceous, and argillaceous constituents are clearly discernable. Geologists have recourse to their usual mode, viz., that they were derived from the wasted materials of older rocks. De La Beche, in examining the mineral structure of the grauwacke, and alluding to some of the difficulties which present themselves, in respect to this mode of derivation, has the following pertinent remarks:—

"The origin of the limestones is of far more difficult explanation than the sandstones and slates in which they are included. We cannot well seek it in the destruction of pre-existing calcareous rocks; for, as far as our knowledge extends, such rocks are of comparative rarity among the older strata. In fact, the quantity of calcareous matter, present in the grauwacke group, greatly exceeds that discovered in the older rocks; and the same remark applies to many of the newer deposits when considered with reference to the grauwacke series. If we take the mass of deposits up to the chalk inclusive, we shall find that, instead of a decrease of carbonate of lime, such as we should expect if that contained in each deposit originated solely from the destruction of pre-existing limestones, the calcareous matter is more abundant in the upper than in the lower parts of the mass; and we may hence conclude that this explanation is insufficient."

"If, as has often been done with other limestones, we attribute the origin of the grauwacke limestones in a great measure to the exuviæ of testaceous animals and polypifers, we must grant the animals carbonate of lime with which to constitute their shells and solid habitations. This they may have obtained either in their food or from the medium in which they existed. The marine vegetables are not likely to have supplied them with a greater abundance of carbonate of lime at that time than at present. Those that were carnivorous might acquire much carbonate of lime by devouring other animals more or less possessed of this substance; but the difficulty is by no means lessened by this explanation; for the creatures devoured must have procured the lime somewhere. It would appear that we should look to the medium in which testaceous animals and polypifers existed, for the greater proportion, if not all, of the carbonate of lime with which they constructed their shells and habitations. Now if we consider the mass of limestone rocks to have originated from the exuviæ of marine animals, we are called upon to consider that carbonate of lime was once far more abundant in the sea than we now find it, and that it has been gradually deprived of it. This supposition would lead us to expect, that as the sea was gradually deprived of its carbonate of lime, limestone deposits would become less and less abundant; and consequently, that calcareous rocks would be most common, when circumstances were most favorable, that is to say, during the formation of the older rocks. This, however, is precisely the reverse of what has happened. Hence we may infer that the origin of the mass of limestone deposits must be sought otherwise than in the attrition or solution of older and stratified rocks, or from the exuviæ of marine animals deriving their solid parts from a sea which has gradually been deprived of nearly all its carbonate of lime. Both these causes may have eventually produced important modifications on the surface of the earth; but the great proportion of lime necessary for the formation of calcareous masses covering a considerable part of it, would appear to have been otherwise obtained."

"It has been usual to consider the lime of the calcareous deposits as derived from limestone rocks through which waters charged with carbonic acid percolated, the cabonic acid dissolving a certain portion of lime, which is thus held in solution by the water until it reaches the surface, where it is thrown down in the shape of limestone. This explanation may suffice for the small deposits we observe in calcareous countries; but is insufficient for the production of limestones generally; for it assumes that the solution of a small quantity of lime obtained from older rocks is, as previously noticed, capable of producing an immense deposit of the same substance."

If the reader will attentively consider the above observations, he will perceive that in reference to the origin of the rocks which now constitute the solid crust of the earth, in whichever way we turn we meet with an insuperable difficulty from which there is no escape; but by considering that the list of chemical elements, commonly considered simple substances, are not, in fact, elementary, but that, by that mysterious process, called vital action, in the vegetable, animal, and mineral kingdoms, every substance becomes so modified and changed, that after having passed through a chain of processes, as vegetable, animal, and mineral, with the intermediate links, it appears to our apprehension to consist of a combination of entirely new elements. It is true, as Professor Phillips justly observes, that "the nature of matter, in the abstract sense, is not given to man to know." But we can observe the changing forms as they pass before us, and that observation leads us to the conclusion, that the solid rocks of a globe, originally fluid, have been formed in the long succession of ages, by passing through the respective vital processes of vegetable, animal, and mineral kingdoms; and that the same process is now in action, as every one may satisfy himself who will be at the trouble to observe the varied phenomena passing around him.

The following is the shell of an animal called a Trilobite, from the shell consisting of three lobes. It is one of the oldest animals whose remains have been found in the earth. If the reader should be startled at being told that this animal lived and died many millions of years ago, he must be reminded that his surprise arises from his ignorance of the geological evidence by which such assertion is supported.

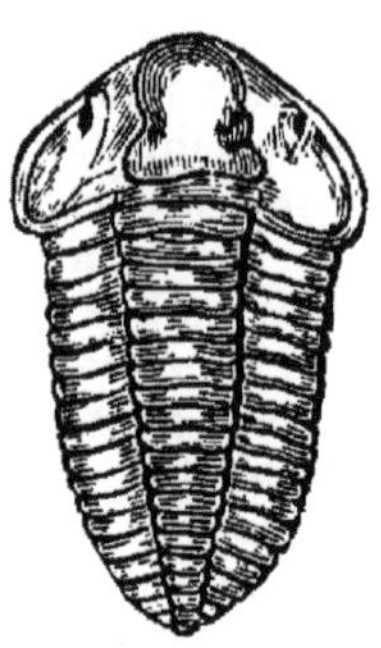

Primary Strata; or, Gneiss and Mica Schist System.—The primary are the oldest and the lowest of the stratified rocks, and, as has already been remarked, contain no organic remains. They are hard and crystalline, lying in immediate contact with the granite floor which supports the whole of the stratified rocks. The following section will convey an idea of the order and manner of superposition:—

The mineral composition of the primary strata is the same as that of all the others; that is, they are composed of calcareous, arenaceous, and argillaceous deposits, more or less intermingled. The principal question, then, is, from what source were the materials derived?

Let us hear what Professor Phillips says, bearing in mind the observations of De La Beche already quoted, with respect to the derivation of the limestones of the grauwacke group:—"If we seek to ascertain the origin of the materials of the oldest or lowest of all the known systems of strata, and take characteristic specimens of gneiss and mica schist for the purpose, we shall be struck with the great resemblance they offer to granite, in the kind, proportionate abundance, and admixture, even color and aspect, of the constituent quartz, felspar, mica, hornblende, &c. So close is the resemblance, that some writers appear disposed to allow for these stratified granitoid rocks, an origin not very distinct from the igneous origin of granite; but careful attention discloses points of disagreement, which are equally important, and tend to a different opinion. Let any one, for example, compare in well-characterized granite and gneiss, the constituents felspar and mica; in granite these are always perfectly crystallized within, and have regular external geometrical figures; in gneiss the external crystallization remains, but the felspar is rounded like sand, or small pebbles, or fragmented like a broken crystal, and the mica is bent and contorted by irregular pressure among the felspar and quartz. Add to these circumstances the lamination of the masses, and we see clearly that the ingredients of gneiss and mica schist resemble granite, because they have been derived from granite rocks; but they differ because they were accumulated under the mechanical influence of water, and not aggregated by chemical forces from a state of fusion."

After some further remarks upon the mineral composition of gneiss, mica schist, chlorite schist, and hornblende schist; of the relative magnitude of the constituent grains; of the laminated structure; and of the general analogies by which the primary group is connected with the stratified rocks above and the unstratified beneath, he proceeds:—

"In this state these silicious rocks become very similar to certain argillaceous slates, which, in fact, in some cases, seem to bear exactly the same relation to gneiss, mica schist, &c., that common clays do to common sandstones: there is every gradation between them; their origin is undoubtedly similar, it may even be called the same; since one land flood or sea storm will form both stratified sands and laminated clays from the same wasted land or cliff, according merely to the difference of circumstances under which the materials are accumulated. Now it is impossible to doubt that clay-slates and grauwacke-slates have been deposited in water; it is equally certain that the gneiss and other felspathic or quartoze rocks, which are associated with it, and occasionally with clay-slate, are also of igneous production; and the composition of gneiss, &c., completes the evidence wanted to prove that the primary strata, analogous to sandstones and clays, were formed from the waste of granitic rocks."

The principal, almost the only, consideration to which this argument is entitled, is derived from the similarity of the mineral composition of the primary strata and of the unstratified granite; but it also appears that there is a similarity of mineral composition upwards as well as downwards,—in short, that this similarity of mineral composition runs throughout the entire series of rocks, stratified and unstratified, of which the solid crust of the earth is composed. That all those rocks, unstratified as well as stratified, have been successively formed in the long course of ages, is beyond a doubt. That solid matter on land, and calcareous rocks in the ocean are now forming, is unquestionable. That the upper rock must have been formed subsequently to that upon which it rests, will not be disputed. And if the earth were originally a liquid, (not by igneous fusion—the supposition of an *entire* earth in a vacuum, in a state of igneous fusion, is nonsense), then it was required that the process of solidification should begin somehow. If we find that by the vital action of the vegetable and animal kingdoms, liquid matter is continually being transformed into solid matter both upon the earth and in the ocean; if we find that the stratified rocks contain within themselves evidence that they also have been formed in a like manner; and if we take this further fact into our consideration, that a specific process which we do not hesitate to pronounce vital action, is also going on in the mineral or crystalline kingdoms, as noticed by Sir David Brewster, (see p. 185), we have before us the chief links of that chain of process, by which a globe, originally liquid, has been for millions of years, and is now, passing onward to the state of a solid world, without the clumsy expedient of breaking up one rock to form another.

It is true that gneiss and other primary rocks bear a close resemblance to granite; it is also true, as has been well shown by Mr. Lyell, that the one set of rocks are transformed into the other. But the process is in the opposite direction to that supposed by Professor Phillips. It is not the transformation of granite into primary rocks, but of primary rocks into granite. The process being viewed in the latter direction, every thing becomes consistent: all the stratified rocks are slowly passing onward to the crystalline or granite form, whilst new strata are constantly forming on the upper surface; and there is nothing unphilosophical in the assumption that the time will arrive when the entire globe will be nothing else than one huge crystalline mass, penetrated in every direction by rich metallic veins. The metal will be abundant in the earth, but there will be no human beings to dispute about its possession.

Mr. Lyell's views concerning the transmutation of rocks may be shortly stated. He considers, and he adduces facts in support of his conclusions, that the primary strata, mica schist, gneiss, &c., are in a state of transition; that they are slowly passing on into the great unstratified mass. It is true he ascribes the change or metamorphosis to the action of internal heat and other imaginary causes; and also he conceives, with other geologists, that the mass of crystalline rock will be again brought to the surface by internal forces,—will be decomposed and the materials again go towards the formation of stratified rocks. But this reasoning, whether it be supposed to be true or false, does not lessen the value of the fact which he has established, that the lower members of the stratified rocks are passing into the unstratified state. Perhaps this metamorphosis would be much more correctly expressed by saying, that the crystallizing principle of the granite (the mineral life already referred to) is pervading and swallowing up the lower members of the stratified rocks,—in short, if we may be allowed the expression, that the stratified rocks are the food, the nutriment, by which the mineral vital action of the crystalline granite is sustained. The following section from Lyell, vol. 4, page 345, will illustrate the position here assumed:—

GRANITE VEINS TRAVERSING STRATIFIED ROCKS.

The ordinary explanation given of these granite veins is, that the granitic matter was melted in the interior of the earth, and forced up into or through the primary strata in a melted state. But besides, that it has not been proved that the granite has been in a state of igneous fusion, granite veins may be seen traversing primary slates, as in the Isle of Arran, and in many other places, as well as in the section immediately before us, without having, as far as can be perceived, caused any serious disturbances in the line of cleavage of the slates, which could not have been the case if a mass of granite had been forcibly injected from beneath. Many circumstances tend to induce an opinion that the granite veins have been formed by the metamorphic or crystallizing process, in the same situations in which they are now found, and have not been forced up in a state of igneous fusion. At the same time, there are cases where the appearances of the granite having been in a melted state are so strong, that we ought to hesitate before we deny that such has not really been the case.

GRANITE.—Little further need be said concerning this well-known rock. It exists in an unstratified mass, and until recently was supposed to constitute in every case the lowest rock upon which all the strata were deposited. Some exceptions to this rule have, however, been lately discovered.

M. Elie De Beaumont has noticed in the western Alps, granite resting upon beds of the oolite group; and in the Swiss Alps, M. Hugi has seen the granite covering the lias limestone. The same inverted order of superposition has also been observed in other localities, not only as respects the granite, but likewise some of the stratified rocks; so that although the order of the different strata is sufficiently regular to enable geologists to determine the age of the rock and other circumstances of geological investigation, yet, upon a review of the whole case, it appears that many rocks are found in positions such as they could not well have been thrown by any force acting from the interior of the earth, even if we grant that such force really existed.

The manner in which the stratified and unstratified rocks are associated together, is the only important question which remains to be considered. We have seen that the stratified rocks have nearly all of them been more or less disturbed from their original horizontality. It being an admitted principle in geology, that *all the strata were originally formed upon a level or horizontal foundation*, in whatever position they be now found, it follows, that they must have been disturbed by some cause, and that cause, whatever it may have been, must necessarily have been adequate to the effects which have been produced, and which are now visible in the disturbed strata. Geologists, in seeking for causes to account for those effects, have confined their researches to the earth itself. They have been precluded from seeking causes external to the earth by the dogmas of astronomy. They have been taught by the Newtonian philosophy that the solar system is a *perpetual motion*, which in itself is an absurdity, for every motion of every kind, whether on the earth or in the heavens, is like a watch or clock, continued only on the condition that it is approaching to a termination. This is an essential condition of all motion, as will be shown more fully hereafter. The clock moves only by "running down;" every swing of the pendulum lets the weight descend *nearer to the centre of the earth;* if the weight cease to descend, the clock stands still. So also every swing or oscillation which the earth makes in her orbit from the perihelion to the aphelion, and *vice versa*, from the aphelion to the perihelion, she is descending towards the centre. The same of the other planets and of their attendant satellites. It is the condition upon which they move. The solar system, like the clock, unless "running down," would stand still. It moves because, and only because, it is running down. Astronomers have taught the contrary, viz., that the system is balanced in all its relations, that it may and will continue in motion forever. Geologists have pinned their faith to the assertions of astronomers, and, therefore, have been compelled to seek the cause or causes of disturbed stratification in the interior of the earth. The following diagram will exhibit the mode of reasoning adopted by modern geologists upon this hitherto difficult point; the explanations and reasoning accompanying which are given in the language of one of the most eminent geologists of the present day:—

"We have shown that the crust of the globe is composed of two great classes of rocks, one of which consists of a series of beds of stone of different kinds, lying upon one another in a certain determinate order of succession, called the *Stratified Rocks*, or the *Strata;* the other of a class of stones distinguishable from the strata by peculiar mineral composition, by never containing pebbles or the remains of animals and plants, and by never being arranged in parallel layers, and from which last character they have been denominated the *Unstratified Rocks*. We shall now proceed to show in what manner these two classes of rocks are associated together. It is quite evident that the mode of formation of the two must have been totally different. While the strata, by their parallel arrangement, the pebbles of pre-existing rocks, and remains of living bodies which they contain, demonstrate that they must have been formed under water, by deposition *from* the surface downwards, the whole characters of the unstratified rocks equally prove that they must have come *to* the surface from the interior of the earth, *after* the deposition of the strata; that is, that they have been ejected among the strata from below in a melted condition, either fluid or in a soft yielding state. Geologists have come to this conclusion, from a careful examination and comparison of the unstratified rock with the products of existing volcanoes, or those burning mountains that have thrown out streams of melted stone or lava, both in past ages, as recorded by history, and in our own time. By this comparison they have discovered a great similarity, often an identity, of composition between the unstratified rocks and lava, and the closest analogy in the phenomena exhibited by the masses of both kinds, and in their relations to the stratified rocks with which they come in contact.

"In every case the unstratified lie under the stratified. This order has never been reversed, except in cases which have been afterwards discovered to be deceptive appearances, and where they have been protruded between strata, as will be afterwards mentioned. But it may be said that this fact of inferiority of position is no proof of ejection from below, far less of posteriority of formation, for they might have been the foundation on which the strata are deposited; their eruption from the interior, and that that eruption took place after the strata were formed, are proved by other evidence, as we shall presently show.

"A section of the crust of the earth, where the stratified and unstratified rocks have been found associated together, has often exhibited the appearance presented by the following diagram:—

"*a* and *b* are mountains of granite or whinstone, with strata of limestone lying upon it. From *a* branches or shoots connected with the principal mass are seen to penetrate into the superincumbent strata, and in the mountain *b* the granite overlies the limestone for a considerable way near the top, as if it had flowed over at that place, and lower down it has forced its way between two strata, ending like a wedge. Now as the penetrating substance must necessarily be of subsequent formation to the body that it penetrates, it is evident that the granite must have been formed after the limestone, although the latter rests upon it. But if any doubt remained, it would be removed by the additional fact that the granite veins in the mountain *a* contain angular fragments of limestone, identical with the strata above, and the fractured ends are seen to fit the places of the continuous stratum from which they have been broken off.

"The posteriority of the formation of the unstratified rocks to the strata is thus made evident from their relative positions; their forcible ejection from below is equally proved by the penetration of their veins or shoots into the superincumbent strata in an upward direction, often with the most slender ramifications to a great distance, and by the portions broken from the strata and enveloped in the substance of the vein. That they were ejected in a soft melted state, produced by the action of heat, is shown by the close resemblance in mineral composition of the unstratified rocks to the products of existing volcanoes, and by remarkable changes often observed to have taken place in the strata where they come in contact with granite and whinstone. Soft chalk is converted into a hard crystalline limestone like statuary marble; clay and sandstone are changed into a substance as hard and compact as flint, and coal is turned into *coke;* all of them changes which are analogous to what takes place when the substances are subjected to a strong artificial heat under great pressure. In the case of coal it is very remarkable; for when a bed of that substance, and a stratum of clay lying next it, come in contact with whinstone, the tar of the coal is often driven into the clay, and the coal loses all property of giving flame, although, at a distance from the whinstone, it is of a rich caking quality.

"We have shown that we are enabled to fix a chronological order of succession of the strata with a considerable degree of precision, and although we have not the same accurate means of determining the relative ages of the unstratified rocks, there are yet very decisive proofs that certain classes of them are older than others, that different members of the same class have been ejected at distinct periods, and that the same substances have been thrown up at different times far distant from each other. *Granite, in veins, has never been seen to penetrate beyond the lower strata;* but whinstone and the lavas of existing volcanoes protrude in masses, and send out veins through all the strata: veins of one sort of granite traverse masses of another kind, and whinstone and basalt veins are not only found crossing masses and other veins of similar rocks, but even of granite. Upon the principle, therefore, before stated, that the penetrating substance must necessarily have been formed subsequently to the body penetrated, the above phenomena demonstrate successive formations or eruptions of the unstratified rocks.

"As the highly elevated, broken and contorted positions of the strata are only explicable on the supposition of a powerful force acting upon them from below, and as they are seen so elevated and contorted in the neighborhood of the unstratified rocks, it is a very legitimate inference that the mountain chains and other inequalities on the earth's surface have been occasioned by the horizontally deposited strata having been heaved up by the eruption of these rocks, although they may not always appear, but be only occasionally protruded to the surface, through the rents produced by the eruptive force. The phenomena of earthquakes are connected with the same internal action, and these have often been accompanied by permanent elevations of entire portions of a country. This theory of the elevation of mountains by a force acting from the interior of the earth, is not a mere inference from appearances presented by rocks, but is supported by numerous events which have occured repeatedly within the period of history down to our own time. In the middle of a gulf in the island of Santorino, in the Grecian Archipelago, an island rose from the sea 144 years before the Christian era; in 1427 it was raised in height and increased in dimensions; in 1573 another island arose in the same gulf, and in 1707 a third. These islands are composed of hard rock, and in that last formed there are beds of limestone and of other rocks containing shells. In the year 1822, Chili was visited by an earthquake which raised the whole line of coast for the distance of above one hundred miles to the height of three or four feet above its former level. Valparaiso is situated about the middle of the tract thus permanently elevated. A portion of Cutch, near the mouth of the Indus, underwent a similar revolution in the year 1819, when a district, nearly sixty miles in length by sixteen in breadth, was raised by an earthquake about ten feet above its original level. A volcanic eruption burst out in an adjoining part of India at Bhoo, at the exact period when the shocks of this earthquake terminated. These cases must not be confounded with the production of new mountains, such as that of Jorullo, in Mexico, in the year 1759, which was raised to the height of 1,600 feet above the table land of Malpais, by eruptions of scoria and the outpouring of lava. The appearance of a new island off the coast of Sicily, in the year 1831, is another phenomenon of the latter class. It rose from a part of the sea which was known by soundings a few years before to have been 600 feet deep, to the height of 107 feet above the water, and formed a circumference of nearly two-thirds of a mile. It was composed of loose cinders, and the part that rose above the level of the sea was washed away in the winter of the same year, but an extensive shoal remains.

"It must not be supposed that these internal movements only took place after the whole series of strata had been deposited. There must have been long intervals between the termination of the deposition of one member of the series and the commencement of that of the stratum immediately above it; and internal movements accompanied with disturbance of the already deposited strata, after they had come to consolidate into stone, appear to have taken place during the whole period that the strata, from the lowest to the uppermost in the series, were deposited. The clearest evidence of this, is afforded by certain appearances exhibited by the strata in all parts of the globe that have yet been examined. The annexed diagram represents a case of very common occurrence, and will explain our meaning. It must be borne in mind that it is an acknowledged principle in geology that all stratified rocks, in whatever position they are now found, must have been originally deposited horizontally.

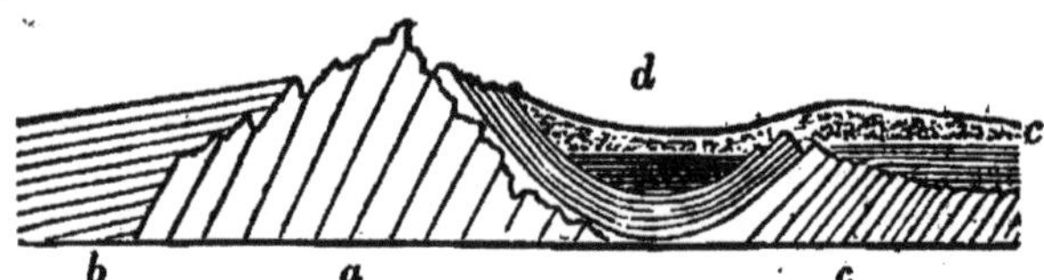


"There are here five different series of strata, *a*, *b*, *c*, *d*, *e*. Now, it is evident, that the series *a* must have been first disturbed; that, after its change of position, the series *b* and *c* were deposited, covering *the ends* of the strata of the series *a*. But *c* appears to have been acted upon by two forces at distant points, when thrown out of its horizontal position, for the strata dip in opposite directions, forming a basin-shaped cavity, in which the series *d* was deposited. In like manner, after the disturbance of *c*, the series *e* was deposited, covering the ends of *c*; but the internal force which raised the beds *e* from the depths of the sea to the summit of the mountain where they are now seen, appears to have acted in such a direction as to have carried up the whole mass without disturbing the original horizontality of the structure. It is obvious that all the interior strata must have partaken of this last disturbance. There are, besides, numerous proofs that there have been not only frequent elevations of the strata, but also depressions; that the same strata which had been at one time raised above the surface of the sea had again sunk down, preserving an inclined position; that they had formed the ground upon which new sediment was deposited, and had again been raised up, carrying along with them the more recently formed strata."

This extract has been given because it contains some of the closest and strongest reasoning which can be advanced in support of the common conclusion, that the mountain ranges of the earth have been upheaved by a force acting from beneath. The reasoning is good, the inferences are fair, so far as they go; but it must not be overlooked that these are sections selected for the purpose of illustrating a point and supporting a particular conclusion. If in all, or in a majority, or even in a great number of cases, equally satisfactory indications could be adduced, the conclusion of the upheaving of mountains by a force acting from within the earth would be tolerably well sustained. But this is by no means the case. One or two sections are found which appear to warrant the conclusion, and upon this narrow basis a general law is founded. In the last diagram, for example, there is nothing to show that the strata were disturbed by the upheaving of melted granite, (indeed, it has not been proved that granite was ever melted by the supposed internal heat); but it is *supposed* that the melted granite has been upheaved beneath the strata, although it has not shown itself above.

But let us look at the mountain ranges of the earth upon the great scale, viewing them as the results of a central force, and let us see whether they are upon those parts of the earth's surface upon which they ought to be found, if their elevation be due to such central force. The diameter of the earth is about twenty-six miles less from pole to pole, than that taken through the equator; that is, as we should imagine, the crust of the globe is *thinner towards the poles* by a difference of thirteen miles. Now, a steam boiler when subjected to a heavy pressure from internal force, always bursts at the thinnest part, and if the mountain ranges had been heaved up by a similar internal force, all the great elevations of the surface ought to be found near the poles. But this is exactly the reverse of the case; they are all within or near the tropics. That is, by the hypothesis, the central force of the earth, unlike that of the steam boiler and all other central forces, has burst through the thickest part, leaving the thinnest part undisturbed. But, although the mountain ranges are not where they ought to be, if we suppose their elevation due to central heat, they are exactly where we should expect to find them, if we suppose them to be the remains of a deposited satellite, which has subsequently been broken up by the earth's rotation and other causes, and scattered over the surface; they are exactly beneath the moon's orbit, and the moon is at this moment approaching the earth. All the other satellites also move in orbits whose axes are nearly coincident with that of their respective primaries, and, therefore, we are justified in supposing, that if at a former period the earth was attended by several satellites, their orbits were nearly coincident with that of the remaining one.

Indeed, an argument in support of the general view may be drawn from the disposition of the mountains on the surface of the moon herself. The mountains of the moon are high cones, with deep and level plains intervening, not in sloping, shelving ranges like those of the earth. How comes this difference in the disposition and characters of the surface of the two bodies? Because no solid matter has been deposited upon the surface of the moon by which the deep vallies should have been filled up, leaving only the peaks of the cones peeping through the surface, as has been the case upon the earth. Nay, even the physical constitution of the moon furnishes an argument. She is a much smaller body than the earth, her diameter being about 2,170 miles; consequently, if, like the earth, she has been passing into the solid condition through a long succession of ages, we should expect that being the smaller of the two bodies, the process would be nearer to completion; and this is precisely what we do find. She is almost devoid of an atmosphere. Why? Because her ocean is nearly dried up. The process—the internal action is nearly complete. She has been the repository of vegetable and animal life, like the earth, and so long as there is moisture to nourish the vegetation, life of some sort, both animal and vegetable, will continue. When that process is finished, she will become a dead mass of rock; her course will be finished; she will have fulfilled her purpose, and, falling upon the primary earth, like her predecessors, the matter will be conveyed with the earth to the central sun, there to be dissolved; again to issue, to form a new world, in which all will be life and activity.

"The surface of the moon as a telescopic object presents a most interesting appearance, indicating that its surface is composed of hills, valleys, and caverns, and perhaps of seas, lakes, and rivers, and all the varieties of distribution that are known to be on the surface of the earth, although the actual existence has not yet been ascertained. That there are mountains and hills in the moon, may be inferred with considerable certainty from those parts which are supposed to be elevations casting a shadow opposite to the sun, as well as from the jagged appearance of the edge of the moon when she is horned or gibbous; the valleys and cavernous parts are distinguished by the shadows appearing next to the sun. Some of the mountains form elevated continuous ridges, others are insulated and conical, having the precise form of the terrestrial volcano. The assertion is startling, but there are lunar volcanoes in different stages; Dr. W. Herschell saw three in a state of ignition at the same time—they resembled a small piece of burning charcoal covered by a thin coat of white ashes, and he further noted a large portion of burning matter, which he supposes was more than three miles in diameter. The height of the lunar mountains was formerly supposed to exceed very considerably that of the mountains of the earth, but the laborious exertions of Herschell and others have determined the fact, that none of them exceeds five miles in height.

"The inhabitants of the moon, if the moon be inhabited by beings whose organization resembles our own, must be capable of living with a very small quantity of atmospheric air and little water. It has been a subject of discussion whether or not she is furnished with an atmosphere. Reason and analogy decide in the affirmative, but it is less than a mile high, and is never clouded, so that the sun must shine for a whole fortnight without intermission on the same spot, without having his heat materially moderated either by the interposition of the atmosphere, or by the evaporation of the moisture. That there is very little water in the moon beyond perhaps springs and small rivers, has been inferred from two remarkable circumstances—the absence of clouds, and the irregular appearance of the margin of the moon as seen in a solar eclipse, no part of it being terminated by a line sufficiently regular to allow us to suppose it the surface of a fluid."

To return to the mountains of the earth. It has been observed from the manner in which the stratified rocks have been distributed, that there have been long periods of repose, during each of which periods nature seems to have gone on in the ordinary course which we witness at the present day upon the earth. But there have also been short periods of violent convulsion, during which the crust of the earth appears to have been rent and shattered by some cause; and when we look around us in the earth to find a cause adequate to the observed effects, we look in vain. M. Elie De Beaumont, who devoted much attention to the ranges of mountains, has the following observations on the subject, which are extracted from De La Beche's Geological Manual, p. 487:—

"The fact of a general uniformity in the direction of all beds upheaved at the same epoch, and consequently in the crests formed by these beds, is perhaps as important in the study of mountains, as the independence of successive formations is in the study of superimposed beds. The sudden change of direction in passing from one group to another has permitted the division of European chains into a certain number of distinct systems, which penetrate and sometimes cross each other without becoming confounded. I have recognized from various examples, of which the number now amounts to twelve, that there is a certain coincidence between the sudden changes established by the lines of demarcation observed in certain consecutive stages of the sedimentary rocks, and the elevation of the beds of the same number of mountain-systems.

"Pursuing the subject as far as my means of observation and induction will permit, it has appeared to me, that the different systems, at least those which are at the same time the most striking and recent, are composed of a certain number of small chains, ranged parallel to the semicircumference of the earth's surface, and occupying a zone of much greater length and breadth; and of which the length embraces a considerable fraction of one of the great circles of the terrestrial sphere. It may be observed respecting the hypothesis of each of these mountain-systems being the product of a single epoch of dislocation, that it is easier geometrically to conceive the manner in which the solid crust of the globe may be elevated into ridges along a considerable portion of one of its great circles, than that a similar effect may have been produced in a more restricted space.

"However well established it may be by facts, the assemblage of which constitutes positive geology, that the surface of the globe has presented a long series of tranquil periods, each separated from that which followed it by a sudden and violent convulsion, in which a portion of the earth's crust was dislocated, — that, in a word, this surface was ridged at intervals in different directions; the mind would not rest satisfied if it did not perceive, among those causes now in action, an element, fitted from time to time, to produce disturbances different from the ordinary march of the phenomena which we now witness.

"The idea of *volcanic action* naturally presents itself when we search, in the existing state of things, for a term of comparison with these great phenomena. They nevertheless do not appear susceptible of being referred to volcanic action, unless we define it with M. Humboldt, as being *the influence exercised by the interior of a planet on its exterior covering during its different stages of refrigeration.*

"Volcanoes are frequently arranged in lines following fractures parallel to mountain chains, and which originate in the elevation of such chains; but it does not appear to me that we can thence regard the elevation of the chains themselves as due to the action of *volcanic foci*, taking the words in their ordinary and restricted sense. We can easily conceive how a *volcanic focus* may produce accident circularly and in the form of rays from a central point, but we cannot conceive how even many united *foci* could produce those ridges which follow a common direction through several degrees.

"Volcanic action, such as it is commonly understood, could not therefore be itself the first cause of these great phenomena; but volcanic action appears to be related (and this is a subject which has long occupied M. Cordier, though he has considered it under another point of view,) with the high temperature now existing in the interior of the globe.

"Now the secular refrigeration, that is to say, the slow diffusion of the primitive heat to which the planets owe their spheroidal forms and the generally regular disposition of these beds from the centre to the circumference, in the order of specific gravity, — the secular refrigeration, on the march of which M. Fourier has thrown so much light, does not offer an element to which these extraordinary effects may be referred. This element is the relation which a refrigeration so advanced as that of the planetary bodies establishes between the capacity of their solid crusts and the volume of their internal masses. In a given time, the temperature of the interior of the planets is lowered by a much greater quantity than that on their surfaces, of which the refrigeration is now nearly insensible. We are, undoubtedly, ignorant of the physical properties of the matter composing the interior of these bodies; but analogy leads us to consider, that the inequality of cooling above noticed, would place their crusts under the necessity of continually diminishing their capacities, notwithstanding the nearly rigorous constancy of their temperature, in order that they should not cease to embrace their internal masses exactly, the temperature of which diminishes sensibly. They must therefore depart in a slight and progressive manner from the spheroidal figure proper to them, and corresponding to a maximum of capacity; and the gradual increasing tendency to revert to that figure, whether it acts alone, or whether it combines with other internal causes of change which the planets may contain, may, with great probability, completely account for the ridges and protuberances which have been formed at intervals on the external crust of the earth, and probably also of all the other planets."

M. Elie De Beaumont, from the most careful and extensive observations, has come to the following conclusions:—

"1st. That in the history of the earth there have been long periods of comparative repose, during which the deposition of sedimentary matter has gone on in regular continuity; and there have also been short periods of paroxysmal violence, during which that continuity was broken.

"2d. At each of these periods of violence or 'revolution' in the state of the earth's surface, a great number of mountain-chains have been formed suddenly.

"3d. All chains thrown up by a particular revolution have one uniform direction, being parallel to each other within a few degrees of the compass, even when situated in remote regions; but the chains thrown up at different periods have, for the most part, different directions.

"4th. Each 'revolution,' or, as it is sometimes termed, 'frightful convulsion,' has fallen in with the date of another geological phenomenon; namely, 'the passage from one independent sedimentary formation to another,' characterised by a considerable difference in 'organic types.'

"5th. There has been a recurrence of these paroxysmal movements from the remotest geological periods; and they may still be re-produced, and the repose in which we live may hereafter be broken by the sudden upthrow of another system of parallel chains of mountains.

"6th. We may presume that one of these revolutions has occurred within the historical era, when the Andes were upheaved to their present height; for that chain is the best defined and least obliterated feature observable in the present exterior configuration of the globe, and was probably the last elevated.

"7th. The instantaneous upheaving from the ocean of great mountain masses must cause a violent agitation in the waters; and the size of the Andes may, perhaps, have produced that transient deluge which is noticed among the traditions of so many nations.

"Lastly. The successive revolutions above mentioned cannot be referred to ordinary volcanic forces, but may depend on the secular refrigeration of the heated interior of our planet." *

But the history of the earth in by-gone ages, as deduced from mountain chains, from the mineral composition of rocks, and from the relative positions of the disturbed strata, satisfactory as it is, to a certain extent, is yet of a secondary character, as compared with that deduced from the fossil remains of animals and plants.

Baron Cuvier remarked, "that without (fossil) zoology there was no true geology."—And this remark is just. By the study of fossil remains, that which was before a high probability, becomes an absolute certainty. If there be any record of the past history of the earth more wor-

*"Ann. des Sci. Nat. Septembre, Novembre, et Decembre, 1829. Revue Francaise, No. 16, May, 1830. The last edition by M. de B. is in De la Beche's Manual, 3d edit.; and D'Aubuisson, Traite de Geognosie, tom. iii. p. 282, 1835."

thy of our credence and confidence than another, it is that which may be traced by the finger of science upon the mountains and rocks of the globe itself, which, we are well assured, was not written by crafty and designing men, whose pens were guided by a desire to realize secular advantages, by imposing a false record upon the multitude. It is indeed a strange and marvellous history to those who have never given their attention to the subject. It is full of wonder; but it is also full of truth. Some geologists, believing the solar system to be a perpetual motion, and seeing before their eyes the clearest evidence that the earth has been in existence as a planet for millions of ages, have, rather hastily, come to the conclusion that she has existed forever. But the study of fossil geology entirely removes this false conclusion.

There are few propositions in natural philosophy more firmly and indubitably established than that this planet which we inhabit had a beginning. We do not appeal to history, sacred or profane, for its confirmation. Geology has established the fact, — not by tracing back to the very beginning of terrestrial things, but by proving that through a long series of ages a slow and silent *progression* has been going forward in the vegetable, animal, and mineral kingdoms, and the earth being a finite quantity, this progression must have had a beginning. Whole races of vegetables and animals have passed away and are no more, — and this has occurred not once or twice, but many times; there has been a regulated gradation of vegetable and animal existence. *But the old forms have never been re-produced.* The specific circumstances favorable to the existence of each of the by-gone races, have ceased upon the earth, and can never again occur, until the solid rocks in which are entombed the remains of former races shall have been dissolved and dissipated in the gaseous form; which gaseous matter, giving rise to new aggregations of cometary and planetary masses, in which again will be called into play all the active circumstances which prevailed in the remotest period of the earth's planetary existence. If this formerly fluid world contain at this time immense masses of solid rocks, those rocks have been formed during the lapse of ages, and the process is still going on; and as certainly as the earth is a finite quantity, that process must come to a termination.

The progressive development of vegetable and animal life, upon which a much more orderly and scientific classification of the stratified rocks, than that of tertiary, secondary, and primary, might be based, is perceived from the following observations by an eminent geologist, and which at the same time shows that there have been four distinct snaps in the chain of that progress.

It has been observed that the time which elapsed from the commencement of the deposition of the older secondary strata, to that of the most recent of the tertiary beds, appears to be divisible into four great botanico-geological periods, of unequal duration, during each of which, vegetation exhibited a common character. Each of these periods, therefore, is characterised by peculiar classes of plants; or, in the language of botanists, may be said to have a flora of its own; and each period embraces a certain number of the series of stratified rocks which compose the crust of the globe. During the continuance of each of those periods, vegetation seems to have undergone only gradual and limited changes — to have been subject to no changes which had an influence upon the essential character of the vegetation taken as a whole; but, on the contrary, there is between one period and another a marked division, a sudden change, in the most important characters of the vegetation. There exists no species common to two successive periods; all is different; and a new *ensemble* of plants which must have been produced under circumstances different from those which pre-existed, replaces the old vegetation. The four great points are as follows:—

A. — *The First Period* includes the coal measures, and all the strata containing organic remains which lie below them. (M to Q, diagram No. 1.)

B. — *The Second Period* comprehends the vast deposits of red sandstone, magnesian limestone, and a sandstone lying above that limestone, called the new red sandstone. (L and part of K.)

C. — *The Third Period* commences with a kind of shelly limestone, that forms a member of the upper part of the group of the red marly sandstone (K,) and includes all the superior secondary strata up to the chalk. (G to I.)

D. — *The Fourth Period* includes all the strata more recent than the chalk. (C to F.)

It is a remarkable circumstance, that the periods are separated by strata, which, if not entirely destitute of *land* plants, contain them in very small quantity. Thus A is separated from B by a formation of coarse limestone (called by geologists the red conglomerate,) in which plants are of rare occurrence, and by the magnesian limestone in which marine plants are almost exclusively found; again, B and C are separated by the shelly limestone (muschelkalk of geologists,) which is almost destitute of vegetable remains; and, lastly, C is separated from D by the chalk, in which, with rare exceptions, only marine plants have yet been found.

*First Period.* — The lowest strata in which animal remains are found, contain also those of plants; so that it would appear that animal and vegetable life were from the first co-existent. The plants in older sandstones are for the most part marine, but the impressions are usually indistinct. Black carbonaceous matter, without any organic form, is by no means unfrequent, and sometimes in considerable quantity; and it is not improbable that it is of vegetable origin, for fossil plants are very commonly found in the state of charcoal. It is in the beds of coal, and in the sandstones, clays, and limestones which accompany them, that vegetable remains first occur in profusion, and there are few phenomena in geology more remarkable than those enormous accumulations of vegetable matter from which the coal beds have been derived. The most distinguishing feature of it is the great numerical preponderance of the third class — viz., the vascular cryptogamæ, and the prodigious size which the plants attain. They constitute five-sixths of the flora of the period, while they do not form the proportion of one-thirtieth in the vegetation of the present time. The ferns of temperate regions are low plants with stems rising scarcely a few inches above the ground, but in the equatorial regions there are what are called tree-ferns, which have a stem from twenty to thirty feet high. Now the different kinds of fossil ferns of this period often correspond with the tree-ferns of the tropics, as is attested by the remains of their stems, which are occasionally met with. The plants called lycopodiums by botanists, constitute another order of this class, and are of a kind intermediate between tree-ferns and the fir-tree tribe. Those now existing never exceed the height of three feet, and are usually weak prostrate plants, having the habits of mosses; but the fossil lycopodiums attain gigantic sizes, stems having been found above three feet in diameter, and seventy feet long. There is in this period a much smaller proportion of the fourth and fifth classes, in comparison with what occurs in existing vegetation; and, with the exception of the fir tribe, which was very common, the existence of the dicotyledonous class is little more than conjectured. The plants which constitute by far the larger proportion of the flora of the first period belong to genera which exist, of such dimensions, only in the warmest countries of the globe; and it is evident, therefore, that the climate of the north of Europe and America must have been at least as hot as the equatorial regions, at the time the plants grew, which are now buried many fathoms under ground in the coal mines of those countries, for all the circumstances attending them exclude the idea of the plants having been drifted from southern latitudes into those situations.

*Second Period.* — The red sandstones, which were deposited so extensively at this period, are even more destitute of vegetable than they are of animal remains. This absence of organic remains is a very remarkable and inexplicable circumstance, considering the great extent occupied by these deposits in all countries, and their vast thickness. The plants hitherto found in the lowest strata of the period have been almost exclusively marine, the few exceptions being vascular cryptogamæ, resembling those of the first period. In the superior beds, a few of the coniferæ or fir-tree tribe have been found, and some that are supposed to belong to the monocotyledonous class.

*Third Period.*— The lowest stratum of this period contains very few plants, and these chiefly marine; but they become more abundant in the sand, sandstones, clays, and limestones that succeed each other in numerous alternations up to the chalk. Many belong, however, to an entirely new race of plants from any which had previously existed. There are no longer the gigantic ferns and lycopodiums of the first period; the same families exist, but the character of excessive luxuriance disappears, and species analogous to plants — now natives of the Cape of Good Hope and New Holland — become common. The whole of the flora of the period consists almost exclusively of the third and fourth classes, and nearly in equal proportions; the rarity of the fifth and sixth classes, that is, of monocotyledonous and dicotyledonous plants, is very remarkable. Among those belonging to the fourth class, viz., the gymnospermous phanerogamæ, there is an extraordinary preponderance of the family called *cycadeæ*, a family scarcely so numerous now over the whole globe as it was then in the small part of Europe where its fossil remains have been found. It constitutes now not above a thousandth part of existing vegetation, whereas it forms one-half of what remains of the flora of this period. The chalk, which constitutes the upper strata of the period, has not afforded as yet more than a few marine plants, and scarcely a trace of land plants, so that a complete change had taken place in the nature of the country surrounding those part where the chalk was deposited, from what had existed immediately before.

*Fourth Period.* — From the termination of the deposit of the chalk formation, we discover in animal and vegetable remains the commencement of resemblances to species which now exist. The proportion gradually increases in the newer strata, until, at last, the flora of the latest tertiary deposits differ very little in character from that of the present time in the same countries. In the beds immediately above the chalk, ferns and cycadeæ again appear, but in greatly diminished proportions; the coniferæ, but very different from those of the older periods, increase in quantity, mixed with palm-trees and others of the monocotyledonous class of tropical regions, associated with dicotyledonous trees, such as the elm, willow, poplar, chesnut, and sycamore. We again meet with local deposits of decayed, or rather altered, vegetable matter, forming thick beds of a kind of coal, which is used in many countries, as on the banks of the Rhine, for fuel,— something intermediate between coal and peat.

Now, the question in this case, is, to what cause are we to attribute this general destruction of organized life at four distinct points, with a sudden and overwhelming force, accompanied apparently by a general deluge, and between each of those points a long period of repose intervening? The fact of the moon's secular acceleration will perhaps enable us to unravel the mystery; for the discovery of which fact we are indebted to Edmund Halley, an English astronomer, whose name ought to stand at the very head of the science he has so much adorned by his discoveries.

"It is to Halley," says the writer of the Treatise on Astronomy, of the Society for the Diffusion of Useful Knowledge, "that we owe the first suspicion of this very important fact regarding the moon's motions. It had been hitherto the universally received doctrine that all the planets, without exception, were subject to such inequalities only as are renewed within a certain space of time, and which, on that account, have been called periodic inequalities. The mean motion is determined by a comparison of the planets' places, at very distant times, embracing a great number of the periods, within which the inequalities are renewed, so that the result obtained is quite independent of these inequalities. No astronomer had ever ventured to doubt the uniformity of these mean motions; and, in fact, we now know that the major axis, and, consequently, the periodic times of the primary planets, are not subject to any but the periodical inequalities of which we have spoken. But this is not the case with the moon. The mean motion of that satellite is continually accelerated; and as this acceleration, though, mathematically speaking, it has a limit, yet will continue for perhaps many thousands of centuries, it is called the secular acceleration, to distinguish it from those inequalities which have a period that falls within the limits of observation. The cause of this phenomena was discovered by Laplace; the fact itself was suspected by Halley. The reality of it was disputed for a long time, but it is now incontestibly established. The mean motion of the moon, as determined by modern observations exclusively, is between three and four minutes more rapid than they found by comparing modern observations with the eclipses observed at Babylon 700 years before Christ; and this result is fully confirmed by two eclipses of the sun, and an eclipse of the moon, observed at Cairo, by Ibn Jounis, towards the end of the tenth century." *

Upon a careful review of the whole of the facts which have come to our knowledge, we are irresistibly led to the following conclusions:—That the earth commenced her career *as a planet* in the liquid state; that solid rocks have been forming upon the earth through a period of duration which to our apprehension appears almost as vast as eternity itself, by the slow, silent, but certain process of that which is rather mysteriously denominated *vital action*, operating throughout the vegetable, animal, and mineral kingdoms, and that this vital action is dependent upon electrical agency. That *all* the solid rocks now upon the earth have not been formed in the situations

* History of Astronomy of the Library of Useful Knowledge, p. 80.

in which they are now found — is already admitted, neither have they been heaved up from beneath, but a certain portion has been deposited from above in the solid form; that as the moon is known to be approaching the earth, we are led to look to that quarter for the materials which have been so deposited, and if it be shown that the earth also is approaching her centre, that such approach is a necessary condition of her motion in her orbit, as well as that of all other bodies in the solar system, then the conclusion to which we have come with respect to the deposition of satellites upon the earth's surface, becomes an absolute certainty.

The facts and arguments tending to show that this is the true nature of the great process, are so many and so satisfactory, especially those exhibited in geology, that it requires but a knowledge of them in order to ensure our assent to the general conclusion.

Minds unaccustomed to geological investigation, are startled at the bare enunciation of a proposition so new, and, to their apprehension, so preposterous, as that the solid rocks of the earth at a former period existed in a soft or liquid form. However stubborn and unyielding our prejudices may be upon this point, they must give way before the still more stubborn and unyielding facts by which they are opposed. The shells and other remains, imbedded in the hard and solid limestone, with which they are so intimately blended that they constitute a part of the stone itself, could not have insinuated themselves, in an entire and unbroken state, into the hard limestone. The matter of which the rock is composed must have existed in a soft and yielding condition at the period at which those remains were imbedded. And this argument applies with equal force to all those rocks constituting the secondary and tertiary formation, and, by analogy, to the primary rocks also, and these three comprehend all the solid matter of which the earth is composed.

Besides which, a very little reflection will enable us to perceive *that the solid earth* must *have been formed from a liquid; and that it is utterly impossible that it could have been formed in any other manner:* because it is impossible to form a solid body of any description whatever, whether large or small, *without a joint* or visible joining, unless the matter of which it is about to be formed, can be previously reduced to the soft or liquid state. Neither can the form of any matter be changed, unless by passing it through the liquid or gaseous state, and in proportion as the liquefaction or gasification of the subject matter is more or less perfectly effected, so in proportion is the separation of the ultimate atoms more or less perfectly effected, and so also in proportion is the change of form and condition more or less perfectly effected. A common tallow candle is a solid body *without a joint*, and has been formed from melted or liquid tallow, and could not be formed *without a joint*, unless from a liquid. The same condition holds with respect to every other piece of art which is formed without a joint. But a chair, a table, a ship, a building, and similar works of art, are formed by *putting together pieces of solid matter*, and are consequently full of joints and visible joinings. A tree or any other vegetable is a solid body without a visible joining, which has been formed from fluid matter, and which could not have been formed from solid matter. An animal is a solid body without a visible joining, which has been formed in a like manner, and could not be formed in any other. A mineral or a crystal is a solid body without a visible joining, which has been formed by the same means. And the rocks and mountains of the earth are but aggregations of crystalline matter, subject to the same laws, and presenting internal evidence in the shells and other fossils which they contain, that they also have passed from the soft or liquid state into their present solid form.

Now, it requires no very great stretch of the reasoning faculty to perceive, that if the deposition of solid beds of earth, sand, or stone, had gone on from the beginning without any disturbing force to interrupt their regular deposition, the different beds or strata must have enveloped the earth in a uniform order precisely like the coats of an onion. But it is not so. They are broken, contorted, and tumbled one over the other, in the most extraordinary manner; and it is the business of geology, viewed as a science, to explain the causes of this seeming disorder. It is an established law in geology, that every bed must have been originally deposited horizontally, in whatever position it may be found at the present day. Now, "if the beds were originally horizontal and afterwards shifted, the supposable causes of this shift are three, and only three. First, an internal force acting from below upwards, so as to raise the crust of the globe. Second, a want of support, owing to internal cavities, so that the beds have fallen, owing to their own gravity. Third, an external shock, which has broken the shell, and made one part tumble over another." * Dolomieu was inclined to the last of these opinions, namely the external shock, in support of which he gives the following: — "A great catastrophe seems to have taken place after the birth of the primitive rocks, and before that of the derivative or parasitical (*couches de transport*) regularity ceased, a fracture took place in consequence of some vast shock; vast it must have been to break through a compact shell 4,000 fathoms in thickness. The strata, which precipitation had arranged horizontally, and crystallization consolidated, were thrown up; some vertically, to a height which, since that period, the water has never attained; others obliquely, in various directions; thus were formed the great eminences of our globe, from which were derived its present irregularities of surface." † Such are the observations of Dolomieu; had he been describing the deposition of a satellite as actually observed, he could not have given a more pointed description.

But if authorities were needed, we have a still greater which we can produce. Mr. Greenhough, president of the Geological Society of London, a gentleman of deep penetration, a practical geologist, in the most enlarged sense of the term, and a man of profound research, after carefully considering the relative portions and disturbed state of the strata over the whole earth, so far as it is known to geologists, has come to the same conclusion with Dolomieu, namely, that the earth must have received a sudden external shock, for he says, it is utterly impossible that the shell of the earth could have been broken and disturbed, as it evidently has been, by any force residing in the earth itself, and therefore we must of necessity look for the cause of this disturbance to some other power external to the earth, and even as he says, although on this point he is in error, we must seek a cause foreign to the solar system.

"If," says Greenhough, "we would discover the cause of this catastrophe, we must look for a cause foreign to our globe —*foreign to the solar system*, capable of inundating continents, and giving to the waters of the deep unexampled impetuosity, but without altering the interior

* Greenhough's First Principles of Geology.

† Journal de Physique, tom. 39, p. 390.

constitution of the earth, or deranging the sister planets; moreover the cause must be transitory, and one which, having acted its part once, may not have had occasion to repeat in the long period of five thousand years. Any supposable cause that would not fulfil these conditions, is insufficient for our purpose." *

Nothing but the deposition and subsequent breaking up of a satellite could fulfil the conditions here required, and required, too, by one of the first geologists of this or any other country. Had Greenhough been aware of the fact that the Newtonian system of philosophy rests upon a fallacy, he would not have felt the necessity of seeking a cause beyond the confines of the solar system, more especially if he had cast his eye towards the long disputed but now established fact of the moon's secular acceleration.

He says, "Did the disturbing cause reside in the mechanism of the solar system?. No; our knowledge of the laws which regulate the motion of the planetary bodies, aided by an experience of 5,000 years, will not allow us to admit that this system contains any seeds either of derangement or decay. The cause must have resided, therefore, *without* that system." †

It is thus that one error in science, as in morals, generates a number of other errors. The reader has seen how much value is to be placed upon the assertion of the "centrifugal force" philosophers, that the solar system "contains no seeds either of derangement or decay," and to avoid a collision with whom, Greenhough was compelled to seek a cause foreign to the solar system. It is established by observations, that the moon has been approaching the earth for the last 2,700 years; that is, as far back as history furnishes any record of eclipses of that body, and if history would carry us further back, we should find that she has been approaching from the beginning; and we know that she is now approaching.

It is true, we have the assurance of Laplace that this approximation has a limit, although he was unable to determine that limit. But Laplace, in his calculations, proceeded upon the basis of "centrifugal and centripetal forces." These were his data, his first principles derived from the Newtonian philosophy; but it has been proved

* Greenhough's First Principles of Geology, p. 196.

† Ibid, p. 195.

that these first principles are erroneous; therefore, the conclusions deduced from them are erroneous also. It has been objected by some, that the whole of the secondary and tertiary strata would not furnish matter sufficient to form four satellites equal in size or volume to the moon; and that, therefore, although the strata may be scientifically divided into four distinct and separate formations, each being separated from the other by a deluge, and each containing within itself fossil remains evidently of a distinct creation, having no connection with the creation belonging to the formation above or beneath; yet, that the proof of these having been depositions of four separate and distinct satellites fails, inasmuch as there are not materials sufficient for the volume of four *solid* satellites equal to the moon. This objection is based upon a condition which has not been put forward in the electrical theory. It is no where asserted that the planets are *solid* bodies; but on the contrary, it is assumed that they are *hollow spheres*, and that the external crust bears but a small proportion to the whole diameter. We have no direct evidence upon this point either way, and very plausible arguments might be adduced on both sides. The opinion that the planets are hollow spheres, must, therefore, for the present, rest upon the general consideration, that such an arrangement is more consistent with the usual economy of nature than that of solid bodies. But however this may be, a little calculation will show us that the matter of the moon, even granting her to be a solid body, (which is granting more than has been proved,) would fall very far short of filling up the present bed of the earth's ocean; whereas, if she be a hollow sphere, which is much more probable, her whole matter would not, if deposited in the South Sea, form an island equal to Australia or New Holland. But whatever may be the quantity of matter contained in the moon, whether she is solid or hollow, we are certain of this,—that she is now, and has been for many ages approaching the earth, and there is no power in the solar system to draw her back to her former position; that at whatever time she is precipitated upon the earth, the earth will receive a large accession of *solid* matter; a general deluge will take place; and in this, nothing more will occur than the repetition of an event which has taken place upon this earth four times already, and in a manner similar in every particular with that which is here anticipated.

That the moon is gradually approaching the earth is now generally admitted, although for a length of time doubted and disputed; and this variation is denominated the *moon's secular acceleration.* We have next to inquire whether the earth be subject to a variation of the same nature, whether in her motion in her orbit she obeys the same law: that is, we have to establish the *secular acceleration of the earth.*

Let us first examine the actual facts of the case, and the explanations given upon the Newtonian philosophy, that is, upon mechanical principles alone, having no reference to any great *process* going forward in the solar system, viewed as a whole; and that we may avoid the imputation of misrepresenting the system which we impugn, we will introduce an extract from Somerville's Connection of the Physical Sciences, a work deservedly held in the highest estimation, and which does not profess to give any original views, but merely a *connected view* of the physical sciences, collected from the writings of the most eminent philosophers of ancient and modern times:—

"A planet moves in an eliptical orbit with a velocity varying every instant, in consequence of two forces, one tending in a direction to the centre of the sun, and the other in a direction of a tangent to its orbit, arising from the *primitive impulse* [the supposed mechanical push,] given at the time when it was launched into space. Should the force in the tangent cease, the planet would fall to the sun by its gravity; were the sun not to attract it, the planet would fly off in the tangent. Thus, when the planet is in aphelion, or at the point when the orbit is farthest from the sun, his action overcomes the planet's velocity, and brings it towards him with such an accelerated motion, that at last it overcomes the sun's attraction, and shooting past him, gradually increases in velocity until it arrives at the aphelion, where the sun's attraction again prevails. * * * * *

"On account of the reciprocal action of matter, the STABILITY *of the system* DEPENDS *upon the intensity of the* PRIMITIVE MOMENTUM [the first push] of the planets, and the ratio of their masses to that of the sun; for the nature of the conic sections in which the celestial bodies move, depends upon the velocity with which they were first propelled in space; had that velocity been such as to make the planets move in orbits of unstable equilibrium, their mutual attractions might have changed them into parabolas, or even hyperbolas; so that the earth and planets might, ages ago, have been sweeping far from our sun through the abyss of space; but as the orbits differ very little from circles, the momentum of the planets, when projected, must have been exactly sufficient to ensure the permanency and stability of the system."—(Page 14.)

We perceive, then, that the stability of the solar system, and, consequently, its eternal duration, depends upon the centrifugal force or momentum of the planets, and that momentum is *supposed* to have been derived from a primitive mechanical impulse, imparted to the earth and other planets about six thousand years ago. Let the reader turn to a previous chapter; he will there see how much value is to be attached to this imaginary primitive impulse and the centrifugal force supposed to be derived from it.

Let us examine this matter a little further:—"The planets are subject to disturbances of two kinds, both resulting from the constant operation of their reciprocal attractions; one kind, depending upon their positions with regard to each other, begins from zero, increases to a maximum, decreases and becomes zero again, when the planets return to the same relative positions. In consequence of these, the disturbed planet is sometimes drawn away from the sun, and sometimes brought nearer to him; at one time it is drawn above the plane of its orbit, at another time below it, according to the position of the disturbing body; all such changes being accomplished in short periods, some in a few months, others in years, or in hundreds of years, are denominated *periodic inequalities*.

"The inequalities of the other kind, though occasioned likewise by the disturbing energy of the planets, are entirely independent of their relative position; they depend upon the relative positions of the other orbits alone, whose forms and places in space are altered by very minute quantities in immense periods of time, and are therefore called *secular inequalities*. In consequence of the latter kind of disturbances, the apsides, or extremities of the major axes of all the orbits, have a direct but variable motion in space, excepting those of the orbit of Venus, which are retrograde; and the lines of the nodes move with a variable velocity in a contrary direction. The motions of both are extremely slow; it requires more than

114,755 years for the major axis of the earth's orbit to accomplish a sidereal revolution, that is, to return to the same stars; and 21,067 years to complete its tropical motion, or to return to the same equinox. The major axis of Jupiter's orbit requires no less than 200,610 years to perform its sidereal revolution, and 22,748 years to accomplish its tropical revolution from the disturbing action of Saturn alone. The periods in which the nodes revolve are also very great. Besides these, the inclination and eccentricity of every orbit are in a state of perpetual but slow change; at the present time the inclinations of all the orbits are decreasing, but so slowly that the inclination of Jupiter's orbit is only about six minutes less now than it was in the age of Ptolomy. The terrestrial eccentricity is decreasing at the rate of about forty-one and a half miles annually; and if it were to decrease equally, it would be 37,527 years before the earth's orbit became a circle.

"But in the midst of these vicissitudes, the major axis and mean motions of the planets remain permanently independent of secular changes; they are so connected by Kepler's law of the squares of the periodic times being proportional to the cubes of the mean distances of the planets from the sun, that one cannot vary without affecting the other.

"With the exception of these two elements, it appears that all the bodies are in motion, and every orbit in a state of perpetual change. Minute as these changes are, they might be supposed to accumulate in the course of ages sufficiently to derange the whole order of nature, to alter the relative positions of the planets, to put an end to the vicissitudes of the seasons, and to bring about collisions which would involve our whole system, now so harmonious, in chaotic confusion. It is natural to ask, what proof exists that nature will be preserved from such a catastrophe? Nothing can be known from observation, since the existence of the human race has occupied comparatively but a point in duration, while these vicissitudes embrace myriads of ages. The proof is simple and convincing."—(Page 19.)

Now here comes the simple and convincing proof:—

"All the variations of the solar system, secular as well as periodic, are expressed analytically by the lines and cosines of circular arcs, which increase with the time; and as a line or cosine can never exceed the radius, but must oscillate between zero and unity, however much the time may increase, it follows, when the variations have, by slow degrees, accumulated, in however long a time, to a maximum, they decrease, by the same slow degrees, till they arrive at their smallest value, and again begin a new course; thus forever oscillating about a mean value."

This proof of the eternal stability of the solar system is, at all events, very short, although we cannot say much in support of its convincing qualities, especially when we reflect that one of the most essential elements entering into the calculation, namely, the centrifugal force, is no force whatever; and also when we recollect that the stability of the system is said to depend upon the original intensity of the primitive impulse or first mechanical push. But it is admitted, that unless space be a vacuum, the motion of the planets must ultimately cease; the centrifugal force must be destroyed by the resistance of any fluid pervading space, however rare that fluid may be. "This," says Somerville, "however, would not be the case if the planets moved in a resisting medium, for then both the eccentricity and the major axis of the orbits would vary with the time, so that the stability of the system would be ultimately destroyed. The existence of such a fluid is now clearly proved; and although it is so extremely rare, that hitherto its effects on the motions of the planets have been altogether insensible, there can be no doubt that, in the immensity of time, it will modify the forms of the orbits, and may at last even cause the destruction of our system, which, in itself, contains no principle of decay."—(Page 20.)

"The stability of our system was established by La Grange," a discovery says Professor Playfair, "that must render the name forever memorable in science, and revered by those who delight in the contemplation of whatever is excellent and sublime."

Little more need be said upon the stability of the solar system. It may be as well, however, to sum the matter up, in order that we may have a clear perception of the case in its present form and condition.

1st.—The aphelion and perihelion points of the earth's orbit, as well as those of the other planets, are moving *forward* on the ecliptic with a slow progressive motion, requiring about 114,755 years to complete a sidereal revolution.

2nd.—The earth's equinoctial points are moving *back-*

*ward* upon the ecliptic, 21,067 years being required to complete their cycle.

3rd.—The eccentricity of the earth's orbit is decreasing at the rate of forty-one and a half miles annually. That of the other planets is also changing.

4th.—The inclinations of all the planetary orbits are decreasing.

5th.—The inclination of the earth herself to the plane of the ecliptic, is changing; as is also those of the other planets.

In short, it may be said, that no body in the entire system ever returns to the same identical position that it had previously occupied in the system; and yet, in the face of all this never-ceasing change, we are gravely informed —and by men, too, holding high pretensions in the scientific world—that the eternal stability of the solar system has been rigidly demonstrated; and to crown the whole, we find that their much vaunted demonstrations are founded upon a fallacy;—the centrifugal force, one of the most essential elements, being no force whatever; and that, therefore, the whole Newtonian system is built upon a false foundation.

If the earth be gradually approaching the sun, it is natural to conclude that the length of the year is becoming less in a relative proportion. Accordingly, we find that the Chinese, Indians, Chaldeans, Egyptians, Greeks, and Romans, however they differed on other points, all agreed in giving to the year a value greater than that which is known to be the true value at the present day. Now, the great object of the astronomers being the calculation of eclipses, unless they had a knowledge of the true time, how could they have predicted the recurrence of an eclipse with any certainty? But the Sothiac period of the Egyptians puts the matter beyond dispute. The Egyptians had more than one calendar, in one of which the year consisted of 365 days; they had no leap-years, but the supernumerary hours and minutes were allowed to accumulate, until they formed a whole year, which was added to the amount, and this they called a Sothiac period, which originally consisted of 1,461 years; at the present day it would require 1,506 years to complete a Sothiac period, the difference being forty-five years. And are we to suppose that the Egyptians (the most eminent astronomers that the world ever produced) could not bring their Sothiac period nearer than within forty-five years of the true time? We cannot come to this conclusion; and yet with this very imperfect time these astronomers could calculate and predict eclipses! To suppose so is an absurdity; it is impossible to calculate an eclipse unless the true time be known.

It is also found that the apparent diameter of the sun is greater at the present day than it is found to be by the ancient Greek astronomers; and this also agrees with the assumption of the earth's approach to the centre. We are too apt to consider that these differences arise from the imperfect modes of observation pursued by the ancients, without considering that it is not only possible, but natural, that there should be an actual difference, seeing there is nothing stationary in nature, and that both the ancient and modern observations may be correct.

The established fact that the moon is approaching the centre, round which she revolves, might lead us to the suspicion that the earth, under the influence of the same law, is also approaching the central sun, independent of any other consideration. But there is no necessity of basing our conclusion upon mere inference, seeing there are abundant facts to substantiate the proposition. This approach to the centre of the earth and other bodies of the solar system is not deduced from the existence of a resisting medium, whereby the motions of the planets are retarded in their orbits. Professor Whewell, of Cambridge, has written a work, one of the Bridgewater Treatises, wherein he endeavors to show that in consequence of a subtle fluid pervading all space, the motions of the planets must eventually be destroyed, and they must be precipitated upon the central sun. That there is a subtle fluid pervading the planetary spaces, is true beyond all question. Indeed, the contrary never would have been imagined, but for the absurd dogmas of the Newtonian philosophy. In order that the planets might continue in motion upon the Newtonian hypothesis, it was necessary that they should move *in vacuo*, therefore, because it was necessary, it was at once laid down as a settled and indisputable proposition that space is a vacuum.

This is a mere begging of the question. Indeed, with the exception of attraction, which had been well known previously, every one of Newton's principles are begged. The *principia* might be aptly entitled the *petitio principia*, so that, as has been already shown, Professor Whewell might have discovered, if he had applied his mind in the proper quarter, that the motion of the planets, if that motion were dependent upon mere momentum, would be effectually destroyed by attraction, without the aid of a resisting medium, and that, too, within a very limited period of time. Besides, the motion of the planets being retarded in their courses, and precipitated upon the sun as a consequence of such retardation, is altogether unphilosophical. What does such a conclusion imply? That the system will come to an end by a kind of failure in nature; that by the laws by which it is moved, it would have continued in motion forever, had it not been for the oversight of the Creator; that it was intended to have moved forever, but in consequence of a certain impediment left negligently in the way, its motion will ultimately be destroyed. Really, this is very simple reasoning, to say the least of it; and yet Professor Whewell has been attacked by Newton's admirers in no very measured terms for having dared to cast a doubt upon the stability of the solar system. His opponents may suffer their rage to cool as regards Professor Whewell. Newton's philosophy will not be overthrown by such reasoning as that advanced in the Bridgewater Treatise of the learned Professor. The system of nature is moved by eternal forces and immutable laws. If the earth and planets be approaching the sun, as they assuredly are, it is not in consequence of the resisting medium by which their motion is retarded. There are other laws to which we shall advert by and by, besides those taken into account either by Newton or Professor Whewell, by which the system is moved, and by which, as a necessary consequence of that very motion, and of the contraction of the earth herself, she must approach the centre, and her existence as a planet come to an end.

But let us advert to the facts of the case. The ancient Chinese astronomers divided the circumference of the circle into 365 1-4 parts, instead of 360°, the division adopted amongst the western nations. By this division the sun moved through one degree daily, so that their solar year was about twelve minutes more in length than that of the present time. The Indians, also, valued the year at a greater length than that which is known to be the true length at present. The following is a synoptical view of the ancient Indian tables, showing the length of the sidereal year, as estimated by the Hindoo astronomers of that time:—

| | days. | hours. | min. | seconds. |
|---|---|---|---|---|
| Siam | 365 | 6 | 12 | 36 |
| Chrisnabouram | 365 | 6 | 12 | 30 |
| Narsapur | 365 | 6 | 12 | 36 |
| Tirvalore | 365 | 6 | 12 | 30 |
| Surya Siddhanta | 365 | 6 | 12 | 36 |

In respect to the Chaldean astronomers, it is mentioned by Porphyry, that Calisthenes transmitted to Aristotle a series of observations made at Babylon, during a period of 1903 years preceding the capture of that city by Alexander the Great, which carries back the Chaldean astronomy to at least 2234 years before the birth of Christ. So that if the Chaldeans were not acquainted with the true length of the solar year, it cannot be said that they were not diligent observers, for here are a set of observations extending over a period of nearly 2,000 years; and, as we shall see by and by, they had the strongest inducements, much stronger than those experienced by astronomers in modern times, to bring their tables to the greatest degree of accuracy, as on the accuracy of their tables depended their success in predicting eclipses. The Chaldeans value the solar year at 365 days, six hours.

The Egyptians, as already noticed, valued the solar year at 365 days, six hours. They are, and with propriety, considered the most ancient of astronomers, as their country is, to this day, esteemed to have been the cradle of civilization. Science, civilization, and *systematized* superstition had their origin in Egypt. According to Dio Cassius, they were the inventors of the division of time into seven days, which we now have by the name of the *week*, the first day of which is still called *sun*-day, and was set apart for the worship of the sun; the other days as *moon*-day (Monday), were named by them after the different planets. Upon the whole, it may be said that the Egyptians were the most ancient astronomers of ancient times, and as their observations extended over a long period, they must have known the true length of the year. They had besides a very deep interest in the matter. The astronomy of Egypt and of Chaldea, as well as that of India, was wholly in the hands of the priesthood, and their chief object in the study was that they might be enabled to predict eclipses. There were three principal classes of the priesthood, the *astrologers*, the *magicians*, and the *soothsayers*. They were *prophets* as well as priests. They pretended to have a knowledge of future events both in the earth and in the heavens. The magicians astonished the multitude with legerdemain tricks, a specimen of which may be seen in the first chapters of Exodus, when Moses and the magicians exhibited their art before Pharaoh. The soothsayers were unriddlers of dreams, &c., such as at the present day would be denominated fortune-tellers. But the vocation of the astrologer, which was more eminent than either of the others, was to disclose the course of events in the heavens. He held the keys of heaven in his art, and maintained his position chiefly by the knowledge which he had acquired of foretelling eclipses of the moon.

This knowledge had been obtained by a long course of observation, and was kept religiously secret from the multitude. It was the priest's art. By this knowledge he was enabled to predict that on such a day at such an hour "the sun would be darkened," or "the moon turned into blood." The prediction was of course verified to the very letter, as he well knew it would be by his calculations, founded on observations. The people were astonished and awed. They honored and obeyed the "wise man of Egypt," who, as was made manifest to their senses, held intimate correspondence with the counsels of heaven. The astrologer was reverenced and almost worshipped as a superior being,—one who was a kind of mediator between heaven and earth, for such he was conceived to be by those who were ignorant of his art. It was therefore of the utmost importance to the astrologer that his calculations should be founded on true data, for on this depended his power with the people, and not only with the people, for kings also bent the knee before the magic power. But if his predictions of eclipses had failed to be verified, his whole power would have vanished. On which account the utmost care and pains were bestowed on this matter; which after all is merely a matter of observation not at all dependent on a knowledge of the true or Copernican theory of the solar system, or that of universal gravitation. But if they had not known the true length of the solar year, they could not have predicted an eclipse with any degree of certainty; and certainty in a matter of so much importance to them was the great desideratum. Accordingly, they were incessantly engaged in correcting their astronomical tables, bringing them in many particulars to within a few seconds of time.—

One of two conclusions is inevitable: either the ancients were not acquainted with the true length of the year, or the year has become shorter by about twelve minutes. The difference is small, but this circumstance more firmly supports the general conclusion; for the smallness of the difference agrees with that of the moon, four minutes, taking into account the difference in the magnitude of the orbits. It also agrees with all the processes of nature in the vegetable, animal, and mineral kingdoms. Every operation of nature is carried forward by slow and almost imperceptible means. It is only by comparing the process at two or more distant points that we are enabled to perceive that it has been really going forward.

Coming down a little later, we find that Hipparchus, of Greece, sometimes called the father of astronomy, devoted a considerable share of attention to the calendar. The astronomers of Greece, previous to his time, valued the year at 365 days, six hours. Hipparchus, by comparing his own observations of the summer solstice with one made 145 years previously by Aristarchus, of Samos, discovered this to be too great. He found that the solstice arrived twelve hours sooner at the end of these 145 years than it ought to have done, on the supposition of the solar year being 365 days, six hours: twelve hours divided by 145, gave him the diminution to be made on the length of the year. In this way he found for the length of the tropical year, 365 days, five hours, fifty-five minutes and twelve seconds: so that from the time of the ancient Egyptians either the year had decreased upwards of four minutes, or the Egyptians were unacquainted with its true length. The discovery made by Hipparchus, that his predecessors had fixed the year at too great a length, has also been made by others, not once or twice only, but several times in each succeeding age. Not to dwell upon the point, we may refer to the introduction of the new style under Pope Gregory.

In the time of Julius Cæsar, the Roman calendar had become considerably confused from the Romans having adopted the year of Numa Pompilius. This defect Julius Cæsar proposed to remedy, and to fix the length of the year, so that a similar confusion might not recur at any future time. The Romans at that time were masters of the civilized world, and could of course command the talents and learning of all the countries east and west. Cæsar accordingly instituted a kind of board to settle the calendar, at the head of which was Sosigenes, the most able astronomer of that day. The length of the year was found in the usual way, by dividing the error which had accumulated during a long period, by which Sosigenes concluded that the true length of the solar year was at that time 365 days, six hours. It is probable, however, that Sosigenes had committed a small mistake in his calculations, for we have seen that Hipparchus, nearly a century earlier, had found it to be about four minutes less. This year, from Julius Cæsar, was named the Julian year. If the Julian year had been fixed at the true value, and the earth had really revolved round the sun without approaching the centre, of course the calendar would have remained correct to the end of time. But at the end of fifteen centuries, whether the year having been fixed too long, or from the orbit decreasing, it was found that the vernal equinox had retrograded on the ecliptic eleven days, in consequence of which, it was considered necessary to reform the calendar.

Thus originated the "new style," or Gregorian calendar, by which it was determined that the true length of the solar year was 365 days, five hours, forty-eight minutes, forty-five seconds. The settlement of the Gregorian year was managed by a body of the most learned men in Europe, at that time; they extended their observations over a long period, and *now* it was thought the length of the year was truly fixed and settled, and therefore the calendar could not again become deranged. But it has again been discovered that the length of the year as fixed by the Gregorian calendar, is too long, as may be seen by reference to Dr. Playfair's "System of Chronology." As usual, the discrepancy is attributed to the reformers of the calendar, and no one seems to suspect that the year is gradually becoming shorter.

From all the facts bearing upon the point, it would appear, taking into account the difference of the magnitudes of the earth and moon, and also of the orbits, they are approaching the centre in a corresponding ratio, by a similar law; and, as will be shown hereafter, they must approach, as a condition of their motion in their orbits.

Now, if the moon be approaching, there was a time when she was much further from the earth than at present; if the earth was really attended by five or more satellites, which have been successively precipitated, the remaining moon must have been the most distant of those satellites. In like manner, if the earth has been approaching the centre for millions of years, there must have been a time when she revolved in an orbit as distant as that of Jupiter; and if at that time no more than one satellite had been deposited, then the earth must have been accompanied by four moons, as Jupiter now is. On the other hand, if the satellites of Jupiter be approaching their primary, as the moon is, and the primary Jupiter also approaching the sun, like the earth, then, when Jupiter has reached the earth's orbit, he may not have more than one moon remaining, in which case he will be in the same condition in that respect as the earth now is, and conversely, the earth must have been at a former period in the condition in which Jupiter is at present. So, also, if the earth be becoming denser, she must have been less dense, when she moved in an orbit as distant as that of Jupiter; and by the hypothesis, Jupiter should be at present less dense than the earth. Further, if the earth be more dense now than formerly, she must be less in bulk, and conversely, when she moved in an orbit as distant as that of Jupiter, she must have been less dense, and consequently, of greater bulk. It is true that by the deposition of solid matter in the form of satellites, her solid contents may be more, but her diameter may have decreased in a much greater ratio. Now let us see whether our hypothesis be borne out by an examination of the solar system.

A slight glance at the planetarium, or scheme of the planets, will at once convince us of the extreme probability of this assumption. Here we see the planets and satellites in the following order and proportion: the number of moons are found in regular gradation with one exception, but even this disappears when viewed in connexion with the other parts of our theory; this exception is Mars, and the asteroids or minor planets. Mars has no satellite; and the asteroids, which are no larger than satellites, and appear, from their situation, as if they ought to have been attached to Mars, revolve in orbits round the sun like the primary planets.

According to our hypothesis, this exception to the general rule admits of an easy explication. From the relative situations of Mars and the asteroids, the former appears to have settled into the system of planets at a period too remote to admit of the latter coming within the sphere of his attraction; nor are they, from their equal magnitudes, capable of attracting each other. If we allow this explication, the whole series will stand as follows, taking Mars and the asteroids as a planet and his satellites:—

| *Primaries.* | *Distances from the sun in miles.* | | *No. of Moons.* |
|---|---|---|---|
| Mercury, | 36,000,000 | | 0 |
| Venus, | 68,000,000 | | 0 |
| Earth, | 95,000,000 | | 1 |
| Mars, | 144,000,000 | asteroids, | 4 |
| Jupiter, | 494,000,000 | | 4 |
| Saturn, | 906,000,000 | | 7 |
| Uranus, | 1,822,000,000 | | 6 |

Had the minor planets been attached as satellites to Mars, it is probable, judging by his distance from the sun, as compared with the Earth and Jupiter, we should not at this time have found more than two remaining. We would also remark, that it is by no means improbable that Mars was attended by one or two satellites during the early stage of his planetary existence. It is further to be remarked, that Uranus, the most distant, and, according to our theory, the most recent of all the known planets, is represented as having only six satellites to accompany her, being one less than Saturn. But this number only represents the satellites of Uranus that have been discovered hitherto. Astronomers are agreed that, with more powerful instruments, it is extremely probable that several more might be discovered. Upon the whole, we are satisfied, if this table be considered attentively in conjunction with the foregoing hypothesis, that the truth, or extreme probability of our theory, is a conclusion that must press itself very closely upon the mind.

Our theory assumes, that the planets and satellites are maintained at their respective distances from the sun and each other by the relative quantities of positive and negative electricity with which each is charged, or, in other words, by the solid contents of matter contained in each, and the quantity of electric fluid with which that matter is charged or saturated. Now, as we can determine by experiment the exact state of two electrical bodies by the attractive and repulsive forces which they exert on each other—and we know that these forces follow the same law as to the intensity of the fluid, namely, the inverse ratio of the square of the distance—this might furnish us with a rough datum for ascertaining the moon's electrical state, that is, how far she has receded towards a complete negative condition; and as the power which she exerts upon the tides is governed by the same law that regulates her own distance, we might, by carefully estimating the *difference* of her attractive and repulsive forces in apogee and perigree, be enabled to obtain a tolerably correct measure of her inductive influence. The ocean may be regarded as a great natural barometer, indicating the state of the electrical atmosphere by which the earth is surrounded; but as it is moved by three forces at the same time—the moon, the sun, and the earth's galvanic circle—all these elements of power must be nicely adjusted before we can expect to arrive at any thing like an accurate calculation.

"It is found to be a direct consequence of the law of electrical induction, that 'if a small body weakly electrified be placed at a distance from another and a larger body more highly charged with the same species of electricity, it will, as usual, be repelled; *but there is a certain distance within which, if it be brought, attraction will take place instead of repulsion.*' This happens in consequence of the inductive influence producing so great a change in the distribution of the electricity as to give a preponderance to the attractive forces of the adjacent parts of the two bodies over the repulsive forces that take place in the other parts, and which would have alone acted if the fluid had been immoveable." From this it appears, that when the moon has approached within a certain limit, the repulsive will be overcome by the attractive force, and she will be precipitated upon the earth's surface. We cannot at present pretend to determine this limit, or to speak with any degree of certainty concerning the period that may elapse before this catastrophe takes place. If the principles of this theory were sufficiently investigated to enable us to deduce with precision the electrical states of Jupiter and Saturn, we might perhaps be able to draw conclusions from the respective distances of their satellites with regard to this point; but, in the present state of our knowledge, we can offer no data that could be at all relied upon. However, we will give a table of all the known satellites in the solar system, with their respective distances from their primaries, as affording a reasonable ground of hope, even granting the truth of our theory, that such a catastrophe will not take place for a very considerable period of time:—

*Mean Distances of the Satellites, the Radius of the Primary being 1.*

| | 1st. | 2nd. | 3rd. | 4th. | 5th. | 6th. | 7th. | DISTANCE IN MILES. | | | | | | |
|---|---|---|---|---|---|---|---|---|---|---|---|---|---|---|
| Earth | 60 | ... | ... | ... | ... | ... | ... | 235000 | ... | ... | ... | ... | ... | ... |
| Jupiter | $5\frac{8}{10}$ | $9\frac{1}{4}$ | $14\frac{3}{4}$ | $25\frac{14}{20}$ | ... | ... | ... | 247000 | 397000 | 632000 | 1113000 | ... | ... | ... |
| Saturn | $3\frac{1}{10}$ | $3\frac{19}{20}$ | $4\frac{9}{10}$ | $6\frac{1}{4}$ | $8\frac{3}{4}$ | $20\frac{1}{4}$ | $59\frac{17}{23}$ | 124000 | 158000 | 106000 | 250000 | 350000 | 810010 | 2394000 |
| Uranus | $13\frac{1}{10}$ | 17 | $19\frac{17}{20}$ | $22\frac{3}{4}$ | $45\frac{1}{2}$ | 91 | ... | 129000 | 297000 | 347000 | 379000 | 779000 | 1569000 | ... |

It appears from this table, that the mean distance of the first, or nearest satellite of Saturn, is three one-tenths the radius of the primary, or 124,000 miles. We may, therefore, consider that this satellite, being the nearest to its primary, will be the first to disappear from the solar system. As its final precipitation will be instantaneous, it is by no means probable that it will be observed from this earth. But at whatever future time it may be discovered that Saturn is attended by no more than six satellites, such discovery must be regarded as a demonstration of the truth of this theory.

We have now adverted to the two distinct propositions, that the moon is approaching the earth, and that the earth is approaching the sun. The first was discovered by that eminent astronomer, Edmund Halley, and is now fully established. The reader has had the evidence upon which the second rests placed before him, and of course can form his own judgment. We now turn to the question, Is the earth becoming denser,—is she contracting into solid stone? There is perhaps no single fact in the wide range of natural philosophy, which rests upon a broader, a more secure and indubitable basis, than this, that the solid rocks of the earth have passed, by a slow and regular process, from the liquid to the solid state.

There is a story told of King George the Third, which places this proposition in a very clear and forcible light. Upon a certain occasion, when apple dumplings had been served up at table, on seeing the dumplings cut open, it is said that the king was sorely perplexed to know how the apples could have been got into the dumplings, seeing there was no opening in the outward covering of dough by which they could have been introduced. This story, if true, only shows that the monarch was not much of a philosopher; otherwise he would have known that there was no great difficulty in introducing an apple, or any other extraneous body, into a soft paste, without leaving any mark or visible joining. But let those who smile at the simplicity of the king, whilst doubting of the original fluidity of the earth, have a care lest they be found sneering at their own folly.

There is not a rock on the face of the earth but contains foreign or extraneous bodies, shells, fossil plants, fossil animals, or pieces of other rocks, firmly imbedded in and forming part of the stone; and these foreign bodies could not by any possibility, have been so imbedded, unless the rock had existed in that time under circumstances precisely similar to those of the apple dumpling; that is to say, that which is now solid stone, must have been at that time soft matter, otherwise these foreign bodies could not have been imbedded. Now, if the earth be contracting, it is obvious that she must have been less dense at a former period than she is at present: if she is approaching the sun, it is also obvious that, at an early period, she must have revolved in a larger orbit, at a greater distance from the sun.

Let us turn our attention to the primary planets, at present revolving in the solar system, and observe whether their different densities corresponds with this process, this progressive action, the density of the earth being 18.

| | |
|---|---|
| Mercury, | Twice as dense. |
| Venus, | One and one-fourth. |
| Earth, | One. |
| Mars, | Seven-eighths. |
| Jupiter, | One-fourth. |
| Saturn, | One-fiftieth. |
| Uranus, | Not known. |

The density of the sun has been estimated at one-fourth of that of the earth; but, as we shall have occasion to notice this great central body in another place, we will pass him over at present.

Turning to the planets, we observe that their increasing density, as we approach the sun, exactly corresponds with all the other known facts. That the earth is contracting or becoming denser, we are well assured: we have sufficient evidence for warranting the conclusion, that she is approaching the sun. That the moon is approaching the earth is an established fact; and from this fact we conclude, that she also is following the same laws in other respects,—that she is contracting or passing into a solid state. Hence all the circumstances come together with so much fitness, that they yield support to each other, and command our assent.

But if the earth has been contracting or solidifying through a long series of ages, it is evident that she must have been previously a very different body to what she is at the present time. If the solid rocks have all been formed by slow degrees, then there was a time when there were no rocks on this earth. In that case, what we now call earth, must have been a vast liquid body; and in such a state we have sufficient chemical knowledge to know, that this liquid body must have been surrounded by an immense gaseous atmosphere, as indeed the earth is even at the present time surrounded by a gaseous atmosphere; although it is extremely probable—nay, it is almost certain—that the constitution of the atmosphere is now totally different, as compared with that which surrounded the earth in the early ages when she existed in the liquid state. Now, what should we call a large liquid body, surrounded with an immense atmosphere, and revolving round the sun, and passing to a great distance from him, as the earth must have done at an early period? *A Comet.* But the form of a comet's orbit, it will be objected, is highly eccentric, whilst that of a planet is nearly a circle. We shall advert to this difference in the orbits by and by; but in the mean time it may be as well to observe, that this difference between the orbits is not in the *form*, but merely in the *degree* of *eccentricity*. The comet's orbit is highly eccentric, and the orbit of a planet is also eccentric, though in a less degree; and the earth's orbit is even now becoming less and less eccentric every revolution, at the rate of forty-one and a half miles annually.

But in order to strengthen the position, that the earth has passed from the liquid, and even from the gaseous state, into her present solid or partially solid condition, we will give an extract from a work by De La Beche, Vice-President of the Geological Society of London, a man eminent in the scientific world:—

"There is," says De La Beche, "so much grandeur and simplicity in the idea of the condensation of gaseous matter into those spheres or spheroids which exist, not only in our solar system, but also by myriads throughout the universe, that we are irresistibly led to adopt some view of this kind, more particularly as it would accord with the unity of design so evident throughout the creation. Encke's comet, that remarkable body of vapor which revolves around the sun in about three and one-third years, proves by its existence that gaseous matter or vapor, of extraordinary tenuity, may float around our great luminary in given times, and in a given orbit, checked only by a resisting medium of still more extraordinary tenuity. There is, therefore, no argument, *a priori* against the hypothesis, that the matter composing our globe may once have existed in a gaseous state, and in that state have revolved around the sun.—(Page 25.)

"The sun and known planets of our solar system are of different densities; it therefore follows that the materials of which these bodies are respectively formed, are either different or do not exist under precisely the same circumstances in each. Hence a given density is not necessary to the existence of a planet; and, consequently, there is no argument *a priori* against the supposition that the density of a planet, such as the earth, may have changed during the lapse of time.—(Page 1.)

"The density of the sun is inconsiderable; it has, therefore, been inferred that great heat exists in the interior, enabling it to resist the enormous pressure exerted upon it. If this mode of reasoning be applicable to the sun, it would also appear applicable to larger planets, such as Saturn, the density of which is considered not much to exceed that of *cork*.—(Page 2.)

"To assume that the earth was once an irregular solid, of a rough and uneven surface, and that it has been ground subsequently and externally by the action of the water into a spheroid, seems but a clumsy hypothesis at best, and by no means accords with that simplicity which so pre-eminently distinguishes all the great works of creation."—(Page 7.)

In addition to these observations of M. De La Beche, it may be remarked, that there is nothing more extraordinary in the formation of solid rocks in a fluid earth, than there is in the formation of a *solid stone* in the fluid contained in the bladder of animals. And further, *we know* that solid rocks are even now forming in the earth by a similar process; neither is there any thing extravagant in the assumption, that a liquid sphere might have previously existed in the gaseous state, since we know that by a natural process all liquids may be resolved into their constituent gases. The chemist can effect this decomposition,— and the chemist is but an humble imitator of the works of nature. Besides all these considerations, it may be noticed, that the *original fluidity* of the earth is the fundamental proposition of the Wernerian theory of the earth, and indeed is now generally admitted by all geologists. The assumption that the earth had passed from the gaseous into the fluid state, requires us to go but one step further; and that step is justified by all the known phenomena of nature.

"Though the mind, unaccustomed to philosophical inquiries, may find it difficult to comprehend that this planet once existed in a gaseous state, this difficulty will vanish upon considering the nature of the changes that all the materials of which it is composed must constantly undergo. Water offers a familiar example of a substance existing on the surface of the globe, in the separate states of rock, fluid and vapor, for water consolidated into ice is as much rock as granite or the adamant; and, as we shall hereafter have occasion to remark, has the power of preserving for ages the animals and vegetables that may be therein embedded. Yet upon an increase of temperature, the glaciers of the Alps and the icy pinnacles of the arctic circles disappear; and, by a degree of heat still higher, might be separated into two invisible gases,—hydrogen and oxygen. Metals may in like manner be converted into gases; and in the labaratory of the chemist, all kinds of matter easily pass through every grade of transmutation, from the most dense and compact to an aeriform state. We cannot, therefore, refuse our assent to the conclusion, that the entire of our globe might be resolved into a permanently gaseous form, merely by the dissolution of the existing combinations of matter.* "

If the earth has passed from the gaseous to the liquid state, and is now becoming more and more dense, it follows as a general principle, that the planets farthest from the sun should be of greater diameter, provided they contain the same quantity of matter, as they are contracting, and approaching the centre in a given ratio. It is by no means to be supposed that all the planets contain the same quantity of matter; however, the bulk of the planets also strengthens the electrical theory. Those nearer to the sun are denser and of less diameter; whilst those further removed, are in these respects in an inverse ratio, as will be seen by the following table, the diameter of the earth being one:—

| | |
|---|---|
| Mercury, | —4-10ths. |
| Venus, | —9-10ths. |
| Earth, | 1 |
| Mars, | —8-10ths.† |
| Jupiter, | 11 |
| Saturn, | 10 |
| Uranus, | 4 |

*Mantell's Wonders of Geology.

† Mars is both less dense and smaller than the earth, and, therefore, has no satellite.

Saturn is one-fiftieth of the density of the earth and of ten times the diameter; therefore, if, when he has arrived at the earth's orbit, he should be contracted to an equal degree of solidity, he would not be much larger than the earth, even if he should in the interim receive a considerable accession of solid matter by the deposition of his satellites, for it is to be presumed that the satellites also are of a density corresponding to that of their primary, and will, in course of things, become contracted into much smaller volume.

It is also maintained in the electrical theory, that the rotation of the planets on their axes is dependent upon the internal activity of the body, the action being exerted through the agency of the sun; that the action is proportionate to the age of the planet, being more active in the beginning, and becoming less and less so as the body advances in age. This will be more fully treated of hereafter; but in the meantime, let us examine how far the facts agree with the hypothesis:

| | *hours.* | *min.* |
|---|---|---|
| Mercury—time of rotation— | 24 | 5 |
| Venus, | 23 | 21 |
| Earth, | 23 | 56 |
| Jupiter, | 9 | 55 |
| Saturn, | 10 | 16 |
| Uranus, | unknown. | |

The centrifugal effect (not force,) no doubt influences the time of rotation; but yet the general law which indicates that the time of rotation decreases, as the density and consequent inactivity increases, is sufficiently obvious. Upon collating all the facts and inferences, whether deduced from astronomy or geology, it is at once perceived that a harmony runs through the whole. Every thing points to one conclusion:—that the earth and all the planets and satellites of the solar system had their beginning in a fluid state; that they are now contracting, and, like the clock, or, perhaps, more correctly, like a river, they are running down towards the centre of attraction; and that they move in their courses only because they are so running down, as the river moves in its course only because it is running down towards the centre of the earth.

If the globe which we now inhabit has really existed in a gaseous state, and in that state has revolved around the central sun, it would seem a solecism still to attach to it the name and character of a planet. A body of gas revolving around the sun, cannot be considered in any other light than that of a comet. We shall, therefore, proceed to notice a few particulars relating to the physical constitution and motions of those bodies, which, although they were observed by the ancients, as wandering meteors, have but recently, comparatively speaking, become known to us as bodies of vapor or gas, forming a constituent part of the solar system, and in which, as we shall see, internal changes are going on as important as those which have been going forward in the earth — as disclosed to us by the study of geology.

Our knowledge of comets is as yet but very limited; we cannot, therefore, expect to find the same amount of evidence in this unexplored region as in the old beaten track of astronomy. It is probable, however, that we shall find a few facts that will serve us as guide-posts in our journey round the *circuit of motion of the solar system*, for that is the great object of our philosophical travels in pursuit of knowledge. Before we begin to draw inferences, it is necessary that we should be in possession of such facts as are within our reach; we will, therefore, present to our readers the substance of the report presented to the French Board of Longitude, in 1831, which is drawn up by that eminent philosopher, M. Arago, and contains within a small compass, perhaps as clear and correct an account of these bodies as can be obtained at the present time:—

"What is that that we call a comet? A comet, etymologically considered, means a star with a head of hair. The most luminous point, seen at or near the centre, is the nucleus. The nebulosity, or foggy luminous aureola, which surrounds the nucleus on every side, is called the hair. The nucleus and this hair together form the head of the comet. The luminous trains, some long, others short, with which most comets are accompanied, whatever direction they are projected in, are called tails.

"Nature of cometary orbits and their elements.

"Comets, which some ancient philosophers considered as meteors, originating in our atmosphere, are, in fact, real stars. The simultaneous observations made on them at different stations in the earth, at a great distance from each other, prove this.

"Since the time of Tycho, who made this discovery, it has been ascertained that comets revolve around the sun, according to regular laws, similar to those that regulate the planetary movements, only that their orbits are very long ellipses, of which the sun always occupies one of the foci. The summit of the ellipse nearest the sun is called the perihelion; the opposite point of the ellipse is called the aphelion. These and all other technical terms should be remembered.

"Comets are seldom seen from the earth except when near their perihelion; and, although it cannot well be given here, a simple calculation demonstrates that three observations made on a comet from the earth are sufficient to determine its orbit.

"On the means of knowing when a comet appears, if it be a new one, or if it has been seen before.

"As soon as a comet has been observed three times, astronomers can calculate its orbit; and they immediately examine and inquire whether or no the elements of this orbit have been previously registered in the catalogue of comets. By following up this inquiry, and by attending to other particulars well known to astronomers, they can decide whether or no the comet under consideration has appeared before or not; and in this way Halley has shown us, that the comets seen by Kepler, in 1607, and by himself in 1682, were identified, that is, they were the same comet. This gives us an interval of seventy-five years; and if Halley's conjectures were correct, this same comet ought to have appeared about seventy-five years before 1607; and, in fact, a comet was observed at Ingoldstadt in 1531—that is, seventy-six years before 1607,—whose inclination, longitude, and other elements of its orbit, agreed with the two succeeding ones, and astronomers no longer doubted the identity of these three comets.

"Halley, on this, immediately predicted that this comet would re-appear at the end of 1758 or the beginning of 1759, the elements of whose orbit would differ but little from those just noticed; and this prediction having been fulfilled, at once gave a new era in cometary astronomy. But Halley was prevented from being very precise as to time, from his belief that the motion of this comet would be retarded by the attraction of two of the planets, and that it would employ about 618 days more to reach its perihelion, than it did in the preceding revolution,—that is, 100 days from the effect of Saturn, and 518 days from the action of Jupiter. The appearance of this comet, therefore, at its perihelion, was calculated by Halley for about the middle of April, 1759. Clairaut, however, discovered that Halley had neglected some small elements, and showed that this comet would be at its perihelion on the 12th of March, 1759; and the event justified these calculations.

"No doubt being left, therefore, as to the identity of this comet, M. Damoiseau, of the Board of Longitude, having by immense labor taken into calculation all the causes of perturbation which will affect this comet on its return, particularly the effect of the planet Uranus, whose existence was not known in the time of Clairaut, this astronomer, our colleague, has lately come to the following conclusion:—'The interval between the arrival of the comet of 1759, and that of its approaching arrival at its perihelion, will be 28,007 days; which, reckoning from the 12th of March, 1759, will bring us to the 16th of November, 1835.' Thus, then, in the middle of November, 1835, we shall see again passing near the sun, that comet, which, in 1456, with a tail of sixty degrees in length, terrified all Europe by its brilliancy, by causing astrological predictions, and by a superstitious application of its appearance to the then fearful progress of the Mahametan arms.

"M. Arago here enters into some details on the comet of 1767 and 1770, whose revolution was fixed at five and a half years by accurate observation; but tells us, too, that in 1767, when that comet approached Jupiter, its elliptical orbit was not of five, but of fifty years, and that afterwards, in 1779, on this comet's emerging from the sphere of Jupiter's attraction, its orbit was so altered from what it had been in 1770, that its duration was of twenty years. 'Hence,' says he, 'we are justified in concluding that this comet of 1770 was brought within the sphere of our vision in 1767 by the action of Jupiter, and that in 1779 its orbit was so lengthened by the same action that we lost sight of it.'

"We now come to the comet usually called 'The Comet of the Short period.'

"This comet was discovered at Marseilles, in 1818, by M. Pons; and M. Bouvard presented the elements of its orbit to the Board of Longitude, in January, 1819. A member of the Board was struck with the similarity of these elements to those of a comet observed in 1805, and no doubt was entertained that these comets were the same. It was then suggested that the comet might have returned more than once in the thirteen years which had elapsed between 1805 and 1818, and this was found to be the truth by M. Encke, of Berlin, who established by indisputable calculations that the elliptical orbit of this comet was completed in about 1,290 days, or about 33-10ths years. This period of its revolution has been since established by actual observation, for this comet of 1818, re-appeared in 1822, in 1825, and in 1829, in the places assigned to it by M. Encke beforehand, with very little variation, of which we shall consider the causes presently. This comet will reach its perihelion on the 4th of May, 1832, but the astronomers of the Cape of Good Hope and of New Holland, will be much more advantageously situated to observe it than those of Europe.

"The comet of 6 3-4 years. We are now arrived in our list at another comet which will re-appear in 1832, and whose proximity to us will be, we are assured, so fatal to the earth and its inhabitants.

"This comet, which astronomers have agreed to call the 6 3-4 years comet, and which has been announced by several writers as threatening our globe with such dreadful ruin during this year of 1832, was first perceived at Johanisberg, by M. Biela, on the 27th of February, 1826, and ten days after by M. Gambert, at Marseilles, who, calculating its parabolic elements, ascertained that this comet had been observed before in 1805 and in 1772. This comet, therefore, is periodical, and it became necessary, in order to determine accurately the time of its revolution, to quit the parabolic elements, and to found calculations on its elliptical elements. M. M. Clausen and Gambart undertook this calculation, and they both came to the result, that this comet revolved around the sun in something less than seven years.

"This result was adopted at once, for in 1826 philosophers had completely abandoned the old notion, that the revolutions of comets must be of necessity, of very great length and duration. However, after the example of the comet of 1770, it would have been hazardous to predict the future re-appearance of this heavenly body, before calculating all the derangements which it might suffer from different planets; our colleague, M. Damoiseau, therefore undertook this long and minute calculation, and the result was, that the comet of 6 3-4 years will cross the plane of the ecliptic, that is, the plane in which the earth moves, on the 29th October, 1832, before midnight. Now, as the earth during its course around the run never quits the plane of the ecliptic, it is in that plane alone that a comet can strike against it, so that, whatever dangers we may have to fear from the comet in question, will be on the 29th of next October before midnight.

"The next consideration is, will this comet, when it crosses the line of the ecliptic, pass near, or over any part of the earth's orbit? for this it must do to cause any mischief.

"On this point, M. Damoiseau's calculations show us that the comet will cross the plane of the ecliptic a little within our orbit, and at such a distance from it as is equal to four radii and 2-3ds of our globe; and, we may say, that this small distance may disappear entirely, if the elements given by M. Damoiseau be submitted to certain minute variations, which it would not be easy to account for or remove.

"Let us take, however, the distance of four radii and 3-4 as the real and true distance. We must recollect that this distance is measured from the centre of the comet, and then let us consider whether or no the dimensions of this body be sufficiently great for some part of it to overlap or lie on our orbit.

"The observations made by the celebrated M. Olbers, of Bremen, on this comet in 1805, gave for the length of its radius (or semi-diameter) five radii and 1-3 of our globe; and as we have just seen that the centre of the comet will be only four radii and 2-3ds of the earth from her orbit, it results clearly that a portion of the earth's orbit will, on the 29th of next October, be comprehended or enveloped within the nebulosity of the comet.

"There remains now only one more question, which is, where, that is, in what part of its orbit, will the earth be at the moment when the nebulosity of the comet rests upon, or embraces a part of that orbit?

"The answer is, the earth will not arrive at that point of its orbit which will be enveloped in the nebulosity of the comet on the 29th of October, until the 30th of November following, that is, rather more than a month afterwards. We have now only to take the mean rate at which the earth travels through its orbit, and this being 674,000 leagues per diem, each league may be taken at about 2 1-2 English miles; a simple calculation will prove that the comet of 6 3-4 years will, at all times of its appearance in 1832, be at more than 20,000,000 leagues from the earth. But if, instead of crossing the ecliptic on the 29th of October, this comet were to arrive on the 30th of November, it would infallibly mix its atmosphere with ours, and, perhaps, even it would strike against us; but I hasten to say, that an error of a month in the calculated arrival of a comet at a given point is not impossible.

"The reader now knows all that can interest him as to the route of the comet in the month of October, 1832. The results which I have given are the same as those which M. Olbers gave in a note, and on which the public, as well as the writers in the newspapers have fallen into such mistakes. I hope I shall be more fortunate, and not be misunderstood. But there are still people who, admitting that the earth will not receive a direct shock from the comet in October next, believe that it cannot touch our orbit without altering the form of it; as if that orbit were a material substance—as if, in short, the parabolic flight of a shell from a mortar could be affected by passing through a space which had been antecedently traversed by other shells.

"On the effect of the resistance of the ether in space on the route of comets.

"Hitherto the routes or courses of planets have agreed exactly with the astronomical tables which have been founded on the supposition that their motion was performed in a perfect vacuum.

"The course of the 'Comet of the Short Period' (Encke's) has just shown us that a new element must be taken into consideration as regards comets; I allude to the resistance which a gaseous substance of great rarity which fills space, and which it has been agreed to call 'ether,' opposes to the movements of bodies traversing it.

"This resistance produces no sensible effect on planets, on account of their density; but comets being generally little more than aggregations of light vapors, are sensibly retarded by this ether.

"In calculating the positions in which the 'Comet of the Short Period' should be found in 1822, 1825, and 1829, M. Encke strictly calculated the derangements it would suffer from the action of planets: nevertheless, at each re-appearance of this comet, there was a difference between calculation and observation, and always on the same side. The cause of these discordances could be found only in the supposed resistance of the ether; and M. Encke has shown this resistance to amount to about two days in each revolution. If this influence on the comet of 6 3-4 years were of the same description, it would not affect essentially the results at which we lately arrived as to the results of the minimum of the comet's distance from the earth in 1832.

"I might have omitted noticing this new cause of perturbation, but I have spoken of it because certain uneasy people have seized on this resistance of the ether, to come to the conclusion, that the moment of the comet's passage through the plane of the ecliptic could not be predicted with certainty; but I will develope this objection in all its force. The comet, if moving in a vacuum, would arrive at a point of our orbit thirty-one days before the earth; but the natural effect of resistance would be to retard, and as the comet moves in ether, it ought to arrive on our orbit later than was indicated, and hence its distance from the earth will be less than was calculated. But let us go straight to the point: according to the objection made, the real position of the comet would be less advanced than its calculated position. What, however, were the facts in the instance of Encke's comet? Why, on its three appearances in 1822, 1825, and 1829, the real comet always preceded the theoretical or calculated comet.

"There is, therefore, no longer any question as to the comet of 6 3-4 years passing the plane of the ecliptic later than was at first calculated. If this comet is governed by the same principles as the comet of Encke, its passage over our orbit must be hastened, and the minimum of the earth's distance would be increased in proportion. I confess that at first sight this acceleration may appear strange, and one would think that a medium which resists could only retard; but this difficulty ceases on our reflecting that the immediate effect of a resisting medium on a body moving in it, is to diminish its centrifugal force, which is just the same as if the attractive force of the sun increased. An increase of this force naturally draws the moving body nearer to the sun, and every one knows that the nearer a celestial body approaches the sun in its orbit, it moves so much the quicker.

"Will this comet have any serious effect on the seasons of 1832?

"This query will, no doubt, awaken the recollection of the grand comet of 1811, which year was so renowned for its vintage, that wines made in 1811 were called 'comet wines.' I know that there are strong prejudices against me, but I will say, that neither the comet of 1811, nor any other comet, has ever had the slightest effect on our seasons. I will begin with facts. Comets, people tell us, warm our globe by their presence. Do they? Nothing is more easy than to refer to the thermometers kept in the different observatories of Europe. Let us take that of Paris, and we shall find the fact, that the medium temperature of the years most noted for comets is less than those of the years in which no comets have appeared. One may here remark, in passing, that the year 1805, with its two comets, was a year in which the medium temperature was low compared with other years; that 1808 may be reckoned amongst the cold years, although few years have produced so many comets; that the coldest year in the table was 1829, in which a comet appeared; and that the year 1831, in which there was no comet, enjoyed a much higher temperature than 1819, when there were three comets, one of which was very brilliant.

"With these facts before us, we cannot attribute to comets any calorific power, as far as our seasons are concerned. But there are other considerations which we keep in view. A comet, in passing, can act on the earth only in three manners:—1. By means of attraction; 2. By its luminous and calorific rays, which emanate from it in all directions; or 3. By the gaseous matter which composes its nebulosity or its tail, and which might fall into our terrestrial atmosphere. This last consideration may be dispensed with as regards the comet of 1832, for it has no tail, and its head will be, as has been shown, at an immense distance from the earth; nor did the tail of the comet of 1811 ever pass over the earth, for, although that tail was 41,000,000 of leagues in length, the comet was never within 47,000,000 of leagues of the earth, and accurate experiments proved that the maximum of light which the comet of 1811 shed upon the earth was not equal to one-tenth of the light of the moon, and when concentrated did not produce the slightest effect on the blackened bulb of the most sensitive thermometer.

"It is, then, to the attractive force of comets that we must look for their supposed meteorological influence.

"Here the moon will serve as a point of comparison. The moon causes the tides of the ocean:—mathematically speaking, the comet of 1811 ought to have produced analogous tides; we must admit that they did not amount to any appreciable quantity. But the height of a tide is proportioned to the attractive power. We know that the lunar tides are very great, and the cometary tides, if any, are insensible; hence it is clear, that the cometary action on the earth bears no proportion to that of the moon; and as to any calorific effects of the great comet of 1811, the most delicate instruments have not shown their existence.

"Can, then, the wine growers expect any result from the comet of 1832?"

*On the physical construction of Comets, that is, their Nebulosity, Nucleus, and Tail.*

"I have before spoken of the nebulosity or hair of the nucleus, and of the tail of a comet. I will now detail all that telescopes have enabled us to discover of their parts.

"Many comets have no visible tail; many have been seen without any visible nucleus; but in no case have comets been seen without their nebulosity—or fogginess, which the ancients called their hair."

On the Nebulosity.—"Amongst the comets having no visible nucleus, and which appeared to be mere globular masses of vapor, slightly condensed towards the centre, I will name only the comets of 1759, 1767, 1798, and the little comet of 1804, whose nebulosity was about 2,000 leagues in diameter. Seneca tells us that stars may be seen through comets, and Herschel saw a star of the sixth magnitude through the midst of a comet without a nucleus in 1795; and Struve, on the 28th of November, 1680, saw clearly a star of the eleventh magnitude through the central part of the 'Comet of the Short Period.'

"When there is a nucleus in the centre of the comet, it seldom happens that the nebulosity extends to this nucleus, with a gradually increasing intensity. On the contrary, the parts of the nebulosity nearest to the nucleus are but feebly illuminated, and appear to be very diaphanous and rare. At some distance from the centre, their light increases suddenly, so as to present a luminous ring round the centre. Sometimes two or three of these concentric rings have been seen, separated by dark lines from each other; but we can easily suppose that this apparent ring is, in fact, a spherical envelope, embracing the centre of the comet. In the comet of 1811, the luminous envelope was not less than 10,000 leagues thick, and its interior surface 12,000 leagues from the centre of the nucleus.

"When the comet has a tail, the luminous ring is closed or complete only on the side next the sun, and forms only a semi-circle. The two ends or horns of this semicircle are the points of departure from which emanates the tail."

ON THE NUCLEUS.—"Comets have often nuclei resembling planets, both in shape and brilliancy. In general they are only small, but not always so. The following is a table of the diameters of nuclei of the several comets:—

| | | | |
|---|---|---|---|
| Comet of | 1798, | 11 | leagues. |
| " | 1799, | 154 | ditto. |
| 2nd comet | 1811, | 1089 | ditto. |
| " | 1897, | 222 | ditto. |

"Some astronomers contend that cometary nuclei, even those which, from their brightness, most resemble planets, are completely diaphanous; that comets, in short, are a mere assemblage of vapors. They found this opinion on observations which I do not think conclusive. The question is important: its solution will decide, to a certain degree, the part we may attribute to comets in the revolutions of the physical world.

"All comets in their courses traverse successively different constellations. The region in which they move is much nearer to us than the fixed stars; therefore, whenever the nucleus of a comet passes between us and a fixed star, we are better able to judge of its composition than in any other position; unfortunately, these exact conjunctions are very unfrequent, but there are some examples:—

"The 23rd of October, 1774, Montaigne saw at Limoges, a star of the 6th magnitude through the nucleus of a comet. This would prove, beyond doubt, that the comet of 1774 had no solid or opaque part, if the star had been seen through the middle of the nucleus; but Montaigne does not say that this was the case, and, in truth, the want of power in his telescope did not enable him to be thus explicit.

"On the 1st of April, 1796, Olbers saw a star of the sixth or seventh magnitude, which lost none of its light, although it was covered by a comet; but he tells us, that the star was a little to the north of the centre of the nebulosity, and if the nucleus disappeared for a short time, it was only because of the stronger light of the fixed star. Other cases which produced no real occultation might be cited, and to which the same doubts would apply.

"On the other hand, if I were to assert that there does exist a solid and opaque body in the centre of the luminous nuclei of comets, the annals of astronomy would furnish me with plausible arguments in support of that opinion. I might cite Messier, who, when he perceived, for the first time, the little comet of 1774, discovered but one star near the nucleus, but some hours afterwards, a second star was seen near the first, and we can hardly help thinking with Messier, that this star might have been at first hidden behind the opaque or solid part of the comet. I might add, that the 'Comet of the Short Period,' on the 28th of November, 1828, as observed by M. Wartman, at Geneva, completely eclipsed a star of the eighth magnitude; and here I will remark, that a positive fact has always an infinite advantage over a negative one, and that the actual eclipse of a star by a comet conveys a proof of a fact, whereas the non-observation of such an eclipse proves only that it did not take place from the probble cause, that the solid or opaque nucleus did not pass exactly over the star. However, as I am not a partisan of any system, I will confess that M. Wartman used too feeble a telescope; and further, that the observation of Messier would have been more satisfactory if the eclipsed star had been seen before its emersion; but the truth is, we have not data whereon to found a general principle as to the physical constitution of very small comets. Some comets have no apparent nucleus, but are generally bright in all parts, and these are no more than aggregations of gaseous matter; a further degree of concentration may cause in the centre of the nebulosity a nucleus remarkable for its brightness, but which, being still liquid, would be diaphanous, and at a more advanced period this liquid having cooled, will be enveloped in a solid crust, and from that moment the nucleus will be no longer transparent. Then, indeed, the eclipse of a star by a comet would be as real as those occultations of stars which so frequently occur in regard to the moon and planets.

"Nothing, then, proves that no comets exist of this third sort, that is,—of solid nuclei; on the contrary, the great brilliancy of some of them justify a belief in the solidity of their nuclei. But those who wish to establish some general canon for the nature and composition of all comets, have only to study, as I have done, the archives of astronomy for the last forty years, to be convinced of the impossibility of finding it.

"Without citing all the wonderful stories which have been told of comets whose light equalled that of the sun, and eclipsed that of the moon, I will here give some facts which are incontestible.

"Forty-three years before the Christian era, appeared 'a hairy star,' which was seen with the naked eye in the day-time. This was the comet which the Romans believed had received the soul of Cæsar, who was assassinated just before its appearance.

"In the year 1402, were two remarkable comets. The first was so brilliant, that the light of the sun at the end of March did not hinder people's seeing at mid-day both its nucleus and its tail, which latter, to use the language of the day, was full two fathoms long. The second comet appeared in the month of June, and was visible long before the setting of the sun.

"Cardan tells us how every body's curiosity was roused at Milan, by the appearance of a star in 1552, which was visible in open day-light. The fine comet of 1577 was discovered on the 13th of November, by Tycho Brahe, before sun-set; but I hasten to a more modern comet, of which we have in a special treatise detailed observations.

"The 1st of February, the comet of 1744 was, according to Cheseaux, more resplendent than Sirius, which is the brightest fixed star of the heavens. On the 18th of February, this comet equalled in brightness the planet Jupiter; some days afterward it nearly equalled Venus in splendor. In the beginning of March, this comet was near the sun, and on the 1st, many persons saw it at midday without glasses.

"To sum up,—We may conclude, from what we have seen, that there are comets without nuclei, comets whose nuclei are perhaps diaphanous, and comets more brilliant than planets, whose nuclei are probably solid and opaque.

"Of the Tail.—The long luminous train by which

comets are often accompanied, has been called at all times 'the tail.' Pierre Apinn ascertained that the comet of 1531 carried its tail in every part of its course, so as to have it always in a prolongation of the line which joined the sun and the nucleus; but this principle has been adopted too generally. It is true that for the most part the tail is placed behind the comet, so as to stream out in a direction opposed to the sun; but the line which joins those two luminaries, hardly ever corresponds with the axis of the tail. Sometimes the want of coincidence of these two lines is very great; indeed in some cases the tail stands out at right angles from the line of conjunction. In fact, it has been ascertained that the tail has constantly an inclination towards the region which the comet has left, as if in its motion through a gaseous medium, the matter of which the tail was formed, had been more powerfully acted upon or resisted, than was experienced by the nucleus.

"The tails become much larger, that is, wider as they lengthen out from the comet. In the middle of them is seen a dark band, which divides them into two distinct, and often equal parts. Ancient observers considered this band to be the shadow of the body of the comet. This explanation cannot be applied to the tails which point towards the sun; perhaps we shall suit our hypothesis to general appearances, if we suppose the tail to be a hollow cone, which, from well known physical causes, might be supposed to present to us two exterior lines of light, separated by a space comparatively dark.

"It is not uncommon to see in comets several separate tails. The comet of 1744, on the 7th and 8th of March, had as many as six, each about four degrees wide, and from thirty to forty degrees long. Their edges were totally light, the lines down their axes gave but a feeble light, and the space between those tails was as dark as the rest of the heavens.

"The tails of comets embrace immense spaces. The following are some of the measurements:—Tail of the comet of 1611, twenty-three degrees long; that of 1689, sixty-three degrees long, and bent like a Turkish sabre, as the cotemporaries say; tail of the comet of 1680, ninety degrees long; that of 1769, ninety-seven degrees long. Thus, these comets of 1680 and 1769 could reach the horizon and set, while part of their tails were still in the zenith.

"I will give here some measurements of comets' tails in leagues, (each league being two and a half English miles.) Tail of the comet of 1680, more than 41,000,000 of leagues; 1769, more than 16,000,000 of leagues; the several tails of the comets of 1744, more than 2,000,000 of leagues.

"I ought here, perhaps, to dilate on the nature of cometary light, on the causes which produce comets' tails, which modify their shapes, &c.; but I will freely confess, that in the present state of science, I could offer on these subjects only gratuitous hypotheses and unsupported theories. It is true, cometary science has made great progress during the last century and a half, but the physical composition of these bodies is still wrapped in great obscurity.

"Are comets luminous themselves, or do they, like planets, only reflect the sun's rays?

"This indeed is a main question not yet answered; but as soon as a comet shall appear, showing to us an evident phasis, all doubts will cease. The phases said to have been seen by Cassini and Dunn, are not substantiated; and in regard to the crescent said to be seen by M. Cacciatore, in the comet of 1819, at Palermo, I will only say, that the line of the horns, instead of being as it would have been in a real phasis, perpendicular to the line joining the sun and the comet, was, on the contrary, parallel to it. On the other hand, the want of phases in the nucleus of a comet surrounded by a thick atmosphere, which might distribute light all over the nucleus, brings us to no certain conclusion; but recent physical discoveries promise us great results, for it has been ascertained that reflected light, when impinging on the eye at certain angles, has some peculiar properties which distinguish it from direct (or primitive) light. In fact, some traces of these properties have been detected by astronomers at Paris, in the comet of 1819; but, after all, nothing certain has been arrived at; and, in fact, were a body ascertained to be itself luminous, it does not on that account lose the power of reflecting the light of other bodies.

"The nebulosity of comets, when attentively considered, presents also inextricable difficulties. Without doubt it seems easy and natural, at the first glance, to suppose comets to be simply masses of permanent gas and vapors, thrown out from the nucleus by the constant influence of the solar rays; but what becomes, under this system, of the luminous concentric envelopes seen round some comets? And why should the nucleus be eccentric, and generally so towards the sun, though sometimes so on the opposite side?

"The different magnitudes of the nebulosities of comets are worthy of deep attention, and Hevelius, rising above all system, announced at once that the diameters of the nebulosities increased in proportion as comets receded from the sun! Pringre had also perceived this, but only dared to announce it in an incidental manner. Although I do not mean to justify Pringre's hesitation, yet in his day, considering too, all the difficulties of admeasurement, &c., we cannot wonder at it; and indeed it was hard to believe that a gaseous mass should, in proportion as it receded from the sun, that is, as it plunged into colder regions, be considerably expanded, instead of being condensed. But, thanks to the 'Comet of the Short Period,' the observation of Hevelius is now established beyond all doubt, and is admitted amongst fully recognized truths. I will now give a table of the variations which the real diameter of this comet underwent in 1826:—

| Dates. | Distance of the comet from the sun. | True diameter of the nebulosity in semi-diameters of the sun. |
|---|---|---|
| 28th October, | 1.4617 | 79.4 |
| 7th November, | 1.3217 | 64.8 |
| 30th November, | 0.9668 | 29.8 |
| 7th December, | 0.8473 | 19.9 |
| 14th December, | 0.7285 | 11.5 |
| 24th December, | 0.5419 | 3.1 |

"The numbers in the second column depend on the supposition that the earth's distance from the sun is in unity. Now, from the preceding table, we see that on the 28th of October, the comet was nearly three times further from the sun than on the 24th of December, but that, notwithstanding this, the real diameter of the nebulosity was about twenty-five times; or in other words, that during the approach of the comet to the sun, the volume of the comet was reduced to the sixteen-millionth part of its original amount, the sixteen-millionth part corresponding with its least distance from the sun.

"It would require a volume to give even an abridgement of the different systems by which astronomers have endeavored to account for, and explain the nature of the tail of comets. Some suppose the lighter particles to be swept away by the impulsion of the solar rays. This might account for tails standing out opposite to the sun, but not for tails perpendicular to that line, nor for six tails at a time, which stand out in all directions: further, some of the comets which appear very thin and light, have no tails at all. The resistance of the ether may have something to do with these tails, but we have yet a long time to wait before any thing can be predicted of this problem so difficult to solve.

"From what I have said of the general tenuity of comets, those who fear the effects of one of them striking the earth, will derive some consolation; and in this we shall be fortified if we study the movements of those planets near which the comets sometimes pass.

"The comet of 1770 is the one which has hitherto passed nearest to us, according to known observations. Its smallest distance from the earth was 602,000 leagues—that is, six times as far as the moon. Laplace has shown that the action of the earth on this comet augmented the period of its revolution by two days, and the re-action of the comet ought in like manner to lengthen the time of the earth's revolution round the sun; but observations have proved that in 1770 the length of our year was not increased by one second. In fact, this comet twice traversed the space in which the satellites of Jupiter move, without causing amongst them the slightest alteration.

"May a comet sometimes strike on the earth, or on some other planet?

"Planets revolve round the sun, according to some primitive law, all in the same direction, and in orbits approaching to circles. Comets, on the contrary, move in very lengthened eclipses, and in every direction. In coming from their aphelia, they constantly traverse our solar system; they pass within the orbits of the planets,—and often they pass even between Mercury and the sun;—therefore, it is not impossible for a comet to come out and strike the earth. Having thus admitted the possibility of a shock, let us hasten to declare that its probability is very small. A mere consideration of the immensity of space in which our globe and comets move, and the small size of these bodies, will show this probability to be very small; but mathematics will go much further, and will give to us a numerical measure of this probability, calculated on the diameter of the comet compared with that of the earth. Let us suppose a comet, of which we only know, that at its perihelion it would be nearer the sun than ourselves, and that it should have a diameter equal to one-fourth of the diameter of the earth; then the calculation of chances shows that it is 281,000,000 to 1 that these two bodies shall not meet, or in other words, 281,000,000 to 1 in our favor. But in this calculation we have supposed to the comet a diameter far too large, and if we strike out the nebulosity, and calculate the chances on the nucleus only, we may multiply the foregoing chances in our favor by ten. This ought to tranquilize the most timid; and as to the comet of 1832, its orbit is known as well as that of the earth, and we have already shown where these two bodies will be when the comet crosses our orbit.

"Do we find, in all we know of astronomical phenomena, any reason to suppose that comets have ever fallen into the sun, or into any of the fixed stars?

"The comet of 1680, at its perihelion, was only one-sixth of the diameter of the sun from its surface. In a region so near this immense globe, the atmosphere which surrounds it may have a considerable density, and may produce on bodies passing through it effects which must not be neglected. This would be true, in particular, in regard to comets whose rapidity of motion at the perihelion is considerable, and whose density is inconsiderable. The necessary effect of such an atmosphere on the comet of 1680, would be to diminish its tangential or centrifugal velocity; but if any celestial body is retarded in its movement, and thereby loses part of its centrifugal force, the centripetal counterbalancing force at once becomes the preponderating force, and the revolving body quits its curve to fall towards the centre of attraction. Thus, then, the comet would pass nearer the sun than it did at its former revolution; and as this approximation will be continued at each return to the perihelion, the comet of 1680 will end by falling into the sun.

"These reasonings rest on demonstrable mechanical principles; we must only admit that in our present ignorance of the density and arrangement of the solar atmosphere, as well as of the orbit and nature of the comet of 1680, it is impossible to calculate in how many ages the catastrophe I have alluded to will occur. The annals of astronomy give us no reason to suppose that any such event has taken place within the time of historical records.

"Let us, however, go into the remotest times, and considering the laws of our own planetary system, let us inquire if there be any thing in these laws which would force us to admit that a comet has, at some former period, fallen into the sun?

"All the planets circulate round the sun from west to east, and in planes forming very small angles from each other. The satellites move round the primaries also from west to east. Moreover, wherever we have discovered a motion of rotation, both planets and satellites turn on their axes from west to east. We shall soon see how extraordinary this phenomenon is, by looking at the enumeration of all these similar motions.

"Astronomers have observed motions of rotation in the Sun, in Mercury, Venus, the Earth, Mars, Jupiter, and Saturn; in the moon, in the four satellites of Jupiter, in the ring of Saturn, and in one of Saturn's satellites, which give a total of sixteen. If to these sixteen motions of rotation we add the motions of translations of these bodies, as well as of those whose rotary motion has escaped notice, we shall find forty-three motions all taking the same direction; but, by calculating the chances, it is more than four thousand millions to one, that this disposition of our solar system is not the effect of accident. We must, therefore, come at once to the conclusion, that some primitive physical law must have been impressed on the motion of these bodies at the moment of their formation.

"Buffon is the first who ventured to mount to the origin of the planets and their satellites, and to account for this similarity of motion. He supposed that a comet falling obliquely on the sun, grazed or furrowed the surface of it, and drove off a quantity of fluid matter, the lighter parts of which, driven to the greatest distance, concentrated and formed the planets Saturn and Jupiter, whose density is, in fact, not great, while the heavier portion, driven to a less distance, produced Mercury, Venus, the Earth, and Mars, and that thus the planets were in their origin so heated as to be in a state of fusion, and that they then all took regular forms, and, in cooling, assumed the appearances we now see. Some of the objections which have been urged against Buffon's system might be answered, particularly those which object to the greatness of the mass to be driven off from the sun by the supposed shock of a comet, for the whole of the planets and their satellites do not amount to one eight-thousandth part of the mass of the sun.

"Celestial bodies, produced as Buffon supposes, would be endued in their motions of translation with that similitude which we remark in our planetary system; but it would not be the same in regard to their motions of rotation, for these might have turned in a direction opposite to the motions of translation. The earth, for example, in performing her orbit from west to east, might, in possibility, have turned on her axis from east to west. This objection may be applied also to the satellites, the direction of whose motion is not of necessity the same as the motion of translation of their primaries. Thus, the hypothesis of Buffon does not meet all the circumstances of the phenomena. Hence it has not disclosed the secret of the formation of the planets, and hence we cannot come to the conclusion that the birth of our system was owing to a comet impinging on the sun.

"But modern discoveries have furnished other objections with which Buffon could not be acquainted. For instance, every solid body, say a cannon ball, thrown into space with a velocity sufficient to make it revolve as a satellite round the earth, must, at each revolution, pass through the point from which it first departed, allowing for the resistance of the air. This may be shown from the first principles of mechanics. If, therefore, the comet of Buffon, in striking the sun, had driven off from it solid fragments which became afterwards our planets, this comet must at each revolution have returned to its original point of departure,—that is, must have brushed against the surface of the sun, where it had before impinged; but every body knows that this is not the case. Moreover, Buffon adopts as a condition that the masses driven off from the sun were hot, and in a state of fusion; and hence the exterior of the sun, at least, must be conceded to be in a state of liquefaction; but the most minute modern observations have by no means confirmed this idea: on the contrary, the rapid changes in the form of the solar spots, both luminous and dark, have of late years led us to suppose, with great probability, that these phenomena take place in a gaseous medium: and now the experiments made at the Observatory at Paris, on the polarization of light, have established this incontestably; but if the exterior and illumined part of the sun be a gas, then the system of Buffon fails in its most essential fundamental point, and is no longer sustainable.

"It might indeed be urged that the dark body of the sun within, which this luminous atmosphere surrounds, and which we occasionally see when the surrounding atmosphere opens,—it might be urged, I say, that this central dark body is liquid; but this would be quite a gratuitous assertion, wholly unsupported by accurate observations.

"To sum up,—and this is the object of this chapter,—nothing proves, whatever Buffon may say, that 'the planets formerly made part of the sun, from which they were separated by a common impulsive force, which still acts on them.' Thus, then, nothing establishes the opinion that a comet had any share in the formation of our planetary system; nothing indicates, in short, that in the beginning of things a comet had fallen into the sun.

"Pliny tells us, that in the time of Hipparchus (about 2,000 years ago,) a new star appeared all on a sudden in the north, which first gave to that astronomer the idea of forming a catalogue of stars. The same phenomenon was observed in 1572 and 1694.

"The new star of 1572 appeared in the north on the 8th of November, in the constellation of Cassiopeia. It was more brilliant than Sirius, and shed almost as much light as the planet Venus. The star of 1604, when seen by the pupils of Kepler, on the 30th of September, at midday was brighter than Jupiter, although only the night before this new star appeared very small. At the end of sixteen months this star was no longer visible. The new star in Cassiopeia was visible for a year and a half.

"The fixed stars seem to be real suns, round which in all probability planets and comets circulate. From what I have just stated we may conclude, that in the heavens there are some stars which, being exhausted, have become dark from being extinguished. Newton believed that stars of this sort become incandescent, and recover their former splendor when comets fall into them, and furnish fresh fuel; but the great name of Newton must not hinder me from remarking that in comparing the incandescence of the heavenly bodies with that of ordinary fires, making comets act, as it were, the parts of logs of firewood in a chimney, he pushed much too far the laws of analogy. In the present day, every body knows that almost all bodies, under certain special conditions, particularly in certain states of electricity, may be rendered luminous, without any thing combining with their substance, and without any thing being disengaged from it. Such is the case indeed with two pieces of charcoal placed in vacuum, of which one touches a wire issuing from one pole of a Voltaic pile, whilst the other communicates with the opposite pole of the same pile; for, as soon as the surfaces of these bits of charcoal are brought very near each other, they become more resplendent than all other known terrestrial fires, and to such a degree, that it has been agreed to call the light emanating from them, 'solar light.' I do not say that this proves that the light of the sun and of the stars is electric, but at least it will be granted that the contrary is not proved; and this is enough to place amongst mere hypothesis, Newton's reasonings in support of his doctrine of comets falling into the sun.

"May the earth pass through the tail of a comet? What would be the consequence of such an event on our globe?

"Newton thought that the exhalations of which the tails of comets are composed, might fall, by their gravity, into the atmosphere of planets in general, and into that of the earth in particular; and there, being condensed, give rise to all sorts of chemical re-action and combinations.

"A few words will be enough to prove, I will not merely say that cometary matter may fall into our atmosphere, but that this phenomenon is of a nature to occur frequently.

"Comets appear generally to be little else than simple aggregations of vapors; but as it is known that attraction is in proportion to the mass, each molecule of the tail of a comet must be very feebly attracted by the body of the comet; and this attraction diminishes as the squares of the distance. Thus, when the distance of a particle from the head of the comet is very great, the attraction must be scarcely sensible. But some comets have tails of immense lengths; for instance, the comet of 1680, whose last visible molecules were 41,000,000 leagues from the nucleus.

One may comprehend then, that a planet, the earth for example, whose mass is often so superior to that of comets, may attract to herself the extreme parts of comets' tails, although at a considerable distance from them; and the introduction into the terrestrial atmosphere of a new gaseous element, may, according to its quantity, either destroy all animal life, or cause epidemics; and thus many authors have attributed to this cause the most part of those epidemic scourges which history has recorded.

"The total number of comets which have been recorded, beginning with the Christian era, is about five hundred. At present, when the heavens are watched with attention, the medium number of comets seen in a year is rather more than two. This frequency of their appearance would cover, or apply to most of the epidemics people might be disposed to impute to comets.

"(M. Arago here enters into a train of reasoning to prove that certain fogs which have overspread the earth, and in particular that the great fog of 1780, were not the tails of comets.)

"*Was the deluge caused by a comet?*

"The numerous and important geological observations for which we are indebted to modern naturalists, prove beyond doubt, that certain regions of our globe have been successively and at different times covered and abandoned by water. In the explication of these cataclysms, people have too often had recourse to comets, for me to refrain from saying a few words on this subject.

"Amongst others, Whiston, in his *New Theory of the Earth*, not only endeavors to show how a comet may have caused the deluge of Noah, but also to explain thereby all the phenomena of the Mosaic account of that event.

"The Mosaic deluge took place, according to the modern Hebrew text, in the year 2349 before Christ, or in the year 2926 according to the Septuagint, Josephus, and the Samaritan text. Let us then consider if at either of these periods any great comet was visible.

"Of all these bodies which modern astronomers have observed, we must at once place in the first rank, as to splendor, the comet which appeared in 1680.

"A great number of historians have mentioned a comet which was very great, imitating the 'light of the sun, and having an immense tail,' and which appeared in the year 1106.

"In going further back we find 'a very large and a very terrifying comet,' designated by the Byzantine writers under the name of *Lampadios*, because it resembled a burning lamp. This comet appeared in 531. Lastly, every body knows that a comet was seen in the month of September, in the year of Cæsar's death. This comet was very brilliant, and was seen by day-light. The date of this comet is forty-three years.

"Since we have no exact observations of these comets, neither in the year 43, nor in 531, nor in 1106—since we have no means of calculating their parabolic orbits—since we are without the only criterion which enables us to pronounce with an entire certainty on the identity or the non-identity of two comets, let us, however, recollect, at least, that the comets of 1680, of 1106, of 531, and of 43, B. C., were all very brilliant, and let us also compare the several states of their appearances.

Before Christ, from 43 to 531, is 575 years.
" " " 531 to 1246, is 577 years.
" " " 1106 to 1680, is 575 years.

"As we do not take into account the fractions of years, these periods may be considered as equal to each other, and therefore it becomes tolerably probable that the comets of the death of Cæsar, of 531, of 1106, and of 1680, were no other than the re-appearance of one and the same star, which, after having completed its orbit in about 575 years, became again visible to the earth. Now, if we multiply this period of 575 years by 4, we shall have 2,300, which, added to 43, which is the date of Cæsar's comet, we are brought back, with the difference of only six years, to the epoch of the deluge, according to the modern Hebrew text, and on multiplying the same period by 5, we find the date of the Septuagint, with the difference of only eight years.

"Whiston, in his theory, required an immense tide to explain the phenomena related in the Bible of the great abyss; he therefore was not content merely to make his comet pass very near to the earth at the moment of the deluge, but he has also given to it a considerable mass, and he supposes the comet to be six times greater than the moon.

"Such a supposition is quite gratuitous; but that is not its least fault, for the supposition is not sufficient to explain the attendant phenomena;—for if the moon produces such effects as she does on the ocean, it is because her diurnal angular motion is not considerable; it is because her distance from the earth scarcely varies in many hours; it is because the moon corresponds vertically with nearly the same points of the globe during a considerable space of time; it is because the fluid which she attracts has always time to yield to her action before she moves on to a region from which her force will act in another direction. But this was not the case with the comet of 1680; near the earth its apparent angular motion across the constellations was extremely rapid; in a few minutes this comet corresponded with a number of points on different meridians of the earth, placed at a great distance the one from the other. As to the distance of the comet from the earth in a straight line, that, no doubt, may have been very small; but then this lasted only for a few minutes. These circumstances taken together are very unfavorable for the production of a very high tide. I am aware that to meet this difficulty we have only to enlarge the comet, to make its mass no longer six times that of the moon, but thirty or forty times; but, I answer, we have not this liberty as far as regards the comet of 1680, in which year it passed very near the earth;—but as in that year it produced neither heavenly cataracts, nor internal tides, nor breaking up of the great abyss; as moreover, neither its tail nor its head of hair inundated us, we may confidently pronounce the theory of Whiston to be a mere romance, —unless, abandoning the comet of 1680, we attribute the part it was to play, to another comet much more considerable.

"His celebrated countryman, Halley, had, however, looked on this subject in a less confined manner. Halley, instead of supposing a comet passing so near the earth as to cause a very high tide, supposes a comet striking perpendicularly on the earth.

"Let us suppose a solid body moving in a right line with a certain rapidity, and that an insurmountable obstacle shall be placed suddenly, all at once on the route of this body, so as to stop it instantly. Let this happen to our earth, the tangential rate of translation of which is eight leagues in a second, and let this effect be produced by a comet of sufficient mass, all bodies resting on its surface, such as animated beings, our carriages, our furniture, our utensils, all objects in short which are not fixed to the ground, would fly towards that point of the earth on which the comet had struck, with the rapidity which had been communicated to them by the earth's motion—that is, with a rapidity of eight leagues per second! One may imagine at once what would be the effect of such an event, when I state that a cannon ball of twenty-four pounds, even at its first departure from the mouth of the gun, moves only 1,200 feet in a second; in a word, every animated being would be annihilated in an instant!

"As to the waters of the ocean, as they are moveable, and as nothing binds them to the solid part of the earth, they would be thrown in a mass towards the point of percussion. This frightful liquid mass would overturn in its impetuous course every object it met. It would rise above the tops of the highest mountains, and, in its reflux, its effects would be hardly less. The disorder which we now remark here and there in the disposition of certain strata on the crust of our globe is, one may say, but a microscopic accident compared with the frightful chaos which would result from the direct shock of a comet sufficiently large to stop at once the earth in its orbit. But another effect would at once result, which would be, that the centripetal force being no longer balanced by the centrifugal, the earth would at once begin to fall towards the sun, into which she would fall sixty-four and a half days after the shock.

"But, taking this shock of a comet under any circumstances and modifications, it is incontestable that the inundations to which such an accident would give rise would not explain the phenomena which have been remarked by geologists, and the effects produced by cataclysms on our globe.

"But let us suppose by the above or by any other cometary influence, vast portions of the continents inundated, and lofty regions buried under water, is it by a violent change such as this that the marine deposits which have been discovered on mountains have been placed there? These deposits are frequently horizontal, very extensive, very thick, very regular. The variegated shells, often very small, which compose these layers, often preserve their projections, their most delicate points, their most fragile parts. Every thing shows the impossibility of a violent transportation—every thing proves that the deposit has been made quietly on the spot. What remains then to be said to explain the observed geological phenomena without having recourse to a violent usurpation of the ocean? We must come to the conclusion that the mountains, as well as the elevated grounds which serve them as a base, have been pushed upwards from below and from under the waters which once covered them. In 1694, Halley brought forward this hypothesis as a possible explanation of the presence of marine animals on the sides and tops of high mountains. This explanation was the true one, and it is now universally admitted. A comet which should materially change either the motion of rotation or the motion of translation of the earth, would produce, no doubt, tremendous overturnings on the crust of our globe; but we must repeat it, these physical revolutions would differ in a thousand circumstances from those which have been noticed, and which at present form the study of geologists.

"*Ceres, Pallas, Juno, and Vesta—are these the fragments of a large planet which has been broken by the shock of a comet?*

"Planetary astronomy has been enriched since the beginning of the present century by the discovery of four new planets, which, not being visible to the naked eye, were unknown to ancient observers. These stars are called Ceres, Pallas, Juno, and Vesta. Their orbits are all between the orbits of Mars and Jupiter.

"Two of these orbits, those of Ceres and Pallas, are nearly equal. The orbit of Juno, and particularly that of Vesta, are much smaller. The four curves, although in different planes, are interlaced. They appear to have had similar elements—in short, every thing leads us to suppose that these planets at each revolution passed formerly through the same point of space.

"This circumstance would be doubtless very extraordinary if Ceres, Pallas, Juno, and Vesta had always been independent of each other; but it will become very simple if we regard the four planets as fragments of a larger one, which one day was broken into pieces. In fact, a planet, properly so called, follows constantly the same route, allowance only being made for perturbation. At each revolution she passes through the same points; but from the instant in which, according to our hypothesis, the large planet was broken, each of its fragments became in every sense of the word a real planet, which began to describe the curve along which its movement was to be directed forever. Some difference of intensity and direction amongst the forces which projected the different pieces, caused notable differences in the forms and in the position of the orbits; but all these elipses must have a common point—that is, the point at which the planetary fragments separated to take their several routes. The common point, therefore, which the orbits of these small planets appear to have had formerly, shows pretty clearly that formerly these four bodies formed but one.

"This theory on the common origin of these four planets was assented to generally; but disagreement arose amongst philosophers, when it became necessary to assign a cause for the splitting of the great planet. Some having recourse to internal gases and commotions, supposed the outer crust of the great planet to be burst, and thus Ceres, Pallas, Juno, and Vesta to be formed. Others reject this doctrine of internal explosion, and declare that a heavenly body can be broken only by the striking of a comet.

"It would be difficult to find in the form and aspect of the four little planets unanswerable arguments for either of these hypotheses; I will, however, give some singular reasons on which the advocates for a cometary shock rest.

"In the larger planets, Mars, Jupiter, and Saturn, we see some traces of an atmosphere, but they are traces only, and can be seen only by the aid of powerful glasses; in the planetary fragments atmospherical phenomena are visible on an immense scale. The atmosphere of Ceres is no less than 276 leagues deep, that of Pallas 192 leagues. Hitherto comets alone had gaseous envelopes so large! Well, then, let us suppose, as people have said, that the large planet which moved between Mars and Jupiter was broken by a comet, and all will be explained! The cometary atmosphere or nebulosity, not having been destroyed by the stroke, will have naturally been divided amongst the different fragments, and will have formed around each an immense atmosphere.

"This theory is ingenious; but unhappily a striking fact comes and contradicts it. Vesta has hitherto afforded us no traces of an atmosphere; but what cause could have thus disinherited Vesta of the share of the atmosphere of the comet, when it was to be divided amongst the planetary fragments?"

Some passages of M. Arago's observations, having reference to the approach of the then expected comet, are expressed in the future tense. This does not in any way interfere with the facts of the case upon which he remarks in a style and manner at once clear and familiar; and therefore, those expressions have been allowed to remain in their original form. It must also be allowed that his reasonings upon those facts are both ingenious and liberal. When, however, he alludes to the probability of the comet of 1680 falling into the sun as a consequence of its moving in a resisting medium, closing his remarks upon that head by saying that the conclusion of the gradual approach of the comet to the centre "rests on demonstrable mechanical principles," we must remind the reader that his reasonings on "mechanical principles" are altogether void, for the "centrifugal force" is one of the elements whereon the calculation and conclusion is founded; and we have already shown that this "force" as it has been denominated, is a perishable element, which upon "mechanical principles" is presumed to endure forever, maintaining a constant and eternal struggle with the imperishable force of attraction. There could be no doubt of the correctness of the conclusions of M. Arago, relating to the comet's precipitation upon the sun, if the data from which those conclusions are deduced could be relied upon; but the data being false, the conclusions are false also. A comet, that is, a body of vapor, a gaseous mass, cannot fall into the sun. It will and must recede or ascend from the sun, not upon merely hydrostatic principles, for even in vacuo it must ascend, because the repulsive principle is now strong within it. A high intensity of the repulsive force is essential to its existence as a gaseous body, and until in the course of ages that force has decreased in intensity upon the great scale, by which the mass will slowly pass from the gaseous to the liquid and solid state, into the form and condition of a habitable world, consisting of rocks and mountains, it cannot fall into the sun. Whilst it continues in the gaseous form, the repulsive is of necessity the predominating force; as on the other hand, in the state of a solid the attractive force is necessarily the predominating. Matter expands or contracts simply as the one or the other of the two ultimate forces predominates.

Now there are one or two circumstances connected with the comet of 1680, which merit our special attention. It passed very near to the sun. Its orbit was highly eccentric, and the tail was suddenly expanded to an enormous length. These three facts, which may apply in a greater or less degree to all similar bodies, will perhaps enable us to arrive at a few important conclusions. First, —the sudden expansion of the tail proves that the physical constitution of the comet was of a character highly volatile. If we conceive of it as a globe of liquid matter in a nascent state, as a condensation or contraction of the solar gaseous fluid, formed in the external, or what may be fitly called, the upper regions of the solar system, in a manner analogous to the formation of a *rain drop* in the upper or external region of the terrestrial atmosphere, we seem to have obtained all that is requisite to illustrate and explain the origin of a comet,—that is, that it has been formed by the *contraction of matter*, which matter had previously *ascended* from the central sun in an *expanded* or gaseous and invisible form; and that as a consequence of this contraction it again seeks the centre, falling towards the sun, until by the excitement or action of the sun upon the nascent liquid, an enormous tail of *expanded* matter is formed, in consequence of which expansion the body again recedes from the centre under the influence of the universal law by which all expanded matter ascends or recedes from the central solid with which it is connected. The matter with which a rain drop is composed recedes from the central earth in an expanded, gaseous, and *invisible* form. This invisible expansion of terrestrial gas is contracted into a *little globe of liquid matter*, in a point of space more distant from the centre of the earth than that at which it was expanded; and this little globe of nascent liquid returns towards the centre in the form of a rain drop, and a portion of this little liquid drop passes onward into the vegetable kingdom, where it takes the *solid* form. The analogy is perfect. An invisible gas assuredly issues from the sun, as otherwise there could not be either light or heat in the terrestrial atmosphere. The sun is but a great retort and gasometer, and if the supply of solar gas were "cut off," the planets would be left in darkness, just as the streets of London would be if the gas companies were to "turn off" the gas upon the main pipes of supply. That portion of the solar gas which penetrates the earth's atmosphere, gives the impetus to all that chain of light, life, and action, which, beginning in the upper region of the atmosphere, descends through many windings to the lowest point of the mineral kingdom. But that portion of the solar gas which penetrates the earth's atmosphere, is an insignificant part of the immense volume which is continually issuing from the sun. The great body of expanded matter passes onward to the outer regions of the solar system, where it must be contracted, again to return towards the centre, for such is the universal law of nature.

The following extract and diagram from the Treatises

on astronomy of the Society for the Diffusion of Useful Knowledge, will be useful here for the facts which it contains, although some of the inferences are not of such value, especially where it speaks of a comet (a volume of gas) being made two thousand times hotter than red hot iron. Page 180-81:—

"The tails of comets are evidently formed of highly rarefied matter, as is sufficiently indicated by their extreme transparency, which permits the smallest stars to be distinguished through them; and there is reason to believe that the nucleus, though in a greater state of condensation, is very far, at least in some instances, from being solid. Astronomers have occasionally distinguished fixed stars of no great brightness through the nuclei of comets. Indeed, when we consider the enormous heat to which many comets are exposed when near their perihelion, it is difficult to perceive that any part of them can escape complete vaporization. Thus the comet of 1680, at its perihelion, was 166 times nearer the sun than the earth. If we suppose, as there is every reason for believing, that the intensity of the solar heat varies, like the intensity of light, inversely as the square of the distance, it appears that the comet must have been subjected to a heat 27,556 times as great as that received by the earth, or 2,000 times as great as that of red hot iron. On the other hand, it must be confessed that in their aphelion, comets experience a degree of cold of which we cannot form any calculation or conception.

"The tail generally begins to appear as the comet draws near the sun; its length increases with its proximity, but does not acquire its greatest extent till after the perihelion passage. Its direction is always from the sun,* forming a curve rather concave towards that body, as in the annexed diagram, where A represents the nucleus of the comet, B the tail, S the sun, M A D the comet's orbit in the direction from M to D.

* The tail is always on a prolongation of the straight line which joins the comet to the sun: thus, if the comet be to the east of the sun, and set after him, the tail takes an easterly direction; but a westerly, if the comet be to the west of the sun, and set before him.

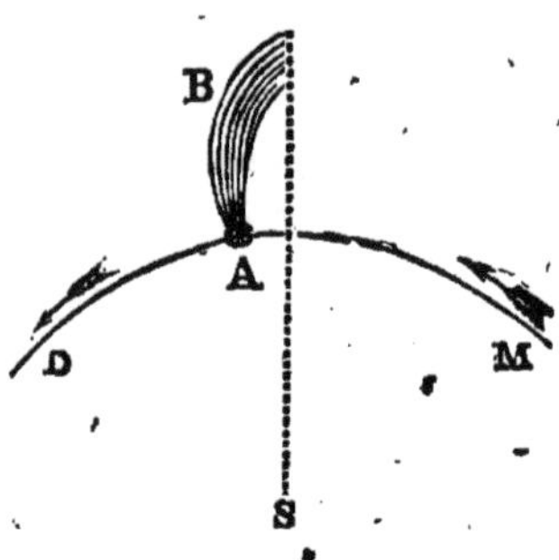


"The position and form of the tail indicate plainly its real cause, which is the vaporization produced in the body of the comet by excessive heat: * how great that heat must be, has been already explained. The tail acquires its greatest size after the perihelion, when the comet has been thoroughly heated, just as the earth does not attain its highest temperature till after the summer solstice."

The comet of 1680 is that from which we propose to deduce our conclusions respecting the recent formation of that body from a gas, as indicated by its volatile and highly expansible character. We have further to show that this volatile fluid is gradually coutracting into a liquid of a more fixed or permanent character, and, during the progress of this change of the physical constitution of the body from the volatile or cometary condition to that of the planetary, that the highly eccentric orbit is continually widening—the aphelion point approaching towards, and the perihelion receding from, the sun; so that the two changes, that of physical condition and of the form of the orbit, proceed together and simultaneously. We have throughout endeavored to draw our facts from independent sources, in order to avoid the imputation of distorting those facts to suit our particular conclusions. For the same reason we will here give a few facts concerning the comet of 1680 from Somerville's "Connection of the Physical Sciences:"—

"Comets when in or near their perihelion, move with prodigious velocity. That of 1680 appears to have gone half round the sun in ten hours and a half, moving at the

* The vaporization mentioned would not produce, however, a tail, without we suppose the comet to move in a resisting medium, which, as we shall presently see, is, from other causes, highly probable.

rate of 880,000 miles an hour. If its enormous centrifugal force had ceased when passing its perihelion, it would have fallen to the sun in about three minutes, as it was then only 14,700 miles from his surface. So near the sun, it would be exposed to a heat 27,500 times greater than that received by the earth; and as the sun's heat is supposed to be in proportion to the intensity of his light, it is probable that a degree of heat so very intense would be sufficient to convert into vapor every terrestrial substance with which we are acquainted. At the perihelion distance the sun's diameter would be seen from the comet under an angle of 73°, so that the sun, viewed from the comet, would nearly cover the whole extent of the heavens from the horizon to the zenith; and as this comet is presumed to have a period of 575 years, the major axis of its orbit must be so great, that at the aphelion the sun's diameter would only subtend an angle of about fourteen seconds, which is not so great as half the diameter of Mars appears to us when in opposition. The sun would consequently impart no heat, so that the comet would then be exposed to the temperature of the etherial regions, which is 58° below the zero point of Farenheit. A body rare as the comet, and moving with such velocity, must have met with great resistance from the dense atmosphere of the sun, while passing so near his surface at its perihelion. The centrifugal force must consequently have been diminished, and the sun's attraction proportionally augmented, so that it must have come nearer the sun in 1680 than in its preceding revolution, and would subsequently describe a smaller orbit. As this diminution of its orbit will be repeated at each revolution, the comet will infallibly end by falling on the surface of the sun, unless its course be changed by the disturbing influence of some large body in the unknown expanse of creation. Our ignorance of the actual density of the sun's atmosphere, of the density of the comet, and of the period of its revolution, renders it impossible to form any idea of the number of centuries which must elapse before this singular event takes place."

The false reasoning from the "centrifugal force" does not require any further notice. The reader must by this time have been convinced that any conclusions whatever which has been deduced from such a "force" is altogether unworthy of attention. This false reasoning does not however alter the *facts* of the case, and amongst these facts there are three which claim our especial attention:

1st. The comet descended towards the sun in an orbit highly eccentric, and with prodigious velocity, 880,000 miles an hour.

2nd. The perihelion point was within 147,000 miles of the surface of the sun.

3rd. The body was rapidly expanded as the comet moved through the perihelion, so that on emerging from the solar atmosphere, the tail extended over ninety degrees of space, being equal to sixty millions of miles.

4th. A comet approaching the sun, when seen at any considerable distance from that body has little or no tail. The tail is thrown out when the body is near the sun, and again drawn in, in the remote regions of the system—that is, in short, that the comet undergoes *one expansion* and *one contraction* during each revolution in its eccentric orbit.

Now, before we attempt to reason concerning the principles by which these appearances are guided and by which the comet is carried through her orbit, let us turn to an analogous case with which we are already somewhat familiar. The legitimate course of investigation is to proceed from things known to things unknown.

In the accompanying diagram, p. 387, let A represent the earth, and B a point forty-five miles above the earth's surface, forty-five miles being the height of the atmosphere, according to those who *imagine* that the space beyond that distance is a vacuum, but as it is now *proved* that space is not a vacuum, the point B may be indefinitely removed to any distance, 45,000 miles or more if required. Now, if a body of solid matter at O on the surface of the earth A be expanded into a gas of greater subtlety, of less density, than the surrounding atmosphere, and the atmosphere be at rest, the expanded matter or gas will ascend in a right line from A towards B, and in proportion as it is more and more expanded, so will it rise to a higher and higher altitude,—that is, it will recede further and further from the centre of the solid body A, from whatever point of that body's surface it may have receded; so that *if sufficiently expanded* it will ultimately reach the point B at whatever distance that point may be situated from the central body A. Now, if the expanded matter at B be again contracted into a solid or liquid globe, as a rain drop is formed in the atmosphere, and the atmosphere being still at rest, it will descend in a right line towards

A with a continually increasing momentum, and will impinge upon the same point of the surface from which it originally ascended in an expanded or gaseous form. But if instead of being arrested in its course by impinging on the solid earth, a clear passage through the centre of the earth be allowed, then the descending body pursuing its original right line, will by the momentum which it has acquired, pass entirely through the earth, and will reach a point beyond the opposite side or surface, at 4 or 12, more or less, as the distance through which it has descended from B to A is more or less. Having arrived at the point 12, the first momentum which it had acquired in falling from B is annihilated by the attraction of A, but this same attraction of A creates a new momentum in the opposite direction, and the body by the new momentum passes from 12 entirely through the body A, and again reaches the opposite surface at O. If the expansion and contraction be repeated, these effects will be repeated; if not, the body will at length come to a state of rest at the centre of A.

Upon the same conditions a balloon will ascend and descend. If a balloon be filled at O with gas which has been expanded from solid coals, it will ascend in a still atmosphere in the right line A B to any given altitude, according as the matter is more or less expanded, and upon contraction of the gas will again descend upon the point O. But if we suppose the balloon to be let fall from a very great altitude, and that by the action of the central earth or any other cause the enclosed matter begins to expand slowly, and continues to expand more and more rapidly as the balloon approaches the central body, the surrounding atmosphere being at the same time not perfectly quiescent, then the descent will be considerably modified. The descending balloon will no longer follow a right line, but will diverge to the right or to the left, according to circumstances; and if the momentum which it has acquired should be sufficient to have carried the falling body along the right line and through the earth to the opposite point 12, then the body having diverged to the right or to the left, will pass upon one side, and will sweep round the earth, being prevented from falling upon the surface by the continually expanding gas. As the ballon sweeps round the earth, the most solid or contracted portion—as the car—will continually point towards the centre of the earth, and the gaseous or most expanded portion will continually point away from the centre, as is shown in the diagram. If the momentum of the falling body would have carried it to the point 12 on the opposite side, then in consequence of the resistance which the body meets in its descent by the continually expanding gas, it will not reach the point 12, but will pass through its perigee or point nearest the earth, (the equivalent of a comet's perihelion or point nearest the sun) somewhere about the point 4; and as the first and second momenta already mentioned continually interfere with each other, the first decreasing, the second increasing, the gas in the meantime continually expanding the baloon, would again recede from the earth towards the point B in a curvilinear sweep and in a very eccentric orbit. Beginning at B in the first instance, it would pass successively through the points 1, 2, 3, 4, 5, 6, 7, 8, 9, 10, 11, 12, 13, &c.; in each successive revolution, the expansion and contraction of the gas going on in the meantime, it would acquire a wider sweep or orbit, the perigee (perihelion) point would continually recede further and further from the centre of A, and the apogee (aphelion) would continually approach towards A; and as by the continual widening of the orbit and shifting of the two extreme points, the gaseous matter would become less and less under the exciting action of the central body, the gas would be less and less expanded as the orbit became more and more circular, until at length, if the orbit should become a perfect circle, these alternations would cease. In order that the balloon should pass through its apogee or point furthest from the earth, at a lower altitude, at each successive revolution, it is requisite that the gas should be less and less expanded; and in order that it should be less and less expanded, if the action of the central body contain within itself the expanding principle, or if the action be reciprocal, it is requisite that the balloon should pass at a greater and greater distance in the perigee or nearest point.

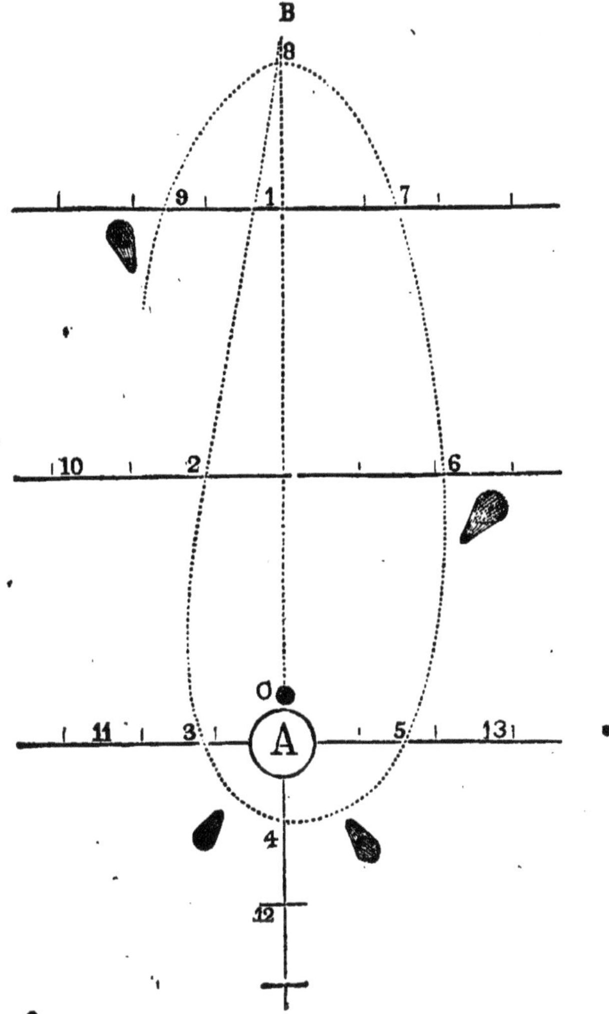


Now, although it is impossible by art to effect those conditions which are here supposed, with respect to the balloon and earth, yet we can very distinctly perceive that if we could surmount all obstacles, such are the courses of motion and action which would follow; and if we turn to the works of nature, so far in every respect above our own, we shall at once perceive that such are the courses of motion and action which comets obey in their orbits. It is true, that in illustrating this point, we have appealed to hydrostatic principles, but when we come to speak of the tides, we shall bring forward a deeper view of the subject, which it is presumed will remove all difficulty on that head.

The facts with regard to comets are these:—The tail begins to be projected as the comet approaches the centre, and continues to increase so long as the body is in the vicinity of the sun. "Immediately after the great comet of 1680 had passed the perihelion, its tail was 20,000,000 leagues in length, and was projected from the comet's head in the short space of two days." Their aphelion distance is continually decreasing, as is proved by Encke's comet, which returns from its aphelion two days sooner at each revolution. They are less and less expanded at each rotation; "not only the tails, but the nebulous parts of the comets diminish every time they return to their perihelia; after frequent returns they ought to lose it altogether, and present the appearance of a fixed nucleus,—this ought to happen sooner to comets of short periods. Laplace supposes that the comet of 1682 must be approaching rapidly to that state."

The following table, by M. G. de Pontecoulant, in which he traces *Halley's* comet from the early ages of history, by the conformity of the periods, will show that this body, which at its last appearance (1835,) could scarcely be discerned without the aid of a telescope, had formerly appeared of such magnitude as to alarm the inhabitants of the earth:—

*Presumed appearances of Halley's Comet in past ages.*

| Appearances. | year. | | Remarkable Events. |
|---|---|---|---|
| 1st, | 330 | before Christ. | Birth of Mithridates. |
| 2nd, | 322 | Christian era. | An interval of six revolutions. |
| 3rd, | 399 | do. | The Comet of horrible aspect, whose tail seemed to touch the earth. |
| 4th, | 550 | do. | Rome taken by Totila; an interval of two revolutions. |
| 5th, | 930 | do. | Five revolutions in this interval. |
| 6th, | 1005 | do. | Three revolutions the interval. |
| 7th, | 1230 | do. | Three revolutions of 75 years each. |
| 8th, | 1302 | do. | One revolution of 75 years. Comet of terrific magnitude; followed by the plague. |
| 9th, | 1380 | do. | One do. do. |

*Appearances of the Comet after the 15th Century.*

| Appear-ances. | | year. | Observations. |
|---|---|---|---|
| 10th, | 1456 | A. D. | The comet of an unusually large size; its tail extended over two-thirds of the interval between the zenith and the horizon. Period 76 years. |
| 11th, | 1531 | do. | Period 75 years. Apian, an astronomer of Ingoldstadt, proved by it that the trains of Comets have always an opposite direction to the sun. |
| 12th, | 1697 | do. | Observed by Kepler and Longomontanus. Period 76 years 8 months. |
| 13th, | 1682 | do. | Observed by Cassini, Hevelius, Halley, &c. Period 75 yrs. |
| 14th, | 1759 | do. | Return predicted by Halley;—calculated by Clairaut. Period 76 years 6 months. |
| 15th, | 1835 | do. | Approach to its perihelion. Period 76 years 8 months. |

Before concluding our remarks on comets, it may be amusing to notice one of the strange conceits of the philosophers of the "centrifugal force" school. The following is from the "Connexion of the Physical Sciences," a work held in high estimation, and under royal patronage, being dedicated by permission to the queen:—"If a comet were to impinge on the earth, so as to destroy its *centrifugal force*, it (the earth) would fall to the sun in 64 1-2 days. What the earth's primitive velocity (derived from the first push) may have been, it is impossible to say; therefore, a comet may have given it a shock without changing the axis of rotation, but only destroying part of its tangential velocity, so as to diminish the size of the orbit,—a thing by no means impossible, though highly improbable, at all events there is no proof that such has been the case." It might have been added "there is no proof that the earth ever received either a shock or a primitive impulse, nor is there any satisfactory proof that the centrifugal force supposed to be derived from that primitive impulse is competent to sustain that tangential motion of the earth in her orbit; that motion must, therefore, be due to some other cause.

The next question is, from what source is the *material* derived of which comets are composed? We have endeavored to show that all the satellites in the solar system are approaching their primaries, and that the primaries are approaching the sun; that comets are gradually contracting and passing into the planetary state, and will follow a similar course; by which it appears that every body at present revolving in, and forming part of, the solar system, will pass into the sun. On the other hand, it is admitted by all scientific men, that matter of some sort is issuing from the sun. Light, it is said, is an imponderable substance, proceeding from the sun at the rate of ninety-six millions of miles in eight minutes. We have attempted to show that no *luminous* matter from the sun reaches the earth or other planets, but that the light which we enjoy is produced in the atmosphere by a specific action going on there continually. But still, whichever of these views we may prefer, it is requisite that matter of some kind should issue from the sun, for that specific action could not be kept up without a constant supply of solar gas; therefore, whether that gas be conceived to be luminous or non-luminous, it does not in any way interfere with the question of a continual issue of *expanded* matter from the central sun. The following converse proportions will place the question in a strong and correct point of view:—

If all the bodies at present revolving in the planetary system be approaching the sun, no new bodies in the meantime being forming, then the planetary system must come to a termination, whatever extent of space or duration we may conceive necessary to such consummation.

Conversely,—If expanded matter be issuing from the sun, however subtle, no supply in the meantime being carried to the sun to compensate the loss, then the sun must at length be dissipated and scattered in space, however large the mass, or whatever length of time may be allotted for its dissolution.

But if the two opposite processes compensate each other, then the system may go on forever; and such reciprocally compensating process is the order of nature in all those miner operations which fall within the scope of our observation.

Now, if the earth and other planets, at present revolving in the system, be approaching and will finish their course as planets by falling into the sun, there to be dissolved and again to issue in the gaseous form, we have a right to suppose that other planetary bodies have preceded them, and are at this moment in the sun in a state of dissolution. The accompanying diagram of spots on the sun's disc, observed by Sir John Herschel, with his remarks upon the physical constitution of the sun, will enable the reader to form some conception of the active processes there going on:—

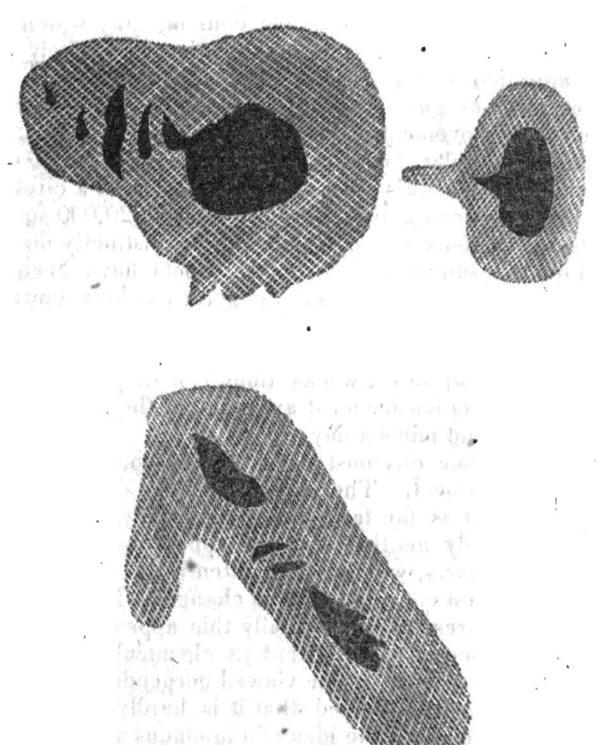

From Herschel's astronomy, page 207, section 330, we shall conclude this by describing what is known of the physical constitution of the sun:—

"When viewed through powerful telescopes, provided with colored glasses to take off the heat which would otherwise injure our eyes, it is observed to have frequently large and perfectly black spots upon it, surrounded with a kind of border, less completely dark, called a penumbra. They are, however, not permanent. When watched from day to day, or even from hour to hour, they appear to enlarge or contract, to change their forms, and at length to disappear altogether, or to break out anew in parts of the surface where none were before. In such cases of disappearance, the central dark spot always contracts into a point, and vanishes before the border. Occasionally they break up and divide into two or more, and in those offer every evidence of that extreme mobility which belongs only to the fluid state, and of that excessively violent agitation which seems only compatible with the atmospheric or gaseous state of matter. The scale on which their movements take place is immense. A single second of angular measure, as seen from the earth, corresponds on the sun's disc to 465 miles; and a circle of this diameter (containing therefore nearly 220,000 square miles,) is the least space which can be distinctly discovered on the sun as a *visible area*. Spots have been observed, however, whose linear diameter has been upwards of 45,000 miles, and even, if some records are to be trusted, of very much greater extent. That such a spot should close up in six weeks' time, (for they hardly ever last longer,) its border must approach at the rate of more than a thousand miles a day.

"Many other circumstances tend to corroborate this view of the subject. The part of the sun's disc not occupied by spots is far from being uniformly bright. Its *ground* is finely mottled with an appearance of minute dark *dots* or *pores*, which, when attentively watched, are found to be in a constant state of change. There is nothing which represents so faithfully this appearance as the slow subsidence of some flocculent chemical precipitates in a transparent fluid, when viewed perpendicularly from above; so faithfully, indeed, that it is hardly possible not to be impressed with the idea of a luminous medium intermixed, but not confounded, with a transparent and non-luminous atmosphere, either floating as clouds in our air, or pervading it in vast sheets and columns like flame, or the streams of our northern lights."

Section 331.—"Lastly, in the neighborhood of great spots or extreme groups of them, large spaces of the surface are often observed to be covered with strongly marked curved or branching streaks more luminous than the rest, called *façulae*, and among these, if not already existing, spots frequently break out. They may perhaps be regarded with most probability as the ridges of immense waves in the luminous regions of the sun's atmosphere, indicative of the violent agitation in their neighborhood."

Section 332.—"But what *are* the spots? Many fanciful notions have been broached on this subject, but only one seems to have any degree of physical probability, namely, that they are the dark, or at least comparatively dark solid body of the sun itself, laid bare to our view by those immense fluctuations in the luminous regions of its atmosphere, to which it appears to be subject. Respecting the manner in which this disclosure takes place, different ideas have again been advocated. Lalande suggests that eminences of the nature of mountains are actually laid bare, and project above the luminous ocean, appearing black above it, while their shelving declivities produce the penumbra where the luminous fluid is less deep. A fatal objection to this theory is the perfectly uniform shade of the penumbra and its sharp termination, both inwards where it joins the spot and outwards where it borders on the bright surface. A more probable view has been taken by Sir William Herschel, who considers the luminous strata of the atmosphere to be sustained far above the level of the solid body by a transparent elastic medium, carrying on its upper surface (or rather, *to avoid the former objection*, at some considerably lower level within its depth) a cloudy stratum, which, being strongly illuminated from above, reflects a considerable portion of the light to our eyes and form a penumbra, while the solid body, shaded by the clouds, reflects more. The temporary removal of both the strata, but more of the upper than the lower, he supposes effected by powerful upward currents of the atmosphere, arising, perhaps, from spiracles in the body, or from local agitations."

Section 333.—"The region of the spots is comprised within about 30° of the sun's equator, and from their motion on the surface, carefully measured with micrometers, is ascertained the position of the equator, which is a plane inclined 7° 20′ to the ecliptic, and intersecting it in a line whose direction makes an angle of 80° 20′ with that of the equinoxes. It has been also noticed (not, we think, without great need of further confirmation,) that extinct spots have again broken out after long intervals of time on the same identical points of the sun's globe. Our knowledge of the period of its rotation (which, according to Delambre's calculations, is twenty-five days, 0.1154, but according to others materially different) can hardly be regarded as sufficiently precise to establish a point of so much nicety."

Sir John Herschel goes on to speak of the sun as being in a state of combustion, of an intensity so great that no conflagration on earth can afford us a medium of comparison with a body in so high a degree of incandescence. We shall not quote his remarks on this head, deeming them to be founded upon principles altogether erroneous. By referring to our remarks on light and heat, it will be seen that so very high degrees of heat as has been contemplated by Sir John Herschel and others, is by no means necessary to produce the effects which we experience on the earth through the influence of the sun. A heat that will convert solid matter into gas is all that is required to produce the ordinary phenomena of light and heat in the earth's atmosphere, by combination with a gas or gasses issuing from the sun. Sir John, after contemplating the sun in the light of an incandescent body, concludes with these words:—

Section 337.—"The great mystery, however, is, to conceive how so enormous a conflagration (if such it be) can be kept up. Every discovery in chemical science here leaves us completely at a loss, or rather seems to remove further the prospect of probable explanation. If conjecture might be hazarded, we should look rather to the known possibility of indefinite generation of heat by friction, or to its excitement by the electric discharge, than to any actual combination of ponderable fuel, whether solid or gaseous, for the origin of the solar radiation."

That the spots are not mountains of the sun laid bare is evident, for *they shift their position*, like a solid body floating in a liquid, and they disappear like a solid body sinking in a liquid,—that is, *they vanish to* a *point*, and they re-appear in a similar manner. The conceit of Sir William Herschel is too fanciful. There is nothing in their appearance which would lead us to conceive them to be a kind of solar clouds, as he supposes. If the reader will attentively consider all that is going on in the cometary and planetary systems, together with the kind of action going on in the sun itself, and will then cast his eye on these *black round spots of* 10,000 *miles diameter, with large fragments apparently broken off from the larger mass, the whole surrounded with a penumbra of a cloudy character, resembling matter in a state of partial decomposition*, he will find some difficulty in the attempt to persuade himself that these spots are not, in fact, old planets in a state of decomposition, the materials by which the everlasting action of the sun is sustained, as without a supply of some sort that action most assuredly could not go on forever.

One circumstance remains to be considered. How is the expanded matter which confessedly issues from the sun gathered together into large globular masses as comets? The efficient cause is attraction. But there are other aids which co-operate in a beautiful manner with that cause. It is a law of nature, little heeded, that all *fluid* matter when in motion proceeds in a spiral or twisting course.

Bore a small hole through the bottom of a pail, and fill the pail with water. It will be seen that the water issues through the hole with a spiral motion; and if the experiment be performed a thousand times in succession, it will be found that the issuing water *always twists in the same direction*, thereby proving that the spiral motion is not the effect of merely accidental or contingent causes, but is due to a constant and immutable law of nature. If the water inside the pail have a contrary motion given to it by the hand, although some disturbance of the spiral may be caused, yet it cannot be made to take the opposite direction, and on withdrawal of the hand it will readily pursue its natural course, even before the internal agitation has subsided. The same effect may be observed on pouring out wine, ale, or water, or indeed any liquid, from a decanter; and watch-makers have taken advantage of this law in their fabrication of fancy time-pieces, by fixing a stem of twisted glass upon pivots, one of which being concealed in the mouth of a lion or other animal, the other behind a little ledge of projecting rock, and the twisted glass kept continually revolving by means of the internal wheel-work, gives a very fair representation of a little fountain. The *twisted glass* renders the illusion complete.

Vegetables are formed from fluid matter, and the spiral vessel is, as is well known to vegetable physiologists, the basis of the vegetable structure. Why does the incipient juicy vessel take the spiral form? Simply because it is formed by the circulation of fluid matter; and as this fluid matter moves with a spiral motion, the vegetable structure condenses or contracts in the form of the moving fluid from which the materials of the structure are derived. With French beans, hop vines, and other climbing plants, this law is manifested upon a more magnified scale. Why does the French bean cling and twine around its support and always in the same direction? This is not the effect of chance, but of a law of nature; and it is a law intimately connected with electrical action, for, as on the one hand, the French bean is attracted and clings closely to the dried and withered stick which is placed for its support, so on the other, it is repelled and turns away from the newly cut branch. Why? Because the juicy newly cut branch and the juicy growing vegetable are in the same electrical states, and consequently repel each other; whereas, the dried branch and juicy vegetables being in opposite states attract each other. There are abundant instances of the spiral motion of fluid matter in the varied processes of nature, and if we turn to the atmosphere, we shall find that the motion of the fluid air is also governed by the same law. The air is invisible, and therefore its motions cannot be followed by the eye, but we can trace the manner of its motion by the effects produced on visible objects. Every millwright knows that there is a right way and a wrong for a windmill to revolve. The right way—as it is called—is generally followed merely from the force of custom, and but few are aware of any reason for the erection of windmills to turn in one way in preference to the other. It is a fact, however, that more power is obtained from the wind or moving fluid atmosphere in one direction than in the other, and this is undoubtedly dependent upon the same law which governs the spiral motion of water and other liquids. The curling motion of smoke is no doubt caused by the spiral motion of the fluid atmosphere, although in towns and cities and hilly countries, the currents must be considerably disturbed, eddies being produced by the various elevated objects on the surface, but still the indications of the general law are sufficiently apparent.

Mr. Green, the aeronaut, in narrating the particulars of his recent experimental trip, has furnished us with some particulars in respect to the spiral motion which his balloon undergoes, which we here transcribe:—

"On our first rising from the gardens, we took a north-westerly direction, and continued that course until we arrived over Vauxhall bridge, when we were at an elevation of 2,500 feet. The line then changed to the north, and shortly after to the north-east. All the time we were passing over the metropolis, we discharged ballast, and rose in proportion. We then pursued our journey, passing over Dalston, Lea-bridge, and Epping, in which direction we continued with but little variation, leaving Dunmow, in Essex, on our left. At this period we had attained our greatest altitude, namely, 19,335 feet, or 3 1-2 miles and 855 feet. It was now that for the first time our view of the earth was intercepted by a stratum of cloud which was apparently somewhere about 6,000 feet below us. In consequence of the vast quantity of ballast that we continued to discharge after having cleared the metropolis, our ascent became very rapid, and from the great expansion of the inflating power, the gas rushed out from the lower valve in considerable torrents. The velocity of our upward progress caused the balloon and car to rotate in a spiral motion on its axis with astonishing rapidity. A similar operation takes place, although not to so great an extent, on all occasions of a rapid ascent or descent. During our ascension, we, at different periods, threw overboard about 1,200 lbs. of ballast, reserving only 100 lbs. by which to regulate our descent. With reference to the fact of there being a supposed natural difficulty of respiration at great altitudes above the earth's surface, as mentioned in the works of Humboldt and other celebrated travellers, by whom it has been painfully experienced in their ascents of high mountains, I am inclined, from the circumstance of an opposite result having been produced upon ourselves on this occasion, to imagine that the fatigue and depression of the muscular powers produced by the accomplishment of their journey, must have led to such an end. Mr. Rush, Mr. Spencer, and myself, at no moment, even when at our greatest elevation, labored under the slightest inconvenience in respect to a difficulty of respiration. We breathed with the utmost ease, and as freely as when walking on the earth's surface. When at an elevation of fifteen thousand feet, we discerned in the so[illegible]-east an extremely vivid flash of lightning."

It is true that the spiral motion of the balloon may be due to merely mechanical causes. The balloon not being a true and perfect sphere, would give it a tendency to rotate upon its axis; but if it should be found that it *always rotates in the same direction*, then it must be considered that the rotation is due to the general law of which we have been treating, and not to any mechanical imperfection in the construction of the balloon itself. In many chemical experiments, the same law is very clearly indicated. Potassium, when thrown upon water, rotates in a spiral course during the continuance of the action which accompanies its oxydation.

Perhaps this curious law will be ultimately solved by that other, no less mysterious, discovered by Professor Oersted, that Voltaic or galvanic currents move in spiral courses around the central and fixed magnet; but to whatever causes such effects may be due, we have the utmost assurance that they are controlled by an established law of nature, as certain and efficient for the accomplishment of its object, as that which governs the rotation of the planets on their axes: indeed, we have reason to believe that the same ultimate principle governs the rotation both of the greater and lesser processes of nature, wherein rotation is manifested. The planets rotate on their axes all in one and the same direction, and this also is due to a law of nature, and is not in any way derived from a "primitive impulse" having been imparted to each at a given distance from the centre, by which they received a whirling motion, like a top, which they have retained unabated up to the present day. The rotation of the earth is due to a natural law of which we shall speak bye and bye, and the spiral motion of fluids, inasmuch as it is constant and unchanging, is also due to a law of nature.

Now, if it be a general law that all fluids move with a spiral or twisting motion, and if there be fluid matter issuing from the sun, we are justified in concluding that such fluid obeys the general law, and having arrived at this conclusion, we shall have little difficulty in perceiving that by the effect of this continually rolling and twisting motion in the distant regions in the solar system, the condensing or contracting mass must be rolled together into globular masses. And these globular masses of partially condensed matter possess all the characteristics of a comet without a tail; and such is the state in which a comet is found to exist when perceived at a distance from the sun. At first there is no tail, but that appendage begins to expand gradually as the loose body approaches the centre, the greatest degree of expansion taking place whilst the comet is in the perihelion, in the immediate vicinity of the great central exciting body, and again decreasing on becoming contracted, as the comet recedes into the distant region of the system.

We have not mentioned the *nebulous theory* of Laplace, which has been supported by Sir John Herschel and others, because it supposes several conditions which are wholly inconsistent with the general and known course of natural processes. It assumes that at a certain remote and unknown period, the whole solar system was filled with an immense volume of nebulous matter; that this nebulous mass, by some cause unexplained, was set in motion in a kind of vortex; that as all the planets move in the same direction, their motion is to be referred to the motion of the nebulous chaotic mass, from which they were formed by a kind of creative effort. That the creation or arrangement of the solar system having been thus effected, not by degrees, planet after planet, but at one birth, the system may remain forever fixed, permanent, and stable, without change, for it is said "it contains within itself no principle of derangement or decay;" although it is now admitted that at some future period it may by some unknown and extraordinary cause be broken up or dissolved into a nebulous mass as at first. These notions are wholly inconsistent with the slow, silent, and progressive movement which characterizes all the operations of nature which have come within the sphere of our observation. It rests upon mere supposition, supported by no evidence, unless the existence of some indistinct masses of vapor, seen imperfectly by the aid of powerful telescopes, in the distant regions of space, be admitted as such. The supposition of the sudden creation of an entire system by an unknown cause, does not come within the range of natural philosophy.

In this chapter under the head "Geology" we have taken a brief survey of the solar system. The earth is a portion of that system; and in tracing the origin of the earth, it was found that astronomy and geology were so intimately connected and blended together, that it became difficult to draw a line of demarcation, on which account the two have been treated under one head. We have thus endeavored to present a brief view of the *great circuit of motion* of the solar system, and will next proceed to the consideration of the manner of operation of the two ultimate forces by which the system is actuated.

## OF FORCE AND MOTION.

A natural force is a power capable of originating motion, supposing every thing to have been previously in a state of rest. All motion on the earth, whether in the physical or moral world, may be traced up, step by step, to the two ultimate and *invisible forces* of attraction and repulsion, or to the primary and *visible effects* of these two forces as exhibited in the contraction and expansion of matter. If the active energy of these two forces were suspended, the whole universe would come to a state of rest; the momentum or quantity of motion existing at the time of the suspension of the two forces would gradually subside, for momentum is not a force, but an effect or accompaniment of motion, which motion has its origin in one or the other of the two ultimate forces. These two forces are the fountains or sources of all motion. Motion, and its accompaniment, momentum, are being continually originated, destroyed, and again originated, but the two forces which originate and annihilate motion and momentum are themselves eternal and indestructible, as matter is eternal and indestructible, for they are essential properties of matter, without which it has never been known to exist.

Some philosophers have held that motion, like matter, is indestructible; that matter and motion are co-existent and co-eternal; that when a body ceases to move, the aggregate quantity of motion in the universe is not thereby diminished, because, they say, the momentum by which it had been moved is simply transferred to other contiguous bodies, or is absorbed into the aggregate of motion or momentum, so that the original quantity of motion or momentum remains forever the same. According to this doctrine, every operation in nature is to be referred to mere motion, without any regard to the forces by which that motion is originated. This doctrine, which is contradicted by the commonest experience, receives a considerable degree of countenance from the Newtonian hypothesis, which affirms that the momenta of the planets will remain forever undiminished, although the attraction of the sun is continually struggling against it, thereby tending to its annihilation. But in addition to our every-day observation of motion; and, consequently, momentum,—for they always go together,—being created and destroyed, a very simple experiment will set the matter at rest. Let two inelastic bodies, containing equal quantities of matter, be impelled with equal velocities, and, consequently, with equal momenta, in opposite directions along the line A B, and let them meet in the point C, then the momentum of each of the bodies will mutually destroy that of the other, and the momenta being annihilated, they will remain at rest in the point C.

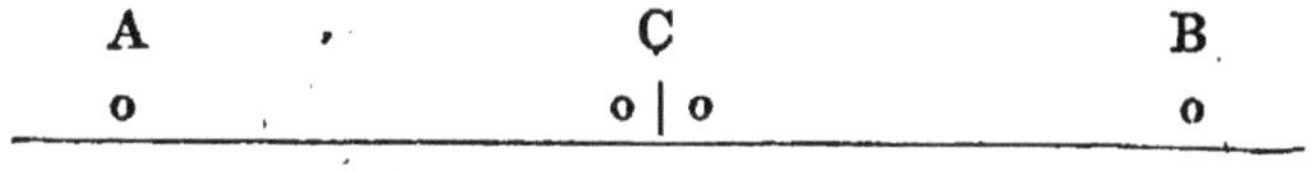

A C B
o o | o o

From the consideration of this case, as well as from a thousand other observations, we perceive that motion with its accompaniment, momentum, is not merely transferred from body to body, but is actually annihilated and continually re-produced, and, therefore, it follows, that both the annihilation and re-production of motion must be referred to natural forces always in action.

Theologians contend that every motion throughout the universe is to be ascribed to the direct or indirect agency of Divine power; but when they find that by the falling of an avalanche, by an inundation, or an earthquake, whole nations are destroyed, involving the innocent and the guilty in one common ruin, they shrink from the conclusions to which their own principles would lead, and with their opponents, fall back upon the laws of nature. However, with the opinions of theologians we have nothing to do in this place. Whenever we attempt to draw inferences from supernatural agencies, we thereby confess that we have arrived at the limits of known causes, our subject becomes mixed and embarrassed with theological disquisitions, and is so far not to be considered in the light of pure natural philosophy.

The Newtonian system is of this mixed character.—Gravity or attraction is a natural force, but the momenta by which it is said the planets are urged forward in their orbits, is presumed to be an effect of supernatural agency; and, inasmuch as the system appeals to supernatural agency, it is so far to be considered rather as of a theological than a philosophical character.

In our present inquiry we are about to trace all motion to the natural forces of attraction and repulsion; at the same time, we by no means attempt to exclude the *Directing Intelligence* from a participation in the works of nature:—viewing him, however, not as the force which moves, but the mind which directs the movement or process to its final termination. As the ship is moved by the natural force of the wind, but is guided or directed in its course into the desired port by the intelligence which presides at the helm; so in the same manner it may be conceived that Intelligence presides at the helm of the universe, directing the motion, whilst the motion itself is due to natural forces. However, in tracing the course of events in the natural world, we are bound by the principles of natural philosophy, to confine ourselves to natural causes only,—those of a supernatural character belonging exclusively to the province of the theologian.

Now, in this case, as in all others, if we desire to derive profit and instruction from our inquiry, we must begin with things known and familiar, and proceed by gradual steps, until we arrive at a knowledge of the unknown and abstruse. We must examine the motions and the causes of the motion of the objects immediately around us, and proceed by degrees, until we find all the motions of the universe comprehended in the same law as that which regulates the most minute process going on at our feet.

In regard to those common and well known instruments or forms called mechanical powers, little need be said in this place. The solar system is not a purely mechanical system; neither are these adaptations of parts usually denominated mechanical *powers* entitled to such appellation. They are not *powers*,—they contain no *force*,—they are merely convenient modes of applying a given amount of force. Nothing is lost by their application except friction, and nothing is gained except convenience. An individual can raise one hundred weight one foot high without the aid of a lever or inclined plane, and this he can do twenty times in succession, by which means he at last has raised twenty hundred weight one foot high. But if he have to raise a cask or hogshead of liquor, weighing twenty hundred weight, he finds it inconvenient to take the cask to pieces so as to raise it in twenty portions; he therefore has recourse to a lever or inclined plane. By the help of these he can raise the twenty hundred weight without dividing it into parts; but in order to raise the twenty hundred weight one foot, he has to apply a force of one hundred weight through a distance of twenty feet, whether he apply the lever or the inclined plane. In respect to the force applied and the resistance overcome, nothing is gained by the application of mechanical forces except the convenience of keeping the cask or hogshead unbroken. All the other mechanical powers resolve themselves into the lever and inclined plane, and therefore do not merit particular notice.

Our object is simply to point out the fact that no force of any kind can possibly be obtained by any combination whatever of those adaptations usually and somewhat improperly named *mechanical powers.* The very name of "*powers*" has tended to mislead many an unfortunate genius into the vain and fruitless attempt to construct a perpetual mechanical motion, and this delusion has been not a little fostered by the confident assurance with which it is continually asserted that the solar system is a perpetual motion, moving upon purely mechanical principles. The numerous losses and disappointments which have been experienced from time to time in this "vain pursuit" will lead us to perceive the inestimable value of correct first principles, for no truth can be more certain or more important than this: that *false principles lead to false conclusions; false conclusions lead to erroneous action; and erroneous action leads to disappointment, loss, and misery;*—and this is true, whether applied to morals or physics.

In our inquiries and examinations concerning force and motion, we must keep this fact constantly and steadily before the mind:—*That the moving body is at all times under the influence of two opposing forces,*—the stronger of the two is the *moving* power, the weaker is the *regulating* power; and the velocity of the motion is in the proportion of the *difference* between the two forces. If the moving power be 12, and the regulating power 8, then the difference 4 is the actual amount of power causing the motion. If the moving power be increased to 16, or the regulating power be decreased to 4, the actual power causing the motion will be increased in a corresponding ratio, and conversely if the moving power be decreased or the regulating power increased, the velocity will be decreased in the same ratio; and if the regulating power be increased so as to become the greater, or the moving power be decreased so as to become the less, then the motion will be reversed, for that which was previously the regulating has now become the moving power, and, as before, the velocity will be as the difference between the two forces.

The actual moving power is at all times attraction or repulsion; but into the regulating power several elements of resistance enter, as friction and the resistance of fluids, besides a portion which is at all times due to the ultimate force of attraction or repulsion. In the works of nature repulsion and attraction are always opposed to each other, the one greater, the other less, in each particular process, expansion or contraction going on as the one or the other is the predominating force; but in works of art this is not the case, for sometimes we have attraction opposed to attraction, and repulsion to repulsion. It may serve to impress this important point more clearly upon the mind to exhibit the relations in the tabular form:—

| *Stronger or moving force.* | | *Weaker or regulating force.* | *Effect.* |
|---|---|---|---|
| Repulsion | *opposed to* | Attraction, | Expansion. |
| Attraction | " | Repulsion, | Contraction. |
| Attraction | " | Attraction, | Mechanical motion. |
| Repulsion | " | Repulsion, | Mechanical motion. |

In order to illustrate these principles in a familiar manner, we will take works of art in the first place, as the mechanical motions consequent thereon are more palpable and obvious, and, therefore, more readily discerned.

## A BEAM AND SCALES.

### *Attraction opposed to Attraction.*

If 16 ounces be placed in each of a pair of scales, attached to a common weigh beam, suspended above the surface of the earth, each scale will be solicited towards the earth by attraction, with a force equal to 16 ounces upon each of the two scales: the whole force pulling upon the fulcrum of the beam will be equal to 32 ounces, (the weight of the beam, scales, and appendages being omitted). But as the two forces are equal on each side of the fulcrum, the whole remains at rest, notwithstanding that there is an absolute force of 32 ounces in actual operation. But they balance each other. The forces are in equilibrio. There is neither a *moving* nor a *regulating* power. But if one ounce be taken from either scale, the equilibrium will be destroyed. The scale from which the ounce has been taken, will no longer be attracted with a force of 16 but 15 ounces; and the other scale, upon which the attraction is but one ounce more, will descend with a *moving* force equal to one ounce, which is the difference of the amount of attraction acting upon each of the two scales. The stronger attraction of 16 ounces is the *moving* power, the weaker of 15 ounces is the *regulating* power. If two ounces be now taken from the moving power, the motion will be reversed, because that which was before the regulating power, has now become the greater of the two. If the regulating power be suddenly removed, then the other scale being no longer resisted will descend with the whole force, as a stone falls to the earth by the force of attraction, meeting with no resistance except that of the atmosphere through which it descends. This experiment may be varied in a number of ways, as by moving the fulcrum to one side or the other of the centre alternately without removing the weights. It is very simple, and for that reason has been introduced, as it illustrates the principle in a plain manner; and if the reader will fix the *principle* clearly in his mind, he will be enabled to follow the reasonings upon all other motions, even those of the solar system, with great ease and satisfaction to himself.

## A COMMON HOUSE CLOCK, WITH WEIGHT AND PENDULUM.

### *Attraction opposed to Attraction.*

The weight is the moving, and the pendulum the regulating power. If the resistance offered by the friction, added to that required to raise the bulb of the pendulum to the highest point of the arc through which it oscillates, be equal to the whole of the attractive force of the earth acting on the weight or moving power, the clock will remain at rest. The two forces are in equilibrio. In order to cause the clock to go, the balance must be disturbed. The bulb of the pendulum, being raised the length of the lever from the point of suspension, is shortened. An ounce is removed from the scale,—the resistance of the regulating power is decreased,—the clock continues to move with a graduated motion,—the attractive force of the earth acting upon the weight or moving power is regulated by the lesser attraction acting upon the pendulum or regulating power; to which must be added the resistance offered by the friction of the works, the whole together being less than the moving power, and the rate of going of the clock is in proportion to the difference. If the pendulum be removed, the weight drops to the earth, the regulating power is removed.

## A CLOCK WITH TWO WEIGHTS.

*Attraction opposed to Attraction.*

If instead of a pendulum, a clock should be constructed with two weights, one at each end of the cord, then, if the weights be equal, the clock will be at rest, as in the case of the scales with 16 ounces in each, with whatever force they may be attracted towards the earth. But if by taking away from the one, or adding to the other, so as to disturb the equilibrium to a sufficient degree to allow the greater weight to overcome the lesser and the friction of the works, then, it is evident that the greater weight will begin to descend with a force equal to the difference between the two. And if when the greater or moving power has reached the earth, and the lesser or regulating power has reached the highest point, the difference be taken away from the lower and greater, and added to the higher and lesser, then the clock will move backwards for a period equal to that in which it had been moving in the opposite direction; and thus, without winding up, by merely changing the *difference* from the lower to the higher level, the clock may be kept in motion, continually going alternately backwards and forwards. It might be difficult to regulate its movement with the same degree of nicety as with a pendulum, but still it would continue to move with a regulated motion. As in the former cases, if the lesser or regulating force be removed, the greater, being no longer resisted, will fall to the earth.

## A CLOCK WITH TWO BALLOONS.

*Repulsion opposed to Repulsion.*

Take a common Dutch clock, and having removed the pallet, place it in an inverted position upon the floor of the apartment. Instead of two weights, as in the former case, attach two small balloons, one to each end of the cord. Now, the balloons must be filled with *expanded* matter, and the matter is kept in its expanded form by the force of *repulsion* acting between atom and atom. If the two balloons be of equal size and weight, and contain the same quantity of matter equally expanded, then their buoyancy will be equal—they will have an equal *ascending* power, just as the two weights had an equal *descending* power; the descending power of the weights was in proportion to the earth's attraction, and the ascending power of the balloons is in proportion to the repulsion between atom and atom, by which the matter or gas is more or less expanded. Now, if all things be equal in respect to the two balloons, the clock will remain at rest. The two ascending powers are in equilibrio; but if the *attractive* force be increased within one of the balloons, so that the enclosed matter shall become more *contracted*, or if the *repulsive* force be increased within the other, so that the gas shall become more *expanded*, then the equilibrium will be disturbed, and motion will ensue. And if when the more expanded body has reached the highest, and the less expanded the lowest point, the conditions be reversed by expanding the lower and contracting the higher, then, as in the case of the two weights, the clock will move backwards for a given time. And this would be accomplished without aiding or diminishing the quantity of matter contained in the balloons, but simply by augmenting and diminishing alternately the forces of repulsion and attraction, whereby the enclosed matter would become more or less expanded or contracted.

## CLOCK WITH BALLOON AND WEIGHT.

*Repulsion opposed to Attraction.*

If the clock be laid in a horizontal position, and the cord being coiled once or twice round the wheel, have a balloon attached to the upper, and a weight to the lower end, then, if the buoyancy of the balloon, which depends upon the internal repulsion, be equal to the attractive force acting upon the weight, the clock will remain at rest. But if the repulsive force be increased, the balloon becomes the moving power, and ascends with a velocity proportionate to the difference between the repulsive force acting within the balloon, and the attractive force acting upon the weight. The weight is the regulating power. If the gas be contracted in a given degree, the conditions will be reversed. The weight becomes the greater or moving power, and the balloon becomes the lesser or regulating power, and consequently the attraction of the earth will draw the weight towards the surface, dragging the balloon, or lesser power, after it.

## A WATCH.

### *Attraction and Repulsion opposed to Attraction and Repulsion.*

In order to understand the nature and manner of action of the attractive and repulsive forces by which a watch is kept in motion, let the reader clench his fist. Now, it will be seen that the skin and flesh upon the back of the hand is *stretched*, whilst that upon the inner surface is *wrinkled*. If now the muscles by which the hand is held clenched be relaxed, but without any voluntary effort to open the hand, it will be found that there is a tendency in the stretched and wrinkled parts to resume their previous state, and in consequence the hand will open to a small extent without any voluntary effort. The *stretched* muscles have a tendency to *draw* themselves together again, until they have reached the point of equilibrium, where they feel to be at ease and rest; and the *compressed* or wrinkled muscles have a tendency to *push* themselves apart, until they also have reached the point of rest or equilibrium. Now, these two forces which *draw* along the external, and *push* along the internal surface of the coiled up hand,—the two forces co-operating, each aiding the other,—are the same forces which actuate the watch, by *drawing* along the *external*, and *pushing* along the *internal* surfaces of the coiled up main-spring. The main-spring is the moving power of the watch; and because the ultimate forces operate conjointly, each aiding the other, the watch-maker is enabled to obtain a great power in a small space.

The attractive and repulsive forces operating upon the main-spring do not oppose each other; and in order that the works may move with a regulated motion, it is requisite that there shall be an opposing or regulating force. This regulating or opposing force is obtained by a small spiral spring, sometimes called the "hair-spring," which is attached to the balance wheel, at the further end of the train of wheel work. In this hair-spring the same attractive and repulsive forces operate conjointly upon the exterior and interior surfaces, as in the main-spring. But the resistance of the hair spring is less than the power of the main-spring. If they were equal, the works would remain at rest. The main-spring has to overcome the friction and the resistance offered by the hair-spring, and the velocity of the movement is in the ratio of the difference between the *moving* power, and the resistance or *regulating* power;—when the watch goes too slow, the resistance of the hair-spring must be diminished, when too fast, the resistance must be increased. If the resistance be removed altogether, by lifting the balance wheel and hair-spring from the point of resistance, the main-spring being no longer resisted, uncoils itself with a rapid movement, the works run down suddenly,—just as the clock weight falls suddenly to the earth when the pendulum is removed. It might be possible to make a watch without a balance or pallet wheel, with two main-springs and fusees, so that the works would move backwards or forwards, as the one or the other of the two springs was wound up,—just as in the case of the clock with two weights. A watch constructed upon this principle, would continue to move until the power of the two springs became equal, and might then be wound up either upon one spring or the other, when it would again move until the equilibrium was again restored.

It does not appear that any purpose of utility would be served either in the case of the watch with two such springs, or of the clock with two weights; neither is it our object to recommend such an arrangement, but simply to illustrate the principles of regulated motion, as depending upon the reciprocal action of two opposing forces.

## ATMOSPHERIC STEAM ENGINE.

### *Repulsion opposed to Attraction.*

The atmosphere is attracted towards the earth with a force of about fifteen pounds to every square inch of surface at the level of the sea, with the mercurial barometer at thirty inches; and, therefore, a piston whose area is 1,000 square inches, fitting air tight into a steam cylinder, sustains upon its *upper* surface an atmospheric pressure equal to 15,000 pounds. But, as fluids press equally on all sides, if the under surface be open to the atmosphere, there is a pressure of 15,000 pounds on the *under* surface also, and consequently the piston remains at rest. The two forces are in equilibrio. Before motion can take place, the equilibrium must be destroyed by some means, either by removing a portion of the resistance on one side of the piston or the other. If the cylinder be made air tight at one or both ends, and fitted with stop-cocks, the piston, or moveable diaphragm, also fitting air tight with the internal surface of the cylinder, and if by means of an air pump a portion of the atmospheric air be withdrawn from either side of the moveable diaphragm, motion will ensue, and the diaphragm will move towards that end of the cylinder from which the air has been withdrawn, until by the compression of the air that remains, the equilibrium is again restored, and the diaphragm comes to rest as at first. Now, the resistance which the enclosed air offers to the motion of the diaphragm in this case is essentially repulsion, because atmospheric air is gaseous or expanded matter. If the repulsive force which holds it in its expanded form could be withdrawn, if the air could be condensed, as steam is contracted into water in the condensing engine, then the resistance would be altogether removed, and the diaphragm would descend to the bottom of the cylinder with the whole force of 15,000 pounds, which is the amount of the attractive force exerted upon a column of the atmosphere, whose base is equal to the area of the piston or diaphragm.

The same object may be accomplished by pumping in air, as well as by pumping it out. If air be forced into the cylinder upon one side of the piston until the pressure be equal to twenty pounds upon every square inch, then there will be a force of 20,000 pounds upon one side of the piston, and 15,000 upon the other, and the piston will move with a force equal to the difference, namely, 5,000 pounds. The 20,000 is the *moving* power; the 15,000 the *regulating* power, to which regulating power must be added the friction of the engine and whatever else may be attached; 5,000 pounds is the *available* power which may be applied to cause motion.

Now, in the atmospheric steam engine, the upper end of the cylinder is open to the atmosphere, and, therefore, upon a piston whose area is 1,000 square inches, there is at all times an atmospheric pressure equal to 15,000 pounds. The lower end of the cylinder is shut in from the atmosphere, but is open to the steam boiler, by means of a pipe connecting the one with the other, usually called the steam pipe. Now, in order that the piston may be raised within the cylinder, it is necessary that the steam pressure within the boiler shall exceed 15 pounds to the square inch. Let the steam pressure be 30 pounds, then there will be a steam force of 30,000 pounds upon the lower side of the piston, and an atmospheric pressure of 15,000 pounds upon the upper side, and the piston will ascend with a force equal to the difference, namely, 15,000 pounds. Now, when the piston has reached the top of the cylinder, the communication between the boiler and the lower end of the cylinder is cut off by means of the valve, or stop-cock. The steam within the cylinder is condensed or contracted into water, and if the condensation be perfect, a vacuum is formed beneath the piston, which being now unresisted beneath, descends by the pressure of the atmosphere with a force equal to 15,000 pounds. By the continued repetition of this alternating process of the expansion and contraction of water into steam, and steam into water, the motion of the engine is continued.

It is an easy matter to trace the motion of the atmospheric steam engine to the two ultimate forces of attraction and repulsion. By the attraction of the earth exerted upon the atmospheric column which rests upon the piston, as well as upon the piston itself, the whole is drawn towards the earth's surface or centre, until the *calorific* repulsion, as it is generally named, has become stronger than the attraction, and the whole column, with the piston for its base, is *pushed* upwards with a force equal to the difference between the two opposing forces; and thus by repulsion the piston is moved from the bottom to the top of the cylinder. The *calorific* repulsion is then decreased, a given weight is removed from the scale, and the whole column, with the piston for its base, is again *drawn* down towards the surface or centre by the force of attraction. The actual moving power is at all times in proportion to the difference between the two forces,—repulsion being stronger during one half of the circuit, and attraction during the other.

## THE HIGH PRESSURE STEAM ENGINE.

### *Repulsion opposed to Attraction.*

After what has been said of the atmospheric, a few words will explain the nature of the high pressure engine.

In this engine there is no attempt made to form a vacuum under the piston. It is named *high* pressure, because it cannot move unless the steam be above the pressure of the atmosphere; and the actual moving power is just as much as the steam is higher than the atmospheric pressure. In high pressure engines it is usual to work with steam of three atmospheres, that is, of 45 pounds to the square inch. Now, as the piston is pressed upon one side with a force of 45 pounds per square inch, and on the other with an atmospheric pressure of 15 pounds, the actual moving power is 30 pounds, that is, the difference. The cylinder is closed at both ends, but for the discharge of the steam after it has exerted its power upon the piston, a pipe is attached, through which, by means of a stop-cock or valve, a communication is opened between the external atmosphere and each end of the cylinder alternately. Now, by means of these valves or slides, when a communication is opened between the boiler and the lower side of the piston, and between the upper side of the piston and the external atmosphere, then, the lower side being pressed *upwards* with a steam force or calorific repulsion of 45 pounds per square inch, and the upper side downwards with an atmospheric pressure, caused by the earth's attraction, equal to 15 pounds per square inch, the piston is forced upwards with an actual force equal to 30 pounds per square inch. By the motion of the engine the slides are now reversed, the upper side of the piston opened to the boiler, and the lower side to the atmosphere, by which the piston is forced downwards by the greater of the two forces, and thus the motion is continued so long as the *calorific* repulsion within the boiler is sufficient to overcome the weight or resistance of the atmosphere caused by the earth's attraction. It is simply moving the weight from the one scale to the other alternately.

## CONDENSING STEAM ENGINE.

### *Repulsion opposed to Attraction.*

In the atmospheric and high pressure engines, the piston works against a resistance of one atmosphere, and consequently with a loss of power or drawback equal to 15 pounds per square inch. In the condensing engine invented by James Watt, by forming a vacuum before the moving piston, by means of an air pump, this loss is attempted to be avoided, and to a certain extent the object is accomplished. An air pump of one-third or even of one-fourth of the capacity of the steam cylinder, will maintain an imperfect vacuum before the working piston, so that the steam in forcing up the piston, instead of having to overcome an atmospheric resistance of 15 pounds per square inch upon the upper surface of the piston, has only to meet the atmospheric pressure on the upper surface of the plunger of the air pump; and as the area of the air pump is less than one-third of the steam cylinder, the atmospheric resistance of 15,000 pounds, which would have resisted a steam piston whose area is 1,000 square inches, is reduced to 5,000 pounds, the saving being 10,000 pounds—that is, supposing the vacuum to be perfect; but as this is not the case, the absolute gain consequent upon the introduction of the air pump is not quite so great. Besides, there are some mechanical drawbacks which reduce the saving still lower; but still there is a decided gain of power with the condensing engine, as compared with the atmospheric and high pressure.

In consequence of getting rid of a considerable portion of the atmospheric resistance, the condensing engine may be worked with steam of a pressure very little above that of the atmosphere, and hence this engine is sometimes named the low pressure engine. The actual loss or drawback is generally estimated at about 6 pounds to the square inch upon the steam piston, so that the gain, as compared with the high pressure engine, is about 9 pounds; but this loss of 6 pounds per square inch does not arise altogether from atmospheric resistance: a considerable portion of it is attributable to the weight of the pumps with which the engine is encumbered. However, in this engine, as in every other case where motion of any kind is discernable, we can trace the motion to the two ultimate forces of attraction and repulsion. By the stronger repulsion or expansive force of the steam the different solid parts as well as the atmosphere are forced up against the force of attraction exerted by the earth, and by means of the slides, the stronger repulsive force being removed, those parts are again drawn downwards by the earth's attraction.

## CONDENSING ENGINE WITHOUT PUMPS.

### *Repulsion against Friction.*

The condensing engine, as an instrument of power, owes its superiority over the high pressure and atmospheric engines chiefly to the vacuum which is constantly maintained *before the moving piston*, by which the atmospheric resistance (the weight in the opposite scale) is, so far as regards the piston itself, got rid of. But, inasmuch as an air pump is required to maintain this vacuum, the power consumed in working this pump must be deducted from the gross amount of gain acquired by the removal of the atmospheric resistance. The *difference* between the whole gain and this drawback is the actual gain. But besides the air pump, there are two other pumps necessary to the common condensing engine of James Watt. There is the cold water pump to supply the condenser with a constant stream of cold water, and the hot water or feeding pump to supply the boiler. The power expended in working these must also be deducted from the gross amount of gain; so that when the whole loss or drawback has been subtracted from the whole gain, it is found to form a very considerable item, often amounting to one-fourth, or, even in some cases, one-third of the gross power. Now, it is plain if the vacuum can by any means be procured in the first instance, and afterwards maintained for any length of time, as in the Torricellian vacuum of the barometer tube, and if the boiler and condenser can be supplied without the aid of pumps, that the *whole gain* would be secured *without any drawback.*

Let us see how this is to be accomplished. It can only be done by arranging the engine so that it shall work in harmony with the works of nature. If the reader has acquired a clear idea of the manner of formation of the rain drop, to which we have already referred so often, and of the axioms, p. 72, he will have little difficulty in discerning the arrangement required in order to obtain so desirable a result. The rain drop is formed by the condensation of steam or vapor in the upper region of the atmosphere, which had been previously expanded at the surface of the ocean or earth. The expanded vapor ascended or receded *from* the surface in consequence of expansion, and the condensed or contracted rain drop descended or returned *towards* the earth's surface or centre in consequence of contraction, having in the ascent and descent performed a circuit,—during one half of which circuit the matter moved in the form of vapor or gas, and during the other in the form of a liquid. Now, the engine must be arranged agreeable to this law, for the whole power of the engine is derived from the circulation going on within it. There is a circuit in every respect analogous to that of the rain drop in continual motion within the engine, during one half of which (from the boiler or point of expansion, through the steam cylinder and eduction pipe, to the condenser or point of contraction,) the matter moves in the form of vapor, and during the other half (from the condenser to the boiler) in the liquid form. The vapor or steam will rise of its own accord in the atmosphere, and even in a vacuum its mere weight can offer no appreciable resistance to the piston, whilst on the other hand the water will fall of its own accord. In the ordinary condensing engine, these things are arranged in an unnatural position. The boiler is placed above the level of the condenser, the steam is drawn down to be condensed, and the water is pumped up to be expanded,—both of which operations are opposed to the ordinary course and laws of nature; for if the water be expanded on the lower level, the steam will rise of itself, and being afterwards contracted on the higher level, the water will fall of itself.

The following plan of a condensing engine without pumps, for which Her Majesty's Letters Patent have been obtained, is constructed upon the principle here referred to:—

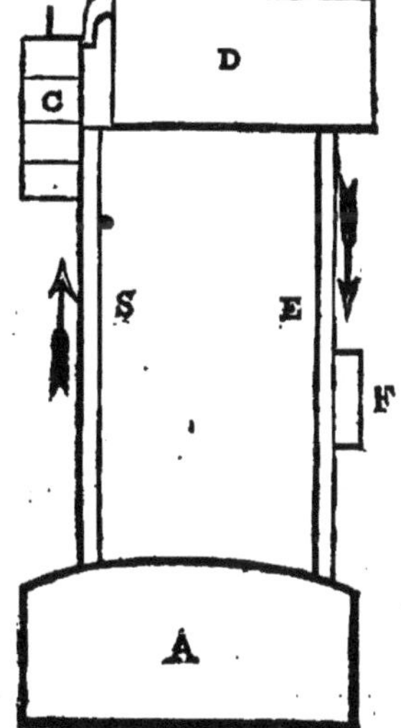

A is the boiler or point of expansion, placed beneath the level of the condenser D, because expanded matter ascends or recedes from the earth's centre.

S the steam pipe. C the working cylinder, in which the steam exerts its power.

D the condenser, placed above the level of the boiler, because contracted matter (condensed steam, or water,) falls of its own weight, or descends towards the earth's centre.

E the water pipe to return the water of condensation to the boiler A; and F an apparatus to cause the boiler to feed itself, without a pump or other appendage attached to the engine, thereby causing a loss of power.

The arrows show the direction of the *circuit of motion* of the circulating fluid, from which the mechanical power is derived. The steam is condensed without a jet, by means of a stream of cold water running continually between a series of metallic chambers, without abstracting from the disposable power of the engine. The valves and other minor mechanical arrangements are not shown.

## ELECTRO-MAGNETIC ENGINE.

### *Attraction and Repulsion opposed to Friction.*

As the motion of the steam engine is continued by a reciprocating action, by the alternate change of the moving power from the one side to the other of the piston by means of the slide valves, so also in the electro-magnetic engine, this alternation is continually effected by means of the "pole changer," by which the attractions and repulsions are successively reversed as the revolving magnet is approaching towards or receding from the fixed points connected with the galvanic battery. In the former case the power (the steam) is generated in the boiler and conducted to the point of mechanical action through a pipe. In the latter the power is generated in the cells of the battery, and conducted along a solid wire to the point where the reciprocating mechanical motion is going on. The circuit of motion of the steam within the engine is broken and renewed by every motion of the slide valve, and the galvanic circle is continually broken and renewed in a like manner.

We have not taken notice of rotary motion in a *continued stream*, without this reciprocating action, as exhibited in some modifications of the electro-magnetic engine,

Hero's steam engine, in revolving street-lamps, and in Barker's water mill. These are all of them analogous motions, and are produced by *re-action.* As the stream of gas issues from the street-lamp, or the steam from Hero's engine, the issuing stream by meeting with the atmosphere, causes a re-action, which, falling upon the area of the aperture from which the stream issues, impels the lamp or engine in a retrograde direction. The immediate moving power is, in fact, repulsion, and may be traced along the stream to the power or pressure which forces that stream out at the aperture. In the case of the street-lamp, it is the weight or pressure of the gasometer upon the enclosed gas, which, by pressing the stream onward, is the remote cause of the motion of the lamp.—The *remote* cause is the attraction of the earth exerted upon the solid gasometer. And so, in the other cases, the motion may be traced up to attraction or repulsion.

## LOCOMOTIVE ON A LEVEL.

### *Repulsion opposed to Friction.*

A locomotive on a level railway with a light load can be urged forward at a great speed, or a decreased speed will drag a very great load, because the power of the steam has only to overcome the friction of the rubbing surfaces and the resistance of the fluid atmosphere through which the engine and load moves,—that is, the friction of the atmosphere. The steam is the moving power, and the friction, in this case, is the regulating power; and the velocity of the engine and train is in proportion to the difference of the two powers. But it can be shown that the attraction of the earth is, in fact, the regulating power, even on a level, and that the friction is but the mode or medium through which attraction exerts its influence. If you increase the load, you increase the friction, and *vice versa*, if you diminish the load, you diminish the friction,—that is if you increase the load, there is a greater force of attraction bearing upon the axles and other moving parts. From this we perceive that the earth's attraction is the chief cause of the friction; and, therefore, a locomotive on a level surface may be said to be under the influence of the two forces: of the repulsive or expansive force of the steam urging it into motion, and of the attractive force of the earth checking and retarding that motion through the medium of friction. These observations with regard to friction will, to a large extent, apply generally.

## LOCOMOTIVE ON AN INCLINED PLANE.

### *Repulsion opposed to Attraction.*

If a locomotive be placed upon a smooth inclined plane, it will have a tendency to run down the incline; and the force which draws it downwards is the attraction of the earth acting upon the carriage, and the amount of force is in proportion to the weight of the carriage and the steepness of the descent. Let the actual force dragging it backwards be equal to one ton, then, if the steam power urging it upwards be also equal to one tone, the locomotive will remain at rest upon any part of the incline; it will neither go up nor down; the two forces are in equilibrio. If the steam force be lowered beneath one ton, the carriage will descend with a velocity equal to the difference. If raised above one ton, it will ascend with the difference. If the steam force be raised to two tons, it will move upwards with a force equal to one ton, the difference.

Having made these remarks upon force and motion as they relate to familiar things, we will now proceed to the forces and motions of the earth and solar system, reminding the reader that in every case of force and motion, we must find the *moving power* and the *regulating power*, for these two are in all cases essential to the motion of an organized machine; and such is the solar system. According to the Newtonian hypothesis, the centrifugal force, or the momentum, derived from the "primitive impulse" is the moving power, and the sun's attraction is the regulating or resisting power; but this view we have already shown to be erroneous, for this moving power is not a force, but an effect which would soon be annihilated by the opposing force of attraction, and the earth's motion would quickly come to an end.

We must still proceed by regular steps from things known to things unknown, for such, and such only, is the legitimate mode of inquiry; and in order that we may obtain a clear and distinct conception of the motions of the planets in their circular orbits—of the motions of the celestial sphere—it is necessary that we should first obtain clear and familiar ideas concerning the motions of bodies on the surface of the *spherical* earth. Before we can acquire a clear notion of these latter motions, we must bring the mind to perceive distinctly the difference between a *plane* and *level* surface.

## DIFFERENCE BETWEEN A PLANE SUPERFICIES, AND A LEVEL SURFACE.

"A plane superficies is that in which any two points being taken, the straight line between them lies wholly in that superficies."—*Euclid's Elements. Definition* 7.

In vulgar language, a plane superficies and a level surface are synonymous; but this notion is incorrect. The surface of the ocean is a level surface; but it is not a plane surface or superficies. The surface of the ocean is spherical. It is a portion of the spherical earth. We find upon reflection that *a level surface upon the earth is a superficies, every point of which is equally near to the earth's centre.* This definition of a level is applicable to a sphere at rest; but as the earth revolves upon her axis, this level surface is in consequence somewhat modified. The earth is not a perfect sphere, but a spheroid of rotation. This difference does not, however, affect the general principle, that a level surface is not a plane, but a spherical superficies.

### A PLANE SURFACE.

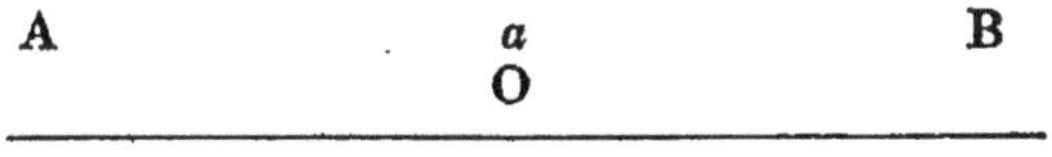

A *a* B
O

---

Now, if a perfectly smooth and spherical body *a* be laid any where upon a perfectly smooth and plane surface A B, the body *a* will have no tendency to move mechanically towards either A or B, or in any other direction.—This is agreeable to Newton's first law of motion:—"That a body at rest will remain at rest, unless disturbed by the action of some external cause." In the case before us, all "external causes," even the attraction of the earth, are supposed to be removed or suspended,—such supposition being necessary in order that all the conditions may be fulfilled. Now, if upon this plane surface we describe an undulating line, or if we describe an undulating line without any regard to the plane surface, strange as it may appear to some minds, a spherical or any other body will remain at rest on any part of that line, just as in the case of the plane surface,—that is, *if the attraction of the earth and all other external forces or external causes of motion be suspended*, a body upon such line being in precisely the same conditions as if in free space. It could have no tendency to move in any one direction more than another.

UNDULATING SURFACE.

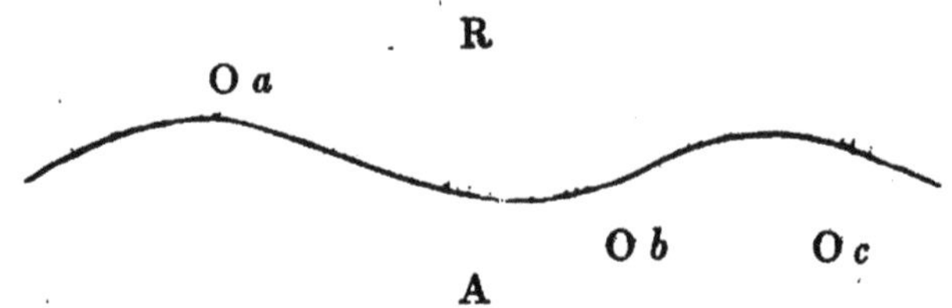


Now, a body placed at *a*, or *b*, or *c*,—that is, on either side of the line, could have no tendency to move in any direction, because the ultimate force or cause of motion is supposed to be suspended. But if, as is the fact in nature, there be an attraction at any distance beneath the point A, then the body *a* would move towards that point, and in obeying that force, would roll down the incline; or if we suppose a repulsive force at R, the body *b* would move away from that point. But the two ultimate forces or causes of all motion being suspended, the bodies remain at rest.

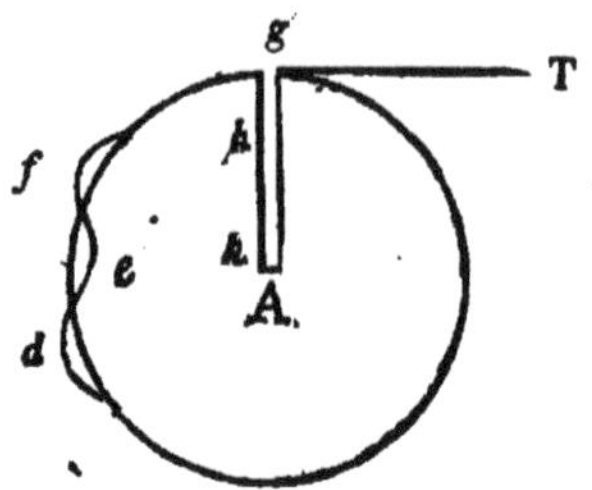


A LEVEL SURFACE.

The circumference of this circle is a faithful representation of a *level surface* upon the spherical earth. The water level of the sea is of this form; and a level railway extending round the earth should follow the curve of the earth's surface. Now, a spherical body, placed any where upon this level surface, could have no tendency to move in any direction; because, although powerfully acted upon by the central attraction at A, yet as every point of the circumference is equally near to the centre A, the body has no tendency to move, because it *cannot move unless by approaching the central attraction which draws it.* The body can move only oncond ition that it shall be running down like a clock, or watch, or river. Now, an undulating line on the earth's level surface, is that which rises and falls alternately above and beneath the circumference, or in other words, a line which alternately recedes from and approaches towards the centre A, as represented by the line *d e f*, and a body placed upon the highest point at *d*, will, by the earth's attraction, descend towards *e*, because *e* is nearer to the centre than *d*—it moves because it is approaching the centre A; and if we suppose all resistance—as friction and atmospheric resistance—removed, the body will, by the momentum which it has acquired in its descent towards *e*, again ascend to the highest point of *f*, and under those supposed conditions might move in this undulating course round the whole globe, just as a pendulum swings upon its centre of oscillation,—the body alternately rising and falling, just as the bulb or bob of the pendulum continually rises and falls. But the pendulum requires a *point of support*, in order that it may be sustained from falling to the earth, and the body rolling or moving either upon an undulating or level surface, requires a point or surface of support also. If the point of support of the pendulum were removed it would drop by its own weight, that is, by attraction, to the earth's surface; and if the surface of support of the moving body were removed, it would drop or be drawn by attraction to the centre of attraction of the earth at A. If the body were in motion at the point *g*, and *the attraction of the earth were suspended*, it would move off in the tangent towards T. If the body were at rest at *g*, and the attraction of the earth in action, it would fall or be attracted towards A through the opening *h h*, being no longer *sustained* by the solid surface of the earth, just as a stone falls down a pit or well towards the earth's centre.

It appears, then, that a body moving upon the earth's surface is *sustained* by the solid earth upon which it moves, and *retained* or held back from proceeding in the tangent by the earth's attraction. It is true, if the body move with sufficient velocity it requires no solid support, just as a cannon ball is carried along by its momentum, without resting upon the surface of the solid earth; but this momentum cannot maintain the motion of the ball forever, if the attraction of the earth be acting upon it; neither could the earth continue in motion by mere momentum whilst the attraction of the sun is acting upon it. The earth is *retained* in her orbit by the attraction of the central sun. This is admitted; and it is necessary to the continuance of her motion that she should be *sustained* in her orbit by some power, as otherwise she would very shortly be lodged in the sun, just as certainly as the cannon ball is dragged to the earth by the annihilation of its momentum. In order that the reader may perceive the principle of motion in a plain manner, we must revert to another case of motion on the earth's surface.

In the following diagram, let the circle *a b c d* represent the external surface of the spherical earth; then, as in the preceding case, a spherical body placed any where upon that surface will remain at rest, having no tendency to move in any direction, *because every point of the spherical surface is equally near to the centre of attraction at* A. In this state of things it may, without impropriety, be said, that the body is held in a state of equilibrio between two forces. The attractive force is drawing it towards the centre A, but the sustaining surface is resisting attraction, so that the body is held down by attraction, and held up by the sustaining surface; which surface is equivalent to a sustaining repulsive force—which, in fact, it really is, for the sustaining matter is not solid, and is only prevented from being so by the force of repulsion. And thus we find that the ultimate sustaining power is the force of repulsion, and that the body is held firmly in its position by being placed between the two forces, as securely as if it were in a blacksmith's vise, and the direction of each of the opposing forces is diametrically opposed to that of the other.

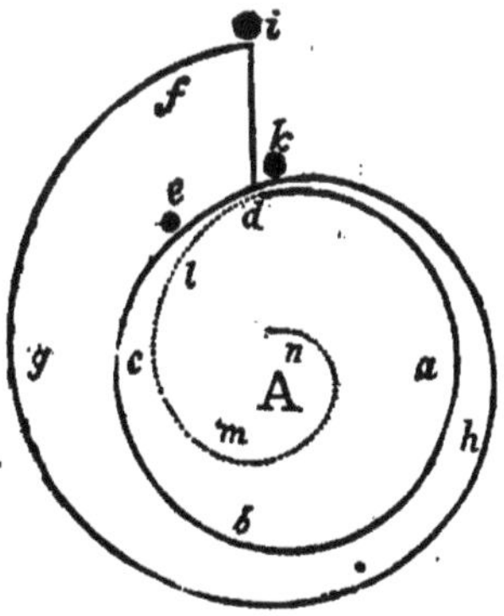


But if the spherical body be placed on the highest or most distant point of the spiral line *f g h*, then the two forces are no longer *diametrically* opposed to each other: the attraction still draws towards the centre A, and the sustaining surface still resists the attraction, but there is a *leaning to one side*. The ball begins to move of itself by the force of attraction, and rolls along the inclined plane, and passing the points *f g h*, it would roll round the entire earth, and ultimately come to rest at the point *k;* and if the spiral line were or could be continued beneath the surface, it would proceed along the dotted line *l m n*, until it reached the earth's centre. Now, the body moves along this spiral line because, and only because, every point of the surface along which it proceeds is nearer and nearer to the centre of attraction at A. Unless this were the case, there is no natural force with which we are acquainted that could put it in motion, or even if it were set agoing that would keep it in motion, if it should meet with any constant obstruction, however small such obstruction might be.

The force of the earth's attraction carries the body down the spiral incline to the point *k;* but there it will remain; the force of attraction cannot raise it from the centre to the higher point *i*. How, then, is the body to be raised? for unless it be raised somehow, the motion is at an end. Whilst attraction is the *moving* force, it cannot continue in motion except by approaching the centre. It is, therefore, necessary, in order that the motion may be continued or repeated, that the body shall be raised to the higher level. Then, what force—what *natural* force, for merely mechanical means are altogether out of the question—will raise the body to the higher level? Repulsion pushes from the centre; but repulsion does not act mechanically,—repulsion will not raise the body in a *solid* mass. How, then, is it to be raised by *natural* means? Let it be *expanded*, and it will rise of itself. And when it has reached the higher level, let it be again *contracted* into *solid* matter, and it will roll down the incline as at first. And as often as the expansion and contraction is repeated, so will the motion be repeated. Now, in this we have, in miniature, all that is contended for in this theory, namely, matter expanding and receding from a centre, and, on the other hand, contracting and returning to a centre; and just in proportion to the energy of the repulsive or expanding force, so will it recede from the centre to a greater or less distance, and just in proportion to the energy of the attractive or contracting force, so will it return towards the centre. The contraction of the earth is exhibited in the formation of solid rocks.

Now, the earth's orbit is not a perfect circle. The orbit is elliptic, like that of a comet, though in a much smaller degree. During one half of her revolution, that is, during six months of the year, she is continually approaching or falling towards the sun, until she has reached the lowest point of her orbit, called the perihelion point. During the other half, she is rising or receding from the sun, until she reaches the highest or aphelion point, so that as she continues to fall, she moves faster and faster, and as she rises she moves slower and slower, —just as a ball in running down one hill and up another is continually accelerated as it runs down the one, and continually retarded as it runs up the other. The principle in both cases is the same, and the causes are nearly the same. The ball is drawn down upon the earth's surface by the force of attraction, with a continually accelerated motion, and by the momentum which it has acquired in falling, it is urged up the opposite ascent; *but it would never rise unless there were a sustaining surface beneath it to prevent it from falling still lower towards the earth's centre.* A river in its bed flows upon a sustaining surface; but as soon as that surface fails, it falls towards the centre of attraction, as the river St. Lawrence descends over the Falls of Niagara in Upper Canada.

We have not forgotten the "centrifugal force" which is said to sustain the earth in her orbit; but we have found that it is quite incompetent to sustain an eternal struggle with the imperishable force of attraction. Now, from the nature of the case, it appears that the earth requires a sustaining force of some kind to prevent her from falling into the sun, as without such sustaining power, the centrifugal force would quickly be destroyed, and she would fall to the centre in a few months. There is, therefore, a natural power which sustains her, whatever that power may be. Now, as it is admitted by all that she is *retained* in her circular path by the force or power of attraction, may she not be *sustained* in her orbit by the power of repulsion? We shall attempt to prove that she is so sustained. The idea that the *invisible* force of attraction retains the earth in her orbit is already established. Thousands will admit the truth of this proposition, who, if they were called upon to prove its truth, would find themselves involved in a considerable degree of difficulty; but the idea of a repulsive force sustaining her is not established, and, therefore, like every new principle, such an hypothesis will be resisted until some facts be adduced whereby it may be substantiated. Before we proceed to the proof of the proposition, we would remark that the notion is not new. It was entertained by the great Kepler, whose laws are considered the basis of physical astronomy, as will be seen by the following extract from Maclaurin's "Account of the Philosophical Discoveries of Sir Isaac Newton." Page 54:—

"Kepler's great sagacity and continual meditation on the planetary motions, suggested to him some views of the true principles from which these motions flow. In his preface to the commentaries concerning the planet Mars, he speaks of gravity as of a power that was mutual betwixt bodies, and tells us that the earth and moon tend towards each other, and would meet in a point so many times nearer to the earth than to the moon, as the earth is greater than the moon, if their motions did not hinder it. He adds, that the tides arise from the gravity of the waters towards the moon. But not having just enough notions of the laws of motion, he does not seem to have been able to make the best use of these thoughts; nor does he appear to have adhered to them steadily, since in his epitome of astronomy, published eleven years after, he proposes a physical account of the planetary motions, derived from different principles.

"He supposes, in that treatise, that the motion of the sun on his axis is preserved by some inherent vital principle; that a certain virtue, or immaterial image of the sun, is diffused with his rays into the ambient spaces, and, revolving with the body of the sun on his axis, takes hold of the planets and carries them along with it in the same direction, as a load-stone turned round in the neighborhood of a magnetic needle makes it turn round at the same time. The planet, according to him, by its *inertia* endeavors to continue in its place, and the action of the sun's image and this *inertia* are in a perpetual struggle. He adds, that this action of the sun, like to his light, decreases as the distance increases; and therefore moves the same planet with greater celerity when nearer the sun, than at a greater distance. To account for the planet's approaching towards the sun as it descends from the aphelium to the perihelium, and receding from the sun while it ascends to the aphelium again, he supposes that *the sun attracts one part of each planet, and repels the opposite part;* and that the part which is attracted is turned towards the sun in the descent. By suppositions of this kind, he endeavored to account for all the other varieties of the celestial motions.

Maclaurin's remark of Kepler's "not having just enough notions of the laws of motion" is of little value, for it is easily shown that the "notions" of Maclaurin himself, as well as those of his master, Newton, concerning the laws of motion are not very "just." In the paragraph immediately following that just quoted, Maclaurin, in attempting to show the fallacy of Kepler's "notion" says, "an attractive force makes it (the earth) descend from the *aphelium* to the *perihelium* in a curve concave towards the sun, but the repelling force which he supposed to begin at the *perihelium* would cause it to ascend in a figure convex towards the sun." From this observation, it would appear that Maclaurin supposes when the sustaining force begins to predominate at the perihelion point, that the opposite attractive force which had previously predominated from the aphelion is altogether annihilated, otherwise he would not have made the remark that the repulsive force "would cause it to ascend in a figure convex towards the sun." It could not describe such a curve unless the force of attraction were destroyed. If that impossible event were to take place, then, no doubt, by the help of the "centrifugal" force the earth would describe such a curve. But attraction and repulsion being natural forces, are never destroyed; and the earth as well as every other body, is at all times under the control of both, the one or the other alternately predominating. That such is the true state of things we will attempt to show by reference to the phenomena of the tides of the ocean :—

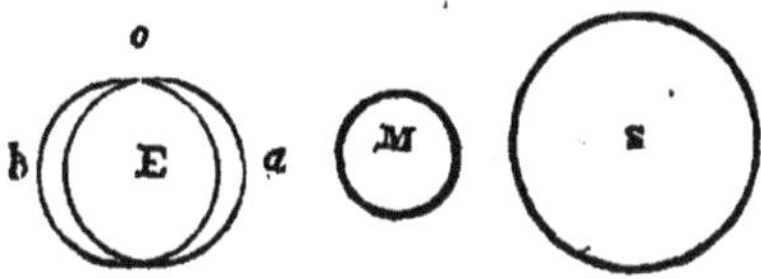


In the above diagram S is the sun, M the moon, and E the earth. Such is the disposition of the three bodies at new moon, at which time we have the highest tides upon the earth—usually called *spring tides*. There are spring tides at the time of full moon likewise; but the position of the three bodies at new moon, as shown above, will more clearly illustrate the conclusion to which we are about to come. Now, the spring tides occur at new moon, because the attraction of the sun and moon are co-operating. The two attractions are pulling in the same direction; and the water upon the surface of the earth at *a* being attracted with greater force than when the moon is in her quadratures as at *o*,—in which position the two bodies do not pull in the same direction, but at right angles—there is, therefore, at new moon, a high or spring tide at *a*. Now, we can very clearly perceive and distinctly understand in what way the conjoint attraction of the sun and moon should cause the surface of the ocean to rise at *a*. It follows from the principles of universal attraction that there ought to be a tide at *a*. The fact and the principle mutually support each other.

But there is a tide at *b* also. How is this produced? By the joint attraction of the sun and moon, say the philosophers of the "centrifugal" force school. This is not so clearly perceived nor so distinctly understood as in the case of the other tide. The assertion that the tide at *b* is produced by the attraction of the sun and moon reminds one of the Irishman's gun that was made to shoot round the corner, for it certainly does appear that if the attraction of those bodies be the cause of the tide at *b*, that attraction must shoot round the corner somehow. Various have been the methods adopted to explain the cause of this tide; and much ingenuity has been expended in order to reconcile it with the Newtonian hypothesis. One attempts to explain it by saying that the earth is elongated or drawn out by her falling towards the moon and sun. This is pure nonsense; she does not *fall* towards those bodies,—at least not at that rapid rate. Another says that the tide at *a* being formed, there must be a tide at *b* in order to restore the equilibrium of the earth;—that the earth would lose her balance by having a tide on one side only, therefore there is a tide on the other side; but *how is it caused* is not so easily deduced from the force of attraction alone. Another mode advanced is, that the earth, moon, and sun, are to be considered as one body, that is, that "these three bodies are not three bodies, but one body." Having thus amalgamated the three into one, the next step is to find a point which is called the "common centre of gravity;" and proceeding in this way the sublime conclusion is at length arrived at, that the centre of the earth is not the centre of the earth's attraction; that the centre of gravity is a little on one side towards *a;* and that, therefore, the water at *b* not being attracted so powerfully as before, *falls away* or recedes from the centre of its own accord, without the aid of any force;—at least none is mentioned. There have been other modes of explanation offered; but those already adduced are generally considered the most orthodox in the scientific world.

Now, before we attempt an explanation, let us endeavor to lay hold of an experimental fact which cannot be disputed, that may throw some light upon the manner of action of the two ultimate forces of attraction and repulsion. Electricity, considered as a branch of science, is that branch which investigates the manner of action of those ultimate forces. Electrical attractions and repulsions are but modifications of the two universal principles which pervade all nature. Now, by experiment with the electrical machine, we have discovered the following law, called the *law of induction*, which will be more clearly understood by the aid of the following diagram:—

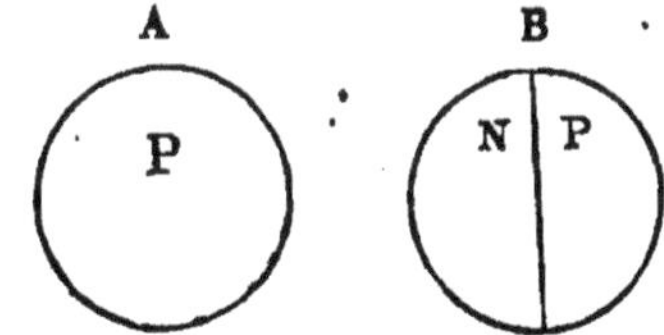


If the body B be presented to any other body in a charged state, as A, *but without touching*, they will mutually induct each other so long as they do not touch. If A be positively charged, then the further side of B will also become positively charged, although it had not been so previously to presenting B to A, and the nearer side (N) will at the same time become negative, and in the same degree; accordingly, if B be composed of two pieces, N and P, which may be taken apart, it will be found on presenting each of the halves to A, that the half P will be repelled, and the half N will be attracted. Now, if attraction and repulsion be universal principles, then the law of induction is a universal principle also. We need not be fastidious about the name, whether it be called electrical induction or the induction of gravitation; it is simply a law which developes itself in the action and reaction of the two forces.

It appears then that Kepler's "notions," when he supposes "that the sun attracts one part of each planet, and repels the opposite part," were more "just" than the notions of those who, rejecting one of the natural forces—and which is required to sustain the earth in her orbit—have introduced a "centrifugal" force, derived from a "primitive impulse." This last is called a sublime discovery, whilst Kepler's natural views are called "notions." If the reader has endeavored to perceive clearly the short explanation which has been given of the law of induction, he will at once discern the cause of *both* tides without any further remark: namely—that the tide next the sun and moon is caused by attraction, whilst that on the opposite side *b* is due to repulsion; and that these particular developments are due to the inductive action which always accompanies the operation of the two forces. He will also perceive as the remote half of the sphere is repelled and the near half attracted, that she is *sustained* in her orbit by the *invisible* force of repulsion, as she is *retained* by the *invisible* force of attraction.

Now, if these forces were completely balanced, if one were not stronger than the other, then the earth would come to a state of rest, as a consequence of the equilibrium,—just as in the case of the scales and weigh-beam, with an equal weight in each scale, or any of the other instances of motion to which we have referred. Motion is at all times the result of the disturbance of equilibrium; and the velocity of the moving body is in the ratio of the difference,—the friction and other resistances being taken into account. Now, in the case of the earth, the attractive or retaining is the stronger or *moving* force, and the repulsive or sustaining is the weaker or *regulating* force; and the resistance to the motion of the earth being small (she moves through a subtle ether), the velocity in her orbit is great, although the *difference* between the moving and regulating forces is not great,—that is, she approaches by very slow degrees; but still she does approach, and must approach, the centre, as otherwise she could no more move in her orbit than a river could continue to move or flow upon a perfectly level surface.

It is true that the earth moves in an undulating orbit. She is continually either rising from the perihelion to the aphelion, or falling from the aphelion to the perihelion; but this does not in any way affect the principle, for exactly the same amount of force is required to carry her round this undulating orbit, as would carry her round a circle,—and a circular line, as referred to the sun as a centre of attraction, is a level surface. In order to move, she must descend upon an incline, as a body moves upon the earth by descending towards the centre. The attractive force is continually gaining upon the repulsive; and the proof that the attractive force is so gaining, is to be found in the *contraction* of the earth into solid stone, as exhibited in the solid rocks which have been forming through a long series of ages,—and the process is still going on, because the attractive or contracting power is continually gaining upon its antagonist.

It is also true, that the tendency to fly off from the centre, in consequence of the momentum—that is, the "centrifugal" force, as it is called—must not be forgotten. There is such a tendency; and, therefore, the earth must by that tendency be carried beyond the neutral line or surface of the two opposing forces. Now there ought to be some fact to corroborate the principle, and the tides furnish such fact.

The nether or remote tide *b*, at Liverpool and some other places where observations have been taken, does not rise so high by one foot or more as the other tide on that side adjacent to the sun and moon. Why is there this difference of the two tides? There must be a cause. Now, if by the momentum the earth be carried out beyond the neutral line of the two forces, then the repulsive force must act with less intensity, and consequently the tide at *b*, being caused by this force, does not rise to as great an altitude. We thus find that the facts and the principles harmonize and mutually support each other. It is likely, indeed it may be considered as certain, that some important things have been overlooked, but still the general facts and general principles corroborate and support each other, thereby rendering the conclusions as positive as any to which men come in the ordinary cases of force and motion upon the earth.

The following diagram of two bodies joined by a spiral spring will represent two bodies held apart by a repulsive force and together by an attractive force at the same time, for such are, in fact, the absolute forces by which the bodies A and B are retained in their relative positions. If the spring be compressed, it will push itself out again, and if pulled out, it will again draw itself back to its former position; and the forces by which this is effected are the ultimate forces of attraction and repulsion, as already noticed in the case of the watch-spring.

Now, if the body A be fixed upon a centre, and the body B caused to revolve round it, then, by the momentum or centrifugal effect, the spring will be elongated, and the body B, whilst in motion, will remain at a greater distance from A than when at rest,—that is, it will be at a greater distance than the point in which the two forces in the spring are in equilibrio. The spring will be stretched by the continual tendency of the body B to fly off from the centre; and such are the conditions of the earth's motion, as confirmed by the tides. If the spring be alternately stretched and compressed, the body B will describe an elliptic orbit, like that of the earth round the sun.

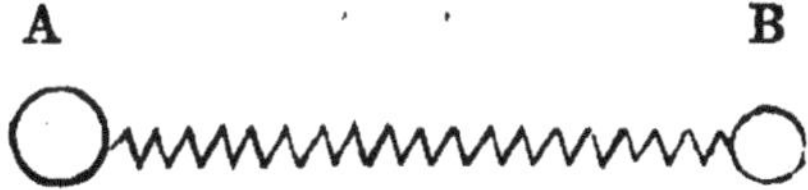

The spiral spring contains within itself the two ultimate forces of attraction and repulsion. If by any means—internal action or external force—the repulsive force be augmented, the spring will be elongated; the body B will recede from the central body A; it will rise to the aphelion point. If, on the contrary, the attractive force be augmented, the spring will be shortened; the body B will approach the centre A; it will fall to the perihelion point. And the motion will be in the ratio of the *difference* of the two forces, just as in the case of the pair of scales and weight, with which we commenced our observations on force and motion, or in any other case, due regard being had to the momentum which *accompanies* the motion.

These are the laws by which the motions of all bodies are regulated which fall within the observation of man—and we can only reason from what we know. If we institute other laws for the regulation of the motions of the heavenly bodies, such as "primitive impulses," "centrifugal forces," or "vacuity of space," we are supposing conditions of which we have no direct or indirect knowledge,—our conclusions rest upon suppositions, the axioms from which they are deduced are mere figments of the imagination.

## THE EARTH'S ROTATION ON HER AXIS.

By the Newtonian hypothesis, the earth is said or supposed to have been set a spinning upon her axis at the same time that she received the "primitive impulse," as will appear by the following extract from the "Connexion of the Physical Sciences:"—

"If a sphere, at rest in space, receives an impulse passing through its centre of gravity, all its parts will move with an equal velocity in a straight line; but if the impulse does not pass through the centre of gravity, its particles, having unequal velocities, will have a rotatory motion at the same time that it is translated in space. These motions are independent of one another; so that a contrary impulse, passing through its centre of gravity, will impede its progress, without interfering with its rotation. As the sun rotates about an axis, it seems probable, if an impulse in a contrary direction has not been given to his centre of gravity, that he moves in space, accompanied by all those bodies which compose the solar system—a circumstance which would in no way interfere with their relative motions; for, in consequence of the principle that force is proportional to velocity, the reciprocal attractions of a system remain the same, whether its centre of gravity be at rest, or moving uniformly in space. It is computed that had the earth received its motion from a single impulse, such impulse must have passed through a point about twenty-five miles from the centre.

"Since the motions of rotation and translation of the planets are independent of each other, though probably communicated by the same impulse, they form separate subjects of investigation."

After what has been already advanced in reference to primitive impulses and centrifugal forces, it would be a waste of time to enter into a serious refutation of the gratuitous assumption contained in the above paragraph. It may be necessary, however, to remark that "the motions of rotation and translation of the planets are" *not* "independent of each other." There is no motion in nature *independent* of other motions, for, as Cuvier justly remarks, "all nature is linked together;—*all is dependent;* —all existence is chained to other existence; and that chain which connects them is infinite in extent, space, and time."

Introductory to the explanations which are about to be advanced in reference to the *natural causes* by which the earth rotates upon her axis, we will give a communication from one of the Journals of the day. Several explanations have been given by different hands, professedly deduced from the principles of the "Electrical Theory," amongst which the following, by a gentleman of liberal education, is, so far as it goes, more correct than any other that has fallen under the observation of the author:—

"Sir,—A subscriber asks if there be any natural cause for the diurnal rotation of the earth and planets on their respective axes? The following, I think, is the best mode of accounting for the phenomena I have yet seen. In a theory of the universe lately propounded by Mr. Mackintosh, the motions and all the phenomena of the universe are attributed to electric and galvanic action, and the diurnal motions of the planets are thus explained: 1st., by referring directly to galvanic influence in the earth itself; 2ndly., it is explained by the reciprocal actions of the sun and planets, for supposing the sun to be charged with electricity of one kind, and the earth with another, an action of the following kind would ensue: during the day that portion of the earth, or any planet, which is exposed directly to the sun's action, would become charged with electricity of the same kind as that of the sun, and the other portion would, during the night, give off that portion of the sun's electricity it had imbibed during the previous day, and the effect produced can be represented by the following diagram:—

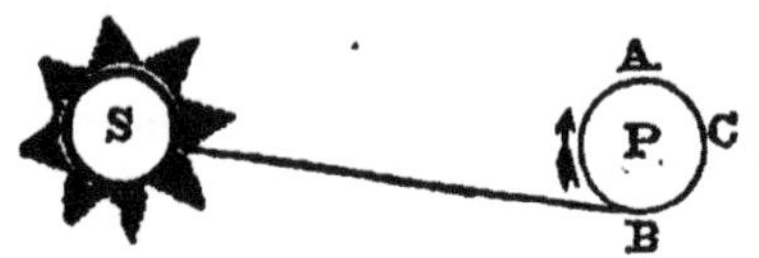


"Supposing the planet to turn in the direction of the arrow, then the portion at point A will be charged with more of the sun's electricity than that portion at B; consequently, according to the well known laws of electricity the portion at A will be repelled on account of the electricity being the same, and the portion at B will be attracted in consequence of the different electric states of the sun and that part of the planet, and so long as electric action exists between the two bodies, so long will they (in proportion to their respective intensity of action) revolve upon their respective axes.

"I remain, Sir, yours, respectfully,

"JOSHUA THORNE."

In order to obtain a clear conception of all the forces connected with the rotation of the earth, it is requisite that we should begin with the most simple elements of rotatory motion, as in the former case with the weigh beam and scales. The first and most essential point to be considered in regard to rotatory motion, is the *fixed centre* upon which the body revolves. It is true the earth does not revolve upon a *solid centre*, but we shall find that the axis of revolution is as fixed and secure as if the opposite poles or ends of that axis were points of polished steel inserted in cups of agate.

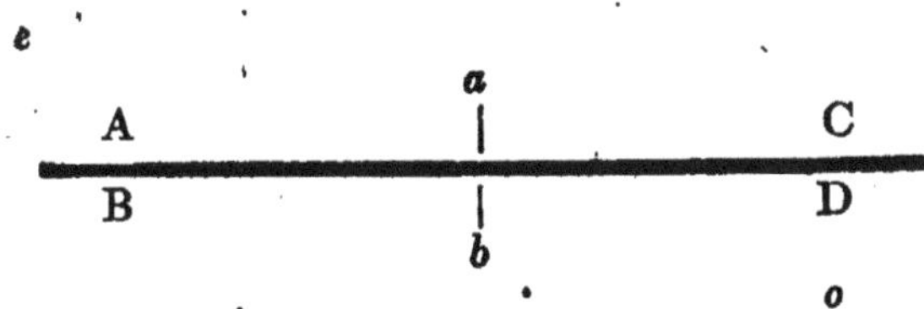


In the above diagram, let A B be a lever, the centre or fulcrum of which is in the point *a b*, then, if an attracting or drawing force be applied at the end A B and on the side A, or if a repelling or pushing force be applied on the side B, the end A B will move towards *e*, and the end C D will move towards *o*. So far this is rotatory motion, and it will be obvious that the rotatory movement depends altogether upon the stability or fixity of the central points *a b*, as will be seen by the following diagram, where the point *a* is removed:—

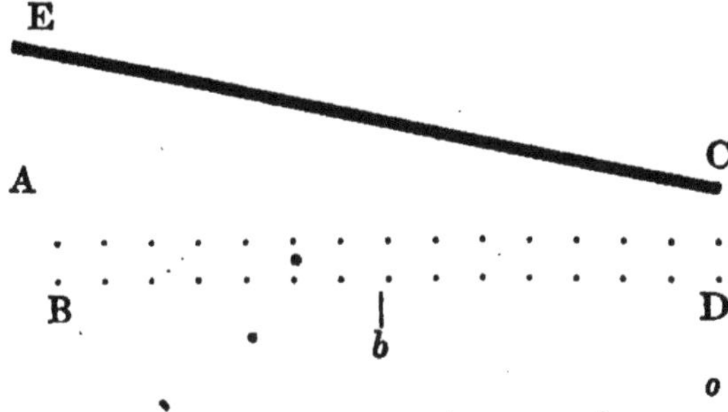


Now, in consequence of the removal of the central point *a*, the end of C D no longer moves towards *o*;—by the application of force at the opposite end A B, the fixed centre, which is essential to rotatory motion, is removed or has given way, and, therefore, the lever can no longer rotate upon its axis as before. It is quite true, that by a sudden impulse being given at the end A B, propelling it in the direction E, there will be a reaction at the end C D, giving that end a tendency to move towards *o*, and that by this tendency the body would revolve upon what is usually denominated its centre of gravity. Indeed, it is from this known tendency that the supposition of the earth's rotatory motion being due to a primitive impulse imparted at a given distance from the centre, has been derived. It is a clumsy mechanical hypothesis at best, to suppose that the earth is flying through space like a great fly-wheel which has been put in motion, and that without any active force being applied to *sustain* that motion it will continue to rotate and fly onward forever, without the guidance of any natural law to control those motions. Such gratuitous assumptions are not entitled to be considered in the light of natural philosophy. Unless we can discern natural laws whereby to account for every phenomena—unless we can perceive the forces by which every motion is produced, it were better to confess our ignorance at once, than to erect systems upon mere suppositions, such as those upon which the Newtonian system is based; for when a system has been thus erected, it stands in the way of further discovery; it becomes a stumbling block in the path which leads to truth, and too often it puts on a character much more mischievous than this. It becomes an embattled tower, from the loop-holes of which the bigoted, the prejudiced, and the intolerant discharge their missiles upon the heads of those who would pass the boundary line, which the keepers of the citadel had marked out, with a view to explore the region which lies beyond that line all unknown, and containing, perhaps, philosophic riches of inestimable value. It were better that we should recognize no system whatever, than that we should allow ourselves to be enslaved by one which says, hitherto shalt thou advance and no further. Besides, even if we were to grant that the earth received the twirling motion and the motion of translation at the same time, by means of an external impulse or "great push," it would not be difficult to prove, upon mechanical principles alone, that the rotatory motion would be modified and controlled by the motion of translation; in short, that if the rotation were attributable to such a cause, we could not have upon the earth those vicissitudes of summer and winter which we now see; and it is for this reason that it has been asserted that the motions of translation and rotation "are independent of each other." The commonest experiment, such as holding a stick by one end and whirling it from the hand, will prove that the two motions are *not* independent of each other.

But to return to the investigation of natural causes. We have seen that a centre of rotation is an essential condition in the case of the lever; and we may further remark, that the lever may be *pushed* or *pulled* (that is, in fact, repelled or attracted, for the ultimate ideas are the same), at either end or on either side; according as it is pushed or pulled on one side or the other, so will it rotate in one direction or the other.

Now, a wheel is a continued or endless lever, as will appear by the following diagram:—

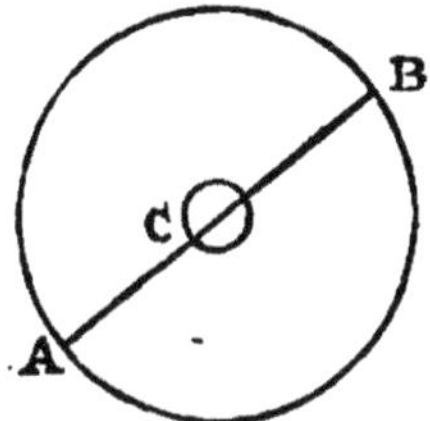


A line drawn across the circle any where, as A B, becomes a lever, and in order that the force may be applied any where upon the circumference, it is necessary that the centre C shall embrace the axle all round, so that at whatever side the force may be applied, the centre cannot be pushed from its place in the manner shown in the case of the lever, page 373.

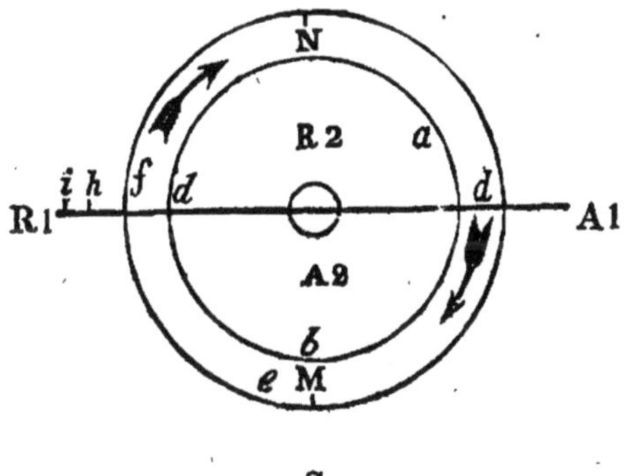


S

In the above diagram, let S represent the sun; let the inner circle *a b c* represent the surface of the earth, and *d e f* the atmosphere. The point M is on the meridian line, and if the earth rotate in the direction of the arrows, the point R 1, that point called evening in common phraseology, or that portion of the revolving sphere upon which the sun is setting, is the part whereon the exciting action of the sun has been longest exerted, or more correctly, that portion of the atmosphere *wherein* the specific solar action, noticed in a preceding portion of this work, has been going on during the whole of the time that that point has been rotating from A1 to R1, that is, during the whole of the day: whilst the point A1 has been during the same length of time removed from the immediate influence of the solar action, namely, whilst that point has been rotating from R1 to A1, or during the whole of the night.

Now that the electrical state of the atmosphere undergoes a specific change during the time that the sun is above the horizon, is well known,—that is, the electrical thermometer, if we may use that expression, rises and sinks according to a certain law, during the period of each rotation. This rising and sinking of the electrical state of the atmosphere is not constant upon any given point of the earth, although the mean may be constant, for the law is obviously determined by fixed principles. Besides which, even if the actuating force be in some degree intermittent, still by the centrifugal momentum of the revolving earth, the motion must be constant, just as the motion of the steam engine is rendered constant by the centrifugal momentum of the fly-wheel, although the actuating force of steam applied to produce that motion is intermittent.

But if the actuating force of steam be suspended, whatever amount of momentum may be in the fly-wheel, the engine will ultimately stop; and if the actuating force which causes the earth to revolve were suspended, her rotary motion would gradually subside, with whatever amount of momentum she might be charged at the time of that suspension:—because the friction of the engine is so great, the momentum with which the fly-wheel is charged would soon be annihilated. If the resistance to the earth's rotation be small, (but it has not been *proved* that it is so), then it would be a longer time before the momentum would be entirely destroyed; but that such would be the ultimate result—unless there were a continued actuating force in operation—is as certain as that the steam engine stops when the steam is turned off.

" No effect without a cause " is an axiom in philosophy which might be considerably improved, at least in its application to the Newtonian philosophy, by the addition of a term which would bring the effect before the mind in the character of a continued operation dependent upon the continued exertion of the actuating cause, by which the axiom would assume the form of "No *continued* effect without a *continued* cause." "Remove the cause and the effect will cease" is an axiom pretty generally received; but not so in the Newtonian philosophy. The cause of the motions of the earth and other planets has ceased to act thousands, nay, if we may put our trust in geology, millions, or as some say, millions of millions of years ago,—and yet the effect is to continue forever. A continued effect without a continued cause!!! According to this kind of philosophy the solar system is a moving miracle.

We perceive, then, that the rotation of the earth requires the continued exertion of an attractive force between the sun S and the point A1, and a repulsive force between S and R1; then the body will revolve in the direction indicated by the arrows. Now, as that portion of the atmosphere situated between M and R1 has been under the influence of the solar action for a longer time, taking the mean, than the portion between M and A1, M R1 being saturated must be repelled, and as the portion or quadrant between N (midnight) and A1 (morning) has been and is undergoing a specific change during the night, by which its previous electrical state has been modified or reversed, that portion of the atmosphere is attracted towards S, the two points of greatest attraction, and repulsion being at A1 and R1. And further, as we have seen, in referring to the tides, that the opposite hemispheres of the earth are attracted and repelled, as suggested by Kepler, that is, the hemisphere R2 is repelled and A2 attracted; then, the central globe being held securely between two forces, the centre of which is in the earth herself, these forces become the pivot or axis upon which she revolves, the solar action going on in the atmosphere being the efficient cause of rotation, the atmosphere embracing the earth as a leathern belt does a wooden drum or cylinder, and thus the rotatory motion is continued, that motion being rendered equable by the centrifugal momentum with which the earth is charged, as the motion of the fly-wheel renders that of the steam engine equable.

Perhaps to some minds the mode of action may be rendered more plain by referring to the general principles of the expansion and contraction of matter. By the solar action the atmosphere is expanded; then the length of the radius or lever is extended at R1, as from *h* to *i*. The sun is the centre of action and of attraction of the system, and as expanded matter always recedes from the centre in proportion as it is more and more expanded, therefore, the atmosphere at R1 being more expanded than it had been previous to the solar action, will recede towards N, where, being contracted, it will again fall towards the sun at A1, thereby impressing a motion of rotation upon the globe which it embraces.

In our notice of the spiral motions, we neglected to notice that every new observation tends more and more to conform an opinion which has been entertained for a length of time, that storms and hurricanes are, in fact, *immense whirlwinds* travelling along the earth's surface; that a ship in a storm is carried round in the vortex in a manner in every way analogous to that in which she would be carried round in the whirlpool called Maelstroom, off the coast of Norway, the difference being only in the dimensions of the spiral curves forming the whirlwind or whirlpool.

But the most satisfactory mode of explaining the earth's rotation, although to the uninitiated the most difficult to comprehend, is by a reference to the principles of electro-magnetism. Electro-magnetic forces act in a manner different from all other known forces. The electro and magnetic forces *act at right angles to each other*. Thus, the magnet being placed in a position north and south, the electric or Voltaic currents will move east and west or west and east on reversing the poles of the magnet, and will return on the opposite side in a contrary direction, thus circumvolving the magnet in spiral courses, as is exemplified in the accompanying diagram:—

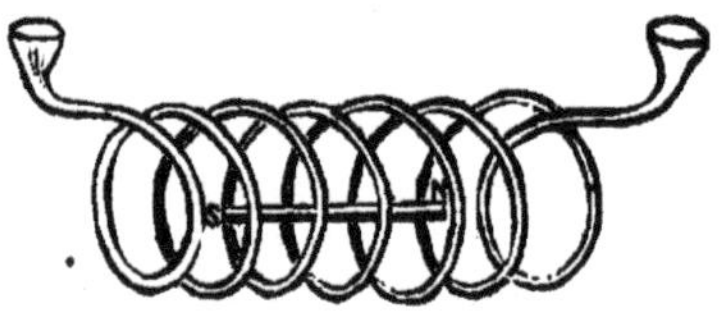

That the earth is nothing else than a great magnet, every mariner who, by the aid of the compass, guides his ship through the trackless deep, can testify. That electric currents are continually circumvolving the earth in the atmospheric regions, is sufficiently manifested by the occasional outbreaks of thunder storms, the aurora borealis, and other phenomena exhibited in the upper regions of the circumambient aerial fluid; and if we are yet in some degree unacquainted with the modes of action of these mysterious principles, it is because we have reposed our faith in a system of philosophy which rests upon a hollow foundation, and have neglected to prosecute our inquiries so as to trace the observed effects to the operation of natural causes.

"So powerful is the action of a helix of this description, that if a small magnetized needle, or bar, be placed within it, so as to rest upon the lower portions of the wire, the moment the connexion is made with the Voltaic battery, so that the electric current circulates through the wires, the needle is seen to start up, and place itself in the axis, remaining suspended in the air in opposition to the force of gravity. This will even take place in a vertical position of the helix, presenting the singular spectacle of a heavy body raised by an invisible power, and maintained, like the fabled statue of Theamides, in a situation totally free from any material connexion and support."

---

## INTRODUCTION TO MORALS.

We are now about to enter upon the second and by far the most important part of our subject—the consideration of the organs and functions of the mind, and of the motive forces by which the living being is actuated. The contemplation of the solar system and of the universe generally, by the harmony of its motions, by the beautifully regulated movements of its parts, affords a pleasing satisfaction to the mind, and so far it is worthy of our study. The knowledge which we acquire by this study is also valuable, as leading us to an intimate acquaintance with the physical laws by which the operations of nature are governed, and thereby we are enabled, to a certain extent, to guide those operations so as to augment the sum of human enjoyment. If this be true as regards the laws of nature viewed upon the great scale, it is equally true and infinitely more important as regards the operation of the physical and moral functions, which, viewed in connexion, constitute man a living rational being,—a being susceptible of pleasure and pain, of happiness and misery. The seat of consciousness of each individual is, in reference to that individual, the centre of the universe, and the objects which immediately surround that centre are to him the objects of greatest importance, and they become less and less important the further and further their locality in space or time is removed from that centre.

In treating of physical operations we have endeavored to show that every motion may be traced to the two ultimate forces of attraction and repulsion. We have next to show that the motions of animated beings also, whether voluntary or involuntary, may be traced to the same ultimate forces, from which it will appear that attraction and repulsion are the fountains or sources of *all motion.*

It must, in the first place, be clearly and distinctly understood, that every thing in nature is relative; that every motion necessarily requires the presence of at least two bodies, which mutually act and react upon each other—one of these is usually considered as the agent or actor, and the other as the patient or subject acted upon. This view is erroneous, because it supposes the *whole force* to proceed from *one* of the bodies, and that the other is altogether passive. But if we examine the works of nature, we shall perceive that that which is called the actor or agent, is wholly powerless, unless called into action by the excitement of that which is called the patient. In short, it is action and re-action throughout the whole chain of process; each of the bodies are powerless without the presence of the other. A stone falls to the earth; but why? Because the attraction of the earth, or rather the mutual attraction, draws it towards the earth, that is, the two bodies approach each other by their mutual or relative attraction. In this case, it is usually considered that the earth is the agent or acting body, and that the stone is the patient or body acted upon; whereas, in truth, the action is mutual.

O

Let O represent a body or atom of matter, existing by itself in infinite and empty space, then, with whatever amount of force the body may be supposed to be endowed, whether attractive or repulsive, it cannot move or be moved, it cannot fulfil the office of either agent or patient.

In the state in which it is, it must remain to all eternity; and no motion of any kind can be produced without the introduction of a second body or being, whether natural or supernatural. By itself it cannot be moved by attraction or repulsion, since there is no second body to draw it towards it, or to push it from it. It remains alone feeble and powerless, whatever amount of force it may possess within itself. "If at rest it would remain at rest, and if in motion it would continue in motion," and upon this supposed case is founded the *vis inertia* of the Newtonian philosophy. It is a case which serves to illustrate our present argument, but it must not be forgotten that it is a case which has no existence in nature. If the *vis inertia* of matter, as assumed by Newton, were a true principle, no change could take place; every thing would remain as it was in the beginning or supposed beginning, for nature never had a beginning.

1 2
O O

If there be two bodies, as O1 O2, then, if there be an attractive force exerted by one and not by the other, the body exerting the force is the agent, and the other the patient. But this is supposing that which does not exist in nature, for all bodies are possessed of an attractive force by which they act upon other bodies; therefore, being guided by the facts as they actually present themselves in nature, we conclude that the attraction is mutual; that the two bodies O1 and O2, or any other, mutually attract each other, and, as a consequence or effect of that attraction, motion ensues, and they approach each other. If, as in cases exhibited upon the earth, more particularly in moral action of which we are about to treat, one body be fixed and the other at liberty to move, then the free body moves throughout the *whole distance* in its approach towards the fixed body. If both are free to move, they mutually approach and meet in the centre, if the power on both sides be equal. If both bodies be fixed or confined or retained with sufficient force, they remain at rest, however great the amount of attraction may be, which is exerted between them. The same observations apply if we take repulsion as the moving force.

If the reader desires to understand morals as a science, it is of the utmost importance that he should have clear ideas of the relative action and re-action of *two bodies*, and that with *one body only*, whether animate or inanimate, there neither is nor can be motion of any kind.

It follows that as all motions are relative, the *terms* which we employ to explain those motions should also be relative; for if we employ positive or absolute terms to express relative ideas, we shall be continually liable to mislead ourselves by the ambiguity of our expressions. The term should be a true *type* of the *thing* typified. The terms *lightness*, *weight*, *levity*, *gravity*, are *absolute* terms, used to typify *relative* things, and are, therefore, improper terms. What does the term *lightness* signify in a philosophical point of view? Nothing. Absolute lightness has no signification; neither has its opposite, *weight*, any meaning, except employed in a relative sense, having a view to the earth's attraction. The weight of a body is the measure of the force of attraction, as mutually exerted between the earth and that body. The term weight taken in an absolute sense has no meaning whatever. A single body of any magnitude placed by itself in space could have no weight; and the weight of any body is the amount of the force with which it is attracted towards any other body. If the attractive force of the sun exerted upon the earth were equal to one pound, then the weight of the earth would be one pound and no more; by itself its weight would be nothing.

The same remarks apply to the terms levity and gravity. They are absolute, not relative; and, therefore, considered as synonymous with lightness and weight, are calculated to mislead the student. When the term gravity is given and received as signifying attraction, it is a proper term; but as its opposite, levity, cannot, with propriety, be given to signify the opposite of attraction, viz., repulsion, it is better to dismiss both gravity and levity from our vocabulary, and confine ourselves wholly to the *relative* and proper terms, attraction and repulsion. We will here give a tabular view of our terms, in which form they will probably fix themselves more distinctly in the mind of the reader:—

---

*Absolute or Improper terms.*

| | |
|---|---|
| Levity | Gravity |
| Lightness | Weight |

*Relative or Proper terms.*

| Repulsion: *from* | Attraction: *to* |
|---|---|
| Repulsion—*Electrical* | Attraction—*Electrical* |
| " *Magnetic* | " *Magnetic* |
| " *Calorific* | " *Cohesive* |
| " *Planetary.* | " *Planetary.* |

*Primary Effects of Ultimate Forces.*

| Expansion of Matter | Contraction of Matter |
|---|---|
| Decomposition of Matter. | Recomposition of Matter. |

*Mechanical Forces.*

| Pushing | Pulling |
|---|---|
| Shoving | Drawing |
| Thrusting. | Tugging. |

*Moral Forces.*

| Repulsion | Attraction |
|---|---|
| From pain (*corporeal*) | To pleasure (*corporeal*) |
| From shame (*mental pain*) | To honor (*mental pleasure*) |
| From hell (*corporeal and mental pain*) | To heaven (*corporeal and mental pleasure*) |
| Antipathy. | Sympathy. |

All the acts of animated beings may be traced to these six fountains or sources of motion or moral action; antipathy and sympathy being compounded of the others, rather than simple or elemental sources of action, and the organs and functions of the animal and mental organizations being so constituted that they are susceptible of receiving impressions of a painful or pleasurable kind. And as *one body* cannot act alone, but must be acted upon by another body, upon which it again re-acts, so also the organ of the living being cannot act alone, but requires to be acted upon or stimulated by another body, upon which also the organ or the sentient being re-acts.

Now, in the physical world we find that the intensity of the forces of attraction and repulsion is inversely as the square of the distance. In proportion as the distance between the two bodies is increased, so the force of attraction or repulsion is decreased; and in the moral world we find that the same law holds with equal propriety. A woman pursued by a ferocious bull, although she may apprehend danger, she does not feel the same degree of fear whilst the animal is at a distance, but as the bull gains upon her,—as he approaches nearer and nearer, the fear, the repulsive force, becomes stronger and stronger; when the animal has come close behind, the fear has reached to its greatest intensity, and the muscular energy also is exerted with the greatest effort. The same may be observed on a race course, where attraction is the actuating force. The prize is the object of attraction, and as the horses approach the winning-post, the force becomes more and more intense, and the energy of the competitors is brought out in a corresponding degree; the whole race-course is agitated by the action and re-action of the contending forces. It is the same in regard to time as space. An attractive object, removed to a great distance in time, has a feeble effect upon the mind, but as the period of enjoyment comes nearer, the feeling of attraction becomes more and more intense; so also, on the other side, a culprit under sentence of death, feels the desire to flee from his fate increase, as his allotted time decreases. If the subject be examined with care, it will be found that the increase or decrease of the intensity of the forces is in a ratio in every respect corresponding to that in the physical world, although from the great diversity of character it may be somewhat difficult to measure the force, as it is plain that the intensity cannot be the same in any two beings who are of a different physical constitution.

In our attempt to penetrate the arcana of the mind, we should endeavor to lay hold of the simple elemental forces by which the moral being is actuated. We are thus furnished with a clue by which we may trace our way with considerable precision through the unseen and intricate labyrinths of the human mind. These elemental forces are few and simple. Every act may be traced to one or other of the six sources of moral motives, given under the head of Moral Forces; and even this small number may be reduced, for the last pair (heaven and hell) have no force whatever upon the mind in the absence of religious faith. The faith and the force always bear a given proportion to each other. If the faith be strong, the moral force is strong. If the faith be weak, the force is weak also. And on this account it is that the teachers of creeds dwell so urgently and unceasingly on the value of faith.

It is literally true, that "without faith they can do nothing;" and on the other hand, if they can raise a sufficient quantum of faith, they can "remove mountains." It may be, and is perfectly true, that there neither is nor can be merit in faith—mere belief or assent to the truth of a proposition—any more than there can be merit in an assent to the plain truism, that two and two make four; neither can there be demerit in dissenting from the contradictory dogma that three make one, and one make three. We presume that he who gives his assent to the truism and dissent to the dogma, has sufficient intelligence to discern the consistency of the former and inconsistency of the latter. He who is led to assent to folly or dissent from plain truth, we may consider less intelligent, more stupid; but there is no merit or demerit in a moral point of view in the one case or the other.

But although there is no merit in faith, it possesses power over the mind. The power of faith is great. It is the root of all the moral forces. *Faith is confidence.* If men had no confidence that the course of action which they pursue would lead to the desired end, they would cease to act; and in respect to the things of this world, their faith or confidence in the future is based upon their experience, the knowledge of the past. The faith or confidence respecting the things of another world, is not based upon experience, but upon the teaching of the priesthood; and unless this faith were continually sustained by the eloquence of the priesthood, it would inevitably die. Even eloquence would fail in sustaining it, were it not supported by that excellent and charitable dogma, "He that believes shall be saved, he that disbelieves shall be damned." Faith is the fulcrum upon which the priest rests the lever with which upon more than one occasion he has shaken the moral world to its centre.

Yet there is a charm in devotion which diffuses a rich and vivid glow of anticipation over warm poetical imaginative minds, by which it obtains a resting place in the affections independent of blind faith. Beings thus constituted, live in the glorious illusion of an everlasting future of happiness, and regard with distrust and repugnance any one who would dispel the visions of their day dreams.

Why, or how is it, that the pleasure and joy of the pious devotee, who lives in the constant contemplation and anticipation of heavenly happiness, is the most exalted, most pure, and perfect of all mental enjoyment? Before this question can be properly answered, it is necessary to put and answer the following, which is nearer home, and therefore more simple:—How is it that a splendid silk shawl appears to the female eye more beautiful, and therefore *more valuable*, in the window of the draper, than it does an hour, or even a minute, after it has passed into the lawful possession of the purchaser? Here is the little principle upon which is founded the deep and intense feeling accompanying heavenly anticipations. The beauties, the joys of heaven, are magnified in the mind's eye a thousand times *because* they have not yet come into possession, and these beauties and joys are magnified a thousand times more by the obscure and indistinct manner in which they are presented to the mind; and such also would be the case with the silk shawl placed in an obscure light; the mind would magnify its beauties far beyond their actual value.

Now, in relation to this shawl, the *point of time* in which the female receives the largest amount of gratification from that object is not at the *moment* when she is *first struck* with its beauty, neither is it *after* it has come into actual possession, but the moment of greatest joy is that in which she *feels* an assurance or *confidence* that she can have this shawl. That is the precise moment of *greatest joy*, and this joy is based upon a *feeling of faith*, or confidence, or assurance, that this or any other desired object will come into possession and can be enjoyed. Now, the religious devotee may be said to live in this extatic moment throughout the whole course of his religious life. But if this principle be true in respect to the joys of heaven, it is equally true with respect to the pains and miseries of hell. He whose existence is spent in the point opposite to the above, does most truly and emphatically suffer the pains of hell.

If blind faith had no other tendency than that of leading to the stability of virtue and its consequent happiness, it ought to be tolerated whether true or false. The grand object is to augment the sum of human enjoyment on earth, and whatever tends to that end is decidedly good, and, therefore, demands the support of all well-meaning men. But unfortunately for faith, happiness has not been its fruit. Ireland is full of faith, and full of misery. In Spain and Portugal faith and bigotry reign triumphant, whilst strife and wretchedness cover the land. Wherever superstition has lighted her fire and put on her seething-pot, the passions of men have boiled over like the lava from Mount Ætna, scattering misery, death, and desolation around. The very names of vice and virtue have been made in many instances to change places. Horrible crimes have been committed under the supposed sanction of a merciful God, whilst the most sacred duties have been neglected under the apprehension of his displeasure.

The mind becomes confused, distorted, and, not unfrequently, totally subverted by the strong excitements induced by a blind superstitious faith; yet, because excitement is necessary to man, forming, as it does, a portion of his very being, devotion in one form or another will always obtain. It may be stripped of blind faith and unmeaning ceremony, it may be rendered rational and subservient to the growth of human happiness, but it cannot be exterminated. Devotion is not faith, but a feeling of the mind,—a deep and intense passion pervading the heart, and mingling with the being of him who has devoted his life to the attainment of a great and good object.

The feelings and affections of human beings, and indeed of all animated beings, constitute a moral soil as diversified in its character in different individuals and different nations, as the vegetable soil which covers the surface of the earth. In the vegetable soil of the earth we find rich fertile spots on which nutritious and poisonous plants grow and flourish luxuriously and indiscriminately, and barren tracts on which hardly any trace of either the one or the other can be discerned; and we find further that by the art, care and cultivation of man, the poisonous weeds may be extirpated from the fertile soil, and the barren land may be improved by the same means, until the whole earth might be converted into a smiling garden. It is the same in the moral world; and here is a ground of hope for the philanthropist, the moral cultivator. Some human beings are rich in feeling: but without culture the feelings and passions of good and evil will shoot up indiscriminately. Others are barren, or almost devoid of all feelings either good or evil; they manifest no disposition to do evil, but neither do they evince a disposition to do good. Their heart is a barren moral soil; their feelings and affections require to be warmed and stimulated in order to bring out a crop of good actions.

Nothing can be done in the way of moral culture with

a being altogether devoid of feeling or passion. The stoics endeavored to extirpate the passions from the human breast. Their object was to destroy vice by drying up its very root, which is in the feelings or passions; but they overlooked this most important truth, that in drying up the feelings, virtue and vice must of necessity wither together. And if they could have succeeded in effecting their object—if they could have formed a perfect man, or wise man, as they called him, according to their own model, that perfect man would have been a mere breathing statue, or animated being possessing the single feeling of consciousness and no more. He could not have experienced the feeling of happiness or misery, because the soil or substratum on which they grow had been dried up. He could not have performed either a good or evil act towards his fellow creatures, because the feelings in which both these acts have their origin had been extirpated from his breast. But the stoics labored in vain, because they worked against nature. The feelings or passions of human nature cannot be entirely rooted out by any art; and it is well that it is so, for they are each and all of them necessary to the happiness and protection of the individual in whose bosom they are planted, and of the society of which he forms a member.

Love and honor are necessary for the support and encouragement of virtue; but hate and dishonor are also necessary for the suppression of vice. A being incapable of feeling cannot feel love and respect for a good man, or hatred and disrespect for a bad man; neither can he be influenced by the love and respect, or the hatred and disrespect of other men, because he is supposed to be incapable of feeling; the moral soil is barren—it will neither grow corn nor tares. A being in whom the social feelings or passions are cold and weak, is indifferent to good and evil—they are almost alike in his eyes. Unless feeling can be found in the breast, or implanted there, the moral cultivator will plough and sow in vain; no moral crop can grow on such a soil.

Now, as it must be perfectly evident, even to the ignorant, that the feelings are some how or other connected with the body, with its organization or physical condition, it must be also evident that the cultivation of morals must begin with the body. When a man is in a fever, his physical organization is in a diseased or deranged state;

and in consequence of the derangement of the body, the mind also is deranged. It would be utter nonsense to *preach* to this individual, or to endeavor to impress upon his mind the necessity of his behaving himself like a wise and prudent man. You might as well preach to the oaks of the forest, and tell them that they ought to bear apples. The physician must come before the priest. The physician can "minister to a mind diseased" by administering to the body, which is the foundation upon which the mind is built; and until this great truth shall be universally known and acknowledged, the teaching of morals must remain in the hands of quacks; in the hands of individuals who have no system—no science of that art which they practise, and which bears upon the happiness and misery of human beings with such immense force. The state of moral science is a disgrace to the age in which we live. There is, in fact, no moral science, properly speaking. There is considerable art of an empirical character, and that art is practised by a body of quacks with a degree of impudent confidence, and even overbearing insolence, which, looking at the ignorance of the body, is truly astonishing, and could not be accounted for, except by the melancholy fact, that the people over whose minds they hold sway, are still more ignorant and debased in intellect than the quacks themselves.

Those who have taken upon themselves the cure of moral maladies, have two nostrums with which they propose to eradicate all diseases. The priest jumps into the middle of the subject with a heaven of everlasting happiness in one hand, and a hell of eternal torment in the other. The former he holds up to the view, in order to induce that course of action which *he* denominates righteous, and with the other, he endeavors to frighten the grown-up children from that course which *he* has determined to be vicious, and thus by coaxing and threatening alternately, he leads the docile herd; but as the ignorance of the herd is essential to the efficacy of his nostrums, he takes every means in his power to prevent the stream of knowledge from flowing in upon them, lest their faith in the medicine should fail. The springs of moral action are to be found in the functions of the animal body; but concerning those springs, or the action and re-action of the mind and body, he does not trouble himself to inquire, so long as mankind are contented to purchase his "*universal medicines.*"

In consequence of this established quackery, the whole subject of morals is in a most confused and unsatisfactory state. Terms have been needlessly multiplied, distinctions of casuistry have been introduced, the simple elementary forces of pleasure and pain, honor and shame, or the hopes and fears which they induce, have been compounded, mixed, and adulterated with extraneous matter, until at length the real acting force has been so disguised, that it requires no small degree of care and consideration to perceive distinctly the most simple case of mental action expressed in the corrupted phraseology.

It has been said that *knowledge is power*, to which it might be added *money is power*, and, with equal propriety, *religion is power*. But the power which these three things give to him who holds them in possession, arises from the *attractive force* which they generate in the minds of other men; from the *desire* which other men have to them, or rather to the fruits or good things which they believe may be obtained by that possession. If no good, no fruits, could be obtained from the tree of knowledge, men would not cultivate the tree; they cultivate the tree only from a desire to eat of the fruit, believing, or rather knowing, that fruit to be good. They desire the possession of money, knowing that money will procure every good, every kind of fruit that can minister to their wants and desires on earth; and they cultivate religion because they believe they shall reap a rich harvest in another world. And, whoever can cause his fellow men to believe that he has the possession of these things and the power to dispense them, will have a power over his fellow creatures proportionate to their belief or confidénce in his power and willingness to dispense them. The philosopher holds the knowledge-power, the rich man the money-power, and the priests the religious-power; and they hold this power simply in consequence of the *desire* which their fellow creatures have to obtain the fruits, the happiness—real or imaginary, it matters not which, for their *desire* is in proportion to their *belief* or *confidence* of the coming harvest, whether on earth or in heaven, and not in the *reality* of the harvest itself.

A man will continue to labor for another man so long as he *believes* that the man has the *power* and the *will* to pay him for his labor. The employer may cheat him at last, it may turn out that he is unable or unwilling to pay him; but so long as the laborer *believes* him able and willing, he continues to labor for him. Men will labor for money so long as they *believe* or have confidence that money will procure them the necessaries of life. Men will not labor for a bankrupt's bill or promissory note. And why? Because their faith and confidence in that note is lost. Before the bankruptcy was published they had faith in the bank, and would labor for its promissory notes; but now they hold them of no value, they can procure nothing in the shape of comforts or happiness from them. If they have learned nothing of the bankruptcy, they will still desire to possess the notes, and will labor for them, although in reality the notes are worthless. Their desire to possess them is founded upon their *faith* of their value, of the power which they give them to procure the enjoyments of life.

The case with respect to knowledge is precisely the same in every particular. Present to a man knowledge, that is, *really useful knowledge*—for no other deserves the name, all other is counterfeit and worthless like the bankrupt's note; but point him to knowledge that may be turned to a profitable account in the business of life, and he will of necessity desire to obtain that knowledge as certainly as he will desire to obtain money, for both give him the same power, the power to procure a larger amount of the enjoyments of life. Those who have no desire to obtain knowledge, have either never seen it in its beauty, or they have been often cheated with the counterfeit. Indeed, there is an immense mass of base coin circulating in the civilized world under the name of knowledge, so much, that it is little wonder that men set so little value upon that which is really good ; the continual presentation of the counterfeit casts a doubt and suspicion over the genuine coinage.

The power of religion is the same in every respect as that of money or knowledge. Men pursue knowledge and money because they *desire* to avoid the *pains of want* and misery, and because they *desire* to obtain the *pleasures of plenty* and enjoyment in this life; and they pursue religion upon the same principle, because they *desire* to obtain the *pleasures of heaven*, and to avoid the *pains of hell* in another life. It matters little whether these pleasures and pains of another life be real or imaginary, they will exercise the same amount of influence upon the individual either way, because their influence depends upon his *faith* or *confidence*, and not in their reality; and supposing them to be imaginary or counterfeit, still the bank of religious faith is safe, because the believer, the holder of religious bank paper cannot present that paper for payment till after *death*. It is not due till then—and even then it must be presented in another world.

Still, faith or confidence is the root of moral action. The laborer toils from Monday morning till Saturday, because, and only because he believes, he has faith or confidence, that on Saturday night he will receive the reward of his toil. The toil itself is repulsive to a certain extent, but the reward is attractive. If the repulsive force be greater than the attractive, he refuses to toil, he "strikes;" and if he were free from the other impelling forces of hunger and want, until the attractive force—the reward of his toil—were made greater than the repulsive force of the toil itself, he would remain firm to his purpose. If the repulsive force of the toil be valued at twenty shillings, then, in order to induce him to act, the attractive force—the reward—must be twenty-one shillings. The odd shilling, the difference, is the moving power, just as in the case of the weigh beam, with fifteen ounces in one scale and sixteen in the other, as already referred to in the chapter upon force and motion.

It is the same in every case of moral action. The farmer expends, in ploughing and sowing, money and labor of the value of £500, in order that he may reap a crop of the value of £600 or £700. The ploughing and sowing is the repulsive force; the crop is the attractive; and the farmer is moved by the difference, or the faith or confidence which he feels that the latter value will be greater than the former, and this faith or confidence is founded upon the experience of former years. If the farmer had no confidence or faith that his toil and care would produce the given result, he would not be moved, he would not act, he would neither till nor sow unless he had faith. But the faith of the farmer differs from religious faith in this: that it is founded upon experience, whereas the other is founded upon traditionary documents which do not accord with experience. The faith of the farmer is supported by facts; the other by preaching. But in either case the intensity of force and action is in proportion to the amount of faith or confidence in the result, and not in the result itself, for that lies hid in the unknown future.

Attraction *to pleasure* and repulsion *from pain* are the

two ultimate principles, forces, or powers that actuate and move animated beings. Every act or motion of living sentient beings has its origin in one or the other of these two ultimate principles or moral forces. Men are not actuated by reason, or judgment, which is but another name for experience or reflection, although their actions, or the effect of these motive powers are, to a very large extent, modified by reflection, or experience, or reason, or judgment, for they are the same. Reflection looks backward into the past, or the experience which is treasured in the memory, and forward into the future which is pictured by the imagination—for the imagination is a duplicate of the memory; and by comparing past events, and referring effects or consequences to their causes, men are taught to submit to a *lesser present pain*, in order to avoid a *greater future pain:* as when a man submits to *present toil* in order to avoid *future starvation*—moderate toil being the *lesser evil.* They are also taught by reason, reflection, or experience to forego a *present lesser pleasure* in order to secure a *greater future pleasure:* as when a man foregoes ease and luxury in his youth, in order to secure those blessings at that time of life when ease and comfort are required;—to discern, discriminate, and determine between the value of present good and future good—present evil and future evil; and to act steadily upon those determinations, constitutes that line of action denominated prudent conduct. Where these differences of value are nicely discerned by an acute reason, and the conduct of the individual is regulated by the decisions of reason, such individual will secure to himself the largest amount of happiness that it is possible to secure in the circumstances in which he is placed.

# ORGANIZATION.

There is perhaps no word in any language, a right understanding of which is so important as this single word, *organization*. The animal body is an organized machine, a combination of organs working together, harmoniously in health, jarring in sickness, each acting and re-acting upon the other. Each organ has a specific function to perform:—the stomach and intestines to digest food and secrete chyle for the support and nourishment of the frame; the liver to secrete bile; the lungs to vitalize the blood, &c. If all the functions are going on harmoniously, and neither too fast nor too slow, then the being whose life is made up of the sum of those functions is in that state which we call health. The functions of the animal body are the seats or roots of the moral or mental feelings. Each specific animal function is the root of a specific mental feeling. The functions of the body are the bases upon which the mental functions are built; each mental function is but a reflection of the base from which it springs.

The feeling of hunger is a mental perception, having its root in the function of digestion, exercised by the stomach—and so of the others; from which consideration it becomes manifest that if we would treat of morals so as to arrive at satisfactory conclusions, we must begin with the animal organization. Those who consider the feelings of the mind only without reference to the functions of the living body, neglect the better half of the subject. They do not begin at the beginning; they jump into the middle of the case. Neglecting the foundation of the fabric they are about to raise, they build a house upon the sand.

The term organization is derived from organ, a musical instrument. Now, what are the materials of which an organ is composed? 1st. A certain quantity of metal for the pipes. 2d. Timber to be cut into boards for the box or body of the organ. 3d. Leather to form the flexible sides of the bellows. Now, let us look at those materials:—A hundred weight of metal in one solid lump, a beam of timber in one piece, and a hide of leather. These are not an organ; they are the materials of which an organ may be formed: but those materials must be organized. The metal must be formed into pipes, each of a given diameter, corresponding to the function which that pipe has to perform in the general organization. Each pipe has apertures with stops for the regulated ingress and egress of the fluid air, which is to circulate through the organ, as the fluids circulate through the animal body. All the pipes being formed, the next object is to cut up the timber; and this also must be done agreeably to a fixed principle of law, otherwise the organization will be imperfect. And lastly, the bellows must be made with a stop or valve, so as to cause the air to circulate in one direction only: similar to those valves which are to be found in the human heart, by which the blood is prevented from flowing backwards. Now, when all the parts have been made,—the pipes, the box, and the bellows, still these several parts do not constitute an organ *until they have been joined together, so as to form one harmonious whole.* If the organ be expected to be a perfect instrument, every pipe, as well as every other part, must be formed so as to execute its particular function duly, and the whole must be put together so as to produce the desired result, namely, the production of modulated sound, which may be called the function of the entire instrument.

Now, after all the parts have been properly formed and put together in a proper manner, we call that arrangement of materials, an organ. But still it is not a living organization. It is a dead organ. It will not perform its functions until acted upon by some external cause. The pipes are filled with air, but that air does not circulate. The circulating fluid is at rest, and the organ is dumb. Set the bellows in action, the circulation begins. Let the stops be acted upon by the fingers of the performer in a given manner, and a succession of melodious sounds grateful to the ear will fill the surrounding space. The perfection or imperfection of the melody is dependent upon the perfection or imperfection of the organization, and also upon the perfection or imperfection of the performer who acts upon that organization. Just so is the character of the human being determined. As the character of the tune is determined by the character of the organ and musical character of the performer, so the character of the individual man is determined by the congruous or incongruous character of his physical and mental organization and the moral influences affecting that compound system.

Much, and much too that is useful, might be advanced upon the subject of organization in a general sense. Into this general view, however, our limits will not allow us to enter. We must proceed to the consideration of the organization of the human being, and the relation of that organization to his moral character, for that is the special subject of our present inquiry. But before we proceed with our especial inquiry, it may be of some utility to give a general definition of an organized machine or system, with a few examples, by which the reader will be enabled to prosecute the general inquiry from the resources of his own mind.

An organized machine or system consists of a certain number of parts, each part having a specific function, more or less connected, and harmonizing with the functions of other parts; all the parts or their functions acting conjointly so as to work out a given result.

In this sense the solar system is an organized machine; a watch, a clock, a steam engine, a tree, an animal, &c., are physical organizations; and the individual mind of man, as consisting of different feelings and functions, is a moral organization. A family, a society, a community, a church, an army, a government, are also moral organizations, being bound and cemented together, not by physical restraints, but by moral or mental ties.

How are the vegetable and animal organizations built up? In works of art, as an organ, a watch, or a steam engine, we put the parts together in solid pieces, one piece after another, until the organization is completed, and the machine may be said to start into life at the point of maturity. It does not increase in bulk like the vegetable or animal. Just as it is formed at first, so it remains till worn out by its own action. But vegetable and animal organizations are built up from a small and invisible point, continually growing and increasing by small increments, until at length the living identity stands before us fully developed, in the form of an oak or a huge elephant. Every organization in the vegetable and animal kingdoms begin their existence in a *liquid state*, and by the circulation of that liquid, the solid fabric is built up.

The tissues of the animal body are formed from fluid matter circulating within the organized frame. This circulation begins at the moment that a new being is conceived. The commencement of that circulation is, in fact, the commencement of the life of that new being; and so long as the circulation continues, the life of the being continues, and no longer. The circulation may go on but for a few hours, or it may last for three score and ten years, or more. It begins upon a small centre, a mere point; a spark—an electrical spark—passes from one excited body to another excited body, where, meeting with a centre excited and prepared for its reception, that vital action which constitutes the very essence of animal life, is set in motion. The new system may be said to begin to spin upon its centre. And what is that power which sustains the motion for three score and ten years? Dr. Wilson Phillip has proved experimentally that galvanic action is the sustaining power. And how does this power, act? By what arrangements can the most intense power be elicited? By forming spiral coils of copper wire of great length, through which spiral coils the galvanic influence is transmitted.

Now, looking at the *manner* of action of electro-magnetic forces, the line of action of each being at right angles with that of the other, it is not difficult to perceive that a *spiral* motion must be the result of their conjoint action. And when we further consider that electro-magnetic forces are every where in action throughout the wide theatre of the world; that all fluids, when in motion, exhibit a tendency to move in spiral courses; and that the solid bodies of the vegetable, animal, and mineral kingdoms have been formed by the circulation of fluids, from which, by secretion, one atom or particle after another is deposited, until at length the solid structure is built up, we at once perceive that the *primitive* tissues of vegetable, animal, and mineral substances ought, in their structure, to exhibit the spiral form; and such, as a general law, we find to be the fact. The spiral vessel is the basis of the vegetable structure. But this spiral basis is subsequently broken up, giving rise to other modifications of the vegetable tissue. So also in the animal kingdom, there are indications that the spiral vessel forms the primitive tissues of the animal frame.

Take the common caterpillar, for example, which in the course of its short life passes through successive changes of structure. In the caterpillar state, the digestive canal is, in proportion to the size of the animal, a huge, spiral coil, completely filling the abdominal cavity. In the chrysalis state the spiral remains, but greatly shrunk in dimensions. In the last or butterfly state, we find new organs developed, as the honey stomach, which do not exhibit the spiral form; but, as in the vegetable world, the spiral vessel is the primitive tissue from which the others derive their origin; and if we turn our attention to the spiral motion of fluids, recollecting that the vegetable and animal solids are formed from the circulation of fluids, we at once perceive that such must be the natural process of formation. These spiral vessels may also be traced in the medullary substance of the human brain, which, by the most eminent physiologists, has been considered the root of the animal system.

A knowledge of the *manner* of formation of the primitive tissues is, however, of little importance, except as a curious speculation. An intimate and familiar acquaintance with the organs and functions of the animated being as they actually exist, is infinitely more to be valued, and happily this is within our reach. If men will consent to forego their antiquated notions respecting the influence of unknown and unintelligible powers acting within the body—spiritual essences which defy the power of physic; if they will but consent to hold a more charitable opinion of our common nature; if they will but reject the false, calumnious, and blasphemous dogma, that man is innately depraved, we might yet hope to see the better feelings and affections of humanity expand, and the sweet fragrance of a more cheerful, more holy, and happier influence arise like the incense of an evening sacrifice from the ashes of a gloomy superstition.

Yet there are parties who, whilst they stoutly maintain the degrading doctrine that man, and indeed all animated beings, are in a fallen and debased state, will violently exclaim against any inquiry into his nature, which would institute a comparison between what are called the lower organizations and that of the fallen, and, by a strange paradox, self-styled lord of the creation. If we would hope to elevate the physical and moral condition of man, we must disregard these cavillers. We must enter into the subject boldly, viewing man and the physical and moral influences by which he is surrounded just as they are.

One thing is plain: he who denies the inherent debasement of the existing order of nature, holds a higher and more exalted opinion of the character of the Intelligence which presides over the course of events, than he who entertains the grovelling notion that the heart of man is deceitful above all things and desperately wicked, thereby casting an imputation upon the Being in whose hands he also affirms are the reins which guide the impulses of that heart. It is better to view man as an organized machine, and to search for the seat of those impulses in the functions of his physical nature, where assuredly they are to be found, than to trace them to sources beyond our knowledge and above our control. If the roots of moral action be in the physical organization, in proportion to our knowledge of that organization we can stimulate or retard that action, and turn it into courses which would lead to a larger amount of happiness both to the individual and to the society of which he forms a member.

We find that a steam engine is an organized machine, through which a fluid circulates actuating the machine, requiring food and drink (fuel and water) to keep up the action, which action is the life of the machine. If the action be too intense, the machine runs riot like a drunkard. If the action be too low, the machine becomes feeble, it cannot perform its functions. If the circulation cease altogether, the machine stops—it dies. It is the same in regard to animal life. The intensity of action indicates the intensity of life; the intensity of life determines the intensity of the feelings; and the intensity of the feelings determines the moral character of the individual. This character may be considerably modified by education, customs, habits, civil and religious institutions, as well as other moral influences by which he may be surrounded, but still the distinguishing characteristics of the individual will manifest themselves, and have their roots in the physical functions of the animal organization.

Dr. Wilson Phillip divides the various functions of the animal body into three orders: the *sensorial*, the *nervous*, and the *muscular*. From a number of experiments he concludes that the muscle retains within itself a certain amount of power; that the muscular power is stored up in the muscle by secretion from the animal fluids, but remains dormant or latent until excited and called into action by the nerves. The nerves are depositories of power, but they require the presence of the muscle before that power can be exerted. Each of the two systems, the nervous and the muscular, is powerless without the presence of the other. Although it is usual to consider the nerve as the agent or active power, and the muscle as the patient or passive subject, this view is not strictly correct; no body or function can act singly and alone, as has been already noticed in this work. Action and reaction is the universal law. The muscles can be excited through the nerves by the agency of galvanic electricity, but the nerves can likewise be excited through the muscles. The two orders of functions do not stand in the relation of cause and effect to each other, but in that of mutually acting powers, the due balance of which constitutes the state of physical health.

The sensorial or thinking power is more difficult of approach; it is placed in a more obscure light, but still it is sufficiently manifest that this power is closely connected with the two preceding. *These three powers, taken connectedly, constitute man a living, thinking being.* Whatever influences the muscle, influences the nerve; whatever influences the nerve, influences the mind; and conversely, whatever influences the mind, influences the nerves and muscles. Further, all three are susceptible of the impress of *habits* more or less permanent, and here lies the power of education either for good or for evil. The impression of good habits in early life upon each of this trinity of functions is almost the only means by which human nature in the aggregate can be reformed and improved; not by operating upon one or the other can the object be obtained, for the realization of the beau ideal of all three is necessary to the formation of a perfect man. Dr. Wilson Phillip considers "that the muscular and nervous functions are the result of inanimate agents acting on vital parts; the sensorial of vital parts acting upon each other; that the sensorial power is not wholly confined to the brain, nor the nervous power to the spinal marrow, both powers in a greater or less degree residing in both organs."

"It is evident, from many observations, however, that the sensorial power chiefly resides in the brain, and that the power possessed by the spinal marrow is chiefly nervous.

"If these powers, it may be said, are thus blended in their organs, what proof have we of their being distinct powers? This proof, it appears to the author, will be found in carefully observing the process of dying, of which what we call death, appears to be only the first stage.

"However blended the organs of the sensorial and nervous powers may appear to be, we are assured that they are distinct organs, by the fact that while those of the nervous power evidently reside equally in the brain and spinal marrow, those of the sensorial power appear to be almost wholly in man, and chiefly, in all the more perfect animals, confined to the former. It may be possible, therefore, to withdraw the power on which the one set of functions depends, without immediately destroying the other, as we find we can withdraw the influence of the nervous from the muscular system without destroying the power of the latter.

"At the instant of death, it is evident the sensorial functions cease, no impression is perceived or followed by any act of volition. It is, however, equally evident to the physiologist, that the muscular power still remains. If under these circumstances the heart or muscles of voluntary motion be stimulated, they still possess the power of contraction, which is only lost by degrees, and not till after the sensorial power has for a considerable time been withdrawn.

"It is also evident to the physiologist, that some part of the nervous power still exists, for if the nerves themselves, or those parts of the brain or spinal marrow from which they originate be irritated, the corresponding muscles are thrown into action. The nerves, therefore, are still capable both of conveying impressions and exciting the muscles."

"It appears from the experiments and observations which have been laid before the reader, that as the muscular is independent of the nervous power, yet influenced by it, the nervous is independent of the sensorial, yet in like manner influenced by it: that the sensorial can be withdrawn without destroying the nervous power, as the nervous can be withdrawn without destroying the muscular power; but in the entire animal, as the muscular obeys the nervous, the nervous obeys the sensorial power; and that they are all so connected, that the existence of each indirectly depends on that of the others. They may, therefore, be justly called vital powers.

"The first observation that strikes us, in comparing the sensorial and nervous functions, is, that the latter bear a striking, the former no analogy, to the effects observed in inanimate nature. The act of secretion and the maintenance of animal temperature, are analogous to the processes of the laboratory, and the transmission of impressions through the nerves, both to chemical and mechanical processes; while the excitement of the muscular fibre is the ready effects of many inanimate agents? But what analogy can we detect between the functions of the sensorial power, sensation and volition for example, and the effects of inanimate agents? We are now in a new world, and at once perceive that it is in vain to look for the analogies which necessarily suggest themselves on reviewing the phenomena of the nervous system. It seems to require but a moment's reflection to teach every sober and unprepossessed understanding, that, in our study of the sensorial power, we must be satisfied with observing and arranging its phenomena without attempting to refer them to any more general principle.

"On a review of all that has been laid before the reader, it is evident that the nervous and muscular powers are, on the one hand, the direct means of maintaining the life of the animal, and on the other of connecting it with the external world; the former receiving impressions from that world, and through the latter communicating impressions to it. All the functions of both powers bear a strong analogy to the properties of the world with which they are thus associated; and we have reason to believe that all these functions, as is evidently the case with many of them, are the results of inanimate agents acting on vital parts.

"As vital properties do not differ from the properties of inanimate nature, in degree or by any other modification, but have nothing in common with them, it follows that when living bodies affect each other only by their vital properties, the result must be such as bears no analogy to any of the properties of inanimate nature; and, consequently, that in all processes which have any analogy, one of the agents must operate by the properties of inanimate matter.

"In the animal body itself, the nervous system alone appears to be the connecting link between the sensorium and inanimate matter. It consists of living parts capable of acting in concert with that matter, receiving impressions from it, and independently of the intervention of the muscular system impressing it; for there can be no stronger analogy than that which subsists between the secreting processes, effected by the nervous power in living surfaces, and the chemical processes of inanimate matter; and if an inanimate agent be employed in the former processes, its supply and application must be regulated by the vital powers of the nervous system. Whether this agent be a distinct being, or only a peculiar state of the constituent parts of bodies, is not the question. All the essential inferences are in either case the same. The phenomena of electric animals are here in point. We see their nervous system collecting or forming and applying, even according to the dictates of the will, an inanimate agent.

"With respect to the sensorial functions, they have only an indirect effect in maintaining animal life, and are excited by no impressions but those communicated through the nervous system. They are, therefore, the results of vital parts acting on each other. Hence it is that they bear no analogy to the processes of inanimate nature, and are the first functions which cease when the vital power begins to fail. In the nervous and muscular functions, an inanimate agent excites the languid powers of life. In the sensorial functions, the functional power and the agent which excites it, being equally vital powers, fail together.

"When the nature of the sensorial functions is kept in view, we cannot be surprised that the attempts to refer them to a more general principle should have proved so futile. To what other principle shall we refer the effects of the vital parts of animals on each other, when it is in animals alone that such parts ever influence each other? Even in vegetable life we find nothing analogous to the sensorial functions. All it possesses bear the same analogy to the properties of inanimate nature which we observe in the functions of the nervous and muscular systems of animals, and are, therefore, the results of inanimate agents acting on living parts. Much less can we look for any analogies of this kind in inanimate nature itself. Such fancied analogies may please in the creations of the poet, but by the philosopher they are justly rejected. While we are charmed with the flights of Lucretius, we see only the perversion of philosophy in the reasonings of Hartley."

Having given this brief view of the connection of the physical and mental functions, and having endeavored to impress upon the mind of the reader the important truths, that stimulants and sedatives applied to either of the three systems of functions will operate a change upon the others; that that which stimulates the body, stimulates the mind, and *vice versa*; and that habits may be impressed upon the body by application to the mind, or upon the mind by impressions upon the body, we will now attempt to reduce the whole into the tabular form, so that by being placed before the eye in one view, the mind may receive the subject in a more systematic form.

plain and undeniable conclusions, —
clusions in systematic language, each term being
propriate and intelligible type of the principle
Such a systematic arrangement of the principles

trut
the
the
late
imp
upo
now
tha
may

# PHYSICAL AND MORAL FUNCTIONS.

The pathway of wisdom lies in the mean,
A vice on each side, and a virtue between,
There are two ways to poverty, two ways to pain:
The mid-path alone leads to permanent gain;
Two ways to death, and two ways to shame:
One way to health, and one way to fame;
Two ways to vice, and two ways to hell:
One way to heaven for those who do well.
In this great game of life from its dawn to its close,
There is one way to win, and there's two ways to lose;
And hence, those who scan mankind and their ways,
Find a great deal to blame, and but little to praise.

The accompanying chart, notwithstanding that much care and study has been expended upon it with a view to render it in some degree perfect, is still to be considered in the light of a rough sketch, rather than that of a finished picture. The principles upon which it is constructed are, it is presumed, plain and intelligible; but the language in which these principles are expressed, is in many instances faulty. Nor is it possible altogether to avoid this faulty expression, unless by forming a vocabulary of terms in accordance with the principles. The practical morals of mankind have not been formed by any rule or principle; they have been shaped and fashioned by the various influences of climate, physical organization, customs, habits, religious and civil institutions, and other contingent circumstances, with the varied actions and re-actions of jarring interests and contending factions. Hence the whole science of morals, if science it may be called, is but one vast jumble of discordant elements and ambiguous expressions, without order, arrangement, or unity of design.

There is apparently no way in which order can be drawn out of this confusion, except by beginning *de novo*, laying down plain axioms, deducing from these axioms plain and undeniable conclusions, and clothing these conclusions in systematic language, each term being an appropriate and intelligible type of the principle set forth. Such a systematic arrangement of the principles and terms of moral science is an all-important desideratum, and until it shall have been obtained, there is little hope of accelerating in any great degree the practical development of moral rectitude, by which, and by which alone, can be obtained the great reward—an augmentation of the sum of human enjoyment. Men are deeply interested in the progress of virtue independent of all ulterior considerations, in reference to punishments or rewards in another life. Individuals or parties may have, or may suppose they have, an advantage in pursuing vicious courses—courses not in accordance with the general weal; but the majority have no interest in doing wrong, for assuredly the consequences of their wrong doing will fall upon their own heads. And when the majority suffer from the wrong doings of the minority, as is the case in civilized and Christian Europe at the present day, still the majority are but suffering the just and natural consequences of their own neglect of duty, for the evil consequences cannot be avoided but by arresting the vicious progress of the minority. This unequal state of things arises, or rather has arisen, from inequalities in the intensity of action of the physical and moral functions; and if it be desirable to reduce the moral world to a more equitable distribution of the pleasures and pains incident to life, we must begin by an investigation of the roots of moral action.

While life continues, physical action must go on. This physical action, after a certain interval, begets an uneasy feeling, and this uneasiness leads to moral action. Thus the function of digestion brings about the uneasy feeling of hunger, and this uneasiness urges the being suffering under that feeling to such course of action, as may obtain that which will allay the uneasiness under which he suffers. In proportion to the intensity of the feeling, so is the voraciousness of the animal; and if under the influence of that feeling only, he continues to devour food until another uneasy feeling, that accompanying repletion, sets in, inducing moral action in a new direction. Thus the feelings are continually vibrating between two points, in obedience to the vibrations of the animal functions. If the vibrations are violent, if the functions and their accompanying feelings oscillate into either extreme, there is diseased action, whether considered in a physical or moral sense; and further, diseased physical action will induce diseased moral action; and conversely, diseased moral action will induce diseased physical action, for mind and body are inseparable, each acting upon the other; but the physical organization is the basis or foundation upon which the mental or moral organization is built up, and therefore demands the first and most careful attention. In the functions of the physical organization are to be found the roots of moral action. If the physical or animal root of carnal desire could be exterminated, as teeth are extracted, there would be no fórnication in the land; but those who may think that such extraction of the root would be desirable, must be content to take all the consequences which would follow such extermination, and those consequences are nothing less than the extermination of the human race. But nature must go on with all her functions, for

> Let the priest say what he will,
> Nature will be nature still.

Tabular view of the animal functions, showing the oscillatory action which accompanies, or rather which constitutes animal life.

| | Limit of Extreme Action. | | Limit of Healthful Action. | | Line of Death, or of Indifference. | | Limit of Healthful Action. | | Limit of Extreme Action. | |
|---|---|---|---|---|---|---|---|---|---|---|
| Death. | | Extreme heat. | | Warmth. | | Coolness. | | Extreme cold. | | Death. |
| Death. | | Disease—gluttony. | | Moderate diet. | | Moderate evacuation. | | Flux—cholera. | | Death. |
| Death. | | Disease—drunkenness. | | Moderate drink. | | Moderate evacuation. | | Excessive evacuation—disease. | | Death. |
| Death. | | Disease—excessive toil. | | Moderate exertion. | | Moderate rest. | | Sloth, torpidity,—disease. | | Death. |
| Death. | | Morbid excitement. | | Moderate nervous action. | | Moderate sleep. | | Morbid drowsiness. | | Death. |

It is of great importance that clear and distinct conceptions should be entertained of the varied functions (referred to in the chart) mental and moral, with the external objects capable of exciting pleasurable or painful sensations upon them, as well as the internal actions and re-actions operating amongst the functions themselves. We will therefore proceed to give a short notice of each, beginning at the lowest point, that of the vital action, which in every case accompanies, or rather constitutes, organic life; although the expletive "organic" is a redundancy when connected with "life," *organic action* is correct. Life, whether vegetable or animal, is a manifestation resulting from, or exhibited in, organic action. This is all that we know of life. Whilst the organic action continues, life continues; when the organic process is finished, life is finished;—nor is it possible, without subverting the laws of nature, to protract that life beyond the completion of the organic process. The river flows because, and only because, it is running down; the clock moves because it is running down; the planetary system moves because it is running down; every system, every motion, every process, is progressing towards a point in which it will terminate; and life is a process which only exists by a continual approach towards death. Eternal life and perpetual motion are almost, or altogether, synonymous.

Consciousness.—Sensation, consciousness, a perception that we exist, is somehow connected with the organic action which constitutes animal life. If the organic action be excited by stimulants, the consciousness becomes more vivid; if soothed or allayed by sedatives, the mental perception becomes more dull. An ardent spirit blazes through a short life and dies; his life is one splendid hallucination. Such is the life of the poet, the patriot, the devotee, and of every other modifidation of enthusiastic character. On the other hand, the phlegmatic man drags through a long insipid existence. The actual amount of life, or its essence, organic action, may be the same in both cases; but in the ardent life, that essence is concentrated, in the other, it is diluted. Both are extremes; both are faulty organizations; both are equally removed from the happy medium. And by the physical treatment the first may be soothed down, and the second may be stimulated, which is assuredly a more natural, more humane, and consistent mode for the cure of moral maladies, than a continued preaching of eternal torments. From this small point, consciousness, the intellect of man grows up as from a root, or germ, until at length its wide expanding branches shoot out to the furthest regions of the universe.

## THE INSTINCTS.

Love of Life.—The instinctive love of life begins with the consciousness of existence, and acts steadily throughout with more or less intensity until that consciousness ceases. It is stronger than reason. We shrink from death, whilst reason acknowledges that life is not worth preserving. The instinctive feeling still prevails; and it is necessary that it should be so, for if the preservation of life were left to the determination of the judgment, it would in thousands of instances most assuredly be thrown away as a worthless thing. The few of our species, who, wrung by a maddening anguish, commit suicide, does not invalidate the general principle, that the love of life is an instinctive feeling stronger than reason. Besides, as in other cases, these few exceptions prove the general law. The unhappy suicide is generally a man of strong mind. An idiot never commits suicide. Instinct has no reason to oppose it in his mind; and for the same reason the lower animals do not commit the act of self-destruction.

Attachment to Sex.—The attachment to sex is necessary to the procreation and perpetuation of the race. This feeling, passion, or instinct, is also stronger than the judgment; and it is requisite for the continuation of the species that it should be so. What single man, looking with the eye of reason alone, upon the cares, the toils, and anxieties attendant upon the rearing of a family, would enter into the married state? The very supposition is preposterous, if the question is to be tried at the bar of cool reason. But the instinct is stronger than reason. In the spring and summer of life, the instinctive feeling pleads for gratification with an irresistible power, and too often breaks down every barrier which reason or remonstrance can oppose to its progress. At length the ardent passions being cooled, reason and reflection resume their sway, and the deluded votary of pleasure is astonished and chagrined at his former impetuosity, and wonders how he could have sought so eagerly a prize which, (like every other) when obtained, appears to yield so small a per centage of that happiness which in prospect appeared so rich and desirable. But it is necessary that it should be so, although at the same time it is highly desirable that this feeling which is so strong should be curbed and kept within due bounds. Unless it be so curbed and controlled, the individual is certain to pay the penalty of his indiscretion in one shape or another.

Fondness of Young. This instinct springs out of the former, and is, especially in the mother, on whom the care of suckling, nurturing, and rearing devolves, much stronger than the judgment. There are few circumstances which evince the adaptation of the means to the end more pointedly than the comparative feebleness of the reasoning faculty and the great strength of the sympathetic feelings in the female of the human race. A reasoning female may be the best of parents, so far as training is considered; but she is seldom the most kind and affectionate of mothers. She may be an agreeable companion to a reasoning husband, but she is not so well fitted to be the nurse of puking infants,—which latter office is the chief end of her existence: it is the niche which she is destined to fill in the great fabric of the world. A puking, crying infant is no fit companion for a mere reasoner, but is the fittest of all creatures for the society and companionship of a being whose sympathies are strong, and attuned to vibrate in unison with those of the helpless babe which leans upon them for protection.

This instinctive feeling is deeply seated in the female breast. The mother clings to her babe to the last. In sickness she watches and tends it day and night without weariness; she heeds not her own comfort; she spares neither toil nor pains that she may restore it to health; and when at length death snatches it away, thereby relieving her from her toilsome fatigues, she sits down and weeps bitterly over the body of her dead child. Why does she weep? Is it because she has been relieved from a load of care and anxiety? That, according to reason, were rather something at which to rejoice. But these instincts, the tone and intensity of which have so large a share in forming the character, disregard the laws of reason, and scarcely can be made amenable to its dictates. There is a very fine illustration of the power of paternal attachment exhibited in the character of David, King of the Jews, when Absalom had attempted to wrest his kingdom and all besides from his hands, even to his life; and when in the midst of his career he was slain by the hand of Joab, thereby relieving David from his dangers and fears. Did David rejoice that his enemy was slain? No; that enemy was his son, and all the feelings of the father burst forth in a full gush of agony. All the kingdoms of the earth sank into nothingness before his eyes; he only remembered that he was a father, and that his son, his beloved son, was slain; and he went up into his chamber and wept and said:—"Oh! my son! Absalom! my son, my son Absalom! would to heaven I had died for thee, Oh! Absalom, my son, my son!" This was the voice of nature issuing from the heart; it would not be stifled, it would not be restrained by any considerations drawn from the deductions of cool reason.

It may be worth while to notice here, that those compositions which take the deepest hold upon the affections have their foundation in those three instincts of which we have been speaking.

Tragedy is based upon the "love of life." This instinct is deeply rooted in human nature, and, therefore, whatever touches it, awakens the sympathies and excites a more intense feeling than can be excited by touching any other function of the mind.

Comedies and novels are based upon the "love of sex." Comedy is not so powerful as tragedy, because love of sex is not so strong as love of life.

Love of young also forms the basis of many tales and pieces of a moving nature. But the most deeply exciting composition is that in which all three are blended; but such blending requires very dexterous management to prevent one feeling from overclouding another.

## ANIMAL APPETITES.

To some readers it may at first view appear strange that *respiration* should be assigned a place among the corporeal feelings or animal appetites. If the regulation of this function had no influence upon the state of the body and mind, it certainly would not be entitled to a place amongst the animal functions. But it has a most extensive and important bearing upon the healthy action of all the other functions of the body, and necessarily of the mind also. Indeed, all the functions re-act upon each other, but the influence of the respiration is pre-eminent. If this function be deranged, the entire organization is thrown into a diseased state.

Neither ought it to have a place unless its regulation be in some degree dependent upon the mind. The action of the heart, or liver, or any of the purely involuntary functions, have no place in morals, because that action is altogether involuntary, and to most persons it may seem that the respiration is also involuntary; but a little consideration will make it appear that this is not the case. Dr. Wilson Phillip has some very judicious remarks upon this point:—

"The muscles of respiration are, in the strictest sense of the word, muscles of voluntary motion; we can at pleasure interrupt, renew, accelerate, or retard their action; and, if we cannot wholly prevent it, it is for the same reason that we cannot prevent the action of the muscles of the arm, when fire is applied to the fingers. The pain occasioned by the interruption of a supply of air to the lungs is greater than can be voluntarily borne. Respiration continues in sleep for the same reason that we turn ourselves in sleep when our posture becomes uneasy. It continues in apoplexy for the same reason that the patient generally moves his limbs if they are violently irritated.

"If respiration continues in apoplexy when no irritation, however powerful, can excite the patient to move them, it arises from the interruption of a supply of air to the lungs producing a greater degree of irritation than any other means we can employ. We have heard of the hand voluntarily held in the fire, but we know of no instance where the breathing has been voluntarily discontinued till the lungs were injured. As the insensibility increases in apoplexy, the breathing becomes less frequent; and when the former becomes such that no means can longer excite any degree of feeling, the breathing ceases.

"By a certain sensation, a wish is excited to expand the chest. This is an act of the sensorium. Till this act take place, the nervous as well as the muscular power, by which its expansion is effected, is inert; it is in vain that these powers remain, if the power which calls them into action be lost. Thus the removal of the brain puts a stop to respiration.

"It is said that the motions of respiration must be involuntary, because we are in general unconscious of them? But do we not become more or less so of all habitual acts of volition? 'If I did so, I did it unconsciously,' is a common expression. If we stop a person who is walking, he cannot tell which leg he last moved, or a person who is playing on an instrument, he cannot tell which fingers he last employed; yet all such acts are strictly acts of volition. If we are reminded of them, we can always interrupt, renew, retard, or accelerate them at pleasure. We have no difficulty in perceiving and changing in any way we please the motions of respiration, when we choose to attend to them; but as there is no other act of volition so habitual, there is none so apt to escape our attention."

A careful attention to the functions of respiration is of greater importance both in a physical and moral point of view than might be supposed upon taking a cursory glance at the subject. This function is the main-spring of the organic action, which, by vitalizing the blood in its passage through the lungs, transmits that vitality to the most minute fibre of the organized frame. In short, to speak in plain terms, the animal body is a *self-sustaining galvanic battery;* the acid oxygen is continually being inhaled from the atmosphere into the blood to support the vital action; and carbonic acid, the *product* of that vital action (which action may be considered a species of combustion), is continually being exhaled from the blood; and this reciprocal action and re-action of inspiration of the active acid, and expiration of the product, is the most essential function of the animal organization, and demands the first and most careful attention.

In order to render the action of this function in a clear and intelligible manner, we will refer to a familiar case which falls under the notice of every individual. The common house fire will not burn unless there be a draught up the chimney. Neither will the *action* of combustion go on in any case unless there be a constant supply of air. When a chimney is on fire, stopping the draught beneath extinguishes the flames, just as stopping the chimney at the top puts out the fire in the grate beneath, or as putting an extinguisher upon a candle puts it out, by cutting off the supply of oxygen which supports the *action* of combustion. Whilst the fire is burning, there is a continued current of air passing into the fire, and a continued current of carbonic acid gas and other vapors passing from the fire up the chimney; and in order that the fire may burn properly, that is, that it may be in a healthy state of action, it is essentially requisite that these two currents shall flow uninterruptedly. If the carbonic acid be not carried off, it will put the fire out more effectually than cold water. If the air be cut off, the fire will go out for want of oxygen to sustain the action of combustion. When a pair of common bellows is applied, the action is increased, because a greater quantity of air is forced in, and a greater quantity of carbonic acid passes off up chimney. To call a burning coal a *live* coal is no figure of speech, it is literally true; and the more intense is the action, the more intense is the life, and the sooner the process comes to a termination. A small quantity of live coals, placed under the boiler of a locomotive steam engine, sets in motion a long train of carriages. It becomes a living machine, whose actuating power is within itself, and the amount of the power which the locomotive is capable of exerting is in proportion to the amount or intensity of action going on in the fire under the boiler. Stop that action and the machine stops—it dies; but it does not begin to decompose, being made of metal, and the organization being perfect, it may be again brought to life and motion by renewing the action under the boiler.

Now the animal locomotive is the same in almost every particular. Unless it receive a constant supply of pure air into the lungs to support the vital action; and unless there be a free discharge of carbonic acid and other vapors generated in the body, and which tend to extinguish the fire of life, there cannot be long either energy, health, cheerfulness, or a disposition in the bosom of the individual to perform the duties of life. He will as certainly flag upon the journey of life as the locomotive engine flags in its speed when the fire fails. Throwing ardent spirits into the machine may cause a short excitement, as when oil is thrown upon the fire; but it is nothing more than a flash, and the action soon subsides into its former state of apathy. It might be affirmed, without much fear of error, that he who attends to the functions of respiration, will enjoy cheerfulness of mind in a healthy body, and will be free from all the distressing maladies incident to pulmonary affections. But unfortunately the avocations of mankind in the present highly artificial state of society almost preclude the possibility of attending to those functions with the care which they demand.

Still something may be done. "Where there is a will there is a way," says the old adage. Muscular exertion, athletic exercises, stimulate and increase the action of the animal functions. How does this effect take place? It is vulgarly supposed that the increase of heat is due to the muscular exertion by a kind of mechanical friction consequent upon the mere motion of the muscles. That some of the effect is due to this cause, there cannot be a doubt, but it is a very small portion. If an individual run briskly for a mile or so, he will excite a genial glow and perspiration, but this is not attributable to the motion of the muscles only. In running he is compelled to breath hard in order to keep up the action of the vital fire which is necessary to urge his locomotive forward with the given speed; and if he were to stand stock still and breath at the same rate, he would thereby increase the action of the functions and the animal temperature to nearly an equal degree. It is better, however, that the muscular action and increased vital action consequent upon increased respiration should go together, for such is the natural order necessary to maintain the healthy action and re-action of all the functions.

As in order to continue the action or life of the locomotive engine, fuel must be supplied to the furnace and water to the boiler, so in the animal machine food and drink is necessary to sustain the vital action, and the supply must be so regulated as to keep the machine in a state of healthy action. Either too much or too little is injurious. If the boiler be completely filled with water, or the furnace completely choaked with fuel, the machine is useless; it is in the first case in the condition of the drunkard, and in the second in that of the glutton. If there be too little water or fuel, there is a loss of power, a loss of strength, which is equally injurious.

Alternate rest and action is also necessary to a healthy state of the animal machine. Too much or too little is in this case, as in every other, equally destructive of health and happiness. The aristocrat is distressed with the heaviness of *ennui*, and the toil-worn laborer is wearied with never-ceasing exertion.

The animal functions are never at any period in a state of perfect repose. In one or other there is at all times a certain degree of uneasiness more or less intense, and this uneasy feeling becomes a spring of moral action. The internal working of the organization never ceases. Whilst life continues, the organic action is always going on; and when that organic action is going on steadily, moderately, and regularly, neither too fast nor too slow, the organs and functions are in a healthy and sound state, and those springs of moral action which have their attachments in those functions may then be considered to be in a healthy tone. The uneasy feeling consequent upon organic action displays itself on two sides, as will be made more plain by a reference to the following table:—

| The uneasiness of* | | Creates a | |
|---|---|---|---|
| | Hunger | | Desire to eat. |
| | Repletion | | Desire to expel. |
| | Thirst | | Desire to drink. |
| | Saturation | | Desire to expel. |
| | Fatigue | | Desire to rest. |
| | Restiveness | | Desire to act. |
| | Suffocation | | Desire to inspire. |
| | Oppression | | Desire to expire. |

The functions never being in a state of repose during the life of the animal, there is always a degree of uneasiness upon one side or the other. No sooner is one side allayed than the opposite sets in, like the alternate attractions and repulsions to the physical world. The allaying of these uneasy feelings is that which we call enjoyment or happiness. The uneasy feeling must be first felt, otherwise there can be no enjoyment. Alternate uneasiness and gratification is the condition on which we hold our animal being, and so that the two sides of the account fairly balance each other, we have no reason to complain; but when the uneasiness of hunger, for example, reaches a point of intensity so as to become absolute pain, without a due compensation of enjoyment, the individual who is so subjected is living at a loss.

* Indolence,—a state of inactivity, is derived from *Indolentia*, a state in which the individual feels no pain or uneasiness: pain or uneasiness being necessary to incite to action.

## EXTERNAL SENSES.

Having already made some remarks upon the senses as instruments for the acquirement of knowledge it will therefore be unnecessary in this place to dwell at length upon their office as connected with the moral being. The chief end at which we should aim in the cultivation of the senses as instruments of power, in fashioning the mind, is to give them a *fine*, *delicate*, yet *firm tone*, so that they may turn away in disgust from gross contact, and at the same time be sufficiently firm not to fret like the Sybarite at the ruffled rose leaf. The senses are the windows of the mind, through which perception passes, and it is highly important that the knowledge which passes through those channels should be presented in the light of unadorned truth; for truth, like beauty, is most beautiful in simplicity, "when unadorned, adorned the most."

## THE PASSIONS.

The passions appear to be the most complicated department of the compound organic being,—man. This complication is, however, more apparent than real. It may be shown, we think, that all the varied feelings of the breast may be reduced to the six elementary passions noted in the chart; and even these might be still further reduced, for they all have their roots in one or the other of two feelings—pleasure and pain. In treating of the passions, terms have been multiplied needlessly, by which a subject, in its nature occult and obscure, has been involved in still deeper obscurity. To take a familiar example—joy and extacy are but different degrees of the same passion, as are also the terms grief and anguish.—Extacy is a higher measure of joy, and anguish is a more intense feeling of grief.

These different degrees of passion will be better exhibited in the tabular form:—

| | | |
|---|---|---|
| Extacy. | Adoration. | Confidence. |
| Joy. | Love. | Hope. |
| ———Line of——— | ———Indifference——— | |
| Grief. | Hate. | Fear. |
| Anguish. | Detestation. | Despair. |

The line separating joy and grief, love and hate, hope

and fear, may with propriety be named the *line of indifference*, for there is a point where the passion passes to the other side. Indeed, a being who is hoping is generally fearing also at intervals. The passion vibrates in his breast, from side to side, like the swinging of a pendulum, as has been shown to be the case with regard to the actions and re-actions of the animal functions. In short, no organ, function, or feeling of the animal being is ever at rest, but like every thing besides in nature is in a state of continual vibration.

Besides those terms representing different degrees of the same passion, there are also terms which are received as representing pure or single passions, which in fact, represent a compound mixture of nearly all six. Jealousy and ambition are of this class of terms representing compound mixture of feeling or passion. Let us analyze jealousy. There is,

Love towards the desired object.
Hatred towards the rival.
Hope that the object may be obtained.
Fear that it may be lost.
Grief for indifference from a loved object.
Joy for indifference shown towards the rival.

Here are all the passions boiling together, and the whole compound expressed by the single term jealousy, thereby inducing the belief that jealousy is a single or elementary feeling or passion; whereas like many others which might be named, it will be found upon a careful analysis, that it is compounded of the six *elements* or passions before named. Indeed, it might be affirmed without much fear of leading to erroneous conclusions, that every passion of the human breast, except those six named in the chart, is a compound; that these six elements, in different degrees of intensity, and mixed in different proportions, give rise to all the varied passions of which the human heart is susceptible.

The passions are of vast importance in an inquiry into the mental capacities of the human being. They are in fact the forces, or rather the points, upon which the forces bear, by which the machine is moved, and have their roots in the animal organization. Whatever stimulates the organic action, stimulates the passions; whatever depresses the organic action, stills them. Indeed, if we examine the passions physiologically, we shall find that love and hate are collective terms, expressive of the organic likes and dislikes of the animal functions. Love, joy, and hope take their rise from the likings; hate, grief, and fear, from the dislikings. The sympathies and antipathies of the organic functions give direction to the feelings or passions in reference to their bearing upon external things.

## MENTAL FACULTIES.

A few words will suffice to show the relative position of the mental faculties with reference to the other parts of the physical and moral organization. The memory receives and retains impressions. The question is not how or by what means this is effected? We take the simple fact that it is so; and the aggregate of the impressions or the ideas resulting from them, is the sum of knowledge possessed by the individual. If the ideas thus treasured in the memory be of a useful kind, and arranged in an orderly or systematic form, such knowledge is valuable, as being capable of being turned to account in the business of life. The imagination is but a reflection of the memory. Without previous knowledge fixed in the memory, there can be no imagination; it has no matter wherewith to operate, for even in its wildest flights it does nothing more than draw its materials from the memory in disjointed pieces, and re-arranges them in fantastic forms. As a general law, the memory points backward into past time, and the imagination forward into future time.

The memory is also the store-house from which the judgment draws the materials of experience, by which it forms its decisions—that is, what we call cool judgment. But sometimes this faculty is biassed in its decisions by the solicitings of the warm imagination, looking forward to the future without the guide of experience from the memory. This is what is called speculation,—a random judgment not justified by a knowledge of the past; not justified by reflection, for reflection is nothing else than looking into the memory for knowledge or experience wherewith to come to a cool decision.

## MORAL POWERS.

Now, the great object of moral science, viewed with reference to the interest, peace, and happiness of society, is to regulate and control the speech and actions of men by moulding, subduing, and modifying the hidden springs of moral action, which have their roots in the animal organization, so to regulate the speech and action, as to secure to the individual himself the highest possible amount of innocent enjoyment. Enjoyment which does not infringe upon the enjoyment of others, but rather contributes to the general stock of happiness, is that mode of action which is and must be acceptable in the sight of both God and man, whatever gloomy misanthropes may say to the contrary.

One point remains to be noticed, that is that the mind, properly so called, pure intellect, does not move the animated being. He is moved by his feelings or passions, and by these only; *but the mind directs the movement*, as the Supreme Intelligence is presumed to preside at the helm of the universe directing the motions, although the motions themselves are due to the ultimate forces of attraction and repulsion.

Upon a review of the whole subject, we find that good and evil have no meaning, except in reference to the pleasures and pains of sentient beings. Good and evil are abstract and collective terms, in which are set forth the sum of pleasurable or painful feelings which sentient beings are capable of enjoying or suffering. But, although good and pleasure, evil and pain, are convertible terms, it is highly important to mark distinctly that every pleasure is not a good, because some pleasures bring a greater amount of pain or evil after them than the good enjoyed. An ounce of pleasure to-day, and a pound of pain to-morrow, will not add greatly to the stock of permanent enjoyment. When the books are made up, and the two sides balanced against each other, he who has enjoyed his ounce of pleasure will find himself upon the wrong side of the account. It is the same with pain. Every pain is not an evil; an ounce of pain to-day, will very frequently bring a pound of pleasure to-morrow. The fool takes the ounce of pleasure, and the pound of pain overtakes him; he shrinks from the ounce of pain, and loses the pound of pleasure. But whilst he takes his ounce of pleasure he does not enjoy it, because very generally he is conscious that the greater pain will overtake him, and this consciousness hangs over him like the sentence over the culprit, and mars his enjoyment. Also in shrinking from the smaller present evil he does not avoid the pain, because being, as he generally is, conscious that he is thereby losing the greater good, the prospective loss vexes his spirit and diminishes the amount of gratification which he had promised himself from the avoidance of the present and lesser evil. By all which we may perceive that vice and folly are synonymous, for he who acts thus is not more a criminal than a fool. Indeed, the unfortunate and irresolute individual generally exclaims at last, "what a fool I was to have acted thus, when I plainly saw or might have seen the consequences!"

The prudent man takes the opposite course. He shuns the little good of to-day, because he plainly foresees that by so doing he will secure a greater good to-morrow; and the mind being fixed upon the prospective good, the present is relinquished without reluctance. The sacrifice becomes easy, because the mind reposes upon the greater recompense in prospect. The rewards and punishments of another world influence the minds and actions of men in the same way. Heaven is a future pleasure, promised to those who will relinquish a present pleasure; and hell is a future pain, threatened to those who shrink from a present pain or duty, for duty includes the idea of pain; and that those future pains and pleasures may overcome the most intense pains and pleasures of this life, they are represented as being eternal in duration and of an intensity greater than can be conceived by the mind of man.

Whatever influence religious views may have in forming and fixing a permanent character, that influence is chiefly due to the *habit of mind* which it induces of looking into the far off future for the reward of present self-denial. This habit of mind grows upon the individual, and generates a tendency to forego the present good for a future good, and this tendency, by mixing itself up with his every-day transactions, gives a fixed and permanent character to the individual. The question is, could not a better, because a more rational, course of conduct be induced, by fixing the mind upon the future as regards his interests and honor in this world, without bending his feelings and affections into an unknown region, to the neglect of the good which may be effected here?

## THE MORAL FORCES.

PLEASURE AND PAIN (ANIMAL).—If there were but one human being in the world, he could not commit an offence against any other human being, for the best of all possible reasons:—there is, by the supposition, no human being to suffer by his aggression; neither could he confer a benefit upon a fellow creature, for the same reason. But this is supposing a case which never had an existence, so far as we know. Let us take a fact. Alexander Selkirk (popularly known as Robinson Crusoe), dwelt for several years alone upon an uninhabited island. For the guidance of this individual, the simple forces of animal pleasure and pain were sufficient. Whatever were his acts, good or bad, he himself must of necessity take the consequences. If he digged or tilled his bit of ground, he had the fruits of his labor to himself, since there was no one else to deprive him of the reward of his toil. There was no lord, who, by virtue of the sword, claimed a rent from the crop which he had raised by his own hands, nor parson or bishop to distrain for tithes in the name of heaven. The fruits of his labor were all his own. If he toiled, he enjoyed the reward of that toil to the full amount. If he neglected to cultivate his land, he had to endure the suffering consequent upon that neglect; he could not help himself from the granary of his neighbor. Honor or shame could not influence his conduct, since there was no human being to confer either the one or the other; nor was it necessary. Honor or respect is given in return for a benefit conferred; shame or disapprobation is awarded for an injury sustained, But Alexander Selkirk, as he could confer no benefit, he could receive no honor; as he could inflict no injury, he could not be the subject of disapprobation or disgrace. He could break no law with any man. He could neither murder nor steal, nor lie, nor covet his neighbor's wife, nor his ass, nor any thing that was his. He had no neighbor. He was all alone, and might be safely left to the laws of nature, or more correctly, to the laws of his animal organization, or, to place the subject on a wider basis, to the laws of God, for the laws of nature are the laws of God, and the only laws of God, since they are the laws by which he governs the universe. Any writings which stand opposed to those laws must be spurious, since they disagree with the declared will of the Governor, as expressed in the unchangeable order of progressive movement by which the world is regulated. Not only this solitary individual, but the whole of the animated creation, is under the influence of the two simple forces of animal pleasure and pain, from the zoophyte that clings to the rock, to the intellectual being—man, who grasps the universe in his wide expanded mind. All are subject to these two moving powers or forces, and it is sheer folly to disclaim those feelings which originate the larger half of our actions. Fanatics may declaim against the lusts of the flesh, but all their declamation cannot destroy them; they will ever remain whilst animated beings remain; they are a part of their existence, and have been implanted for beneficial ends. All that can be done, or ought to be desired, is to regulate their action so as to produce the greatest amount of happiness. To subdue them when too strong, to stimulate them when too weak, is the highest point of cultivation to which we can attain, and with this we must be contented.

Honor and Shame.—As soon as two human beings come to live together, the forces of honor and shame come into play. And they are powerful forces; the right understanding and direction of which, is of the highest value in the progressive civilization of the human race. Two beings cannot live together for any length of time without performing acts of kindness to each other. A kindness conferred necessarily begets a feeling of gratitude in the bosom of the individual receiving the benefit, and of respect towards the benefactor. Indeed, these feelings are almost identical; and that which we call honor, respect, or approbation, is nothing more than giving expression to the feeling which has been thus generated. On the other side, an unkind act begets a feeling of dislike, which being expressed, becomes the language of disapprobation, disrespect, or dishonor. If we analyze the feelings thus generated, and the roots from which they spring, we shall find at last that they grow out of the universal feelings of like and dislike to pleasure and pain, respect being addressed to sentient beings who confer pleasure, and disrespect to those who inflict pain. And if the same expressions are not directed to inanimate objects from which we derive pleasure or pain, it is because such expressions have no effect in arresting the evil or advancing the good; whereas when applied to sentient beings, they have such effects. Hence their value—hence their power for good or for evil, just as they are wisely or unwisely directed.

In the present state of things these powerful moral forces are most unwisely directed. An individual who stalks forth to commit murder upon the large scale, under the name of a General, is applauded by the ignorant multitude. This ignorant and unmerited applause fans the flame of ambition in other minds, and thus the horrid trade of war, rapine, and oppression is spread and encouraged. In this respect Homer's Iliad and such works have done incalculable mischief, by stimulating the incipient gems of latent ambition. Let things be called by their right names. Let such characters be known as ringleaders of a gang of banditti, and the trade of wholesale butchery, by being made disgraceful, will cease to be followed. No man likes to follow a degraded employment; whilst on the other hand, he will follow any avocation, if the world will but admire. The very throne might, by the voice of public disapprobation, become so degraded, that few or none would be found willing to incur the odium attached to the office of a king; and unless a speedy change come over the administration of the laws, that office will at length, of a certainty, be buried beneath the execrations of a long suffering people.

Whilst, on the one hand, individuals are honored and rewarded for pursuing courses of action subversive of the peace and happiness of society; on the other, worthy characters, whose lives are spent in the most useful avocations, are despised and neglected. The honest ploughman, whose labor furnishes food for his species, is held in low esteem. Eternal rewards in another world may continue to be preached as inducements to virtuous conduct, and eternal punishments as discouragements to vice; but so long as splendid wickedness is rewarded by the honor and respect of men, whilst lowly virtue suffers neglect and contempt, vice *will* flourish, and virtue will wither and decay. The forces of honor and shame are near at hand and act upon the mind with promptitude and decision, whilst heaven and hell are seen afar off; and as the moral forces, like the physical, act inversely as the square of the distance, these extra-mundane forces produce a feeble effect upon the mind and conduct.

It may be, and indeed is true, upon the apparent approach of death, that the moral forces of reward and punishment in another world begin to act upon the mind of the believer with energy and effect; but the death-bed repentance of an individual whose life has been spent in the prosecution of evil designs, is a poor recompense to those of his fellow creatures who have suffered by the wickedness of his practices. Still, if those moral forces were applied to the propagation of virtuous conduct, *and of that alone*, they ought to be considered in the light of useful auxiliaries to the more certain, because more prompt forces of honor and shame, and on that account should not be abrogated, even although the foundation upon which they rest were not of the most satisfactory kind. But when we find that the individuals who teach the dogmas by which these forces are sustained are the veriest tools of tyranny and oppression, the firm supporters of dominions, principalities, and powers by which the lowly virtuous are cheated of that modicum of enjoyment which of right ought to fall to their share in this life, it is not surprising that some spirits should arise, who, sympathizing with the sufferings of the many for the exclusive benefit of the few, should lay hold of these two pillars which sustain the temple of Dagon, and bending themselves with their whole strength, should endeavor to drag the edifice to the earth, even at the risk of being buried in the ruins, like Samson of old.

Honor, respect, or approbation, for a good act done, is a cheap reward. It costs the giver nothing, and is to the receiver a high, an ample, and solid gratification. In rightly constituted minds, both the giver and receiver partake of the enjoyment. Indeed, it may be questioned whether the giver does not enjoy the largest share of the mutual gratification. But in awarding approbation to any single act or general line of conduct, circumspection is eminently needful. We should be well assured that the act or line of conduct of which we approve is calculated to augment the sum of human happiness. Misplaced approbation or disapprobation is, in fact, weakening the cause of virtue, and strengthening that of vice. It is putting the weight in the wrong scale. It is also of importance that the approbation should be commensurate with the intrinsic value of the act. Too much respect is apt to generate unseemly pride, whilst too little produces indifference, apathy, and debasement of mind. Respect awarded in the wrong place, gives a wrong direction to the course of human action, whilst too much or too little given to particular acts, stimulates or retards too much or too little in a like degree. These nicieties are too subtle to be left to the discrimination of every individual member of society, and, therefore, it is requisite that there should be erected some general standard by which all should judge; and this standard should be based upon the common consent of men, as deduced by investigation of the consequences, good or evil, which follow or flow from a general line of conduct.

The standard at present appealed to, is to be found in the ancient writings of barbarous nations. In these writings we find characters set up as models of imitation, whose conduct, if submitted to an honest and unprejudiced English jury, would, it is to be feared, be deemed of that flagrant kind, to entitle them to a life settlement in one of the penal colonies. Whilst such standard continues to be maintained and such models held up for the imitation of youth, there need be little wonder that vice and misery curse the land.

Heaven and Hell.—Little need be said upon this pair of moral forces. They are compounded of the other four. Hell is described as a place of corporeal punishment by fire and brimstone, and of weeping, wailing, and gnashing of teeth—that is, of mental and corporeal anguish. Heaven is not so distinctly described. Delicious music to charm the sense, crowns of glory, honor, and power, are amongst the rewards held forth, these being the descriptions of things which act most powerfully as inducements upon the minds of men. They have, however, no force whatever, as has been already observed, in the absence of faith. The amount of force and the amount of faith, always bear a relative proportion to each other; they rise together and sink together. In the wild, enthusiastic fanatic, the faith and the force is strong, and exercises a corresponding influence, whether for good or for evil, over his speech and actions. We will now proceed to notice the action and re-action of the different moral forces, and the relation in which they stand to each other, as co-operating or counteracting agents, beginning with the most simple case, that is, with one force.

ANIMAL ATTRACTION, ACTING ALONE.—If there be a number of hungry dogs scattered around the skirts of a large field, and a piece of flesh meat be dropped in the centre of the field, then this point becomes the centre of attraction. The dogs rush to this point and are gathered around it in a mass. This is analagous to the contraction of expanded matter into solid in the physical world. The force is of the same kind, namely, attraction; and the effect the same, the contraction of matter.

ANIMAL REPULSION, ACTING ALONE.—If now a firebrand be dropped in the midst of the assembled mass of dogs, they will be instantly dispersed and scattered around the field as at first. This is analogous to the expansion of solid matter into gas, in the physical world. In both cases the ultimate forces and the effects are the same, and throughout all animated nature it is the same, although amongst men, in what is called civilized society, the course of action is much disguised by the invention of money, which, being the vehicle or medium through which animal gratifications are procured, men seem to seek that alone; but they pursue money only because it is the means by which they can procure gratification of their animal and other wants, natural or artificial.

ANIMAL ATTRACTION AND REPULSION CO-OPERATING.—If an attractive or pleasure-giving object be placed *before* an animal, it will run towards it with a given amount of energy, say at the rate of three miles an hour. If at the same time a repulsive or pain-giving object be placed *behind* the same animal of equal intensity with the attractive, the moral force actuating the animal is doubled, and if the animal be capable of so great speed, he will move forward at the rate of six miles an hour. This case is founded upon the supposition of no other forces interfering with the two here spoken of. The two forces are acting together in the same direction, and the effect is consequently doubled.

ANIMAL ATTRACTION AND REPULSION COUNTERACTING EACH OTHER.—Let the attractive force which a given object exerts upon the animal organization be equal to 12, and let there be an object of a repulsive character placed near the first, exerting a force upon the organization also equal to 12, then the animal will hesitate to remain at rest (like the beam with equal weights in each scale), because although there is a force of 24 acting upon the organization, the one side balances the other; the two forces are in equilibrio, and the animal remains at rest until the one or the other forces predominates *in the mind*, and according as the attractive or repulsive force predominates, the animal advances or recedes.

If the subject of moral force and action be carefully examined, it will be found that in every case the organization, both physical and mental, is under the influence of contending forces, soliciting it to move in different directions, and that the energy of moral action is due to the *difference*, as in the physical world. Every function of the organization is a point upon which a force may be exerted, and before we can draw a correct conclusion with respect to the direction of the action, we must be in possession of both the amount and kind of force exerted upon every particular function. This renders the problem extremely difficult, but still an approximation may be obtained if we will carefully examine the subject.

If the functions be 12, (see chart), and if upon nine of these there be a force of 27,—3 upon each, and if upon the other 3 there be exerted a force of greater intensity, 9 upon each, then the 3 will balance the 9, because 3 multiplied by 9 equal 27, and 9 multiplied by 3 equal 27; but such equilibrium as is here supposed can never take place whilst the action which constitutes animal life continues, for that action continually destroys the balance. No living function ever remains during two consecutive instants of time in exactly the same condition; one feeling is gaining, another losing, and thus the mechanism of the body and mind is kept in a state of never-ceasing vibration or oscillation, from one side to the other.

Honor Opposed to Pain and Death.—Two gentlemen, having had some difference, one demands of the other what is called satisfaction, that is, they agree to fight a duel. They part for the night, and are to meet at the appointed place of rendezvous early on the following morning. Neither of them it may be presumed, has any particular wish to be shot. The contemplation of such a consummation is calculated to raise a feeling of the repulsive kind. If he were actuated by no other feeling than this, it is very certain that he would not appear at the time and place of meeting. What then is the force that draws him to the place? for it is equally certain that if there were no force of any kind to move him, that he would not appear. The attraction to honor is stronger than the repulsion to death, and the difference between the two forces moves him to the place with a reluctant step.

The attraction to honor is the moving power, and the repulsion to death is the regulating power. We say nothing here of the propriety or impropriety of such meetings; we have given the case simply by way of illustration. The conditions are precisely the same with a General or other officer who leads an army into the field; the honor and reward which he receives from those who employ him is, *in his mind*, greater than the toil and danger which he incurs, and the difference moves him forward into the action.

Shame Opposed to Animal Pleasure.—An opportunity is presented to a youth of strong animal propensities by which he might gratify those propensities at the expense of female virtue; but he refrains. Why? There must be a force of some kind restraining him. He feels within that by giving way to the lower feelings, he will lose the respect, not only of his fellow creatures, but also that inward approbation of his own conduct which passeth all understanding, and thereby he is restrained. This repulsive force of shame is continually contending against the lower animal feelings, holding them back and restraining them, whilst the attractive force of honor urges forward to the performance of noble deeds.

The great object, indeed the only object is, to direct these forces so as to produce the greatest amount of good. Like physical attraction and repulsion, these moral forces of pleasure and pain, honor and shame, are inherent and indestructible.

"That the human mind is *powerfully* acted upon by the approbation, or disapprobation, by the praise or blame, the contempt and hatred, or the love and admiration of the rest of mankind, is a *matter of fact*, which however, it may be accounted for, is beyond the limits of dispute. Over the whole field of morality, with the exception of that *narrow part* which is protected by penal laws, it is the only power which binds men to good conduct." *

Self-love, or love of self-good, is the ruling power or moving principle of human nature. Honor and shame appeal to the moving principle or ruling power by making honor *more loved* than pleasure, shame *more hated* than pain. By proper cultivation upon a good organization, honor and shame become the ruling powers. The love of honor becomes stronger than the love of pleasure; but in a faulty organization, where the sense of honor cannot be brought out sufficiently strong to counteract sensual pleasure, where the sense of *moral* or *mental pleasure* derived from honor, is weaker than the *sensual* or *corporeal pleasure*, we are compelled to appeal to corporeal sense to make it act upon itself in the shape of reward and punishment. It were needless to appeal to the moral sense, so long as the corporeal sense is the master, and controls the actions of the being to whom we appeal.

Heaven and Hell.—We have already alluded to these forces incidentally, and shall not, therefore, dwell upon them.

Their power is fast declining with the faith by which they are sustained. They have, however, exercised a powerful influence upon the destinies of the human race. Indeed, it might be questioned whether the original savage races could have been tamed without the powerful aid afforded by these forces. In the savage state men were merely animal, and could not be influenced unless by forces which appealed to their animal nature. Hence, by holding up heaven and hell as places or states of intense pleasure and pain awaiting those who restrained themselves from the pleasures or endured patiently the pains incident to the present state, the animal feelings were, as it were, turned against themselves. The same forces of animal pleasure which urged the individual on to the commission of any acts, were thus turned against him, restraining him from seizing a present enjoyment in the hope of receiving a greater future enjoyment, and urging him to endure a present pain in the hope of avoiding a greater future

* James Mill, author of British India.

pain. If these hopes and fears had been applied by the priesthood for the protection of the weak against the strong, for the protection of virtue against the ravages of vice, and for these purposes only, the wise and good would have continued to wink at the factitious forces employed, seeing the beneficial results which accrued from their operation. But when, instead of this salutary operation of these imaginary forces, we find the priesthood leagued with the oppressor to rob and crush the feeble, it becomes the duty of every one who feels a sympathy for the sufferings of his fellow creatures, to expose the trick by which the minds and bodies of men are retained in worse than Egyptian bondage. Whilst the mind is free, though the body may be enslaved, there is hope of an ultimate emancipation; but when the mind is enslaved, the body must be enslaved also, and until the mind be delivered from the shackles which bind it, there is no hope of an effective emancipation of the body. The hopes and fears of heaven and hell have had their use in the process of civilization; but their day is gone. In the childhood of the race they were influential in guiding the unruly natures of the uninformed; but now that man approaches his majority they appear to be wholly supererogatory, and altogether unavailable, except as a means of enabling the cunning and powerful to impose upon the weak and credulous.

The following, from the pen of Mr. James Hill, of Wisbeach, exhibits the ancient and modern value and direction of these forces in a very distinct and impartial point of view:—

"FORCE, FRAUD, WEALTH AND WISDOM.—The poets of old chaunted of the Four Ages, the Golden Age, the Silver Age, the Brazen Age, and the Iron Age; but in doing so they entirely reversed the order of sequence. Progression appears to be the course of nature; and although to a casual observer symptoms which appear to be those of retrogression are occasionally manifested, he who takes a comprehensive view of things will come to the conclusion that what is apparently a retrograde movement, is only the precursor to a future advance.

"Let us take a survey of what has been, and what probably will be the course of human advancement. In the infancy of mankind, the superiority of man to man depended on the physical strength and powers of the individual. He who was fleetest in the chase, he who possessed the greatest strength in combating the wild animals, became a chief—the Nimrod of his day. In those early times there were neither game-keepers, nor lords of the manor. No one claimed to himself any portion of the ground on which he trod, much less did he claim an individual right to the beasts of the field, the fowls of the air, or the fishes of the sea, so long as they were roaming at large in their native element.

"The only property known was strictly personal property. He who slaughtered the boar appropriated it, and it became his own. But that which was obtained by force, by force only could be maintained—the vindictive feelings of man which were called into exercise in these combats, tinged his whole character. The weak and the feeble were imposed upon by the strong—right was might, and might was right. This must have been the 'iron age.'

"But beyond those fierce chieftains, under the shadow of the palm tree, do you not perceive the man with outstretched arms and with flowing beard? He has kindled a fire and is making grotesque movements with his limbs and uttering strange sounds; at his bidding the warriors lay down their spears; at his bidding the hunters carry to him the choicest of their four-footed prey; though to all other persons they are so overbearing, to him they are submissive and humble; and ought they not to be?—he is the priest. He can call down the vengeance of heaven on those who dare to question his authority—at least so he tells them and so they believe. He performs sundry feats of sleight-of-hand and legerdemain, and then he tells the ignorant savage that he has the power to alter the course of nature, and they call his strange doings miracles. Shrewd in intellect, as must have been the early priests, (however deficient may have been some of their successors), he has observed that a certain state of things has invariably succeeded certain previous events, and though he knows not why, yet the result of many years' experience having shown him that such has always been the case, he naturally concludes that it always will be. Hence, when he observes a recurrence of events which have always been followed by certain other events, he ventures to predict with confidence what will occur, and this is called prophecy. And now having attained a very advanced age, his experience being proportioned to his age, he is consulted by the tribe on all occasions of interest, and he gives his opinion both to what he does know, and what he does not; in the latter case he couches his answers in ambiguous phrases of double meaning, so that whatever may be the issue he does not stand committed. This is called oracular.

"But this state of things was not without its use. So long as the post of priest or prophet to the tribe was occupied only by men of purity of purpose, who exercised their knowledge in a way to harmonize their fellows, to protect the weak from the attacks of the strong, their influence was beneficial; but when in process of time these patriarchs were succeeded by men of contrary character—men who lent Fraud to Force for the most diabolical purposes, assumed that they were the vicegerents of heaven with unparalleled assurance, properly might it be designated the AGE OF FRAUD OR THE BRAZEN AGE. If the brass had been applied only to break the iron rod, it would have been valuable; but when the brass and the iron blended for the purpose of crushing those who resisted the iron rule, fearful indeed were the results. When Force attempted to take from man his liberty, Fraud insisted to keep him in ignorance, and to tell him it was the will of heaven. In cases where Iron Force was too feeble, Brazen Fraud aided in the conflict; and when Brazen Fraud was insufficient, she called to her aid the Iron Hand of Force; thus was this fair earth converted into one great prison-house.

"This state of things was fitly illustrated by the figure of the beast whose head was of brass and body of iron, but, like all *unholy* objects, it rested on a bad foundation; fortunately for persecuted man—the feet were of clay.

"And shall not this clay undergo transformations, and be converted into something to destroy both the brass and the iron? It shall. Behold the clay moulded into small cubical dies, baked in the furnace, and tens of thousands of these pieces of baked clay piled one on the other perpendicularly, and connected by coverings under which the Lords of the Brass and Iron are protected from the violent tempest and the storm, by the forced labor of their vassals; and cities arise, and men are congregated together, and buildings are extended, and even the vassals, in due time, are graciously allowed to build for themselves humble habitations, provided they will fall down and worship the beast, whose head is of brass and body of iron; but, if they shall dare to call in question the beauty of the beast, how shall they escape from being crushed by its blows? But time progresses, and cities multiply, and the humble vassals make many discoveries, which they, the lords of brass and iron, were unable to do. Whilst these vassals have been employed in constructing cities, in tilling the earth to provide food for their rulers, their wives and daughters have been employed to spin and to weave for the wives and daughters of their rulers; and, during their few hours of cessation from toil, invention has been at work to diminish the labors of both; gradually indeed, but steadily, have these inventions succeeded each other. Rather than stoop down to grub the earth with his hands at the bidding of his rulers, he preferred to stand erect in the dignity of manhood, and he invented the spade. Still finding this too toilsome, he invented the plough, by which human labor was diminished many hundred fold. In all the productive departments of life, inventions to diminish human labor followed each other in quick succession. Instead of one wheel, spinning one thread, thousands of wheels spinning thousands of threads, were set in motion by one mighty wheel; and instead of this being propelled by muscular effort, the mind of man, noble, beautiful and powerful, was able to set it in motion by his will; the powers of nature were rendered subservient to his purposes, and, abandoning his first step, that of employing the horse, the ox, and other animals to labor for him, the winds and the waters became his slaves. Using the knowledge he possessed, as the instrument to obtain further knowledge,—refinement on refinement,—when it was found that the winds and the water could not always be obtained at the right time, or the right place, he substituted the intangible vapor—steam, to obtain a power infinite and eternal. Did darkness interfere with his proceedings, he called light out of darkness; another intangible vapor—smoke—was converted into a medium of brilliant brightness—gas. The ocean, which seemed a barrier separating country from country, he made the high road to connect distant regions.

"But all the inventions, first intended as an abridgement of labor, have been perverted to a less worthy object, that of amassing wealth for the few; and hence have followed a train of evils—avarice, envy, hatred, and all uncharitableness; properly may it be called the SILVER AGE, for the extension of a man's silver or wealth is, with some very few exceptions, the extent of his influence. He of the greatest muscular strength, he who was the chieftain of the first ages of the world, the man of Iron, is now powerless. And the men of Brass—fast is their influence diminishing, the age of superstition is passing away. The men of Brass have taken possession of part of the Silver; but their influence is now or mainly in proportion to their Silver, not to their Brass.

"We have seen, then, that power, built upon sheer force, has passed away; that it was only perpetuated by the union with fraud; we have seen both yield to wealth. Contrast the influence of a Rothschild on the affairs of the world with the influence of the Irish or Yorkshire giant, or the Pope of Rome, or both united. As men progress in knowledge, they will learn to estimate things rightly, and the influence of wealth will be held in as great contempt as that gigantic strength, or fraudulent assumption of Divine origin. They will not need Poor Law Acts, nor Poor Law Amendment Acts. Then shall the store-houses of Nature open their vast treasures. Oh! Nature! how magnificent are thy stores. Oh! Knowledge! thou only key for unlocking the store-houses of Nature. Instead of condemning and abusing human nature, (for human nature and inanimate nature must be in harmony), would man but attend to the course of nature, shape his institutions and proceedings in accordance with her perfect operations—would he but cultivate knowledge, and use that knowledge as an instrument for obtaining more, how different a state of things would ensue! Men will learn that happiness is the only object of intrinsic excellence; that wisdom, not wealth, is the high road to happiness, and instead of schemes of amassing large quantities of what is called wealth, by individual and competitive efforts, where each man conceives his neighbor a rival or a foe, magnificent schemes will be undertaken by united masses of men to obtain all the luxuries of life, by the aid of mechanical powers employed for the benefit of the whole; and it will be found that he is the wisest and the happiest, who contributes the most to the common stock of knowledge, by employing the discoveries of science and philosophy to the inexhaustible treasures of nature. Like the air we breathe or the light which shines upon us, there may be enough to spare for each, so that no one need wish to appropriate an extra quantity, and if he did so, it would be a source of unhappiness, not of pleasure. The distinction between man and man will not be the extent of his acres—not the measure of his possessions, but the measure of his mind. Does not every one see that this is the real standard by which men even now are estimated after their decease? True, a few vulgar minded men, whose only ambition is to die rich, ask, when they hear of the death of a cottager, 'What did he die possessed of?' But who measures the greatest and wisest of past ages by such a standard? Though seven cities contended for the honor of the birth-place of Homer, the probability is, that he was not possessed of a household in any. Who now estimates Euclid, or Virgil, or Locke, or Bacon, or Newton, or Shakspeare, or Milton, or the really great men of any age or any country, by any measure but that of their intellectual and moral attainments? When this shall become the general standard —not merely of the dead but the living, then and not till then, will commence the GOLDEN AGE."

That the "Golden Age" of wisdom, virtue, and happiness will arrive, sooner or later, there cannot be a doubt. Wisdom declares that happiness can be reached by no other path than virtue; and men are beginning to take heed to her declaration.

The wages of vice is misery, and of virtue happiness. But unhappily, in the highly artificial state of society, as at present constituted, happiness does not always follow in the track of virtue, nor misery in that of vice. Individuals and classes are suffered to follow vicious courses, drawing certain misery after them, but the suffering is artfully turned aside from falling upon the head of the wrong-doer, and comes with unmitigated weight upon that of the lowly virtuous. On the other hand, the enjoyment consequent upon a course of virtuous action, is diverted from its natural channel, and appropriated by those who neither "toil nor spin." So complicated, distorted, and purposely confused and entangled is the social texture become, that it might be doubted whether in some respects we should not be enabled to reach the goal sooner and with less toil, if we had to start in the race from the primitive state of the wandering savage, than from the supposed high point which we at present occupy in the scale of civilization. What is civilization? If the question should be answered by a reference to the comparative happiness of the rude Indian, and the so-called enlightened European, it would probably be found that the lot of the latter is the least enviable of the two.

The following is the opinion of Joseph Brant, otherwise Thayendanega, Indian, Chief of the Six Nations:—"To give you entire satisfaction, I must, I perceive, enter into the discussion of a subject of which I have often thought. My thoughts were my own, and being so different from the ideas entertained among your people, I should certainly have carried them with me to the grave, had I not received your obliging favor. You ask me, then, whether in my opinion civilization is favorable to human happiness? In answer to the question, it may be answered, that there are degrees of civilization, from Cannibals to the most polite of European nations. The question is not, then, whether a degree of refinement is not conducive to happiness; but whether you, or the natives of this land, have attained this happy medium. On this subject we are at present, I presume, of very different opinions. You will, however, allow me in some respects to have had the advantage of you in forming my sentiments. I was, Sir, born of Indian parents, and lived while a child among those whom you are pleased to call savages. I was afterwards sent to live among the white people, and educated at one of your schools; since which period I have been honored much beyond my deserts, by an acquaintance with a number of principal characters, both in Europe and America. After all this experience, and after every exertion to divest myself of prejudice, I am obliged to give my opinion in favor of my own people. I will now, as much as I am able, collect together, and set before you, some of the reasons that have influenced my judgment on the subject now before us. In the government you call civilized, the happiness of the people is constantly sacrificed to the splendor of the empire. Hence your codes of criminal and civil laws have had their origin; hence your dungeons and prisons. I will not enlarge on an idea so singular in civilized life, and perhaps disagreeable to you, and will only observe that among us we have *no prisons*; we have no pompous parade of courts; we have no written laws; and yet judges are as highly revered amongst us as they are among you, and their decisions are as much regarded. Property, to say the least, is as well guarded, and crimes are impartially punished. We have among us no splendid villains above the control of our own laws. Daring wickedness is here never suffered to triumph over helpless innocence. The estates of widows and orphans are never devoured by enterprising sharpers. In a word, we have no robbery under color of the law. No person among us desires any other reward for performing a brave and worthy action, but the consciousness of having served his nation. Our wise men are called fathers; they truly sustain that character. They are always accessible, I will not say to the meanest of our people, for we have no mean but such as render themselves so by vices. The palaces and prisons among you form a most dreadful contrast. Go to the former places, and you will see perhaps a *deformed piece of earth* assuming airs that become none but the Great Spirit above. Go to one of your prisons; here description utterly fails! Kill them, if you please; kill them, too, by tortures; but let the torture last no longer than a day. Those you call savages, relent; the most furious of our tormentors exhausts his rage in a few hours, and despatches his unhappy victim with a sudden stroke. Perhaps it is eligible that incorrigible offenders should be cut off. Let it be done in a way that is not degrading to human nature. Let such unhappy men have an opportunity, by their fortitude, of making an atonement in some measure for the crimes they have committed during their lives. For what are many of your prisoners confined? But for debt? Astonishing! And will you ever again call the Indian nations cruel? Liberty, to a rational creature, as much exceeds property, as the light of the sun does that of the most twinkling star. But you put them on a level, to the everlasting disgrace of civilization. I knew, while I lived among the white people, many of the most amiable contract debts, and I dare say with the best intentions. Both parties at the time of the contract, expected to find their advantage. The debtor, we will suppose, by a train of unavoidable misfortunes, fails; here is no crime, nor even a fault; yet your laws put it in the power of the creditor to throw the

28

debtor into prison and confine him there for life! a punishment infinitely worse than death to a brave man! And I seriously declare, I had rather die by the most severe tortures ever inflicted on this continent, than languish in one of your prisons for a single year. Great Spirit of the Universe! and do you call yourselves Christians? Does then the religion of Him whom you call your Saviour, inspire this spirit, and lead to these practices? Surely, no. It is recorded of Him, that a bruised reed he never broke. Cease, then, to call yourselves Christians, lest you publish to the world your hypocrisy. Cease, too, to call other nations savage, when you are tenfold more the children of cruelty than they." *

However, amidst all the misery, degradation, fraud, and false civilization of our race, one consolation remains. Knowledge is advancing; superstition, ignorance, and intolerance are falling back; and so certainly as true knowledge progresses, virtue and happiness must follow in her train. This is our anchor of hope.

As the church is the right hand of the government, so the army may be considered the left hand. Its power as an instrument of government, is much inferior to that of the church. The church exercises its influence upon the *minds* of men, the army upon their bodies; and inasmuch as the mind is master of the body, the church, by chaining down the mind, fetters the body at the same time. If the mind be enslaved, the body must be enslaved also;—the body under the direction of an enslaved mind, is doubly enslaved—it is the slave of a slave.

Such are, generally speaking, the minds and bodies of the individuals constituting the armies of despotic powers. In order that they may become subservient to the purposes for which they are embodied, it is requisite in the first place that they should be ignorant almost to brutality. Into these ignorant minds a moral system, or rather military code of laws is instilled, inculcating duties entirely distinct from, and in many instances opposite to, the duties of civil life. The chief duties of a soldier are to coerce and kill his fellow creatures at the bidding of those whom he is diligently and unceasingly taught to believe to be his superiors. "The duties of a soldier" are rung in his ears incessantly, and preached, too, by a chaplain who hesitates not to enforce and strengthen the military

* Stone's Life of Joseph Brant.

code by appeals to Divine authority, thus investing the horrid trade with the sanctions of heaven.

By this system of training, the mind of the soldier is fashioned to suit the purposes of his "superiors;" and the mind being subjugated, it requires small art to enchain the body so as to render the individual the ready tool of tyranny and oppression. "A little learning is a dangerous thing," it has been said. Whether this be true in regard to civil life might be questioned, perhaps; but it is certainly true in respect to an army retained for the purposes of oppression. A little knowledge let in upon the minds of the soldiery would break the tyrant's rod, and destroy the whole machine. Let the soldier but once see and *feel* that he is a *tool* in the hands of his "superiors," and he will hate himself, and those who have enslaved him. There is no physical force in an army or any other body of animated beings independent of the mind. The mind is, after all, the fountain—the spring of every physical effort, whether of an individual or a congregated body of individuals; and unless the *minds* of those individuals be first subjugated, it will be vain to attempt to subjugate the bodies.

If we would obtain a distinct perception of the moral forces which bind an army together and actuate it in its movements, it is to the officers that we must direct our attention. The common soldier is a mere animal. The attraction which draws him in the first instance, is generally the paltry bounty of a few pounds, which is wasted in drunkenness and debauchery. The attractive force which holds him to the body is the mess pot and the licentiousness of a barrack. He is nothing. Fill his trough and you have him. Let it be empty, the animal attraction fails, and he runs away. No pay, no soldier, is his motto. He is actuated by no principle.

But the officer is moved by other forces besides those springing out of the mess pot. "Honor is the subject of his story." It may be that he entertains very erroneous notions concerning those actions which are honorable or dishonorable. He may conceive that in order to sustain the splendor of tyranny, oppression, rapine, and murder upon the great scale, are very honorable deeds, so long as they are committed under the sanction of military law: or he may conceive that that line of conduct which is called virtuous in civil life, is beneath the dignity of a "military officer." But still honor of a certain sort forms a large portion of the power or force which moves him. It is to be sure a strange notion of honor which he entertains, but still, such as it is, he is moved by it. When at length he is covered with scars and stars, ribbons and titles, and a few other matters, he thinks himself a very fine animal; and such no doubt he is in the eyes of the fools who shout and cheer the creature who has trampled on their liberties. So long as the people continue to sing to the honor and glory of conquerors and tyrants, so long will the trade of the tyrant flourish. Neither have the people a right to complain of the oppression which they foster by their ignorant adulation. As they sow, so shall they reap. Let respect and honor be the reward of humanity and virtue. Let degradation fall upon the head of inhumanity and vice, and the moral world will assume a different aspect.

The crown or council is the centre of the army, as it is of the church. The gift of generalships, colonelcies, and every grade of commission, to which is attached honor, emolument, and power, is at the disposal of the crown. Hence the whole chain of organization is in the hands of the centre, which is thus enabled to direct the motion of the entire military machine in a manner every way analogous to that which obtains in the church. The most humble subaltern *hopes* to be one day commander-in-chief, or at least to hold a commission of some importance; and these being in the gift of the crown, he cannot expect to realize his hopes except by supporting the centre from which, in return for that support, he looks for the reward in prospect. Besides, military commissions are generally placed in the hands of those families whose private interests are in a great measure identical with those of the crown—that is, in the hands of the dominant party, of which party the crown is but the nominal centre.

The organization of the civil power, judges, magistracy, constabulary, police, &c., also centres in the crown. Here the influence of the centre upon the different branches of the organization is less powerful than upon those of the church and army; but still by giving the more important places to persons whose interests are identical with those of the crown—that is, to persons belonging to the dominant party; and the higher offices of the civil department being held up as prizes to those who most actively serve that party, like the bishropics in the church, and generalships in the army, the whole civil power leans towards and gives its support to the crown or centre, round which the whole organization, civil, ecclesiastical, and military revolves.

There is another engine of government which ought not to be forgotten—the *public press*. This portion of the civil power leads, or rather misleads, the public mind, and in a great measure supplies the place of that influence which has been hitherto exercised by the priesthood, but which is at present rapidly declining. If the public press were organized like the army or the church, it would be found a more efficient instrument of power than both these put together. It is almost the only power which sustains the tottering crown of Louis Phillippe, of France. Happily, however, for public liberty, such organization is almost, or altogether, impracticable. The dissenters in the press, as in the church, are sufficiently numerous and powerful to keep in check any combination of this kind, which might be attempted with a view to stifle the voice of the nation.

From this short sketch it may be perceived that a large amount of all the moral forces by which the minds of men are moved, are in the hands and under the direction of the government or centre of the national organization. Honor and shame, rewards and punishments in this world, (and through the influence of the priesthood in another world, also,) are at their disposal, and in proportion to their power to wield and direct these forces is the strength of the government. There are, however, one pair of these forces in the hands of the people, and which no power can take from them,—the forces of honor and shame. These two forces *wisely directed* are competent to overturn the most stubborn tyranny that ever was erected upon earth. But so long as the multitude are content to worship and honer at the bidding of others, without considering whether the objects of their adoration are really worthy of worship and honor, so long will they remain the slaves of those who direct their minds. It is vain to hope that an ignorant people ever can be free and happy. They must become the prey of the crafty, and even if they were left to themselves, they would still remain in a miserable and degraded state, from a want of the knowledge requisite to place themselves in a more elevated and happier position.

In forming a society of any given magnitude, from a family upwards to a kingdom, much depends upon the fitness and firmness of the centre upon which the moral organization is to revolve. This may be witnessed in a public meeting. Until a chairman is appointed, the meeting is a mere mob, a moral chaos, it has no centre. And the subsequent order of the meeting is very greatly dependent upon the fitness and firmness of the chairman or moral centre. As a general principle, it may be said that the strength of a society is in proportion to the perfection of their moral organization rather than their numbers. Twenty men, firmly knit together as one body, will effect more, either in civil or military affairs, than a hundred or even a thousand, who are not united by any common tie or principle, or centre of action. The necessity of a centre has been so strongly felt in military affairs, that even inanimate objects have been set up;—flags, standards, or banners have been set up, round which to rally in the day of battle.

What is a military banner? A long pole, with a piece of calico fastened to the top; the whole being of, perhaps, the intrinsic value of half-a-crown. But this pole and rag (the more ragged the better,) has upon more than one occasion saved a kingdom. Instances are recorded in which the soldiers have fallen in heaps round the standard, until their dead bodies have formed a wall of defence. But it is not however the pole and the rag for which the soldiers fight so strenuously. The loss of the flag, is, they are persuaded, the loss of their honor, and for this ideal entity—the spirit of an army—they fight to the last. The value of an inanimate centre is chiefly due to this circumstance: The men, by some strange association of ideas, will rally round it as round a leader, without bearing towards the inanimate object those jealous, envious, or angry feelings which often at the critical moment damp the ardor, and not unfrequently turn the heart of the soldier in the wrong direction. Indeed, all symbols, mitres, sceptres, crowns, thrones, images, relics, &c., derive a great portion of their efficacy and power from the same or a similar principle.

Every moral principle is a centre and the individual embodying in himself that particular principle in the greatest perfection, will *naturally* become the centre of action in the working of the principle, whether it be good or bad. Thus, according to the pious devotee, God is the abstract moral centre of goodness, virtue, and love. He is the bond of sympathy, by which all the purer and better spirits of human nature are knit together. He is the centre, the standard, or point of attraction 'round which they rally; and in proportion as each spirit of the body corporate becomes more and more assimilated to this abstract standard of moral perfection, so does the body become stronger and stronger,—more firmly united, more closely drawn together in the bond of moral sympathy.

"Evil be thou my good."—MILTON.

The devil is the abstract moral centre of evil, vice, and hatred. He is the embodiment of the force of antipathy. He is the representative of the moral repulsive force. In proportion as each member of the body corporate becomes more and more assimilated to the abstract standard of moral evil, so does the body become weaker and weaker, more and more scattered; for the spirit which actuates them is moral repulsion or hatred. Men who are wholly depraved (if such a thing could be) hate one another even with more vehemence than they hate the virtuous. Their body corporate is only held together by the slight attraction of the little moral goodness which may be among them. Take this away and they are scattered to the winds; for the spirit of their system—the central point upon which it turns, and from which it is actuated, is the concentration of antipathy, of hatred, of moral repulsion.

Now, take a hundred men, and if you wish to form a system upon the spirit or principle of moral evil, pick out the greatest villain of the number, and let him be the leader or moral centre. The other ninety-nine will by degrees begin to be assimilated to his character, and the system (whilst it lasts) will continually approximate towards the centre or point of perfection of moral evil. But in proportion as it becomes more and more perfect, it becomes more and more disunited. The spirit of sympathy or moral goodness becomes weaker and weaker. The spirit of antipathy or moral evil becomes stronger and stronger. The attraction is weakened, the repulsion is strengthened, and the body corporate is scattered to the winds. Perhaps the best and most just punishment which could be inflicted upon the wicked, would be to separate them from the virtuous and place them by themselves. They would be a punishment to each other by their mutual vices.

To form a system of moral goodness, is, of course, the converse of the last. Place the most virtuous man in the centre, and rally round him as round a standard.

If the object be to meet the enemy, give the leadership to the most daring. His daring spirit will be transferred throughout the body.

If the object be to get away from the *immediate* danger, give the leadership to the greatest coward. He will *lead* the body out of the field, for he will be sure to be foremost in running away; and the body will catch his spirit and run after him.

The wise and prudent man is neither *daring* nor *cowardly*. He weighs the consequences of the action. He considers the future good or evil which are likely to follow as consequences of his standing or running; and he acts accordingly, without the foolhardy daring of the one or the weak and feeble cowardice of the other.

## RIGHTS AND DUTIES.

A duty is something which an individual or body is expected to perform. The duty itself is not of the attractive, but rather of the repulsive character, and unless the individual can be bound to its performance by some other force, the duty will certainly be left undone. There are two ways by which the repulsive force connected with the duty is to be overcome. 1st. By bringing a stronger repulsive force to bear against that which is supposed to to be attached to the duty. Fines, disgrace, and other punishments for neglect of duty act in this manner. The pain inflicted for neglect is greater than that attending the performance of the duty. Therefore, the duty is performed, except in the case of a few thoughtless individuals who do not look beyond the present moment. 2nd. by bringing an attraction of greater power to overcome the repulsion to the duty. This is the most natural, and, therefore, the preferable mode, whenever it is practicable.

Honor is a cheap force; let the duty be esteemed sufficiently honorable, and it will be performed. If the attraction to the honor, act more powerfully upon the mind than the repulsion to the duty, then the honor overcomes the pain; if less powerfully, the pain overcomes the honor, and the duty is left undone. This may be expressed in the tabular form. Thus:—

| Repulsion from duty. | Attraction to honor. | |
|---|---|---|
| Value 12. | Value 10. | 12—10=2, the difference 2 is the moral force or moving power. |
| Value 5. | Value 6. | 6—5=1, attraction to honor is the moving, repulsion to duty is the regulating power. |

By the above it will be perceived that the moral action is determined by the greater overcoming the lesser force, as in the physical world.

Rights and duties are reciprocal. Wherever there is a duty to be performed, there also is a right to be asserted. A right is something claimed of another, and both the claimant and the granter are governed by the same principles as in the case of duties. As the object of duty is an evil, real or imaginary, so also is the object of right a real or imaginary good. The granter gives up the real or supposed good, or retains it, just as his mind is actuated on one side or the other by opposing forces. He parts with the attractive object, because it is considered disgraceful to retain that which is the right of another; and the disgrace is a stronger repulsive force than the attractive force of the object in question. We have not referred to the legal force by which individuals are compelled to pay their debts, &c.,—for still it is at last the same forces; for the laws derive their sanction from the approbation and disapprobation of men. Take away this sanction and the law becomes a dead letter.

A duty on the one part implies a right on the other.—To give even a list of the varied rights and duties of civilized life would occupy a large volume, and would exhibit in a condensed form the spirit which ought to guide the legislature in the enactment of laws. Our limits compel us to confine ourselves to one general or fundamental principle, from which all the secondary laws may be deduced. That moral axiom given by Jesus Christ and other legislators previous to his time, "Do unto others as you would that others should do unto you," is perhaps the most general principle to which the *duties* of life could be referred. It is established by the universal assent of mankind; indeed, no reasonable being could dissent from it, for that all men ought to so act may be considered a self-evident truth. The axiom is simple, beautiful and perfect in itself *so far as it goes*—that is, so far as relates to *duties*. But it announces one side of the question only. It says nothing whatever of *rights*. Throughout the whole of nature, in physics and in morals, we have two opposing principles—attraction and repulsion, pleasure and pain, honor and shame, rights and duties; and any general axiom which refers to one of these only is one-sided, and does not embrace the whole case. The two sides must be placed in contrast or opposition to each other, in order that we may perceive clearly the mutual bearing of the two, as thus:—

Duty.—Yield unto other men the same measure of good which you desire that they should yield unto you.

Right.—Claim from other men the same measure of good which those other men claim from you.

Even these converse axioms do not express the whole subject, for they relate to the good, pleasurable, honorable, or attractive side only; whereas there being *two principles*, good and evil, and at least *two men* entering into the question, we cannot render the subject complete in all its relative bearings, unless we introduce at least *four axioms*, two having reference to the mutual relation of the men or actions, and two to that of the principles.

Duty.—Forbear to injure other men, as you would that other men should forbear to injure you.

Right.—Claim the same forbearance from other men, as other men claim from you.

There is quite as much virtue in asserting a right, as in performing a duty. He who attends to the one side and neglects the other is but *half-virtuous*.

## NECESSITY AND RESPONSIBILITY.

A careful review of the physical and moral functions of the compound organization, and of the external influences by which they are stimulated to action, whereby motives are generated and action induced, leads at once to the conclusion, that the feelings, thoughts, words, and actions are the necessary and inevitable results of predisposing causes, and that, therefore, man is not a free agent in the usual acceptation of the term, that is, that the will is not free; that the act, or more correctly, the effect, which we denominate volition, is determined by causes over which the individual or patient has no direct control. The individual can act as he wills, it is true; but he cannot will or determine what shall be the motive by which the will itself shall be awakened or called into action. The motives present themselves, and the will is determined by that which makes the deepest impression. Some men contend that the doctrine of necessity destroys the principle of moral justice, and has a tendency to evil, by inducing a belief of the irresponsibility of man.

But this is to take a limited view of the subject; for whilst it is allowed on the one hand that the individual man is necessitated to feel, think, and act as he does, it must not be overlooked on the other, that the society of which he forms a member, is necessitated to feel, think and act likewise, and that if the individual is necessitated by the laws of his nature to do that which has a tendency to injure the social body, that body is also necessitated by the laws of their associated nature to restrain or to punish, if need be, for the preservation of the society.—Not, however, upon the principle of anger or revenge, as conceiving him to be a free agent, and that he might have willed to act in a different manner, but upon the principle of necessity; the corrective is applied in order to bring into play counteracting motives, by the influence of which the evil conduct may be restrained in future, not only as regards the individual in question, but others also, so that the society may be secure against the evil consequences of such acts. The doctrine of necessity leads to forbearance, charity, and forgiveness to the unfortunate delinquent on the one hand; whilst on the other it moderates that puffed up pride and self-conceit of the over-righteous, who would claim the exclusive merit of their own great goodness as being the sole product of their good-will and self-determination.

When a criminal is punished, it is not, or ought not to be, to satisfy the vengeance of the law, but that the punishment may create a counteracting motive, and *necessitate* others to avoid a course of conduct which leads to pain and ignominy. The punishment for crime is itself an evil which all humane minds must deplore; but if the causes which led to that cannot be removed, then society is necessitated to institute punishment, as being the lesser evil of the two. But every effort should be strained to remove the causes of crime, for by this course the evils of crime and of punishment are removed together. This is the course which wisdom and humanity alike point out. Every punishment inflicted for crimes, the causes of which might have been removed, is a savage and wanton, because an unnecessary cruelty; whilst on the other hand, it must not be forgotten that society requires to be protected against the evil deeds of individuals, whether necessitated or not, and no overstrained benevolence must be allowed to interpose a shield for the protection of the guilty, if thereby the innocent and peaceable are left exposed to fresh attacks from the impunity or misplaced mercy which has been extended to the evil doer.

## CUSTOM AND HABIT.

It must be confessed, after all that can be advanced with respect to reason and law as guides to moral action, that at least nine-tenths of the acts of human beings may be referred to habits and customs. Habit and custom are the two greatest tyrants upon earth. They control every thing, without paying the slightest regard to reason or common sense. When a child is born, a midwife must not be called in, as of old. Why? Simply because it is the custom to have a male practitioner. Next the infant is swathed and swaddled, and gruelled and slopped, not by any rules of common sense, but according to custom, It is taken to the baptismal font to be sprinkled, being accompanied by god-fathers and god-mothers, and a certain round of ceremonial observances are gone through, not enjoined by any law or ordinance of scripture, but merely agreeable to custom. If the child be a female, and in England, after a time its tender chest is squeezed into a pair of stays; if in China, its foot is crammed into a small iron shoe, in obedience to the tyrant, custom. At school the young mind is stuffed with French and foppery, not because of any utility which can be perceived in that mode of training, but it is the custom.

The business of courtship and marriage is also carried on after a given ceremonial established by custom. The most trivial affairs, as well as the greatest, are under the sway of this universal tyrant. If a king or queen is to be proclaimed or crowned, or a pauper passed from one parish to another, the ceremonial established by custom must be observed. Christmas day comes round, and general feasting and drunkenness prevails, according to custom. Two friends meet each other in the street, neither of whom have any desire to drink, but one must invite, and the other must accept the invitation to the tavern, because it is the custom. So it is through the whole journey of life from the cradle to the grave. The time and manner of eating, drinking, sleeping, clothing, and acting of every kind is established by custom. The multitude follow in the beaten track without inquiring why or wherefore, or whether a more convenient and expeditious road might be discovered, by which they might reach the desired end.

People live, and even die, according to custom. And after death, the body is put in an expensive box, covered with silk and trimmings. Mutes and paid mourners, empty coaches, and towers of black Ostrich feathers, form a part of the mock solemnity. At length the box and body is lowered into the earth, amidst the gabbling of an almost unintelligible jargon, all of which is done agreeably to the established custom of the country, and every part of the unmeaning ceremonial is deemed by the multitude of the most vital importance.

Habit.—As custom is the great tyrant which rules the nation, compelling the king and the peasant to bend to his yoke, so habit is the little tyrant which sways the individual. The great value of education, of discipline in determining the future character of the individual, is chiefly due to the power which it possesses to establish permanent habits of mind and body. Every function is capable of the impress of habit; and the habit once formed, whether good or bad, remains fixed, and can scarcely be eradicated by any power which reason or argument may oppose to it.

There is a story told of a man who, from a habit of gluttony, became afflicted with indigestion, and in consequence applied to a physician. The physician examined his case, and perceiving that his disease arose entirely from his habit of immoderate eating, gave him the following advice:—"Sir," said he, "I perceive the nature and cause of your complaint very clearly, and in order to remove that complaint, I will tell you what you must do—you must steal a horse." "Steal a horse!" said the patient, astonished at so strange a recommendation, "what effect would the stealing of a horse have upon indigestion?" "I will inform you," said the doctor; "your indigestion arises solely from a habit of gluttony which you have contracted. This habit is rooted; it is vain to tell you that you must break it, you cannot do so with the little resolution which you possess on this point. But if you were to steal a horse, you would get into prison, and there your diet would be so regulated that you would soon recover from your indigestion."

There is an important and serious truth contained in the above, and a severe stricture upon the imbecility of human nature. The drunkard acknowledges with sorrow and shame the folly and wickedness of the course which he pursues, but still he returns to his cups, like the dog to his vomit. So also is it with any bad habit which has been formed. No one is more thoroughly convinced of the evil tendency of the habit, because no one suffers so much by it as the unfortunate individual in whom it is formed, but still the effort to overcome it is too great for his resolution, until he sinks under its power, unless by some fortunate combination of circumstances, of which none is more powerful than that of forming new associations, he is relieved from the thraldom of the habit by which he has been enslaved. Man is said to be lord of the creation,—a being of reason and reflection. Those who look at his present condition with a philosophic eye, might be apt to suppose that such expressions were meant in irony and derision; for with all our boasted advancement in science and civilization, there is still a long way to travel before we reach that goal of happiness for which all are straining.

In the majority of minds, the reasoning faculty is so

low, that the individual cannot connect even the two last members of the series—that is the result with the preceding action. Such minds have no reasonable rule of action; they perpetually fall into error and its consequent misery. If they act with any thing like consistency, it is only from habit and example, and hence the great value of good examples; they tend to the establishment of good habits in that large class of mankind whose reason is not competent to trace for themselves a just course of action from previous conclusions, deduced from fundamental principles.

Yet the almost slavish obedience which mankind yield to habit and custom is not to be viewed in the light of an unmixed evil. It begets uniformity of feeling, thought, and action amongst that large class who reason indifferently upon moral subjects. It also relieves us from the necessity of debating within ourselves as to the consequences of every particular act. The things appertaining to habit and custom are done or avoided by the individual, as it were, involuntarily, and in very many cases, almost unconsciously, without any effort of the mind; and the mental faculties being thus relieved from the continual necessity of weighing, balancing, and determining concerning that large class of actions which are already determined by custom and habit, are left at liberty to concentrate themselves upon those particular points in which are involved the progressive advancement of the species.

Besides which, as habit and custom rule the civilized world with a steady hand, the reformer is enabled to perceive that if he would introduce moral improvements which shall be permanent, he must labor to establish new customs and habits; for however clear and convincing may be his moral or political reasonings, they will produce but a transitory effect, unless he can sustain the reasoning effort until he gives a new direction to the customs and habits of the people.

Those who conceive that the world cannot be reformed until all are convinced of error by the voice of reason, neglect to consider that the mass are not moved by reason, in the course which they now pursue. They are but followers and humble imitators of the higher intellects even when they profess to reason; and so soon as those higher intellects are convinced of the necessity and practicability of introducing a better state of things, their course of action will be changed by the force of conviction, and the great mass of mankind will follow in the new track as they do at present in the old.

## SYSTEM.

That which we call a system is, in fact, an organized arrangement, whether physical or mental. The solar system is a physical organization, the centre of which is the sun. All the parts have a mutual dependence on each other; but the *centre* is the most important or main point in the organization of the system. The moon, the earth, or indeed any single planet might be entirely removed, and still the system would go on—(a limb only has been removed—the vital part has not been touched); but if the sun—*the centre*—were removed, the whole would fall into confusion. The system would fall to pieces—it would become a chaos, or rather, it would fall into a new form, totally different from that in which it had previously existed; in which form the varied processes of nature in the vegetable, animal, and mineral kingdoms could not be carried forward as at present.

These remarks apply to every organization in the physical world, and also—and with the same force—to every organization in the moral world. An army is an organized moral system, (that is, a system governed by the *mind*,) the centre of which is in the general or commander. A private soldier, a non-commissioned or commissioned officer, or a colonel, or even a general of brigade may be removed, and yet the organization may continue to work. But if the *centre*, the commander-in-chief give way, the whole falls to pieces. That which was before an army, is now a *mob*, a chaotic, confused mass, without order or arrangement, and altogether unfit to accomplish the objects for which the materials were brought together. Napoleon Bonaparte was a centre of this description, and much of the scattered elements of his system are yet in existence, but they are wholly powerless without their centre of action.

The Christian church is, or was, an organized moral system, the *centre* of which was in the Pope of Rome, who is still the centre of the Catholic church; and the efficient working of the ecclesiastical organization, like every other, is essentially dependent upon the *fitness and firmness* of the centre round which it revolves. A centre well fitted to the church, would be ill adapted to the army, and *vice versa*. The centre of every moral system should embody within himself the principle which is to govern the organization. He should, in fact, possess the concentrated essence of the moral spirit which is to actuate the whole body corporate, of which he forms the centre, which spirit, like the sun's rays, radiate from the moral centre, warming and invigorating every part of the system. Such was the principle and spirit of Napoleon's system, by which he subjugated some of the old established governments of Europe.

A civil government is an organized system, the centre of which is in the king or first magistrate, and the stability of the government is, to a large extent, dependent upon the fitness and firmness of the centre. Although in this, as in every other system, each part has a mutual relation and dependence on every other part, so that it may be said the harmonious adaptation of the whole, and the firmness of the centre, determines the stability of the system.

The solar system is a physical organization, and is actuated by the purely physical forces of attraction and repulsion. Man, considered as an isolated animal organization, is actuated by the animal forces of attraction to pleasure and repulsion from pain. Considered as a portion of society, or of the social organization, he is further subjected to the forces which actuate that organization—namely, the social forces of attraction to the approbation, and repulsion from the disapprobation of his fellow associates. And considered as a religious being, he is subject to the forces of the religious organization—that is, attraction to heaven, and repulsion from hell.

Now the art of governing mankind, is simply the art of directing these six moral forces, and the strength of the British government is mainly attributable to this circumstance. It holds in its hands the reins of all the six forces. The king, *in council*, is the centre of the church, and directs its movements for political purposes. He is the centre of the army and navy, and of the civil power. All the powers centre in the king, or rather in the council or ministry, for the king is but the nominal centre, and it is necessary that the power should nominally centre in one individual, in order to secure at least apparent unity of action. Preferment in the church is in the gift of the crown nominally, in reality in that of the governing party, of which party the ministers are a committee of delegates, suffered to remain in office only so long as they support the interests of the party whom they represent, of which party they are generally the most able and active members; and as church preferment is in the gift of the crown, every priest, from the most petty curate of a country hamlet, upwards to the archbishop of York (the highest but one in degree), supports by his preaching and by the moral forces of heaven and hell which he wields, that government from which he hopes to obtain preferment. And as he is aware that preferment is obtained either for money or for work done, he labors to extend his influence over the people, and to make manifest to the governing party his *usefulness*, by unceasingly inculcating the duty of submission to the powers that be. By these means, he hopes at length to obtain the golden mitre of Canterbury, which is held up as a prize to every priest who will faithfully serve the "lords of the land."

The emoluments of the church as at present constituted, may be considered as a lottery scheme, in which are a great number of small, and a few very large prizes. These few large prizes can fall into the hands of a few only; but still every priest *hopes* that one or other may become his by political subserviency, just as every purchaser of a ticket in the state lottery hopes that he may be the fortunate holder of the number which will obtain the £40,000 prize. Thus the church works as a political machine, playing into the hand of those who hold the power of dispensing the greater prizes. A party amongst the dissenters have been clamorous for a separation of church and state, and for an equalization of church livings, with a view to remove from the Christian religion the contaminating influence of secular interests. Such separation and equalization would no doubt purify the Christian church, but it would spoil the political machine, and, therefore, the governing few will resist it with all their might, for the church is the right arm of the government. If the aid and support of the priesthood were withdrawn, the government of this country as at present constituted and administered, would crumble to pieces—it would fall by its own weight. The unholy connexion of church and state cannot be dissolved except by pointing out to the people the fraud by which they are held in subjection and misery; neither the state nor the church desire the dissolution of their adulterous union. The church supports the state by fraud; and the state supports the church by force. It is fraud and force combined and leagued together to cheat and plunder the people.

## SYMPATHY AND ANTIPATHY.

These are collective terms of large and comprehensive signification, under which may be traced a reflection or *fac simile* of the whole of the moral functions referred to in the chart. As the moral functions are faithful reflections of the physical functions of the animal body, so the sympathies and antipathies, which may be properly termed the *social functions*, are faithful reflections of the moral and physical organizations in which they have their origin. Some philosophers have affirmed that self-love and social are the same. Had they said that the latter is a reflection or image of the former, as the face seen in the mirror is a reflection of that which is placed before it, they would have been nearer the truth. If the face before the mirror be fair and beautiful, and the mirror be free from distortion, then the reflected image will be fair and beautiful also; but if either the face or the mirror be distorted, the image also will be distorted. And so it is in regard to the mind. Society, with all its customs and laws, is the mirror; the compound physical and mental organization of the individual, with all its habits and tendencies, is the figure placed before that mirror, and, as in the former case, the reflected image expressed by the *social functions* will exhibit all the beauties and flaws of the mirror, or of the figure placed before it. In order that the reflected moral image may be perfect, it is requisite that both the individual figure and the mirror of society should be perfect.

Sympathy, in common or vulgar language, is generally given and received in the limited sense of commiseration. Sympathy has a much wider extension of signification. It

Loves with the loving—hates with the hating;
Hopes with the hoping—fears with the fearing;
Joys with the joying—grieves with the grieving.

The individual who is moved by sympathy, partakes of the feeling of the being with whom he sympathizes, whatever that feeling may be. A pain inflicted upon the child awakens the sympathy of the mother. The mother does not feel the actual bodily pain which the child feels, but by sympathy she feels pain or pleasure in the pain or pleasure of the child. Sympathy is a concordant or harmonizing state of feeling between two or more animated beings; as on the other hand, antipathy is a discordant or jarring state. A tory sympathizes with a tory; a whig with a whig; a radical with a radical; a Turk with a Turk; a Catholic with a Catholic; a Protestant with a Protestant; a dissenter with a dissenter; an Englishman with an Englishman; an Irishman with an Irishman; a Scotchman with a Scotchman, &c. Between the radical and the tory there is no sympathy or harmony of feeling; but on the contrary, there is a strong antipathy. These two parties do not love and hate, hope and fear, joy and grieve, in harmony; whilst the one rejoices, the other grieves. The objects which excite love, and hope, and joy on the one side, excite hate, and fear and grief on the other.

Sympathy is the bond of party, the social centre round which it moves. Antipathy is the embattled wall which surrounds and circumscribes it. Sympathy is the attractive force which draws men together into social union. Antipathy is the repulsive force which preserves the health and purity of the spirit (of whatever character that spirit may be) which actuates the body, by the rejection and expulsion of discordant elements—elements which could not sympathize or harmonize with the actuating spirit or principle. As a stone thrown into a pond gives rise to rings which radiate and spread from a centre, one succeeding another, until at length they extend to the very margin; so, in some cases, an act either of oppression or of magnanimity will awaken and set in motion the social sympathies or antipathies, until ultimately the vibration spreads to the margin of the society, whether that society comprise within its limits a family, a parish, a country, a kingdom, or an empire, or even the entire habitable globe. When Caroline, consort of George IV., was persecuted, the sympathies of the nation were awakened towards the queen, and their antipathies towards the king, and the feeling spread from bosom to bosom, until at length the whole nation was in one universal commotion, and this commotion had its centre and origin in the private difference of two individuals. No other human being was in any way affected by this difference except through the influence of sympathy and antipathy.

Like creates like by sympathy. Yawning begets yawning; drunkards make drunkards; cowards make cowards; love begets love; hate begets hate; hope begets hope; fear begets fear; joy begets joy; grief begets grief;—in short, every feeling of the whole frame may be moved by the sympathies and antipathies.

There are two ultimate principles which stand in opposition to each other, and which run throughout all nature, actuating both mind and matter. Attraction is the binding principle of the physical world, by which every organization is held together, from the least to the greatest. Sympathy is the attracting and binding principle of the moral or mental world, by which the social organization is cemented. The sun is the centre of the physical attraction of the solar system, and God is the personified centre of that sympathetic attraction by which animated being are drawn together into the bonds of love and fellowship. In the breast in which this sympathy resides, there is a *feeling* of assurance that there is a benevolent God who cares for the well-being of his creatures, and this feeling is a stay and comfort to the heart. As this feeling has not been implanted by reason, neither can it be rooted out by reason. The feelings cannot be moved by syllogisms. But as concerning this power, whatever the heart may feel, the understanding can perceive little or nothing, it would be more seemly for those who pretend to a familiar knowledge of the attributes and character of that Being, whom no man hath seen at any time, to confess their ignorance at once, that thereby we might hope to have peace from the long continued strife which has prevailed amongst men concerning the *unknown*.

Home is the place where the sympathies are satisfied.

A youth *feels* at home with his father and mother, sisters and brothers, wherever the place may be, or whatever degree of comfort may be attainable in that place. A father *feels* at home with his wife and children in the same way;—that home may be under a hedge or a tree, it may be in a hovel or a palace. The formation of that *home* is not in the external circumstances, but in the gathering around him of the beings in whom the social sympathies find a solace and a resting place. That alone constitutes home. Let us hope that the day may yet arrive, in which the whole human race will constitute but one great family, and the world one vast home.

## ACTION AND RE-ACTION.

If there be two boats or other vessels, in all respects equal, in one of which is a man with a pole or boat hook; and if he push the empty boat from him with the pole, both vessels will move. The empty boat is considered to move by the *action* of pushing, and that in which the man is standing is considered to move by *re-action.* So also if the one vessel be drawn towards the other by means of a rope, both will move equally,—the action and re-action is mutual and equal. This case illustrates *mechanical* action and re-action;—the pushing of the two vessels apart by means of the pole is equivalent to the expansion of matter, and the drawing of them together by the rope to the contraction of matter. In the works of nature every thing is in motion, expanding or contracting; if the *action* of expanding be extreme, the *re-action* of contracting must also be extreme. If the oscillation of the pendulum be great on one side of the perpendicular, it will be great on the other side also by re-action. In the physical world action and re-action is the universal law; and the same holds in morals.

War begets poverty, poverty begets humility, humility begets peace; peace begets plenty, plenty begets pride, pride begets war; war begets poverty, &c., and so on round the circuit, like the rain drop in the atmosphere, or the earth in the solar system. Again: monarchy leads to oppression, oppression leads to resistance, resistance leads to liberty, liberty to licentiousness, licentiousness to anarchy, anarchy to suffering, suffering to submission, submission to monarchy, and monarchy to oppression. It is the same in manufactures and commerce; action and re-action regulates and controls every operation. To prevent these actions and re-actions is altogether impossible; for the system of nature is a system of motion or action—nothing is standing still—all is in motion—going and returning, like the ebbing and flowing of the tide. The life of man is itself but a portion of the universal process; and all that remains for us to do is to press forward, avoiding violent action, that thereby we may escape the violent re-action which is sure to follow.

THE END.

Milton Keynes UK
Ingram Content Group UK Ltd.
UKHW022320170124
436226UK00005BA/161